REALIZING PEACE

Realizing Peace

A CONSTRUCTIVE CONFLICT APPROACH

Louis Kriesberg

OXFORD
UNIVERSITY PRESS

OXFORD
UNIVERSITY PRESS

Oxford University Press is a department of the University of Oxford.
It furthers the University's objective of excellence in research, scholarship,
and education by publishing worldwide.

Oxford New York
Auckland Cape Town Dar es Salaam Hong Kong Karachi
Kuala Lumpur Madrid Melbourne Mexico City Nairobi
New Delhi Shanghai Taipei Toronto

With offices in
Argentina Austria Brazil Chile Czech Republic France Greece
Guatemala Hungary Italy Japan Poland Portugal Singapore
South Korea Switzerland Thailand Turkey Ukraine Vietnam

Oxford is a registered trade mark of Oxford University Press
in the UK and certain other countries.

Published in the United States of America by
Oxford University Press
198 Madison Avenue, New York, NY 10016

Library of Congress Cataloging-in-Publication Data
Kriesberg, Louis.
  Realizing peace : a constructive conflict approach / Louis Kriesberg.
    p. cm.
  ISBN 978-0-19-022866-8 (hardcover) — ISBN 978-0-19-022867-5 (paperback)
1. Peace-building—United States—History. 2. United States—Foreign relations—1945–1989.
3. United States—Foreign relations—1989– I. Title.
  JZ5584.U6K75 2015
  327.1'720973—dc23

                    2014033535

9 8 7 6 5 4 3 2 1

Printed in the United States of America on acid-free paper

Contents

Preface and Acknowledgments

I HAVE SPENT much of my life preparing to write this book. I wanted to apply my understanding of the fields of conflict resolution and peace studies to find better ways to resolve conflicts than large-scale violence. My concern particularly was with how Americans could constructively manage engagements in foreign conflicts. I wanted to confront challenging problems and suggest specific actions that persons inside and outside of the U.S. government might take that would have more constructive results.

Friends and colleagues who know that I often point to possible paths to positive changes in terrible international conflicts, often point to a current international mess and ask me challengingly, "What would you do NOW?" My deflective response often would be, "You should have asked me five years ago." I wrote this book to think more systematically of serious answers to questions about what to do now.

I am indebted to innumerable persons for their help over many years in understanding the conflicts about which I write in this book. They include former students and now colleagues who do research and writing on the matters discussed in the book and those who try to apply the ideas of conflict resolution and peace studies. I owe much to associates in community organizations, colleagues from many countries in professional organizations, and colleagues in many conflict resolution centers in the United States and abroad, as well as to several programs at the Maxwell School of Citizenship and Public Affairs at Syracuse University.

In particular, I want to mention the Syracuse Area Middle East Dialogue group (SAMED); the Peace Studies Section of the International Studies Association; the Peace, War and Social Conflict Section of the American Sociological Association; and the International Peace Research Association. I have benefitted from my engagement in several Maxwell School programs, including Executive Education and National Security Studies. I especially am grateful for the support and friendship of Catherine Gerard, Elizabeth Myers, Deborah A. Toole, and all others associated with the Program for the Advancement of Research on Conflict and Collaboration.

I thank colleagues who read chapters of this book in earlier drafts, providing valuable information and insights: William Banks, Frederick F. Carriere, Bruce Dayton, Miriam Elman, Galia Golan, Robert A. Rubinstein, Brian Taylor, and Stuart Thorson. I appreciate the support and excellent editorial handling of the manuscript by Angela Chnapko, Oxford University Press editor.

I value the interest and comments of my sons Daniel Kriesberg and Joseph Kriesberg and of their families about this book, and I acknowledge the incentive they give me to try to make their world safer and less destructive than mine was. I thank especially Paula Freedman, my partner, who added so much joy to writing this book, as she read and re-read every chapter with enthusiasm and critical editing.

Glossary

AFL	American Federation of Labor
AFSC	American Friends Service Committee
AIPAC	American Israel Public Affairs Committee
ADR	Alternative Dispute Resolution
AU	African Union
AUB	American University of Beirut
BDA	Banco Delta Asia
BDS	Boycotts, Divestment and Sanctions
CIA	Central Intelligence Agency
CIO	Congress of Industrial Organizations
CORE	Committee of Racial Equality
CSCE	Conference on Security and Cooperation in Europe
DOD	Department of Defense
DPRK	Democratic People's Republic of Korea
DLC	Democratic Leadership Council
DOP	Declaration of Principles
DOS	Department of State
EC	European Community
EU	European Union
FOR	Fellowship of Reconciliation
FRG	Federal Republic of Germany

FSA	Free Syrian Army
GDR	German Democratic Republic
GRIT	Graduated Reciprocation in Tension-Reduction
GWOT	Global War on Terrorism
HCNM	High Commissioner on National Minorities
IAEA	International Atomic Energy Agency
IBC	International Branch Campus
ICC	International Criminal Court
IFOR	Implementation Force
IGO	International Governmental Organization
IR	International Relations
IRI	International Republican Institute
INGO	International Nongovernmental Organizations
IMF	International Monetary Fund
ISI	Inter-Services Intelligence
ISIS	Islamic State in Iraq and Syria
KGB	Committee for State Security (Soviet)
KLA	Kosovo Liberation Army
LDF	Leaders for Democracy Fellowship Program
LDK	Democratic League of Kosovo
MEK	Mujahedin-e Khalq Organization
MENA	Middle East and North Africa
NATO	North Atlantic Treaty Organization
NDI	National Democratic Institute for International Affairs
NED	National Endowment for Democracy
NIAC	National Iranian American Council
NSC	National Security Council
OAU	Organization of African Unity
PA	Palestinian Authority
PDD	Presidential Decision Directives
PLO	Palestine Liberation Organization
PRC	People's Republic of China
R2P	Responsibility to Protect
RPF	Rwandan Patriotic Front
SALT I, II	Strategic Arms Limitation Treaties
SFCG	Search for Common Ground
SDI	Strategic Defense Initiative
UAE	United Arab Emirates
UN	United Nations

UNESCO	United Nations Educational, Scientific and Cultural Organization
UNMOVIC	United Nations Monitoring, Verification and Inspection Commission
UNPROFOR	United Nations Protection Force
USAID	United States Agency for International Development
WMD	Weapons of Mass Destruction

REALIZING PEACE

1 Toward More Constructive Conflicts

HEATED DEBATES ABOUT American foreign policies arise from widespread dissatisfaction with the results of U.S. governmental involvements in foreign conflicts. Officials who pursued policies that did not work out well defend their decisions, while political opponents deride them and propose quite different policies. This is evident in the partisan arguments about the neoconservative policies implemented during George W. Bush's presidency, and the quite different policies adopted in Barack Obama's presidency. Similar debates, sometimes with much less partisanship, go back to the early years of the Cold War.

Actual American engagements in foreign conflicts, however, have varied on a case-by-case basis in the strategies chosen and in the degree of their success. Moreover, Americans who are not governmental officials also engage in foreign conflicts, and their actions should not be ignored. The variability in strategies and in results provides the evidence used in this work to assess the possible effectiveness of different strategies. My assessments are made from the constructive conflict perspective, synthesizing ideas and practices from the conflict resolution and peace studies fields. This enables me to suggest alternative strategies to those that had been tried and proved to be unsuccessful.

The world military, economic, cultural, and political preeminence of the United States since the end of World War II has enabled U.S. government leaders to shape many aspects of the world system. They have led, for example, in greatly influencing the formation and workings of the international governmental organizations dealing with economic activity. American governmental and nongovernmental actions have hugely influenced technological innovations, political ideals, popular culture, and much more.

Despite this dominance, it is striking that on many occasions U.S. involvement in specific foreign conflicts has been unsuccessful and sometimes counterproductive. In the case of many other foreign conflicts, however, the intended benefits of engagement were attained to a significant degree. Three kinds of engagements in foreign conflicts are examined in this book. First, Americans may fight in conflicts in which they view their country as opposing a significant adversary such that deadly violence occurs or is threatened. Second, Americans may intervene in conflicts abroad in which two or more large-scale coercive adversaries are in contention, and the intervention is not simply in support of one side in opposition to an opponent, as when the intervention is for humanitarian considerations. In actuality, such interventions may be viewed as partisan by the contending sides, and indeed to some degree often are supportive of one of the adversaries.[1] Third, some Americans may provide mediation services in foreign conflicts between adversaries who have resorted to violence or seem likely to do so. These three kinds of involvement are not always clearly distinct; rather, a particular American involvement often blends two or three kinds of actions, and the primacy of one or another changes over time.

American officials and private citizens have used a wide variety of methods of engagement in foreign conflicts. In principle, this should make it possible to assess the effectiveness of different methods and approaches in achieving desired constructive results. In practice, every step in making such assessments poses challenging problems. I will try to confront the problems carefully and openly.

To focus and delimit this analysis, I draw heavily from the constructive conflict approach, which is outlined in this chapter. This approach is based on empirical research and the analyses of conflict resolution applications. It offers a comprehensive perspective for all kinds of conflicts at all stages of their manifestation, including emergence, escalation, de-escalation, settlement, and peacebuilding. Furthermore, based on that approach, I make suggestions of possible alternative policies that would be more constructive than those used in foreign conflict engagements that did not go well.

Aims of the Book

I do not dwell on military operations in this book, but recognize their possible constructive roles in various contexts. There is a large body of literature on military force applications and I hope that my analysis here will help make better alternatives more visible and enhance the constructiveness of all kinds of engagements in foreign conflicts. Military personnel recognize that they are sometimes tasked by civilians to undertake assignments for which they are not well suited. It is useful to expand the repertoire of policies beyond doing nothing or using military force.

Certainly, U.S. involvement in foreign conflicts has frequently entailed the use of U.S. military force, or at least the threatened use of military violence.[2] America fought in high-casualty wars in Korea, Vietnam, and Iraq, none of which could be regarded as highly successful. The United States often has borne extremely large costs to win small benefits in fighting enemies, in intervening on humanitarian grounds in wars, or even in mediating international conflicts. This is also remarkable given the generally high regard Americans and American society are held in the world.

This is even more puzzling when the trends of declining deadly violence in the world are considered. There is substantial evidence that rates of violent deaths among humans have been trending downward from prehistoric times, despite increasing capabilities for killing people.[3] More recent periods clearly have had declines in rates of violent deaths, notably since the end of the Cold War. International wars have become rare; domestic wars have decreased and occur at a low, fluctuating rate; and deaths in wars have also declined.[4] Despite these realities, U.S. engagements in armed conflicts have increased since the end of the Cold War.[5]

Accounting for relatively effective involvements is important and useful, but so is accounting for ineffective and destructive engagements. Admittedly, judging whether a particular American involvement was a success or a failure is frequently controversial, and varies with the time frame of the assessment and the point of view of the person making the assessment.

Assessments of what went well and what went poorly are made in this book in order to derive ideas useful for engaging more constructively in future conflicts. Such retrospective and speculative analyses, however, are difficult and certainly disputable. Analyses of past policies usually focus on describing what happened and sometimes venturing explanations for those events. Such analyses usually tend to suggest that whatever happened was inevitable, given the circumstances at the time. Considering alternative options that might have been feasible in the past can foster fresh thinking about future choices.

In assessing specific American participations in foreign conflicts, it should be kept in mind that strategies are never wholly failures or successes, wholly destructive or constructive. Every particular set of actions has both beneficial and adverse consequences, in different proportions, for different parties in a conflict. The intention here is to understand how particular strategies under specific circumstances had significant broad and enduring beneficial consequences, and could reasonably be regarded as such for the persons who chose the strategies. Furthermore, constructive and destructive are comparative terms. I often am explicit about designating a particular action as constructive or destructive compared to a particular alternative, but sometimes that is implicit, for the sake of brevity.

In this book, I examine American involvements in foreign conflicts that have been relatively effective and beneficial and others that were not. I do not attempt to examine all aspects of American foreign policies, which pertain to a wide array of matters, including foreign trade, humanitarian assistance, engagement in the United Nations (UN), and bilateral relations with allies. The focus is on three kinds of American relationships to large-scale foreign conflicts in which deadly violence is or threatens to be extensive. As identified earlier, the three kinds of relationships are as an adversary confronting another adversary, as an intervener in an ongoing conflict abroad, and as a mediator in a foreign conflict.

I analyze a variety of such American involvements and assess whether taking a constructive conflict approach would have yielded better consequences than using more traditional coercive approaches.[6] Actual policies that were relatively ineffective or counterproductive are occasionally compared to plausible positive policies that might have yielded more beneficial results. The result of such assessments should provide the grounds to determine whether more efforts to develop and employ the constructive conflict approach would be beneficial for the American people.

The constructive conflict approach derives from the ideas and practices of the developing conflict resolution field and from the field of peace studies. It is not presented as a comprehensive theory of social conflicts, but as a perspective in analyzing and conducting conflicts.[7] It is distinctive in emphasizing how to wage struggles well and bring about generally desired outcomes.

In the course of this book, I will trace the approach's evolution and growth from its emergence in the 1950s—how work in the constituent fields of peace studies and conflict resolution contributed to the official and non-official American participation in foreign conflicts, as well as the way the fields were affected by the experience of Americans in foreign conflicts. Learning from that interaction will enhance our understanding of each. Of course the way conflicts are waged and the fields of conflict resolution and peace studies are not purely American phenomena, and some attention will be given to ideas and practices from elsewhere.[8]

This treatment should help readers reflect on past American international involvements and infer lessons useful for current and future international policies. Even familiar events are seen in a new way when looked at from different points of view. The interpretations people make of their past actions help guide their future conduct. Unfortunately, mistaken interpretations are poor guides and contribute to failed and counterproductive strategies.[9] This is particularly true in foreign conflicts, since people generally have only indirect experience and limited knowledge of those complicated events occurring over long periods of time. The consequences of the ways the U.S. government as well as private American citizens have engaged in such conflicts are examined. The consequences relate not only to effects on external actors in the conflicts, but also to internal impacts upon American society.

Throughout the book, the diversity of Americans and the impact this diversity has on their views of American participations in foreign conflicts are considered. This diversity derives from more than the ideological differences between the Right and the Left. In addition, interests and perspectives vary by regions of the country, by religious and ethnic communities, by class and occupational positions, by generations, and by genders. Special attention is given to different actions and perspectives between American officials and American private citizens. I shall try to keep this diversity in mind and avoid assuming a false unity and uniformity of views and actions manifested by U.S. government leaders and various groups of private American citizens.

The Constructive Conflict Approach

The constructive conflict approach is a realistic perspective to understanding the dynamics of all social conflicts, and thereby provides ways to improve the benefits and efficacy of Americans' participation in foreign conflicts. This approach is an increasingly influential alternative to conventional adversarial thinking. Elements of this approach are becoming increasingly adopted in some social arenas, or at least particular terms from it have become frequently used, such as "win-win," "conflict transformation," "stakeholders," "mediation," and "dialogue." In order to assess the potential advantages and disadvantages of applying this approach, it must be set forth clearly.

The concept of peace, as used here, should be defined at the outset. It is commonly understood in two meanings: negative peace and positive peace.[10] Negative peace refers to the absence of direct physical violence, of wars. Positive peace includes the absence of structural violence, the institutionalized inequities in basic living standards. It is also sometimes extended to include harmonious relations. My usage is close to negative peace, with the addition that relations are not unilaterally and coercively imposed by one group upon another within the same social system.

The evolving constructive conflict approach has emerged from the conflict resolution and the peace studies fields. Since the end of World War II, and especially since the 1970s, research, experience, and theorizing about how conflicts can be waged and resolved so they are broadly beneficial rather than mutually destructive have greatly increased.[11] An overview of the perspective is presented in this chapter, and later chapters analyze, illustrate, and apply the various beliefs and practices more fully so that their adequacy can be better judged by the reader.

Early work in conflict resolution and peace research focused on why wars broke out, why they persisted, and why peace agreements failed to endure. Knowing why bad things happened was assumed to suggest how good things could occur (by avoiding doing what preceded the destructive escalations). This has some obvious limitations. Later research and theorizing have focused on what actions and circumstances actually have averted destructive escalations, stopped the perpetuation of destructive conduct, produced a relatively good conflict transformation, or resulted in an enduring and relatively equitable relationship among the former adversaries. A comprehensive approach to accounting for such transitions that integrates many factors and processes is still evolving.

These conflict resolution ideas have steadily evolved from the early years of the conflict resolution field in the 1950s, when it became identified as an area for research, theory-building, training, and practice. Much of the research and theory-building was based on studying the actual practice of peacemaking and peace-building by officials and by private citizens. That kind of work was a central part of the field of peace studies, which preceded the emergence of contemporary conflict resolution. For both, at the beginning, research methods included single or multiple case studies of decision-making in crises, effective international mediation, nonviolent conflict escalations, peacemaking negotiations, and peacebuilding.[12] They also included quantitative analysis of arms races, international mediation, international conflict negotiations, and building peaceful international relations (IR).[13]

In addition, two other research methods were used to study basic ideas and practices in the fields of peace studies and conflict resolution. One method entailed interpersonal and small group experiments related to negotiation styles and outcomes, maximizing mutual gains, and the formation of superordinate goals.[14] The other major research method was the analysis of interactive problem solving workshops by scholar/practitioners. In these workshops participants come from countries or other entities that are in conflict and engage in analyses of the conflict and explorations of possible ways to overcome contentious issues. The sessions are guided and facilitated by conveners of the workshops, often academics.[15]

The fields of peace studies and conflict resolution and many related fields of study continue to evolve in interaction with each other.[16] As these fields have grown in scope and empirical grounding, the lessons learned have been taught and have spread into the public arena. As workers in these fields learn, teach, and apply what they have learned, these ideas continue to be tested and refined.

Those ideas have evolved in tandem with the episodes of American participation in foreign conflicts that are examined in this book. The interactions between those involvements and the fields of conflict resolution and peace studies during the last several decades are central in this work.

Realities of the Constructive Conflict Approach

The fundamental idea of the constructive conflict approach is that conflicts are inevitable in human social life and they can produce widespread benefits. Conflicts are a major way people seek to challenge and rectify injustices, to win autonomy and more control over their own lives. In many cases, other people are likely to feel threatened by such efforts and resist them. Therefore the outcomes of conflicts are widely viewed as yielding gains to one side at the expense of the other.

Indeed, the benefits of a conflict generally are not equal for all the contenders, but some benefits may accrue to many contenders, and highly destructive consequences for the contenders can be avoided. Underlying this belief that conflicts can be resolved constructively is the recognition that conflicts often result in minimal mutual losses and even have substantial mutual benefits. Assessments of these outcomes may change over time, as relations among the former adversaries change. Of course, the different parties in a conflict may also differ as to their relative benefits from the conflict's outcome.

The possibilities of waging conflicts in relatively constructive ways are based on seven inter-related realities. These realities are empirically grounded, being inferred from experience and research. They are discussed here as guides for analysis and practice, not as dictated applications. Individually, they can be drawn upon to advance goals that are likely to have beneficial consequences for many people, including many opponents. Some ideas may be applied in the wrong circumstances and yield unwanted results. Nevertheless, combined they can guide strategies that avoid self-defeating behavior and illuminate paths out of seemingly intractable, mutually damaging fights. Together they provide the empirical grounding for the constructive conflict approach.

VARIETY OF INDUCEMENTS IN WAGING CONFLICTS

The first basic reality is that social conflicts are usually conducted with varying methods that inflict greater or lesser damages on the other side and with varying costs borne by each side. In a severe conflict, all sides are likely to suffer some degree of unwanted impacts. In this book, the severity of the losses and the broader the range and number of people so impacted constitute indicators of a conflict's destructiveness. Furthermore, different ways to wage a conflict have different chances of yielding significant and widely shared benefits. How damages can be minimized and gains maximized for various stakeholders in waging and settling conflicts will be examined throughout this work.

One reason that conflicts can be waged constructively, and have some good consequences entailing some mutual benefits, is that there are a great array of ways to conduct a struggle. Three kinds of inducements can be variously combined by each adversary to affect its opponent so that it changes its objectionable conduct.[17] One obvious kind of inducement is coercion or negative sanctions, applied to compel the desired change in the other side's conduct. The coercion may be threatened or implemented and may be violent or nonviolent. Another kind of inducement is the use of positive sanctions, offering rewards for the desired changed behavior. The third kind of inducement is persuasion, the use of appeals, justifications, and arguments that the desired changed behavior by the other side will be in that other side's own best interest and help fulfill shared values. Persuasion is often based on the attractive attributes of the persuader who possesses what has come to be called "soft power."[18]

In actuality, each strategy synthesizes these three kinds of inducements in shifting proportions. Richard L. Armitage and Joseph S. Nye, Jr. have written of the value of combining soft power and hard power (negative and positive sanctions, particularly military power) to constitute smart power.[19] These terms were often used by Hillary Clinton in her confirmation hearings as Secretary of State and in subsequent addresses.

The possible good effects of conflicts are widely recognized within societies, and conflict management is institutionalized in political and legal systems so as to derive benefits and reduce the costs of raising and settling contentions. This is at the heart of American political institutions and its adversarial legal system, which are designed to manage many conflicts, but they do not cover all kinds of conflicts and are ineffective at times. The constructive conflict approach focuses on the less formal and institutionalized means of managing struggles, which are largely the means used in foreign conflicts.

SOCIAL CONSTRUCTIONS

The second reality is that social conflicts are socially constructed by the antagonists, but not as any one of them would determine it.[20] Members of each adversarial side in a conflict strive to construct their own identity and the identity of the enemy; disagreements about that tend to be contentious. Members of each adversarial party consider which issues are at stake and how the antagonists are endangering or hampering the realization of their hopes. Within each contending party, political, religious, and intellectual leaders help generate different visions of the fight in which they are engaged. Furthermore, each side's conception of the opponents and the conflict influence the opposing side's self-conceptions. Such interactions can have varying implications.

HETEROGENEITY OF ADVERSARIES

The third reality is that each party in a large-scale conflict is heterogeneous in many regards. Most relevant here are the different interests and concerns that are held by leaders and among all the other people in a contending country or adversarial entity. Indeed, it is a common theme in conflicts for leaders on each side to assert that they have no quarrel with the people in the opposing camp, but only with their bad leaders. Leaderships themselves are not uniform and unitary; there are different interests among rivals and even allied groups. Furthermore, every person and group has many interests and values that are to some degree at stake in a given conflict. Consequently, as the relations among the groups within any one side change, a shift in the course of a conflict is feasible. Different factors or parties change in their relative power and influence—regularly through electoral politics, and in many other ways. Notably, in foreign conflicts, relations among allied governments are particularly subject to changing character, and therefore to possible conflict escalation or deescalation. Each party or faction on each side of a conflict can decide to act relatively constructively or not.

INTERCONNECTEDNESS

The fourth reality is that conflicts are interrelated and embedded in larger settings. Many conflicts are linked over time, each waxing and waning in scale and intensity. Others are linked in social space, small ones being nested in a series of ever-larger conflicts. Additionally, each side in a major conflict is engaged in its own set of internal and external fights. Shifts in the salience of one or another conflict affect the significance of other interconnected conflicts. The primary enemy may be downgraded to enemy number two, or even become an ally, when a new conflict and enemy become pre-eminent. Very significantly for the way a conflict is waged, it is not waged as a totally closed system. The social context may be the source of interveners who exacerbate a destructive conflict by helping to perpetuate it and/or to use more lethal weapons. On the other hand, external actors may serve as intermediaries who help constructively transform the conflict; for example, through mediation.

DYNAMISM

The fifth reality follows from the other four. It is that conflicts are dynamic; they move through stages and can be transformed to be better waged. They emerge, escalate, begin to de-escalate, and move toward an ending (imposed or agreed-upon), and the resulting outcome becomes the ground for renewed conflict or a stable new relationship. At each conflict stage, members of each contending party can behave with a greater or lesser degree of constructiveness: to stop destructive escalation, minimize outcomes that are destructive, and avoid destructive conflict legacies. There are no clearly demarcated stages with all members of the antagonistic sides moving together in lock-step, in an unvarying sequence. Some members of each side may lag behind in the transitions, while some may resist a particular transition and bring about a regression to an earlier step, either of escalation or de-escalation.

MEDIATION

The sixth reality is that mediation can contribute to beneficially changing a wide range of conflicts, from settling a dispute to transforming a complex conflict. Conflict transformation is generally understood as a broad positive change in the relationship between adversaries. Conflicts that are in early stages of escalating contention or that have become locked into self-perpetuating contentions can benefit from mediation.

Mediation varies greatly in form and content and its effectiveness is greatly dependent on the fit between what is attempted and the circumstances of the conflict. Generally, the conflict circumstances set parameters for what mediation can achieve. Nevertheless, the possibilities of mediation in improving the efficacy and quality of transforming and settling specific conflicts are well documented.[21] The study and practice of mediation is a central component of the field of conflict resolution, as discussed later in this chapter.

CONSIDERATION OF OTHERS

Finally, the seventh reality is that considering the other side's concerns often has shared benefits. Such considerations can guide contentious conduct toward stable, mutually acceptable accommodations among adversaries. This is the idea that establishing enduring legitimate relations among adversaries is more likely when they take a long-term time perspective and take into account each other's concerns and interests. This empirical generalization must be understood in conjunction with the fourth idea about the heterogeneity of each adversary. It is not the interests and concerns of oppressive autocratic leaders that must be considered so much as those of the great majority of people within each side in the conflict. It is undoubtedly the most challenging guiding principle for leaders of each side to apply, since it risks losing support from their own constituencies and making themselves vulnerable to demagogic rivals. Of course, consideration of the opponent does not require abandonment of one's own concerns and interests.

Building on these realities, the constructive conflict approach provides a comprehensive framework for analyzing and conducting all kinds of conflicts. This begins with the very definition of conflict. A social conflict occurs when two or more persons or groups manifest the belief that they have incompatible objectives.[22] Note that a conflict is not defined by the way in which it is manifested. In everyday speech, conflict sometimes refers only to relations marked by harsh coercion or violence, and sometimes only to undesirable conduct between people. The objectives that are viewed as incompatible, however, may not be of great significance. They may refer to disagreements about the means to achieve shared goals and contested with little resort to coercion.

Since conflicts change and move through stages, particular kinds of conflict resolution methods are appropriate for different conflict stages. Specific sets of explanatory conditions and processes are important at each conflict stage. In trying to explain how certain members of each party in a conflict move from one stage to another, analysts and partisans point to different factors. Partisans often point to characteristics of their adversary to explain why the conflict arose and why it is waged destructively. Many observers and analysts emphasize how the adversaries are associated and interact with each other to account for escalations and de-escalations. Still other observers and analysts focus on the system or context within which the antagonists exist.

In reality, all three sources of factors and processes combine to explain a specific change in a conflict's trajectory. For certain conflicts at particular times, one combination or another will provide the most valid accounting. On the basis of that understanding, suitable strategies may be adopted to avert destructive escalation, to move toward constructive de-escalation, to reach mutually acceptable agreements, or to build enduring good relations. Such considered choices are made by conflict partisans and intermediaries to maximize the chance of making efficient and effective progress.

Constructive Conflict Methods

The field of conflict resolution is sometimes viewed simply as a set of techniques used by intermediaries who regard themselves as conflict resolvers. In reality, constructive conflict methods are often applied by conflict partisans themselves, and also by interveners who do not think of themselves as being in the field of conflict resolution.[23] Indeed, evidence for various conflict resolution ideas and practices is based upon the actual experience of diplomats, political leaders, social movement organizers, and many other kinds of people engaged in conflicts.

In this book, the constructive conflict approach refers to the concepts and practices consistent with the seven realities previously outlined and are applied wittingly or unwittingly by partisans or by intermediaries. Three sets of methods of practice warrant attention at the outset: negotiation, escalation, and mediation.

NEGOTIATION METHODS

A large number of methods relate to how adversaries may negotiate a settlement of a particular dispute or to take steps that positively transform a major conflict. A core focus of analysis includes practices such as each negotiator listening attentively to what negotiating partners say, uncovering the interests and concerns that underlie stated positions, separating the persons in the negotiations from the conflict, and thinking creatively of new solutions to solve the problem constituted by the conflict.[24] These practices can be learned and are taught in conflict resolution courses.

To increase the likelihood of reaching agreements effectively and maximize shared benefits, fairness, and durability, the parties represented in the negotiations and the settings for the negotiations, as well as the methods of negotiation, need to be appropriate for each particular conflict. Empirical research indicates many ways to reduce asymmetries in resources between opposing sides that will enhance the outcome of negotiations.[25]

ESCALATION METHODS

Although much attention in the field of conflict resolution relates to settling disputes and reaching agreements, the constructive conflict perspective recognizes the importance of reaching outcomes that are regarded as legitimate and fair by significant stakeholders in the conflict. Very often, for that to occur, one or another side in a conflict reasonably believes that it must fight before the outcome will be fair. Indeed, escalating a conflict often is necessary to gain rights that have been denied or to defend one party's members from grave threats to what they deem to be highly significant for them. As should be obvious, each side in a conflict may believe that it must defeat its opponents to safeguard itself. In seeking victory, they may cause each other great injuries and severe mutual losses. Misperceptions of the balance of resources that each side can bring to bear regarding the matters at stake certainly can contribute to unanticipated losses.

Utilization of constructive escalation strategies is more likely to occur insofar as the adversaries share and recognize that they share common identities, values, and interests. Adversaries are in a relationship that in reality has some such qualities and is not simply and wholly characterized by incompatible and antagonistic qualities. They usually share an interest in avoiding the costs of a highly escalated violent fight. They often also share some possible gains that working cooperatively might provide.

Developing and adopting ways to escalate a fight with minimal destructiveness is central to the constructive conflict approach. The use of violence in conflicts has been the subject of immense attention. There is a great deal of experience and research regarding the horrors of war and the tendency for violence to be reciprocated and generate escalating exchanges of hurting behavior with fewer and fewer restraints. In many times and places in the past, recourse to violence in combat has been glorified and celebrated. This has become less widespread in human history, and at present, recourse to violence is often regarded as regrettable, although necessary under certain circumstances.[26] Relatedly, wars in recent decades have become less frequent and actually less deadly. One set of reasons for these developments, as discussed in later chapters, has been the increasing efforts to circumscribe and outlaw certain forms of violence. This is illustrated by international norms, laws, trials, and interventions proscribing the use of land mines, the commission of genocides, and gross violations of human rights.

Adopting the constructive conflict approach does not mean advocating that the United Sates never use military force in any engagement in foreign conflicts. At present, there are times and places where its use can be constructive. Much depends on its magnitude, its purposes, and the context of its use. As will be examined in this book, too often its use has been excessive and even counterproductive.

In the fields of peace studies and conflict resolution, considerable attention is given to nonviolent forms of coercion and to noncoercive inducements. In recent decades, the effectiveness of various nonviolent forms of action in bringing about contentious changes has been documented through considerable theorizing, research, and experience. As a result, knowledge is growing and diffusing about what conditions and policies make for effective nonviolent actions.[27]

MEDIATION METHODS

Mediation, a core component of the constructive conflict approach, includes a great range of mediating services or functions. In this discussion, they are roughly sequenced from largely facilitative to highly intrusive. A major service of mediation is helping adversaries communicate with each other, even when they are engaged in deadly conflict. Mediation sometimes entails helping the adversaries reframe their conflict, perhaps by helping them see shared threats of other problems that they can best manage by working together. This can help result in a constructive transformation of the conflict.

Mediators may help ease the negotiation process by proposing rules and techniques that enable disputants to discuss differences and minimize adversarial argument. These actions may include ensuring time constraints on speaking, sequencing of speakers, and encouraging disputants to ask questions of each other to learn the other side's underlying interests and concerns.

Mediation often helps opposing negotiators discover new options that are mutually acceptable to settle the conflict. This may result from bringing together a few members of the different sides to informally discuss their relationship and identify plausible steps to settle their conflict, as may occur in problem-solving workshops.[28] It also may be fostered by brainstorming, during which members of the negotiating sides suggest possible solutions, putting aside difficulties in implementing them for a short time.

Mediation sometimes takes the form of a mediator shuttling between opposing sides, learning what each side wants, what each may give up, and what each will not surrender. On that basis, a mediator may develop a possible settlement and present it to the opposing sides for their approval.[29] A mediator may be more or less active in formulating the settlement, varying from simply combining elements of each side's position to creatively constructing a new solution that he or she tries to sell.

Some mediators actually add resources that sweeten a settlement deal, resources that none of the adversaries will or can credibly contribute to the settlement. Mediators sometimes can alter the payoffs for each side's acceptance or rejection of a deal by pressuring one or more of the adversaries to reach an agreement.[30] Mediation often provides support for an agreement, which helps give it legitimacy for the negotiators' constituencies. Finally, mediators, insofar as they represent a broader community, frequently are seen as validating the fairness of the agreement and protecting the interests of parties not at the negotiating table. This also contributes to a more constructive conflict outcome.

In summary, many mediating services can enhance constructive de-escalating processes. They may speed initiating and concluding settlements, and may contribute to the fairness of a resulting agreement and help ensure its implementation. However, it is difficult (if not impossible) for the same person or group to perform certain functions simultaneously, but some may be done sequentially, as a mediator increases his or her level of participation. Of course, mediating efforts are often ineffective and sometimes counterproductive, as when they are poorly done or undertaken with methods that are not appropriate for the circumstance of the conflict. Mediation can fail to be significantly helpful when the mediators' wishes to get any kind of agreement are paramount or their desires to enhance their own interests are too great.

To maximize the potential benefits of mediation in mitigating destructive conflicts, mediation should be understood and conducted in accord with the contemporary conflict resolution field. However, in actuality, heads of countries and major institutions who may be acting as mediators in large-scale, major conflicts are not likely to have had any formal exposure to the ideas and practices of mediation in the context of the conflict resolution approach. Nevertheless, their associates and staff increasingly may have had such exposure.[31] The understandings of the public at large are also important. Insofar as the public is familiar with and supportive of the conflict resolution ideas and practice, its members will support their leaders acting in accord with them.

The approach also embodies many methods that are relevant to averting the outbreak of social conflicts, particularly ones that are conducted destructively. These methods relate to building social relations that are not oppressive or harshly unequal and to establishing legitimate ways of managing inevitable disputes. The methods are wide ranging, including training in conflict resolution practices, promoting curricula that strengthen mutual respect across societal divisions, and building social institution, cross-cutting ethnic, religious, and class divisions.

In recent decades, constructive conflict practices have expanded greatly in programs to recover from the traumas, hatreds, and fears resulting from destructively waged conflicts. The techniques to avert destructive conflicts before they arise are relevant here. In addition, dialogue methods and education to bolster reconciliation are expanding. The choice of these methods will be examined in many contexts throughout this book.

International Conflict Perspectives

The varying ways Americans think about international affairs and how the United States should engage in foreign conflicts are certainly highly relevant for this book. Their ways of thinking guide their own conduct, and the public's views influence elected federal officials' foreign policy choices.[32] Americans widely share many general values and preferences about America's place in the world. However, they also differ in their beliefs about how to actualize their values and prioritize their preferences. In subsequent chapters, this will be discussed in relation to specific foreign conflict involvements.

Undoubtedly, Americans differ in their beliefs about the necessity and efficacy of force and particularly of resorting to various kinds of violence in foreign affairs. Those beliefs affect the feelings Americans have about U.S. military personnel, in peace and in war. In addition, Americans vary in their beliefs and feelings about diplomats and diplomacy, about formal treaties and business contracts, and about international governmental organizations. They also differ in the relative importance of various interests and values they seek to protect or advance in foreign affairs. Obviously too, beliefs and attitudes change over time and vary regarding particular issues.

IR is a large academic field encompassing several schools of thinking about international affairs, with varying influence upon the attentive public and elite actors. Many of the disputes among adherents of these different schools are not germane to this book's purpose, but they do provide important insights that are useful for it. Therefore, I briefly note these diverse schools of thought, but do not discuss them in detail.

These IR approaches are often referred to as theories, but they are not comprehensive, formal deductive systems. Adherents of different schools generally emphasize one or another factor that is deemed to explain the workings of the international system, and some adherents attribute normative implications for the factor they stress.[33] These broad approaches change over time, partly as the world changes. The prominent schools include realism, liberalism, constructivism, and institutionalism, and critical approaches such as Marxist, feminist, post-colonial, and ecological.

Realists emphasize power because states seek security in an anarchic world. State leaders generally are viewed as acting rationally, weighing costs and benefits of different policies, and giving little weight to international law and institutions. There are variations among realists, some emphasizing that states seek to maximize power and to dominate, while others emphasize more defensive strategies.[34] Interestingly, realists recognize that some state leaders do not behave realistically, but reason that this will result in trouble for them.

Adherents of liberal IR theory stress that the domestic and transnational social context fundamentally shape state conduct in world politics. The society members' ideas, values, interests, and institutions impact state behavior by shaping state decisions.[35] Some adherents have stressed the empirical finding that democratic countries do not make war against each other and reason that a liberal economic and political world order of democratic countries will be peaceful. The primacy of persons over states also lessens respect for state sovereignty and supports the propriety of interventions into countries where people are suffering mass violence or harsh oppression.[36]

Institutionalism shares some of realism's assumptions, but it stresses how international rules and norms can and do reduce international insecurity and promote cooperation. Empirical research demonstrates how international organizations and regimes can provide greater efficiency and security in conducting international affairs.

Constructivism emphasizes how meanings are derived from ways of thinking about the world, and therefore it focuses on issues of identity and beliefs. State behavior depends on socially constructed perceptions of in-groups and out-groups, of justice, and of threats.[37] Constructivism also emphasizes the role of non-state actors who promote ideologies and beliefs that influence state behavior.

In addition to these IR approaches, there are several schools of thought that are critical of them, particularly of realism. These critiques stem from broad theoretical perspectives that have implications for the field of IR, particularly for international conflicts. For example, feminism is a wide-ranging perspective relating to all realms of social life, but it makes many contributions to understanding international conflicts that have been ignored or underestimated in mainstream IR work.[38] For example, strict gender roles for men and women are sustained by childhood socialization and adult institutions so that masculine ways of making decisions and of interacting are dominant. The result is support for hierarchical controls and ready resort to coercion or even violence in conflicts.

Marxism and other critiques of capitalism or of any large class, status, or power inequalities provide grounds for criticizing IR approaches that ignore state decisions being made to protect the economic or political interests of the ruling elites.[39] It should not be surprising that states do not have "interests" that are equally shared by all their citizens and which their leaders disinterestedly try to secure or even advance. IR theories that assume that the world is made up of such states warrant criticism, and the criticism can and do come from many directions and with different solutions.

Post-colonial critics take another stance, from the point of view of the developing, non-Western worlds. They view much of the mainstream IR theories as looking out from and looking out for the Eurocentric position.[40] That position was the core of the global economic system and it established the rules governing the system, but the post-colonial critics argue that as the world is changing, the Western world is becoming less dominant.

Finally, dealing with specific issue areas can be the source of critiques of the quite general IR perspectives identified here. For example, this is manifestly the case for the field of ecology and environmental challenges at local and global levels. Attention is being given to ecological issues, but theoretical convergence has only recently begun.[41]

The application of any of these ways of viewing a specific international conflict is not a simple matter. It might seem reasonable to expect that realist thinkers would be prone to support resorting to warfare and liberal thinkers less so. On the other hand, some analysts and practitioners stressing the importance of protecting and promoting American values of freedom and democracy have supported undertaking wars in order to expand those values. That was the hallmark of the liberal Democrats who became neoconservatives in the Republican Party or even those Democrats who supported going to war against Saddam Hussein's regime in Iraq.[42] At the same time, noted realist analysts were opposed to that war for such idealistic purposes.[43]

Scholars and practitioners in using the constructive conflict approach who are based in the fields of peace studies and conflict resolution have at times been critical of some aspects of IR perspectives. However, they also draw ideas and understandings from the IR approaches. Peace studies is one of the long-standing sections within the International Studies Association. After all, the IR theories emphasizing particular factors are important complements. The constructive conflict approach also is complementary to them. Indeed, in some degree there is a convergence between the conflict resolution and constructive conflict approaches with conventional national security thinking.[44] After all, the recent changes in the global system need to be recognized by those who would try to act effectively in it.

What is relatively distinctive about the constructive conflict approach as presented here is that it emphasizes the agency of persons engaged in conflicts, not general immutable forces. It is about changing conflicts and not only about understanding how they came to be the way they are. Furthermore, its adherents are less likely to regard a particular world system or international relationship as the right one. Their emphasis is on the process for changing and improving the world and relations in it.

These qualities of the constructive conflict approach could make it useful for policy-makers and activists engaged in foreign conflicts. Certainly, official U.S. foreign policy decisions do not flow out of any broadly conceived theory stressing one or another factor determining conflicts. The decisions are tailored by many considerations and understandings of particular circumstances at home and abroad. Some people and organizations may be highly ideological and adhere to strict interpretations of their dogma. However, American political leaders traditionally have been relatively pragmatic. Many presidents have staked out a general approach to their foreign policy orientation to differentiate themselves from predecessors from the other political party and to lend coherence and rally support for their decisions. This will be apparent in later chapters.

The United States is characterized by many voluntary associations, including many that are active in international affairs or have interests or values that bear on

U.S. policies regarding engagement in foreign conflicts. Their own participation in foreign conflicts and their efforts to influence U.S. foreign policy will not be ignored in this book. They may be based on ethnicity, religion, occupation, military veteran status, political ideology, or any number of other bases.

The constructive conflict approach, as I discuss it here, assumes some agency, some capacity for persons to affect the course of events by choosing one course of action over another. It suggests guides to conduct and provides an expanded repertoire of possible actions with broad beneficial consequences. It draws not only on the fields of peace studies and conflict resolution, but on academic theories of IR, other academic disciplines, reflections by engaged practitioners, and the common sense thinking of people everywhere.

Overview of the Book

Without a doubt, American involvement in foreign conflicts frequently has been ineffective and even counterproductive. The engagements in foreign conflicts have often been justified and supported as serving humanitarian needs and advancing universal norms and values. Yet many people in many countries think of the United States as interfering and dominating in their affairs, while serving crude American interests. Having sacrificed in relying upon highly coercive strategies, there is a natural tendency to want to believe that the sacrifices were worthwhile. It is painful to do otherwise. And there are often some benefits to claim, but too little thought or discussion is devoted to consider how those benefits or greater ones might have been attained with considerably lower human and material costs.

Whatever the good intentions may have been for coercive strategies and recourse to military engagement, those actions often have not produced sustained good results. This tends to be true in large-scale conflicts, where necessarily no single actor has full control of events. There are many contenders in every conflict, and each conflict is interconnected with many others. Therefore, some unintended consequences of any single conflict stakeholder's actions are inevitable. In this book, I offer some reality-grounded alternatives to the failed coercive strategies that have been pursued.

The constructive conflict approach emphasizes the importance of trying to analyze a conflict thoroughly and considering possible policy options before undertaking any one of them. In the following chapters the approach will be applied to analyses of possible application of the perspective. Those applications will test the usefulness of the approach. Judgments of the effectiveness of the approach are not only factual matters. Values and preferences are relevant as well. However, determining which values are good and how they should shape conduct is not an easy matter. Such issues have been the subject of debates at least since the time of Aristotle. Even now, sometimes it seems we face the unhappy choice between moral absolutes or moral relativism. In our actual conduct, however, other choices do exist.

To examine those other possibilities, I begin with considering the relationship between values and facts.[45] According to a very influential perspective in the social sciences, facts and values are deemed to be separate phenomena, independent of each other. This has been debated and contemporary work has found contrary evidence. Facts are affected by the values of the people discovering and reporting them. Values affect the factual questions asked and they influence the theoretical interpretations made for the facts. On the other hand, values are affected by what are considered facts, as we learn from experience and from studying the consequences of different conduct and policies.

Still, there many sources of morals, norms, and standards of judgment that people access and apply.[46] They are experienced in some degree as external to individual cognitions. Two major sources are faith in divine injunctions and in cultural traditions. These of course are limited to believers and are not universal, which may limit their applicability in conflicts between different communities of believers. Another possible source may be identifiable universal human needs, but these are usually quite general and fulfilled in many ways, often culturally prescribed. In addition, recent research on inherent standards of social conduct indicates that the human species and many other animals reward those who act fairly and punish those who do not.[47] Finally, I draw attention to global social norms. The diffusion of shared norms may be seen in the growing acceptance of the existence of universal human rights and the condemnation of torture, rape, and genocidal acts.[48] They are particularly relevant for large-scale social conflicts.

Synthesizing the multiple sources of values and moral standards with attention to the experience and research about the consequences will enable making judgments about the constructiveness and destructiveness of particular actions in specific circumstances. Instead of proclaiming broad moral principles, the analysis here will consider which policies are better in specific conditions. The analysis can then recognize changes in global political, cultural, technological, and normative conditions over time.

In the following chapters, actions that have contributed to progress toward peace will be noted, and their consistency with the conflict resolution approach assessed. Actions that were followed by destructive developments will also be noted and the possibility that those actions were inconsistent with the conflict resolution approach will be discussed. This analysis should help assess the value of the conflict resolution way of thinking in deciding how to pursue a constructive foreign policy.

Furthermore, the results of such an analysis should provide guidelines for actions to be taken and actions to be avoided under various circumstances.

In judging certain past actions as faulty, I do not mean to simply exploit the easy benefits of hindsight. The persons choosing the actions they did were doing so with limited knowledge and were experiencing pressures that could not be ignored; they were doing the best they could often within terrible circumstances. Viewing the actions with present knowledge and experience, however, can illuminate possibilities that will be more available when similar choices must be made in the future.

The chapters that follow trace the development of the constructive conflict approach and of American involvement in foreign conflicts in their historical sequences. This is useful since the approach evolved from prior work and each conflict involvement had legacies affecting subsequent conflicts. In Chapter 2, the first 24 years of the Cold War, 1945–1968, are discussed, focusing on episodes of adversarial contention and of conflict intervention. In Chapter 3, the transformation of the Cold War, 1969–1988, is analyzed. Chapter 4 examines the ending and immediate aftermath of the Cold War, 1989–1993. Then in Chapter 5, American interventions and other involvements in foreign conflicts during William J. Clinton's presidency, 1993–2000, are examined. Chapter 6 is focused on the war on terrorism and other conflict engagements during the years of George W. Bush's presidency. Chapter 7 analyzes the foreign conflict engagements in the years of Barack Obama's presidency. Finally, in Chapter 8, I discuss how the prevailing ways of thinking in America, conditions of civic institutions in American society, and the American political system can be changed so as to make constructive actions increasingly likely to be realized.

2 Escalations and De-escalations in the Cold War, 1945–1968

FOR MANY DECADES, American engagement in foreign conflicts was dominated by the adversarial relations with the Soviet Union, the so-called Cold War. There were frightening escalations and occasional reassuring de-escalations, and ultimately a remarkably nonviolent ending. The focus throughout this account is on American actions that affected these escalations and de-escalations and related foreign conflicts. Certainly, Americans alone did not determine the course of the Cold War, yet often they did influence its trajectory in significant ways, sometimes constructively, but often not. In conjunction with this examination, I discuss the emerging and evolving conflict resolution field that would contribute to more constructive ways to handle major international conflicts.

Initial Escalation, 1945–1952

World War II produced legacies that hugely affected the Cold War. Grotesque horrors were perpetrated during the Second World War, including the Holocaust, massive deaths in the Soviet Union, carpet bombing of German cities, and the nuclear bombing of Hiroshima and Nagasaki. Unlike the aftermath of the First World War, pacifist sentiments were not a widespread reaction to those and other horrors. Indeed, the cruelty and brutality of German Nazis and Japanese imperialists sanctified the extreme violence deemed necessary to destroy the organizations and people who committed dreadful acts. The military forces of the United States, Great Britain, the Soviet Union, and their allies were regarded as heroic by the peoples in their homelands and by the people they liberated from German and Japanese occupation. Having great military capability seemed to be a necessary safeguard against calamity. This view also derived from the general interpretation that British and French appeasement and military unpreparedness in the 1930s resulted in Fascist aggression.[1]

In addition, the extreme way the war was fought and the Allied insistence on total victory with unconditional surrender served as a model of modern war. The realities and value of concessions that were made, or of using particular elements from the former regimes in post-war governance, received little public attention. Thus, the Allied concession to retain the emperor of Japan on his throne greatly facilitated the surrender and the occupation of Japan.[2]

Soon after the end of World War II, and despite the wartime alliance between the Soviet Union and the West, the Cold War quickly erupted. Fierce disagreements arose between the U.S. and Soviet governments about which groups would govern in different countries. This was notably the case in Poland and in Greece, where a civil war between the government and Communist forces was waged. Crises related to the control of Berlin recurred, including the 1948 Soviet blockade of West Berlin. The Cold War was socially constructed by American and Russian leaders as an ideological conflict—between Freedom and Totalitarian Communism according to the Americans, or between Socialism and Capitalist imperialism according to the Russians. This masked more parochial constructions of American and Russian ambitions and interests.

In 1949, after many years of civil war in China, the Communist armed forces led by Mao Tse-Tung drove the Nationalist government headed by Chiang Kai-shek from mainland China to Taiwan. Mao proclaimed the establishment of the People's Republic of China (PRC). Communists could understandably believe they were on the march, which contributed to their overreaching at times. The need ultimately to rely on armed force as an agent of change or to prevent change was in the forefront of most political leaders' thinking. This contributed to mutual miscalculations among the government leaders of the United States and of the leaders of the USSR, PRC, and North and South Korea.

For example, the developments in the Korean peninsula after the Japanese surrender in 1945 had destructive consequences partly due to each side's overreaching and failing to give adequate attention to the concerns of their adversaries and of local populations. Korea had been a colony of Japan beginning in 1906. Japanese domination and exploitation of the Koreans produced resistance that the Japanese labeled communist, which contributed to the identification among Koreans of nationalism with communism.[3] President Franklin Delano Roosevelt's vision of the postwar world incorporated anticolonial nationalism, and he favored the idea of trusteeship as a transition to independence. The British and French governments, however, effectively opposed any trusteeship for their colonies. The disposition of Korea was not clearly agreed upon at Allied conferences about postwar arrangements. The U.S. government recognized the Soviet interests in Korea as a neighboring state, preferred a Korea administered as a single unit, and desired to play a leading role in the Korean occupation and government. The contradictions in these purposes were complicated by the recognition that Korean farmers felt exploited by Japanese and Korean landlords and sought sweeping land reforms. At the Potsdam Conference in July 1945, the United States was still planning for a land invasion of Japan and expected that Soviet military forces would advance into Manchuria and perhaps Korea. The idea of a unified, neutralized Korea with no foreign intervention might have been agreed upon, but it was not broached.[4]

When the Japanese military forces collapsed before U.S. military forces landed in Japan, the United States proposed a division of Korea between Soviet and American military forces before Korea was overrun entirely by the Red Army. The 38th parallel was as far north as the U.S. leaders thought they might secure Soviet agreement, and the Soviets did accept it.[5] Both sides thus obtained what seemed essential for their own national security interests. The concerns and interests of the Korean people were not given attention, partly due to the military exigencies of the time. However, moving quickly to a single Korean entity might have forestalled the great problems that arose from dividing Korea, but undoubtedly that would have been extremely difficult to establish at that moment. A unified Austria, however, was accomplished even with zones of occupation, as discussed later in this chapter.

The possibility of a unified Korea was discussed at the December 1945 meeting in Moscow of U.S. Secretary of State James F. Byrnes, Soviet foreign minister V. M. Molotov, and British foreign minister Ernest Bevin. The idea of a trustee arrangement with a provisional unified government seemed acceptable to them. But what transpired in Korea were actions by particular American, Russian, Korean, Chinese and Japanese officials who produced two states, which would become hostile.[6] Koreans were certainly not united, and many rejected the idea of a trusteeship. This included Syngman Rhee, who had been an exile in the United States and had long campaigned for Korean independence from Japan. He was strongly anti-Communist and closely associated with Korean landlords and other conservatives. General John R. Hodge, the U.S. occupation commander, himself quite conservative, was supportive of Rhee. In the north, the Soviets were hesitant about choosing some leading Korean Communists and chose one they could trust, Kim Il-sung, to chair a central People's Committee in the North, effectively a provisional government.[7]

Kim Il-sung had been a guerilla fighter in Manchuria in the 1930s and lived in the Soviet Union during most of World War II. He depended on Soviet support and had no base in the South. Both North and South Korea were to be led by fiercely nationalist leaders, determined to reunify Korea under their own rule.[8]

In 2002, professor William Stueck reflected on what policies the United States might have pursued to avoid the tragic path that was followed by many stakeholders.[9] He suggested that the best opportunity to form a unified Korean government was in September 1945. Just before Americans arrived in Seoul, some Koreans had formed the Korean People's Republic, a leftist organization with links to local people's committees. Stueck contemplated that if the Americans had encouraged a rightist party to form broader coalitions, the vision of a unified Korean might have become credible. Admittedly that would have required more persistence and trust-making steps than perhaps were then attainable. Stueck reasoned that would have necessitated replacing Hodge with General Joseph Sitwell, who was more knowledgeable about the region and more sensitive to the economic discontents among the local populations. That would have averted a South Korea led by Rhee and opened the possibility of forming a coalition government acceptable to the Soviet Union as well as to the United States.

This reasoning resonates with the constructive conflict approach. U.S. political leaders would be attending to long-term consequences and concerns of all the other primary stakeholders. They would take into account the felt needs of common people in the countries engaged in the region. Instead of risking self-focused, short-term, and confrontational actions on the ground, a broader approach with attention to the many interlocking conflicts linked to Korea might have had better consequences. The Communist victory in China in 1949 made such an approach even more unlikely.

Instead, the Korean division deepened and became more militarized, cross-border attacks occurred, and guerrilla fighting arose in the South.[10] Then, on June 25, 1950, North Korean military forces crossed the 38th parallel demarcation line and invaded South Korea. The attacks had been well-planned and approved by Stalin and Mao, and they anticipated a quick military victory.[11] However, they had overplayed their position and provoked a profound response. The attacks were a tactical surprise to the Americans and South Koreans, so the larger and better-equipped North Korean forces swiftly advanced. President Truman, with the sanction of the United Nations, ordered U.S. military operations to defend South Korea.[12] After being pushed far back, the U.S. and allied military forces successfully carried out a massive landing above the battle lines and rapidly recovered the lost ground, but then continued to move north beyond the 38th parallel. Chinese leaders warned that they would intervene to stop a continuing military advance up the peninsula.

Enticed by the military success and dismissive of the Chinese warnings, the U.S. and South Korean forces advanced close to the Chinese border. Massive Chinese armed forces entered the war and drove the allied forces back down the peninsula; the war entered a long bitter stalemate close to the former demarcation line. U.S. military casualties included 36,574 deaths in the Korean theater.[13]

The United States, if it had pursued a more constructive conflict resolution approach, might have given more weight to the likely reaction of the Chinese and earlier consideration of a mutual accommodation.[14] The risks of overreaching by the side that is winning are likely to be recognized and treated seriously if thoughtful conflict analysis is undertaken, including giving consideration to the opponents' likely reaction and to prior relevant experience in other conflicts.

Overall, the initial period of the Cold War was marked by important ideological differences, but the conflict also was characterized by mutual fears of military threats. Each side believed that the other sought to impose its form of government and to use its military power to expand its domain.[15] Each side insisted it was acting defensively as it strengthened its military capability; but those actions seemed to confirm the adversary's belief in the reality of the threat.

The way the Cold War was waged in its initial years, when Joseph Stalin ruled the Soviet Union, established patterns of conduct and structures that in many ways proved to be counterproductive for both sides. The heavy-handed Soviet domination of Eastern Europe generated resistance that was harshly suppressed, and which ultimately became untenable. Covert actions by each side to subvert the other's rule or influence were to prove damaging to many of their own long run interests.

The fundamental U.S. strategy toward the Soviet Union was generally discussed in terms of containment, derived from the analysis of George Kennan.[16] Although he regarded the Soviet Union as expansionist, he reasoned that if it were contained and its expectations of capitalism's failure were not fulfilled, it would change and adapt to that reality. He argued, "We must have courage and self-confidence to cling to our own methods and conceptions of human society . . . [T]he greatest danger that can befall us in coping with this problem of Soviet communism, is that we shall allow ourselves to become like those with whom we are coping."[17] In implementing this doctrine, however, the reliance on military strength quickly became paramount. This was expressed in the 1950 National Security Council Report 68 (NSC-68), which called for a powerful military capable of offensive operations against Soviet warmaking capacities. Kennan was critical of this undue militarization of the containment idea, confident that the Soviet leaders would not start a general war in Europe.

The American preponderance of economic and military power in the world after the end of World War II fostered the expectation among many Americans that the century of American global primacy had come. The expectation was enhanced by faith in the significance of the American monopoly of atomic weapons, although the monopoly was short-lived. Even when the Soviet Union developed its own atomic weapons, American superiority in number of warheads and in the quality of delivery systems endured.

Given the overwhelming American power, some Americans attributed unwanted foreign developments to Communist subversion and acts of betrayal by high-placed Americans. Thus, the defeat of the Nationalist government of China by the Chinese Communists was characterized as the "loss of China," caused by the U.S. government's lack of continued support. The American supporters of Chiang Kai-shek, the "China Lobby," and some Republican political figures made this argument. An enduring legacy was the wariness of many Democrats to being seen as "soft" and "weak" in foreign affairs.

Some political leaders, notably Joseph McCarthy, Republican senator from Wisconsin, charged widespread Communist infiltration of the State Department and elsewhere in the government. He and others claimed that Communist spies and sympathizers contributed to the loss of China and the Soviet acquisition of atomic secrets. Although there were several agents of Soviet espionage, the sweeping and generally unfounded accusations had a chilling effect and hampered accurate assessments of international affairs and thoughtful consideration of policy options. In addition, the careers of people in many areas of endeavor, including entertainment, scholarship, and government service, were severely damaged. The experience of accusations and shattered lives produced a legacy of fear among some people that they must not appear to be "soft" about Communists or other enemies of America. Yet, McCarthy so overreached that he was censured by the U.S. Senate, and the term "McCarthyism" became an epithet that served as a caution against wild accusations.

Despite the widespread American support for the goals and methods of waging the Cold War, many alternative perspectives were advanced in the first decade after the Second World War. Some were continuations of long-standing views. They included religiously based pacifist beliefs and socialist concerns about capitalism and imperialism. The war helped produce a new cadre of activists; for example, as a consequence of the experience of conscientious objectors to military service. They developed new social goals and means of struggle as civil activists after the war.[18]

The idea of advancing world federalism gained popularity in the United States and many other countries manifested in a substantial social movement, which included the formation of several organizations, supportive statements by major public figures, and a draft constitution for a world government.[19] However, after a few years of widespread interest, a general decline in attention occurred, perhaps because of the primacy of the Cold War paradigm.

Potential supporters of a peace movement were divided and relatively inactive in the early 1950s. The divisions were exacerbated by the 1948 presidential elections, with five contenders: Harry S. Truman, Thomas E. Dewey, Strom Thurmond, Henry A. Wallace, and Norman Thomas running as the nominees of the Democratic, Republican, States' Rights, Progressive, and Socialist parties, respectively. Although the States' Rights and the Progressive parties represented different elements of the Democratic Party, Truman won re-election. Wallace campaigned against the militancy of the Truman administration's anti-Soviet policy that threatened to result in war. At times critical of Soviet communism, he also sometimes explained its bad behavior as a consequence of Western antagonism. Most leaders of the liberal wing of the Democratic Party and pacifists in the peace movement attacked Wallace as a tool of American communism.[20]

The North Korean invasion of South Korea consolidated the broad American consensus supporting Truman's conduct in the Cold War. Truman's characterization of the Korean War as a police action undertaken under the authority of the UN gained wide support. Norman Thomas favored it, and even Henry A. Wallace lent his support. No clear and plausible alternative was articulated. American discussions of limiting the objectives and the methods of waging the Korean War might have avoided the overreaching military advance and the prolongation of the war that occurred. As discussed later in this chapter, only at the end of the 1950s did attention to the specific issue of nuclear weapons testing become a catalyst for a massive peace movement.

The Cold War was not rigidly frozen; it went through several periods of intense escalation, then of thawing followed by renewed freezing. Thus, the first few years of the Cold War were marked by the Berlin blockade and the Korean War. Yet, understandings and institutionalized ways to manage the Soviet-American conflict gradually developed and helped moderate the intensity of crises.[21]

Early Moderations of Confrontations, 1953–1959

Following the death of Joseph Stalin in March 1953, the possibility of substantially reducing the intensity of the Cold War arose.[22] The new collective leadership in the Soviet Union, soon headed by Nikita Khrushchev, was concerned about the state of the Soviet economy and the burdens of military preparedness. Worried by what the leaders saw as continuing Western military encirclement, they wanted to reduce the tensions of the Cold War and find areas for cooperation with the United States. They undertook a wide array of domestic reforms and a variety of foreign policy initiatives under the rubric of peaceful coexistence. At the same time, they continued to believe that Communism would triumph and they should support revolutionary movements, as a post-colonial world began to emerge.

On the American side, Dwight D. Eisenhower was inaugurated as president in January 1953, and he too was concerned about the burdens being placed on the American economy by the Cold War arms race.[23] He considered the possibility of responding to the Soviet peace overtures, but that was not the course taken. Secretary of State John Foster Dulles and other officials advising the president developed strategies that Eisenhower adopted to contain, deter, and even roll back Soviet control. Reliance would be placed upon nuclear weapons to manage military expenditures and to counter Soviet expansionist threats. Political, economic, and covert measures would be taken to "create and exploit troublesome problems for the USSR, impair Soviet relations with Communist China, complicate control in the satellites, and retard the growth of the military and economic potential of the Soviet bloc."[24]

In the context of these diverse considerations and expectations, some important steps to reduce Cold War contentions nevertheless were taken by the Soviet and the American governments. In July 1953, after two years of stalemate and deadly battles in Korea, difficult negotiations produced an armistice. However, a peace treaty and mutual diplomatic recognition were not achieved. This failure bedeviled relations between the United States and North Korea, yet serious efforts to reach a peace treaty have not been pursued, despite many North Korean expressions of great interest. Again, a more constructive approach would point to undertaking explorations of that possibility in subsequent years.

OFFICIAL ACCOMMODATIONS

Using elements of the constructive conflict approach contributed to lessening Cold War intensity when the circumstances were suitable. For example, in May 1955 the Austrian State Treaty was signed by the United States, the USSR, France, and the United Kingdom, ending the four-power occupation of Austria and a matter of contention between the USSR and the West.[25] Unlike the division of Korea, Austria had one government, despite being occupied. Two considerations were crucial in reaching an agreement to end the four-power occupation. The Soviets had recognized that the Communist Party in Austria had very little electoral support and that was not changing. The Austrian government provided credible reassurances to the Soviet leadership that Austria would not join any Western alliance opposing the USSR, and it would remain neutral in the Cold War. The value of creative reassurances between opponents in settling conflicts is an important element in the constructive conflict approach.

Face-to-face meetings between the highest officials of the United States and the USSR were renewed.[26] A summit meeting of the "Big Four" was held in Geneva in July 1955, including President Dwight D. Eisenhower of the United States, Prime Minister Anthony Eden of the United Kingdom, Prime Minister Edgar Faure of France, and Premier Nikolai A. Bulganin of the Soviet Union, with Nikita Khrushchev also attending. However, no substantial progress was made in settling major issues in contention during these years. Germany remained divided and West Germany was militarily and economically integrated within Western Europe. Disarmament negotiations were conducted for appearances' sake, and efforts to find mutually acceptable steps to control the arms race were unsuccessful.[27]

The National Security Council judged that U.S. disarmament policy was in disarray, which could be rectified by appointing someone to do a comprehensive policy review. In March 1955, President Eisenhower appointed Harold Edward Stassen as his special assistant on disarmament, with cabinet status. Stassen worked diligently and creatively with Soviet officials to forge proposals that could be mutually acceptable. However, Dulles effectively countered his efforts, negotiations were not successful, and Stassen resigned in February 1958. Subsequently, however, Stassen's gradualist approach was adopted by Dulles and his successor, Christian Herter.[28]

In September 1959, Nikita Khrushchev visited the United States, met with Eisenhower at Camp David, Maryland, and traveled to Iowa to visit Roswell Garst's farm. Garst had visited the Soviet Union privately in September 1955 to promote and sell hybrid corn seed and met with Khrushchev at that time; they agreed that Soviet agriculture would benefit from adopting some of America's agricultural methods.

Khrushchev was back in the United States in September 1960 to attend a UN session in New York, at which he pounded his shoe on his desk to demonstrate displeasure at a delegate's speech. His behavior was ridiculed by many Americans, but he showed a human face in representing the Communist system. Finally, negotiations regarding disarmament, conducted for competing propaganda benefits, gave way to achievable arms control measures.[29]

Several developments within the Soviet Union in the 1950s and 1960s were critical for the future transformation of the Cold War. In February 1956, Khrushchev delivered a shocking secret speech at the 20th Party Congress denouncing Stalin's cult of personality and crimes, including the terror of the mass purges of the 1930s.[30] News of the speech soon spread beyond the high ranks of the Communist Party, spreading disillusionment about Stalin and Stalinism throughout the Soviet Union, the Soviet bloc, and beyond. It helped foster a period of liberalization known as the "Thaw," reducing censorship and enabling greater expression of independent thought. These were exciting times for many young intellectuals who debated how to change the Soviet system and retain the Communist Party's rule. Foreshadowing future developments, the young Mikhail Gorbachev and his wife Raisa were active in these circles.[31]

In April 1956 the Soviet government established the Institute of World Economy and International Relations to conduct research on the economy and politics of contemporary capitalism; it was a step toward more objective and less ideological analyses. Other institutes were soon founded, focusing on various regions in the world; most notably, the Institute of U.S. and Canada Studies was founded in 1967.

NON-OFFICIAL LINKAGES

Soviet participation in international nongovernmental organizations opened during this period, enabling academics and artists to meet and exchange ideas with colleagues outside the Communist world. For example, in August 1956, as I began a year as a Fulbright Research Scholar based in Cologne Germany, I attended a meeting of the International Sociological Association in Amsterdam. For the first time, delegations from the Soviet Union and some countries of Eastern Europe came. The Western sociologists wondered who would appear, since Soviet leaders had previously denounced sociologists as "running dogs of capitalist imperialism." Among the delegation members were philosophers, ethnographers, journalists, Communist Party ideologues, and some actual sociologists, particularly from Poland. Some long-lasting connections were begun between attendees from the East and the West.

In January 1958, an American-Soviet agreement was signed to begin officially organized cultural exchanges in various domains.[32] Its scope included exchanges in science and technology, agriculture, medicine and public health, radio and television, motion pictures, exhibitions, publications, government, youth, athletics, scholarly research, culture, and tourism. It was an executive agreement rather than a treaty, thereby not requiring ratification by the U.S. Senate, which might have resulted in a prolonged debate. The Soviet and Eastern-bloc participation in international nongovernmental organizations and in these exchanges enabled collegial relations to grow across the Cold War divide.[33]

During the 1950s, what came to be called Track Two diplomacy also was initiated, which has become an important component of the conflict resolution field. This channel refers to non-official meetings between persons from opposing sides, often possessing good connections with officials within their sides. For example, in July 1957, nuclear physicists and others involved in the development of nuclear weapons and strategies about their possible use, from the United States, Great Britain, and the Soviet Union, began to meet and exchange ideas about ways to reduce the chances of nuclear warfare. The first meetings were held in Pugwash, Nova Scotia in Canada, at the summer home of Cyrus Eaton, who provided the initial funding for these meetings. This evolved into the Pugwash Conferences on Science and World Affairs.[34]

American and Soviet physicists were well positioned to forge transnational connections and to influence government officials, particularly related to the dangers of nuclear weapons. They knew of each other's research through publications; the Soviet nuclear scientists read the *Bulletin of the Atomic Scientists*, which discussed proposals related to the arms race. In April, 1955, the Hungarian-born American nuclear physicist Leo Szilard discussed with the Soviet ambassador to the United States the idea of establishing a small committee to study Soviet-American disagreements about nuclear weapons and recommend ways to overcome them. He later wrote to Khrushchev and met with him in September 1960, when Khrushchev was in New York. In 1957 and 1958, Andrei Sakharov, a leader in the development of Soviet nuclear weapons, participated in efforts in the Soviet Union to spread information about the risks of nuclear weapons tests.

Discussions at Pugwash meetings over many years contributed to the signing of the Partial Test-Ban Treaty, the Nonproliferation Treaty, the Biological Weapons Convention, and the Anti-Ballistic Missile Treaty. Later meetings helped build consensus for the Strategic Arms Reduction Treaties I and II, the Intermediate Nuclear Force Treaty, and the Chemical Weapons Convention.[35] In recognition of these contributions, in 1995 the Nobel Peace Prize was awarded to the Pugwash Conferences and to Joseph Rotblat, its executive director.

The establishment of the Dartmouth Conference is another important example of Track Two diplomacy during this period.[36] President Dwight D. Eisenhower urged Norman Cousins, then editor of the *Saturday Review*, to bring together a group of prominent American and Soviet citizens as a means of keeping communication open when official relations were especially strained. The first meeting was held at Dartmouth College in October 1960, and many meetings followed, providing a venue for the exchange of information and the exploration of options that might be useful in official negotiations.

Beginnings of Conflict Resolution Field, 1950–1960

Within the United States, after World War II, many nongovernmental organizations began to engage in the emerging fields of peace studies and conflict resolution and to advocate actions and policies that their participants believed would reduce the chances of war between the United States and the Soviet Union.[37] Colleges associated with the peace-churches, Brethren, Friends (Quakers), and Mennonites established peace studies programs, and later conflict resolution programs, and many Catholic institutions of higher education established peace and justice programs.

The field of contemporary conflict resolution began to emerge in the mid-1950s, drawing upon theory and research from many academic disciplines and experience in many arenas of conflict. Within the United States, the Center for Advanced Study in the Behavioral Sciences at Stanford in Palo Alto, California, was a catalyst for the field's emergence. The center was intended to foster major new undertakings in the behavioral sciences. In its initial year, 1954–55, several scholars were invited who reinforced each other's thinking related to peace and conflict theory and research. They included social psychologist Herbert Kelman, economist Kenneth E. Boulding, mathematician Anatol Rapoport, political scientist Harold Lasswell, and general systems theorist Ludwig von Bertalanffy.

In the next year, Boulding and Rapoport returned to the University of Michigan and joined with other colleagues to begin *The Journal of Conflict Resolution* in 1957. Then, in 1959 they and others established the Center for Research on Conflict Resolution at the University of Michigan, with the sociologist Robert C. Angell as the first director. Scholars at the Center and in other institutions published a variety of works that might contribute to formulating a comprehensive inter-disciplinary theory of social conflicts.[38]

In 1959, the International Peace Research Institute was established in Oslo, Norway, with Johan Galtung as director for its first ten years.[39] Galtung founded the *Journal of Peace Research* at PRIO in 1964, and in 1969 he was appointed professor of conflict and peace research at the University of Oslo. His work was highly influential throughout the world; for example, his analysis of structural violence was important in the conflict analysis and resolution field in Europe and in the economically underdeveloped world.[40]

The concept of structural violence is crucial to the proposition that in a social system in which some people are not inflicting direct physical violence against other people there still may be groups of people living impoverished, shortened lives. People with such lives are suffering structural violence. This underlies the distinction made in peace and conflict studies between negative peace, the absence of war, and positive peace, the absence of structural violence as well, as discussed in the previous chapter. For some workers in the field, positive peace refers to high levels of well-being, justice, or liberty.

The relations between negative and positive peace are complex, and workers in the peace and conflict resolution fields vary in the emphasis they give to each concept.[41] Some analysts stress that societies and relations characterized by negative peace will not be enduring if they have high levels of structural violence or unjust domination of one side by another. Violence may even be viewed favorably as a way to bring about a high degree of positive peace. In this work, peace is not a quality of a relationship that is either present or absent. Group relationships are complex and dynamic, with varying degrees of many dimensions of peacefulness.

In a sense, the constructive conflict approach has evolved from responding to the contradictions about advancing both negative and positive peace. It offers an approach for developing and employing peaceful ways to overcome violent and oppressive relations, including escalating struggles, so that the relations become productive and just.[42]

A wide variety of research and theorizing relating to conflict and to peace started in the 1950s and 1960s. Some work examined the bases and escalation of conflicts in various arenas. Other work focused on particular aspects of conflicts; for example, psychological and social psychological processes, the functions of social conflict, and negotiating in conflicts.[43]

Much attention was given to conflict escalation, which was generally regarded as disruptive and undesirable.[44] Thus, considerable work was focused on community conflicts, in which fluoridation of drinking water was opposed or where protests erupted against "left-wing" books in libraries. In 1954, the Twentieth Century Fund commissioned the Bureau of Applied Social Research at Columbia University to review the literature about outbreaks of community conflicts.[45] Then, conflicts relating to the social movements of the late 1960s changed the stance of many social scientists about the desirability of social conflicts, as examined in the next chapter.

Research that was to be influential in the emerging field of conflict resolution examined industrial conflicts and the ways that labor-management conflicts could be ameliorated. This research included studies of the institutionalization of collective bargaining, and the processes of negotiation, mediation, and arbitration.[46] It included management processes that attended to the emotional needs of workers, the human relations approach in management. It also included regular meetings of executives, managers, and workers in which significant problems in the organization were discussed and solved.[47] The idea that conflicts posed problems that required innovation and creativity to be solved came to play an important role in the conflict resolution approach.

Another body of work during this period that was to play a significant role in the development of conflict resolution involves experimental research pertaining to small group dynamics and group relations. For example, analyses were made of how leaderless groups function and manage themselves, which could bear on interactions among persons from antagonistic collectivities seeking to solve their conflicts.[48] Beginning in the late 1940s, Morton Deutsch conducted and synthesized experimental research about many aspects of conflict resolution. This included research about the conditions conducive to building cooperation and trust and to pursuing constructive negotiation.[49]

Influential research and theorizing was also done about the structural and cultural features of societies that affect the way international and domestic conflicts are conducted. For example, analyses of the military-industrial complex revealed the self-serving interests of the managers and investors in corporations producing military weapons, of members of Congress who received campaign contributions from them, of workers employed in these industries and their union leaders, and of military leaders who gained status and power by controlling the weapons.[50] The research indicated how these interests were served by developing newer and more powerful military weapons, often independent of security needs for them. The analyses were conducted about the U.S. and Soviet military-industrial complexes and served to demystify the alleged need for increasing the size and budgets of military establishments in those and allied countries.

Another matter of study pertained to nationalism, loyalty, and communal identities and their roles in large-scale conflicts. For example, Morton Grodzins examined the making of disloyalty as well as loyalty, prompted by studying the World War II internment of Americans of Japanese descent.[51] In addition, studies of the outbreak of revolutions began to draw attention.[52]

Numerous research projects were also undertaken analyzing quantitative data about interstate wars, notably the Correlates of War project, initiated in 1963 under the leadership of J. David Singer.[53] Robert C. North led a project examining why some international conflicts escalated to wars and others did not, and Richard Snyder analyzed foreign policy decision-making.[54]

The logic of game theory and the research based on it also has contributed significantly to conflict resolution thinking.[55] The associated vocabulary has spread into much popular parlance, although often unconnected to that source. Two basic types of two-sided games or conflicts with different kinds of payoff matrices are often distinguished: zero-sum and mixed-sum. In zero-sum games, such as matching pennies, what one side wins, the other loses. People engaged in intense fights often think and act as if they are in a zero-sum conflict.

In actuality, all conflicts can be reframed and reconfigured into mixed sum conflicts. The payoff matrices in such games or conflicts have four outcomes: one side (A) wins and the other loses (B), B wins and A loses, both A and B lose, and both A and B win. However, how much each side wins or loses varies from one payoff matrix to another.

The payoffs often are such that individually rational conduct can result in collectively self-defeating losses. In a conflict with such a payoff, each side may have two choices: to cooperate with the other side or to try to gain an advantage over the other side. In this case, the payoffs are such that each side reasonably would choose not to cooperate in order to protect itself from the other side, whatever the other side does. As a result, both sides lose more than if they trusted each other and chose to cooperate and thereby have a win-win outcome. Thus, leaders of two neighboring countries may each spend great sums for military defense in fear of being attacked and defeated by the other side. That is costly and dangerous, but seems rational for each side; however, if they could agree to limit their spending to clearly defensive weapons, both sides could be winners.

A great deal of research and theorizing has and continues to be done about this kind of a mixed-sum payoff matrix, which is identified as represented by a hypothetical prisoner's dilemma.[56] Much research has been based on reiterations of this game, including different strategies played by computers. The computer program that most dependably resulted in stable cooperation and greatest common gain is a simple *tit-for-tat* strategy. In this strategy, the opening choice is to cooperate and in every subsequent choice, the other side's cooperation or noncooperation was reciprocated. Other research using historical examples has been interpreted to confirm the positive effectiveness of reciprocating with equivalent actions, and not persisting in cooperation or noncooperation regardless of the other side's actions.[57] Of course in actuality the opposing sides may differ about when the exchanges began and what is equivalent.

In actual conflicts, as the constructive conflict approach emphasizes, each side is not a single unitary entity engaged in a single conflict. Each entity includes internal factions and external allies, and also other antagonists in other conflicts. Those complexities necessarily affect each player's actions.

Finally, a variety of research and theorizing was done about ways conflicts could be overcome. For example, Muzafer Sherif researched not only how groups readily develop in-group solidarity and antagonistic attitudes toward other groups, but also on how the antagonism is overcome when the group members are in situations that foster superordinate goals (goals that they share).[58]

Charles Osgood examined how unilateral actions could result in reciprocal interactions that de-escalate a conflict, a process he termed Graduated Reciprocation in Tension Reduction (GRIT).[59] The initiating side announces the policy and takes a series of steps that are conciliatory but do not endanger its own security. As a result, mutual reassurance and mutual confidence can help transform a conflict.

Other research focused on preventing violent conflicts from recurring or emerging, such as Karl Deutsch's examination of the formation of security communities between countries and David Mitrany's analysis and Ernst Hass's research about the way cooperation in one functional area can foster increased integration in other areas.[60] Such research promised to aid in formulating policies that bind societies together, even former adversaries, so that wars would not recur between them. For example, as a Fulbright Research Fellow, I spent the academic year 1956–57 in Germany studying the newly established European Coal and Steel Community and how it affected German opinions and institutions so as to foster a European identity and Franco-German reconciliation.[61] These matters became highly salient again after the end of the Cold War, with its attendant increase in collective interventions to stop wars and aid in reconciliation and peacebuilding after mass violence.

Related work dealt with nongovernmental activities as well as government policies; for example, attention was given to the expanding roles of international nongovernmental organizations.[62] This recognized the emergence of transnational social ties that could be the basis of sustainable governmental institutions, regionally and globally. The importance of non-state actors has increased in many regards and now is the object of considerable research and policy concerns, as will be discussed in later chapters.

These activities generated a multitude of ideas and empirical findings, but they did not form a unified theory or even a clearly formulated approach to mitigating social conflicts. They were the sources, nevertheless, for an emerging alternative way of thinking about and managing American relations with the Soviet Union and engaging in other international conflicts. They provided a reservoir of strategies to be applied in similar circumstances and interpersonal networks that could be mobilized for specific policies under opportune conditions.[63] The soil was well prepared and many seeds had been planted for future growth.

John W. Burton, for example, drew on small group and organization experimentation in developing facilitated workshops to help resolve international conflicts.[64] Burton had held important offices in the Australian government, including Secretary of External Affairs. In 1963, he resigned from government service and established the Centre for the Analysis of Conflict at the University of London. Beginning in December 1965, Burton, with several colleagues, organized a series of meetings with representatives from Malaysia, Indonesia, and Singapore about a bitter dispute relating to Malaysian independence. The academic facilitators were analytic and nonjudgmental, helping the representatives to interact noncoercively and analyze the roots of their conflict, which was followed by cooperatively searching for new shared options and their own solution. The meetings concluded in May 1966 when official negotiations had produced an ending to the dispute. The facilitated problem-solving workshop helped in developing an alternative to the conventional international relations approach to resolving international conflicts.[65]

Escalating and De-escalating Events, 1955–1968

Despite steps toward de-escalation of the Cold War, many events in the 1950s and the 1960s demonstrated that the great rivalry between the United States and the USSR continued. The rivalry was waged on several related fronts, including an arms race, economic and scientific competition, and an ideological struggle. Thus, Soviet leaders asserted that the USSR's success in becoming a powerful industrial and military power and providing for the basic needs of the Soviet people was a wonderful model for people in economically underdeveloped countries. The underdevelopment of the Third World was explained by Marxism and its analysis of capitalist imperialism. In practice, the Soviets supported regimes allied to them, rather than waiting for the economic changes in the underdeveloped countries that would generate a revolutionary condition. On the other hand, American leaders claimed that political democracy and individual freedom together with a capitalist free market system account for American wealth, global power, and high standard of living. In practice, economic policies were pursued in Third World countries that it was thought would eventually produce democratic societies.

To some degree, both sides used persuasive inducements, based on their soft power, to compete and did not rely solely on coercive power. To strengthen America's soft power, overcoming the discriminatory treatment of African Americans would be important. Some steps in this regard were taken by the federal government. For example, in July 1948, President Harry S. Truman signed Executive Order 9981, which ordered racial integration of the armed forces. The civil rights struggle, waged in the courts and in Southern lunch rooms and streets, won admiration for America around the world. It bolstered American soft power.

Several grave international crises occurred as leaders on each side sought to advance goals that challenged and constrained the other side, and employed coercive threats in doing so. Furthermore, sometimes particular factions and groups within one or both camps spurred the conflict's escalation and the resulting crises, and at times internal changes resulted in unanticipated dangerous crises. In addition, governments and peoples in various regions of the world, while pursuing goals of their own, tried to take advantage of the U.S.-Soviet rivalry, thereby exacerbating the Cold War.

These processes and circumstances often combined to produce Cold War escalations, which seriously undermined constructive efforts that were beginning to transform the Cold War. Sometimes, on the other hand, the very changes that signaled a relaxation of tensions actually prompted acts that provoked an intensification of the Cold War. Thus, the "Thaw" in the Soviet Union, which allowed for the expression of more diverse views, was taken very seriously by people in Poland and Hungary, including leading members of their ruling Communist parties. Fiery flare-ups in tension also spurred efforts to dampen the flames quickly or over time, producing conditions better suited to peaceful growth.

In October 1956, the Polish Communist Party surprisingly selected Wladyslaw Gomulka as its leader, someone who had been imprisoned (1951–1954) for "nationalist deviations."[66] Khrushchev and other Kremlin officials tried to coerce the new Polish leadership to adhere to Soviet positions and decided to deploy Soviet troops to replace the Polish leadership. However, this was not done when Gomulka made a speech pledging that Poland would fulfill its obligations to the Warsaw Treaty Organization and build socialism.

During the same time, the Hungarian attempt to move toward a more humane and autonomous society followed a different course.[67] On October 23, 1956, perhaps having taken too seriously the possibility of U.S. and Western assistance in breaking away from Soviet domination, uprisings broke out in Budapest and elsewhere in Hungary. Soviet leaders argued about how to respond and decided to try negotiations, but this decision was reversed on October 31. Hungarian Communist Party leader Imre Nagy's declaration that Hungary would withdraw from the Warsaw Pact was probably decisive in that reversal. On November 4, 1956, the Red Army invaded Hungary and suppressed the uprising. The consequences in Poland and Hungary included changes that over time contributed to social movements that would hasten the end of the Cold War.

THE ARAB-ISRAELI CONFLICT

The Cold War rivalry sometimes worsened regional conflicts, which in turn intensified the Cold War. This happened with the 1956 Arab-Israeli warfare, which was part of an interconnected tangle of conflicts.[68] In telling the story of any conflict, the choice of the starting point is socially constructed and often controversial. In this case, one might begin with the 1948 establishment of the state of Israel and the defeat of Arab military forces that sought to stop it; or begin in 1952 when Arab nationalist military officers, led by Gamal Abdel Nasser, took power in Egypt; or begin with the February 1955 creation of the Baghdad Pact, a regional military alliance to constrain the anti-Western governments in the Middle East.[69]

Initially, the new Israeli leadership saw possible affinity with the new Egyptian leadership, since they both had struggled against British rule and shared beliefs in socialism. Indeed, there were peacemaking overtures through nonofficial channels. The American Friends Service Committee (AFSC) and other Quaker organizations, having done humanitarian work in the Middle East with Jews and Arabs, had good relations with both. Consequently, in July 1955, Israeli and Egyptian government leaders invited the AFSC to attempt to reach a settlement between their countries.[70] Elmore Jackson led the Quaker response and travelled back and forth between Egypt and Israel. These efforts helped contain episodes of cross-country violence and avoid large-scale escalations. President Eisenhower and members of his administration were consulted and possible meetings between Eisenhower and Nasser as well as between Eisenhower and Ben-Gurion were discussed. They did not materialize before Nasser decided that negotiations about an arms accord with the U.S. government were stalemated and he must turn to East European countries for military assistance.[71]

Leaders of both sides in the Arab-Israeli conflicts generally acted in ways they deemed defensive against what they felt were serious threats. Their actions were often coercive and taken with too little regard to the perceptions and possible reactions of the other side. Consequently, great reliance on military force, which was lightly constrained by consideration of likely adversarial responses, resulted in policies that proved ineffective and counterproductive for many actors.

American accounts of the escalating crisis that culminated in the 1956 Suez war usually begin with the September 1955 agreement of Czechoslovakia to provide Soviet military materials to Egypt. But that agreement followed several prior developments.[72] Egyptian leaders regarded the agreement as a needed response to the French sale of Mystere IV jet airplanes to Israel and to the threats posed by the Baghdad Pact.[73] In addition, Egyptian-Israeli relations were deteriorating and hostile actions were escalating, including increasing interference with Israeli-bound shipping going through the Suez Canal. The Egyptian government had sought and believed it might receive some military aid from the U.S. government, but became convinced that was not going to happen.[74] The Soviet government could view the arms deal as a way to become a significant player in the Middle East, yet it limited the sale to older Soviet weapons to reduce the chances of seeming to upset the military balance in the region.[75]

The Egyptian-Czech arms deal did not precipitate the crisis that produced the Suez War. Indeed, Secretary of State Dulles continued policies that might result in Egypt's peaceful cooperation with Western powers and prevent Egyptian reliance on the Soviet Union. Thus, the U.S. government supported building a high dam across the upper Nile River, at Aswan, to generate electric power and extend irrigation. However, believing Egypt required U.S. financial assistance to build the dam, Dulles then seemed to condition financial aid upon Egyptian agreement to curtail arms purchases from the Soviet Union and move toward an accommodation with Israel.

With mutual mistrust hampering reaching an agreement, the United States abruptly withdrew its offer of financial aid for building the Aswan Dam on July 19, 1956. Even earlier, American support for the Dam was not always clear, and was viewed with doubts by Egypt. The withdrawal of the offer changed what had been a noncoercive inducement into a highly coercive one. To have been effective, the policy of assistance needed to have been applied with more awareness of Egypt's options and perceptions.

Following the withdrawal, Nasser quickly decided to do what he had long considered: he announced on July 26, 1956 that Egypt had nationalized the Suez Canal.[76] He asserted that earnings from the Canal would help finance building the Aswan Dam. The U.S. attempts to prevent close Egyptian-Soviet relations collapsed. Britain and France, America's close allies, were outraged at the nationalization and they planned to overthrow the government led by Nasser.[77] While conducting negotiations about future operations of the Suez Canal, British and French leaders secretly encouraged the Israeli government to attack Egypt and promised they would then militarily intercede and ensure victory. Israeli Prime Minister David Ben-Gurion agreed, and Israeli military forces invaded Egypt on October 29. Britain and France issued an ultimatum to Egypt the next day and began a bombing campaign the day after that. On November 5th, a British parachute regiment occupied the El Gamil airfield and the next day British and French commandos landed in the Port Said area. Israeli military forces moved swiftly to seize the entire Sinai territory.

Strikingly, the assault upon Egypt coincided with the Soviet military suppression of the Hungarian revolt. The Eisenhower administration decided to adhere to international norms against aggression and sought a UN resolution calling for a cease-fire and the withdrawal of the invading military forces, which an emergency session of the General Assembly passed. The resolution also established the United Nations Emergency Force, and peacekeepers were stationed along the length of the Israeli-Egyptian border, on the Egyptian side. The United States had forced a cease-fire in Egypt and the speedy withdrawal of the invading forces. The Soviet government added its threats of intervention if the invaders did not exit Egypt.

The United States' forthright opposition to the British, French, and Israeli invasion salvaged some political benefits from the damages the United States had suffered as a result of the crisis and war. The United States was now the dominant Western power in the region, but Egypt had become solidly aligned with the Soviet Union. Moreover, Nasser was a hero in Egypt, in other Arab countries, and in the Third World in general. The Soviets could and did claim they had effectively threatened Britain, France and Israel, and obscured their own aggression in Hungary.

American policies preceding the war had proven inadequate. Perhaps this was inevitable after Nasser's rise to power. Certainly, coordinating policies with allies and anticipating shifting relations among adversaries is extremely difficult, even for a great power. In retrospect, nevertheless, the policies seem to have been overly reliant on American economic and military coercive power, and insufficiently attentive to the interests and perceptions of the many parties with a stake in the region's affairs.

The Suez crisis and war were conducted without any notable public engagement. Only a few officials in the U.S., Egyptian, Israeli, British, French, and Soviet governments were involved in the misjudgments, misunderstandings, and attempted manipulations that created the crisis and the war. The many governments often acted with little communication with each other and sometimes with great secrecy. Broader participation in decision-making with greater discussion among the governments and publics might have averted the war and its unfortunate consequences. It would have yielded more options, including noncoercive ones, a basic idea of the constructive conflict approach.

COVERT COLD WAR INTERVENTIONS

In addition to visible military and diplomatic moves, from the beginning of the Cold War the U.S. government aided friendly governments that were challenged by opposition groups, especially if the opponents were associated with the USSR. Assistance was also given to groups opposing governments deemed to be unfriendly to American interests, or which were considered overly sympathetic to communism and the Soviet Union. U.S. government assistance sometimes included covert operations to replace governments considered harmful to U.S. interests with friendly governments. Covert operations, however, are prone to have unintended consequences, including harming the side carrying out the operation, a phenomenon that is referred to as "blowback."[78]

More generally, conducting covert U.S. operations against popularly chosen governments makes the United States vulnerable to charges of hypocrisy and spreads suspicion about a wide range of U.S. undertakings. In the context of the Cold War, moreover, such interventions were justified among American leaders as necessary defensive moves against Communism.[79] Such covert operations were not likely to be a secret from the Soviet leadership and would be regarded as evidence of aggressive American imperialism. Of course, Soviet covert operations had parallel dangers. On the other hand, taking open actions would allow for explanations and explorations that might mitigate conflict escalations.

During the Cold War, the American and Soviet governments secretly aided various nonmilitary activities against each other. These political and intellectual activities were directed to win support for the government's policies and to counter the efforts of the adversary. Most famously, beginning in 1948, the Communist Information Bureau supported cultural conferences for world peace and against the United States' foreign policies. The CIA soon countered and began covert support of anti-Communist intellectuals of the Left through the Congress for Cultural Freedom and related conferences and publications.[80] This continued until 1967, when the CIA support became known and those covert activities were stopped.[81]

Often nongovernmental organizations, advancing their particular interests, acted consistently with official U.S. policies. For example, in the early years of the Cold War, American trade union leaders engaged in intense efforts to help organize non-Communist trade unions in developing countries and to counter Communist Party–controlled trade unions in Western Europe and Latin America. Leaders of the American Federation of Labor and the Congress of Industrial Organizations (CIO) and their constituent unions had a variety of reasons for their anti-Communist work, aside from helping their government in its foreign policy. Some of the CIO union leaders, like Walter and Victor Reuther, had battled American Communists for influence and control of some unions. The AFL's anti-Communist policies were influenced by Jay Lovestone, a former leader of Communist Party USA, who had broken with it and became a militant anti-Communist.[82] Trade union activities demonstrated the critical importance of nonmilitary methods in waging the competitive struggle against Soviet influence in countries around the world. The attractiveness of American society—its abundant soft power—was an additional source of influence in winning and holding allies in the rivalry with the Soviet Union.

Covert U.S. actions were sometimes undertaken to overthrow an existing government. Well-known actions during this period include Iran, Guatemala, and Cuba.[83] In March 1951, the Iranian Parliament nationalized Iran's oil industry and seized control of the Anglo-Iranian Oil Company. Negotiations between the British government and the Iranian government, led by Prime Minister Mohammad Mossadegh, failed to resolve their differences, and a costly economic stalemate ensued. The Mossadegh government also introduced many socialist reforms. British and American intelligence officials developed a plan to overthrow the government, and on August 19, 1953, a coup forced Mossadegh from office. Shah Mohammed Reza Pahlavi returned to power, having been driven out earlier as Mossadegh consolidated power to counter the plot against him. For over two decades, the U.S. government supported the Shah's rule and Iran's role as a major regional power. But the Shah's rule became increasingly repressive and the population more resistant until the revolution of 1979 overthrew the Shah and established a theocratic regime hostile to the United States. The U.S. installation of the Shah and support for his rule fueled anti-American sentiment, which was exploited in the outbreak of the 1979 revolution and in the subsequent consolidation of the Aya-tollah Khomeini regime.

The CIA also covertly organized a military coup that in June 1954 ousted the democratically elected president of Guatemala, Jacobo Arbenz, and replaced the government he headed with one led by Colonel Carlos Armas. Arbenz had forced the United Fruit Company to sell portions of its land to be distributed to peasant farmers, which was treated as if it were a sign of Communist influence. Partly sus-tained by Cold War antagonism, more than 200,000 people died in the 36-year civil war that followed. This covert action was not secret for long and contributed to the view of many people in developing countries that American interest in aiding and encouraging democratic reforms was hypocritical. Such actions diminish America's soft power.

THE CUBAN MISSILE CRISIS, 1961

The Cold War shaped U.S.–Cuban adversarial relations and had far-reaching ef-fects on it. In January 1959, a small group of revolutionaries led by Fidel Castro es-tablished a new government, having induced Fulgencio Batista, the self-appointed president of Cuba, to flee. The new government's leaders soon declared themselves to be Communists and the Soviet Union began to provide economic and ideological support. Subsequently, Cuba energetically encouraged and aided revolutionaries in other countries.[84]

Many Cuban refugees in the United States were eager to overthrow the Castro-led government, and the CIA secretly assisted them in that endeavor.[85] Plans were drawn up for an invasion of Cuba during the Eisenhower administration and when John F. Kennedy became president, he was informed of the plans and approved them. On April 17, 1961, about 1,300 exiles landed at the Bay of Pigs, on the southern coast of Cuba; but no uprising of supporters occurred and they were quickly de-feated by the Cuban army. This ill-conceived invasion understandably substantiated Castro's sense that he and his government faced an existential threat from the United States. Indeed, the CIA conducted covert efforts to assassinate Castro.[86] This was the beginning of what the Soviet Union called the Caribbean Crisis and Americans called the Cuban Missile Crisis.

Khrushchev decided on the bold and risky strategy of secretly placing intermedi-ate-range nuclear-armed missiles in Cuba, by which he could provide security to the Cuban government, demonstrate international socialist solidarity, and quickly strengthen Soviet nuclear capability relative to the United States.

Immediately after U.S. intelligence-gathering flights discovered that Soviet mis-sile bases were being constructed in Cuba, President Kennedy called a meeting of the Executive Committee of the National Security Council to discuss how to re-spond.[87] From October 16 to October 29, 1962, participants at the meetings dis-cussed a wide range of possible strategies. The president was rarely present at those meetings, which helped ensure the discussion would not be influenced by inferring his inclinations, and so more alternatives would be kept open for examination. The diversity of views and the conduct of the meetings helped the participants avoid fall-ing into the trap of "group think," which would exclude consideration of ideas that were not quickly part of the group consensus.

After those deliberations, Kennedy decided to avoid a sharp escalation and in-stead chose the limited option of imposing a quarantine blocking Soviet vessels from completing the construction of the bases. What ensued was a series of meas-ured exchanges that were monitored to avoid unwanted escalations.[88] This also pro-vided the breathing space needed to negotiate a way out of the crisis, which entailed mutual concessions and face-saving. That desire to avoid a potential mutual disaster set in motion a series of constructive exchanges, including messages between Ken-nedy and Khrushchev, which produced a face-saving mutually acceptable agree-ment. The agreement included the Soviet withdrawal of the missiles from Cuba and the U.S. government's pledge not to try to overthrow the Cuban government. An-other part of the negotiated resolution of the crisis was kept secret at the time: the U.S. government agreed to take its missiles out of bases in Turkey.[89]

The conflict resolution approach generally stresses the value of having groups with a stake in the outcome of a conflict represented in negotiations to settle a con-flict. That increases the likelihood of producing an equitable and enduring resolu-tion. The exclusion of important stakeholders can result in the excluded groups undermining whatever agreement is reached. But there is also recognition in the conflict resolution field that no agreement may be reached if highly intransigent parties are at the table. In negotiating the end of the Cuban Missile Crisis, the Cuban government was fortunately excluded and its objections were disregarded. The Soviet and American governments agreed that the UN would monitor the Soviet missile withdrawal. When Fidel Castro denied entry of UN monitors into Cuba, the Soviet government simply loaded the missiles on the decks of the ships taking them away, which allowed U.S. aircraft to oversee the removal. Determining who is to be included in negotiations requires balancing many considerations and the specific conditions relevant to any settlement.[90]

The fear and anxiety during the crisis and its peaceful resolution greatly contrib-uted to a significant interlude of de-escalation in the Cold War. In some regards, the steps taken were consistent with Osgood's GRIT strategy, but probably were not planned as such.[91] John F. Kennedy's June 1963 speech at American University did convey some of what would be the initiation of GRIT. In that speech he gave a reassuring context for de-escalating acts. Kennedy said, "Let us reexamine our attitude to the Cold War . . . We must deal with the world as it is." He declared that the United States would not conduct nuclear tests in the atmosphere as long as other states did not and he announced a high-level meeting would take place to reach agreement on a nuclear test ban treaty. A hotline was established between the United States and the USSR, enabling the leaders of the two countries to quickly communicate directly with each other in an emergency, which could avert a runaway escalation in a crisis.[92] In August 1963, the Partial Test Ban Treaty was signed by the governments of the United States, USSR, and the United Kingdom, ending nuclear weapons testing in the atmosphere. Other arms control agreements were subsequently negotiated, signed, and ratified. In January 1967, the United States, Soviet Union, and sixty other countries banned nuclear weapons in outer space. In July 1968, the United States, Soviet Union, and many other countries signed the Non-Proliferation Nuclear Weapons Treaty.

U.S. agreements to these arms-control measures, as well as to subsequent ones, were not simply top-down decisions made by government leaders. Major citizen actions were undertaken by American organizations opposing U.S. government policies regarding nuclear weapons. Some of the scientists who created the first atomic bombs, who had quietly opposed their use against Japanese cities, later campaigned for international control of nuclear weapons. They joined the social movement campaigning to end nuclear weapons testing in the atmosphere.[93]

In 1957, The Committee for a SANE Nuclear Policy was founded by Coretta Scott King, Benjamin Spock, and others, focusing on the dangers of radioactive fallout from nuclear weapons tests.[94] Numerous rallies were held, addressed by notable persons from many public spheres; full-page ads were placed in leading newspapers; and government officials were lobbied and petitioned to stop nuclear weapons testing and end the arms race. A broad-based peace movement had emerged that had wide support on this issue. In the 1956 presidential election campaign, Democratic candidate Adlai Stevenson suggested a halt to nuclear weapons testing.[95] Later, in the mid-1960s, SANE and many other organizations also began to mobilize opposition to the U.S. engagement in the Vietnam War.[96] Peace movement organizations exerted influence on elections, Congress, and the executive branch bureaucracy, with different pathways being important for different arms control cases.[97]

These de-escalation moves did not transform the Cold War, but they helped establish understandings that aided managing subsequent confrontations. Indeed, escalations were generally constrained and direct warfare between the United States and the USSR was avoided. Leading groups on both sides learned about others' concerns and modes of operation, even with leadership changes.[98] Kennedy was assassinated in November 1963, and Lyndon B. Johnson became president. In October

1964, Khrushchev was forced out of office by his colleagues, who thought he had taken too many risks and had acted with too little regard for the judgment of his colleagues.[99] He was followed by a more collective leadership group, which Leonid Brezhnev gradually came to lead. They were less willing to take risks. They were committed to building up the Soviet Union's nuclear weapons capability, and they strove to produce a correlation of forces that would enable them to negotiate from strength, or at least as an equal.

THE ESCALATING VIETNAM WAR, 1961–1968

When Johnson became president, he vigorously introduced a broad spectrum of social programs to advance his vision of creating a Great Society. Indeed, remarkable progress was made in reducing poverty in America and overcoming the long-entrenched discrimination against African Americans, particularly in the southern states. These policies were spurred by massive popular movements of low-income groups, African Americans, and people acting in solidarity with them. The policies also fostered the activism of many people in numerous social movement organizations. Once activated and having experienced achieving significant social change, many Americans became involved in other nonviolent struggles to advance social justice and to resist waging war in Vietnam. These movements also contributed to the future growth and development of the conflict resolution field, as discussed in the next chapter.

The low-level U.S. military engagement in the war in Vietnam taking place at the time Johnson became president was not successful. Kennedy had been convinced of the need to wage anti-guerrilla warfare to combat the Soviet Union's aggression, and upon becoming president expanded the U.S. capacity for conducting counter-insurgency wars.[100] Increasingly, military personnel and covert operations personnel were trained in special warfare methods. That capacity then began to be deployed for fighting in Laos and Vietnam, and the number of U.S. personnel stationed there steadily increased.[101]

Johnson could see no better alternative to the policy that was underway. The U.S. policy in Vietnam, although fashioned by "the best and the brightest," was not appropriately guided or executed.[102] It was largely framed in the context of the Cold War in terms of a bilateral zero-sum competition with the Soviet-led Communist camp. The U.S. escalation was guided by the belief that military capability was fundamental in determining the course of international conflicts. It was based on the conviction that the Vietnamese opponents would rationally calculate the costs of the increasingly coercive escalation being imposed and accept the outcome sought by the United States, whereby Vietnam would be divided and the south would have a government friendly to the United States.

Furthermore, as a Democrat, Johnson did not want to be vulnerable to Republican charges that he had "lost Vietnam."[103] He shared the belief that American credibility was at stake and the fall of South Vietnam would be followed by neighboring countries falling like dominoes. The situation was viewed by U.S. political leaders within the Cold War framing. The nationalist character of the North Vietnamese government and its antagonism to China was not recognized.[104] The complexity of interlocking conflicts was ignored, and too little effort was made to understand the concerns and interests of the adversary. A military escalation seemed to be the only possible course of action, and he began to send more ground troops to Vietnam. The desired result was not achieved and U.S. military operations grew.

For the United States to escalate military coercion, it was important to gain domestic backing for it. Johnson achieved an important measure of support by the congressional passage of the Tonkin Gulf Resolution on August 7, 1964. On August 2 and 4, Johnson had received reports about possible North Vietnamese attacks upon two U.S. destroyers in the Tonkin Gulf. Although there were some doubts about the matter, the judgment was made that they did occur and retaliatory action was taken.[105] On August 5, Johnson came to Syracuse University to dedicate a building and spoke of the Tonkin Gulf attacks, the Communist challenge in Southeast Asia, and the U.S. commitment to repel the North Vietnamese aggression. On August 7, 1964, Congress passed the Tonkin Gulf resolution authorizing the president "to take all necessary measures to repel any armed attack against the forces of the United States and to prevent further aggression."[106]

As the war escalated and American casualties rose, popular opposition to the war grew and various organizations articulated alternative courses of action. In June 1962, Students for a Democratic Society issued a manifesto for what was soon referred to as the New Left. This Port Huron Statement was written largely by Tom Hayden, then the editor of the University of Michigan student newspaper. It decried the military-industrial-academic establishment, but initially focused on domestic concerns, notably the Civil Rights struggle. In the academic year 1964–65, the Free Speech Movement emerged at the University of California–Berkeley campus, gaining new capacities and rights for student political activism. The large-scale bombing of North Vietnam that was begun in early February 1965 was a catalyst for marches and teach-ins against the war.

Martin Luther King Jr. and other civil rights leaders joined in the antiwar cause, as the war undercut needed domestic programs. The civil rights movement, the student movement, and countercultural movements added energy to the antiwar movement. But that conjunction also aroused opposition to them, which increased in the late 1960s. The resistance to the war was condemned by many political leaders, and the tactics of some opponents to the war offended other Americans. Nevertheless, the ongoing military escalation prompted increasing American organized resistance to the war and to military service. The sense of frustration by those who wanted the United States to stop the American killing and dying in Vietnam and by those who wanted to win the war in Vietnam intensified the anger they directed at each other.

Particular events contributed to a feeling that the country was spinning out of control. Martin Luther King Jr. was assassinated on April 4, 1968, in Memphis, Tennessee, where he was to join a march of sanitation workers protesting poor wages and working conditions. The killing was followed by riots in many cities across the country, by African Americans in predominantly African-American neighborhoods.

President Johnson tried private and public peace overtures, but unconvincingly. For example, on April 7, 1965, Johnson gave an address at John Hopkins University, "Peace Without Conquest." He explained, "We fight because we must fight if we are to live in a world where every country can shape its own destiny. And only in such a world will our own freedom be finally secure."[107] He went on to argue that Communist China is the real enemy. "The rulers in Hanoi are urged on by Peking . . . It is a nation which is helping the forces of violence in almost every continent. The contest in Vietnam is part of a wider pattern of aggressive purposes." This was hardly the way to influence the leaders of North Vietnam to consider any settlement with the United States, dismissing their goal of national unification as part of Communist China's aggression. Yet he asserted that, "It should be clear that the only path for reasonable men is the path of peaceful settlement. Such peace demands an independent South Vietnam securely guaranteed and able to shape its own relationships to all others." Having stated that, he continued, "And we remain ready, with this purpose, for unconditional discussions."

Much of the speech was devoted to holding out the promise of future economic well-being for all people in the region, who were suffering from poverty and disorder. Johnson proposed a great cooperative effort for development that he hoped that North Vietnam would join "just as soon as peaceful cooperation is possible." He detailed wonderful projects for economic development and to provide food and medical care, for which he would ask Congress to contribute $1 billion.

Under the circumstances, this offer would not be an effective step toward peace. The North Vietnam leaders would be mistrustful of such vague offers in exchange for giving up their strongly held nationalist goals. It was not presented with signs of respect or understanding, or with acknowledgement of any responsibility for the war (unlike the 1963 John F. Kennedy American University speech addressing the Soviet Union).

In any case, North Vietnamese leaders would regard their suspicions as warranted when a week after the speech a thousand tons of bombs were dropped on Viet Cong positions. Indeed, massive bombing became a major method to defeat the Viet Cong in the south, and the North Vietnamese government that was supporting the Viet Cong against the South Vietnamese government. However, doubts about the effectiveness of bombing were widespread, particularly against a non-industrialized economy; Johnson privately shared the doubts even as he continued to heavily rely on bombing.[108]

Congressional questioning of the war's objectives and strategies became manifest as the fighting escalated. Thus, senators Ernest Gruening and Wayne Morse voiced their opposition to the war's escalation, but they were the only senators to vote against the Gulf of Tonkin resolution. From 1966 to 1971, Senator J. William Fulbright, chairman of the Senate Committee on Foreign Relations, held hearings about U.S. engagement in Vietnam. The hearings gave legitimacy to opposing the war, and also offered detailed defenses and critiques of the reasons for continuing U.S. policies or for changing course. In addition, the television coverage of the war brought images to American dinner tables of American casualties, of frightened Vietnamese women and children, of burning villages, of shootings, and of corpses. They were not reassuring images about the value of what the United States was doing or of future success. Opposition was growing but the policy was not changing.

Johnson himself had grave misgivings about the correctness of the path being taken, but he felt that he had no choice but to continue on it. This is clear from the numerous telephone conversations he had with associates, which he taped.[109] He explained the problems that he faced, and those with whom he spoke generally commiserated with him, but rarely offered a way out. He was trapped, believing he could not quit and he could not win.

By the end of 1968, the tragic escalation of the Vietnam War had cost the lives of over 30,000 U.S. military personnel killed in action.[110] The number of U.S. casualties rose in 1966, 1967, and in 1968; in those 3 years 28,980 U.S. military personnel were killed in action. In addition, in those years, 53,469 persons from the Republic of Vietnam forces and 413,211 persons from the North Vietnam and the Viet Cong forces were killed in action. Early in 1968, the Viet Cong and the North Vietnamese forces launched a massive attack on South Vietnamese, U.S., and allied forces throughout South Vietnam, generally referred to as the Tet Offensive. Although the attack was militarily defeated, it convinced many people in the United States that a military victory could not be achieved at any acceptable cost.

As the war went on, the Democratic Party became deeply divided. Senator Eugene McCarthy challenged Johnson for the Democratic Party nomination for the presidency and did surprisingly well in the New Hampshire primary election on March 12, 1968. Senator Robert F. Kennedy entered the race on March 16, and Johnson dramatically declared on March 31 that he would not run for re-election. Kennedy went on to win the California primary on June 5 but then was fatally shot, eliciting immense grief and despair.

Vice President Hubert Humphrey later joined the race for the nomination. Although he did not compete in the primaries, he had the support of many Democratic Party leaders. In August 1968, at the Democratic Party convention in Chicago, protestors against the war chanted "the whole world is watching," while the police tear-gassed and beat them. Humphrey won the nomination, and initially ran as a supporter of Johnson's foreign as well as domestic policies; the polls showed him far behind Richard M. Nixon, the Republican nominee. George Wallace also ran, as the candidate of the pro-segregationist American Independent Party, hoping to win enough electoral votes to place the choice of president into the House of Representatives.

In October, Humphrey began to break away from Johnson's Vietnam policies and called for a bombing halt. Then, on October 31, 1968, Johnson announced ending all air, naval, and artillery bombardment of North Vietnam and revealed that discussions with the North Vietnamese government had been underway in Paris since May and sufficient progress was made so that productive talks that included the government of South Vietnam and of the National Liberation Front could begin.

Nixon, viewed as a fierce anti-Communist, campaigned as a president who would restore "law and order"; he pledged to end the military draft and suggested he had a plan to end the war. On the whole, however, he did not campaign on a new policy regarding Vietnam. The election results were close as measured by the popular vote, Nixon receiving 43.4%, Humphrey 42.7%, and Wallace 13.5% of the votes. However, Humphrey won only 191 electoral votes, Nixon won 301, and Wallace won 46 (with 270 electoral votes needed to be elected).

Certainly, the American social-political circumstances and election season were not conducive to expeditious and effective peace negotiations ending the war in Vietnam. The negotiations were begun late in Johnson's term and the positions of the adversary sides were very far apart. One important issue for the United States in negotiations with North Vietnam was the extent of its commitment to maintain the government of South Vietnam, headed by President Nguyen Van Thieu. It is doubtful that any agreements among all the major parties in the fight could have been reached at that time, but the contacts between Thieu and confidants of Nixon probably helped reduce those chances.[111] Anna Chennault conveyed to Thieu that he would have a better deal with Nixon as president, and Thieu became more resistant to the understandings Johnson was trying to reach with the North Vietnamese.

Before closing this chapter, it should be noted that the overwhelming attention to the war in Vietnam hampered the U.S. government's engagement elsewhere in the world. Thus, the Israeli-Arab conflict was neglected after the end of the 1956 Suez war, until the crisis and war of 1967.[112] The eruption of the crisis after Egypt called for and obtained the withdrawal of UN peacekeeping forces along its border with Israel got Washington's attention. But the belated U.S. efforts were not adequate to avert the June 1967 war. That war resulted in the Israeli occupation of the West Bank, the Gaza strip, and part of the Golan Heights, and the unification of an expanded Jerusalem. After extensive negotiations, on November 22, 1967, the UN Security Council passed Resolution 242, which became the basis for all future official discussions about making peace between Israel and the Palestinians and the Arab states. The resolution, however, does not mention Palestinians (only referring to refugees); it calls for the withdrawal of Israeli armed forces from territories occupied in the recent conflict and for the right of every state in the region to live in peace within secure and recognized boundaries.

Reflections Deriving from the Constructive Conflict Approach

The constructive conflict approach can suggest alternative policies that might have been less destructive for Americans during the foreign engagements of the 1960s. During that period, particular elements of the approach were in the minds of some analysts and practitioners who were developing this perspective. They and later analysts drew lessons from the mistakes made in the escalation of the war and applied them to building the conflict resolution field.

First, the constructive conflict perspective could foster thinking about potential alternative framings of the conflicts related to the U.S. engagement in the war in Vietnam. Rather than an over-constraining Cold War structure, attention to the many interconnected conflicts active at that time could have opened new options. Thus, more attention could have been given to the intensifying conflict between the Soviet Union and the People's Republic of China that was becoming evident in the late 1950s.[113] Furthermore, the importance of Vietnamese nationalism, aside from adherence to Communist ideology, could have been given more weight. Consequently, fears of a domino effect if the U.S.-supported South Vietnamese government fell would not have weighed so heavily, nor would fear of losing face or credibility appear so serious. These points were made in 1966 by George Kennan in his statement at Senator Fulbright's Vietnam War hearings.[114]

The constructive conflict approach gives much attention to the use of nonviolent and noncoercive means of struggle and sensitizes those who use that approach to the frequent counterproductive results of heavy reliance on violence. In the course of escalating U.S. involvement in the Vietnam War, the range of means tended to be limited, as if the choice were simply between increasing military force or withdrawing from any engagement. It was often said at the time that the United States was trying to "win the hearts and minds" of the Vietnamese people, which should have meant reliance on other strategies than bombing and military pacification.

One strand in the broad peace studies and conflict resolution approach is the importance of the relationship between means and ends. Means that are consistent with the end tend to be more effective than ones that are not, since the means shape the end. Moreover, certain ends may not be attainable by any acceptable means that are available, in which case the ends might best be modified. As the political problems in South Vietnam mounted in the early 1960s, the challenge of securing an anti-Communist South Vietnam by U.S. military intervention was becoming insurmountable.[115] As became evident after the Vietnam War was finally over, that outcome was not a vital U.S. interest. A comprehensive examination of an attainable alternative outcome that would have been acceptable should have been undertaken by U.S. government leaders. Instead, the possibilities of formulating achievable goals with acceptable means were not seriously and widely examined.

Such a comprehensive examination, adopting a constructive conflict perspective, would give serious consideration to the interests and concerns of all the major parties in the conflict. In this instance, that would certainly include Vietnamese government leaders. That could be enhanced if they had encouragement to envision how they could solve the civil war in Vietnam and deal with the North Vietnamese government's engagement with limited U.S. military support for a short time. Limiting the U.S. commitment to the South Vietnamese leaders might have helped them concentrate more on winning the Vietnamese people's support.

A version of such thinking was made contemporaneously by Richard Russell, Democratic senator from Georgia and chairman of the Senate Armed Service Committee, and confidant of President Johnson. In a taped telephone conversation on November 9, 1964, Russell raised the specter of Chinese intervention in the war, and mentioned a political way out of Vietnam for the president. He said that he thought the CIA "ought to get somebody to run that country [who] didn't want us in there ... [Then] we could get out with good grace."[116]

Whatever the goals may be, the conflict resolution approach offers much guidance on communicating effectively with adversaries and constituents. Some recent research bears on the formulations Johnson used in his April 1965 address, "Peace Without Conquest," discussed earlier. He held out the promise of economic development assistance to the North Vietnamese leaders if they peacefully acquiesced to South Vietnam's independence. Recent research provides evidence that when sacred values are contested, offers of material benefits are not effective in reaching an agree-ment.[117] Indeed, matters regarded as sacred are not to be sold; that would be highly dishonorable. Offers of compromises or material benefits then may be viewed as insulting and increase reliance on violence. National unification is often felt to be a sacred cause.

Roger Fisher and his co-authors reflected upon and analyzed the problems in the United States using bombing in North Vietnam as a method to get that nation to change its conduct.[118] They applied conflict resolution ideas related to negotiations, and pointed out the differences in the intended message and the way the message was probably received. The ostensible purpose of the bombing was to induce the North Vietnamese government to stop providing military assistance to the anti-government fighters in the south; bombing the trail that was being used for that purpose was intended to stop that activity. But bombing does not in itself clearly convey what is being demanded and what is threatened or offered if the demand were met. For example, the action demanded was meant to be "stop aiding the rebels in the south," but that was probably received as "stop supporting your comrades." The offer, if the demand were met, probably was intended to be "we will stop bomb-ing and soon talk about helping establish a government in South Vietnam," but what was probably received was "we will consider explaining how we are going to set up a puppet government in the South."

Clear and credible communication between enemies is very difficult to achieve, given the likely high levels of mistrust and fear. Conflict resolution research and experience have produced a substantial literature on how that can occur, and how conflict de-escalation can begin and be sustained, which is discussed throughout this book.[119]

Finally, applying the constructive conflict approach to American engagement in Vietnam, from 1961 to 1968, would entail giving weight to the views of diverse groups in the United States. Strategies that bear a high cost in lives and financial burdens cannot be sustained if the goals are not deemed sufficiently important and the means are not perceived as likely to be effective by the American public. Robert S. McNamara, reflecting on the mistakes made while he was Secretary of Defense during this period, inferred several lessons. Among them, he noted these:

We failed to draw Congress and the American people into a full and frank discussion and debate of the pros and cons of a large-scale U.S. military in-volvement in Southeast Asia before we initiated the action.

After the action got underway and unanticipated events forced us off our planned course, we failed to retain popular support in part because we did not explain fully what was happening and why we were doing what we did.[120]

Instead, it may be noted, dissenting voices were ignored or silenced. In turn, many doubters and critics of the policy became increasingly vehement. Some of them might have contributed better to civil discussions and generated public support for less disastrous policies. Some activists within the peace movement used rhetoric and committed actions that were offensive to those with whom they disagreed, and even to neutral bystanders. Mutual recriminations and derogatory name-calling became counterproductive for all sides. As discussed later in this book, peace movement activists learned from such mistakes and adopted a different style in challenging later U.S. military engagements. The conflict resolution approach to negotiation provides numerous methods to win a hearing from opponents and to discover common ground.[121]

The persistence of the U.S. engagement in the Vietnam War illustrates some of the dangerous processes that research in the field of conflict resolution has analyzed. One is "groupthink," the tendency for members in a decision-making group to quickly settle on a preferred option and stay with it.[122] This occurs as members disregard, marginalize, or cast out those members who challenge the emerging consensus and as would-be dissenters quickly give their assent in order to get along and remain connected. Entrapment is another common process that makes for persevering even when a policy is failing. It is the tendency of people to increase their commitment to a course of action, once it is undertaken, in order to justify or redeem prior investments and costs.[123] Thus, a fight may be continued so that the dead would not have died in vain.

Conclusion

The Cold War was marked by numerous crises, confrontations, and periods of intense conflict, such as the Vietnam War. However, it should be recognized that even in the first two decades of the Cold War, mutual understandings and shared interests were developing that constrained and contained dangerous escalations between the United States and the USSR. Major processes underlay the gradual change in Soviet society and its relations with the United States. At times, American actions contributed to the management and gradual transformation of the Cold War. These actions generally have been consistent with a conflict resolution approach, which was emerging during this period.

On many other occasions, however, American and Soviet actions contributed to risky escalations, which often exacerbated tensions and slowed the transformation of their relationship. These were often the result of leaders in each society catering to their own domestic interest groups and constituencies. The prevailing ways of thinking and the great capacities for doing violence also sometimes favored adopting policies that proved to be destructive. Too often, having the capacity to act coercively becomes an invitation to do so. Considering alternatives, monitoring and correcting failing policies, and exchanging information with adversaries were underutilized ways to avoid destructive escalations.

The world context was also important in shaping the early course of the Cold War. Many of the advances and setbacks in the course of the Cold War's transformation resulted from actions taken by persons other than Soviet and American officials. They were the result of transnational governmental and nongovernmental organizations, of policies of Koreans, Egyptians, Vietnamese, Israelis, and Cubans, and of changing global norms and beliefs. These considerations also are examined in later chapters, which are concerned with subsequent conflict episodes during and after the Cold War.

3   Transforming Conflicts, 1969–1988

THE REALITY OF conflict dynamism is demonstrated by the transformation of the Cold War and other conflicts between 1969 and 1988, during the administrations of presidents Nixon, Ford, Carter, and Reagan. The Cold War's intensity varied considerably, with episodes of fierce escalation but also of substantial de-escalation, sometimes occurring simultaneously in different arenas for different groups. Several of the developments discussed in this chapter laid the groundwork for the ending of the Cold War. Simultaneously and in interaction, new developments in thinking and in practice within the field of conflict resolution were occurring.

Escalation, Détente and Confrontation, 1969–1973

The degree of American-Soviet hostility varied greatly during the presidential terms of Richard M. Nixon and Gerald Ford. The escalations and de-escalations resulted from developments in linked conflicts and as a result of actions by officials and private citizens in the United States and in the Soviet Union. Reviewing what they did and the consequences of their actions can help assess the effectiveness of different American approaches to realizing peace.

Nixon and his national security advisor, Henry Kissinger, undertook a highly activist and tightly controlled global foreign policy, which they viewed in the context of the Cold War. To an unusual degree, they decided on actions without broad official engagement, and implemented many of them without informing the American public or officials with authority to oversee or conduct such actions. They adhered to what they regarded as a "realist" approach, relying greatly on coercive power.

As a Harvard professor, Kissinger had been an influential analyst and proponent of traditional realism applied to contemporary conditions, marked by the existence of nuclear weapons.[1] He reasoned that the American and Soviet nuclear weapons made an all-out war between them unlikely since it would destroy their societies. However, local wars would still be fought, which might include use of nuclear weapons on a local scale. Developing a range of military capabilities could then make flexible responses possible, accompanied by diplomacy. In many books and articles, he articulated an approach to policymaking that he sought to implement. Successful statesmanship, he believed, is innovative and requires that the constraints of bureaucrats, primarily concerned with minimizing risk, be overcome. Consultation with other governments cannot resolve major differences and he believed that the United States should retain as much freedom of action as possible. Once in office, he tended to act on these beliefs. Ideas have consequences.

THE VIETNAMS, USSR, AND PRC COMPLEX

The U.S. engagement in Vietnam was the most critical foreign policy issue Nixon and Kissinger confronted upon taking office. Their desired outcome of the U.S. involvement differed little from Johnson's.[2] The strategy to achieve it was more complex and included three policies. Nixon increased the emphasis on the Vietnamization of the war, and reducing U.S. military engagement in ground fighting. This had the benefit of reducing U.S. military casualties and buying more time from the U.S public, which might help convince the North Vietnamese that the United States could persevere in the fight. This was consistent with the recognition of a basic idea of the constructive conflict approach, that every adversary is heterogeneous with diverse concerns, including the United States.

Second, Nixon undertook a massive bombing campaign in Cambodia to interdict North Vietnamese supply routes to South Vietnam (Republic of Vietnam). This would demonstrate to the Vietnamese and the Soviets that he could resort to extreme means.[3] Such extreme violence, without credible reassurance of benefits from any proffered deal or serious consideration of the other side's interpretation of the action was not consistent with basic constructive conflict ideas and might undermine the achievement of the desired goals.

Third, Nixon tried to induce the Soviet leaders to pressure the North Vietnamese leaders to accede to a settlement acceptable to the United States. This entailed a policy of sticks and carrots directed at the Soviet Union. He made it clear to the Soviets that arms control agreements and trade would be linked to developments regarding Vietnam. These policies were more congruent with the realities of inter-connected conflicts and reframing socially constructed conflicts.

This mixture of coercive and noncoercive escalating actions by the Nixon admin-istration did not bring about the desired changes in Vietnam. The military escala-tion in Vietnam and neighboring countries reached a new height with Nixon's decision to attack an allegedly large Communist headquarters in Cambodia with-out consulting Congress.[4] On April 30, 1970, Nixon announced that he was sending a U.S. military force of 32,000 into Cambodia, in a joint operation with South Viet-namese forces. He asserted that failing to do so would demonstrate that the United States was a "pitiful helpless giant."

The anti-war movement, which had subsided considerably, was massively aroused. Students in colleges and universities across the country demonstrated in opposition to the expansion of the war. On May 4, 1970, at a demonstration on the campus of Kent State University in Ohio, four students were killed and eight wounded by Na-tional Guard troops. On May 15, at Jackson State College in Mississippi, two more students were killed in connection with anti-war protests. Student protests erupted and about 20% of the country's college and university campuses were shut down, some for a few days and some until shortened semesters were ended.[5] Many students demanded that the semester simply be concluded and they receive grades and cred-its. But in many cases students sought and achieved curricular changes that would contribute to peace and justice. For example, at Syracuse University, numerous stu-dents demanded they be taught nonviolence; in response, workshops were organized in the summer and in the fall a program in nonviolent conflict and change was estab-lished.[6] Congressional and editorial opposition to Nixon's actions was widespread, and he withdrew the U.S. forces from Cambodia by the end of the month.

A different grand strategy was also underway that would contribute to a remark-able de-escalation in U.S. relations with the USSR and also with the People's Re-public of China (PRC). The desire to extricate the United States from Vietnam was an incentive to reduce tensions with the Soviet Union and the PRC. Nixon and Kissinger thought that the United States could reduce Soviet and Chinese support for North Vietnam by improving relations with the two major Communist powers. At that time, China and the Soviet Union were highly antagonistic, even having bloody border skirmishes.[7] By improving relations with both the Soviets and the Chinese, the United States would increase competition between them as they each sought to improve relations with the United States. As a result, each would reduce its support to North Vietnam; which would put pressure on the North Vietnamese to settle the Vietnam War on terms acceptable to the United States. Furthermore, the rivalry with the Soviet Union was viewed as the primary conflict, and the opening to China would increase U.S. leverage against it.

This new strategic configuration meant that the conflict with North Vietnam was reframed, or seen in a new context. Such redefining of a conflict is a manifestation of a basic idea in the constructive conflict approach.[8] No longer was the United States fighting a war against a monolithic Communism, in which "losing Vietnam" would set in motion a series of falling dominos. Rather, China and the Soviet Union were recognized as having opposing national interests, and the United States could play one off against the other by warming relations with each. The reframing of the U.S.–North Vietnam conflict may not have produced North Vietnam's acceptance of peace on U.S. terms, but it probably helped contain repercussions harmful to the United States of the North's later unification of Vietnam. It also contributed to long-term benefits in U.S.-Soviet and U.S.-PRC relations.

Peace negotiations between the United States and North Vietnam, begun In Johnson's administration, were renewed by Nixon. The negotiations between Kissinger and Le Duc Tho, representing the North Vietnamese government were begun in August 1969 in Paris, and conducted secretly as a back channel. Later, publicly-known meetings included representation of the South Vietnamese government and the Provisional Revolutionary government (the Viet Cong), in addition to the United States and North Vietnamese governments, which had primary standing.

The negotiation issues in contention related to the timing of U.S. troop withdrawal, the release of U.S. and Vietnamese prisoners of war, the presence of North Vietnamese military forces in South Vietnam, and the re-supply of military materials to the contending forces in South Vietnam. Tough bargaining ensued simultaneous to ongoing military operations. The emerging terms of agreement would not ensure the survival of the South Vietnamese government, and Nguyen Van Thieu, its president, resisted them, but he ultimately had to accept Washington's decision. On October 26, 1972, at a press conference, Kissinger discussed the key provisions of the emerging agreement, declaring that, "Peace is at hand." Public and congressional opposition to U.S. military engagement in Vietnam was strong and withdrawal was necessary. Nixon and Kissinger claimed to be achieving "peace with honor," and this was accepted by much of the American public.[9]

Nixon was re-elected in November, easily defeating George McGovern. McGovern had run a campaign that repudiated the American engagement in the Vietnam War, and he was widely regarded as holding extreme views by the American electorate. The negotiations continued, marked by an 11-day strategic U.S. bombing operation over North Vietnam, the so-called Christmas bombing.[10] The North Vietnamese recognized that the U.S. terms would enable them to unify Vietnam not very long after the United States withdrew. Finally, on January 27, 1973, an agreement was signed in Paris to settle the war; U.S. military forces were soon withdrawn and U.S. prisoners of war released. However, the Nixon administration continuing the war as long as it did, the way the war was waged, and the settlement that was reached all contributed to the deep divisions in the United States about American governance and foreign policies.[11] Many harsh judgments have been made about U.S. conduct, including the following:

> By any fair standard, Nixon and Kissinger had treated their Vietnamese ally with contemptuous disregard, and their Vietnamese enemies with bad faith and brutality. In doing so, they had almost certainly magnified the enormous difficulties of enforcing the peace they had finally succeeded in negotiating.[12]

As part of the Paris agreement, Nixon promised reconstruction aid to North Vietnam tentatively up to $3.25 billion over five years.[13] But this was not discussed with Congress and there was little preparatory work to win support for it. Furthermore, the stories that former prisoners of war told upon return to the United States of their hardships and torture aroused great anger toward the North Vietnamese. In the end, the terms of agreement were not implemented and, as was widely anticipated, the South Vietnamese government fell. Vietnam was unified by North Vietnamese military forces that marched unopposed into Saigon on April 30, 1975.

Would a more constructive conflict approach have produced a better outcome than the Paris agreement? The terms agreed upon were not much different than the terms that could have been had earlier, which would have saved many lives on both sides. An earlier settlement might also have averted the horrors of the genocide in Cambodia and avoided the disasters of the war in Laos. The settlement terms, their implementation, and future relations with the Vietnamese and among the American people might have been better if the strategies to wage and to settle the war had been more attentive to the local circumstances. Despite Nixon and Kissinger's recognition of the significance of the Soviet-Chinese antagonism, the war in Vietnam seemed to be regarded as a subordinate part of the Cold War. The significance of Vietnamese nationalism was not fully appreciated; the nationalism that would spur resistance to China, as well as to the United States. Furthermore, the South Vietnamese government had a marginal role in the negotiations, presumably in order to reach a signed agreement. But if the civil war character of the struggle had been given more credence much earlier and if the limits of U.S. military forces to impose a solution been better understood, the burdens and responsibilities of resolving the civil war would have required more substantial and realistic conduct by the South Vietnamese leadership.

The Nixon administration's decision-making about how to conduct the U.S.-Vietnam engagement was remarkably closely held and secretive. Greater participation by the Department of State, Congress, and the American public would probably have improved the decisions made and lessened the troubled implementation in the aftermath of the decisions. Greater transparency and consultation would have reduced the recriminations, mistrust, and bitterness of the war's aftermath in the United States. Instead, efforts were made to intimidate and discredit persons who disagreed with the decisions. Some of these efforts were counterproductive and hampered policymaking; ultimately they resulted in Nixon's impeachment and resignation.

The story of the Pentagon Papers is illustrative.[14] Daniel Ellsberg was a former U.S. Marine who served in the Pentagon in 1964 and then in Vietnam as a civilian in the State Department. He became convinced that the United States could not win the war, and while working at the Rand Corporation he obtained and photocopied classified papers that revealed that the Pentagon was convinced that victory was not possible and the casualties would be much higher than publicly acknowledged. In 1970 he unsuccessfully tried to convince a few U.S. senators to read some of the papers into the Senate record, for which they could not be prosecuted. Ultimately Ellsberg, although believing he would be convicted for releasing secret materials, leaked the documents to the *New York Times*. In one effort to discredit Ellsberg in September 1971, G. Gordon Liddy and E. Howard Hunt were directed to break into the office of Ellsberg's psychiatrist. They were the leaders of the break-in at the Democratic National Committee offices in the Watergate complex in June 17, 1972. This covert action and many others, including CIA and FBI operations to disrupt organizations opposed to the Vietnam War, finally led to proceedings that would certainly have resulted in Nixon's impeachment. To avoid that, Nixon resigned as president on August 9, 1974. He was succeeded by Vice President Gerald Ford.

EUROPE AND DÉTENTE

Importantly, political changes in the Federal Republic of Germany or West Germany, made possible new accommodations in Europe that helped transform the Cold War. In 1969, for the first time in the history of West Germany, the Social Democratic Party led in forming the country's government. Under the leadership of Willy Brandt, West Germany undertook a new policy, OstPolitik, toward the German Democratic Republic or East Germany, Poland, and other countries of Eastern Europe. This policy of rapprochement entailed the recognition of East Germany, which previous West German governments had rejected. Furthermore, the OstPolitik meant that the Soviet, Polish, and German borders, established after the end of World War II, were accepted. This provided assurance that West Germany would not attempt to regain the territories transferred to Poland. German reunification would be put off and it would not be imposed by the West. This German reorientation initially was not welcomed by Nixon and Kissinger, but they accepted its reality and made use of it to forge better relations with the Soviets.[15]

Trade relations expanded between western and eastern Europe and between the United States and the Soviet Union. All this helped Eastern European economies, but that also made the successes of the Western societies more visible to the Soviet and East European people. East-West mutual accommodation, or détente, promised benefits for many people in the West and the East.

The Soviet leaders saw value in détente with America. The Soviet economy had stalled; indeed, its rate of growth was falling relative to the United States after years of high rates of growth. Remarkably among industrialized countries, in the 1970s Soviet life expectancy began to decline and infant mortality began to rise.[16] Détente presented the possibility of moderating the arms race and the competition in newly independent and developing countries around the world. Moderation would reduce the economic strain that the rivalry was causing. Furthermore, increased international trade was seen as a way to improve Soviet domestic economic conditions.

The convergence of these developments enabled several agreements to be negotiated between the United States and the USSR, and in some instances with other governments as well. These agreements were viewed as mutually beneficial, enhancing the security of all the signers. They pertained to arms control and other matters: namely, seabed arms control (with other governments) in 1971, anti-ballistic missiles, strategic arms limitation (SALT I), basic principles for conduct between the United States and USSR, biological weapons convention (with other governments), prevention of incidents on the high seas, trade agreements (all in 1972), and the limitation of the size of nuclear weapons test in 1974. They were negotiated using traditional diplomatic methods, but blended with highly visible summit meetings and with secretive back channel procedures. In addition, the dangerous nuclear alert associated with the 1973 war of Egypt and Syria against Israel was well contained.

Kissinger spent a lot of time in back-channel diplomacy, particularly with the Soviet ambassador to the United States, Anatoly Dobrynin. This often entailed linking different matters about which formal and relatively open negotiations were underway, making grand trade-offs possible about disparate issues.[17] Such back-channel negotiations helped reach agreements, but they sometimes also had adverse consequences for the quality of the agreements and for their implementation.[18] Reliance on back channels meant that pertinent knowledge, which might have been provided by officials in the major relevant departments and agencies, including the Department of State and the CIA, was missing. In addition, the essential public support for the agreements and the overall approach they embodied was weak in this case, which left the officials favoring arms-control agreements vulnerable to opponents.[19] Attacks against the agreements and the approach grew in Congress and also in conservative Republican Party circles. The reaction was strong enough that Gerald Ford, upon succeeding Nixon as president, avoided referring to détente. The antagonism to détente contributed to the rise of Ronald Reagan in the Republican Party.

A major de-escalating agreement was the result of the 35-country Conference on Security and Cooperation in Europe (CSCE), which began in 1973.[20] The CSCE produced the Helsinki Accords in 1975; they incorporated a remarkable tradeoff with profound consequences. The Soviet Union gained the important assurance, finally, that the borders established at the end of World War II (shifting the Russian, Polish, and German borders to the west) would not be changed by force. The Soviet Union made concessions regarding the rights of journalists, the movement of people across borders, and exchanges of publications and information. These concessions strengthened the claims of dissidents in the Soviet Union and in the countries of Eastern Europe. New civil society organizations began to develop; for example, the Committee for the Defense of Workers in Poland and Charter 77 in Czechoslovakia.[21] Consequently, the hegemony of the Soviet ideology was weakened. At the insistence of the European Community (EC), the CSCE stressed the importance of governments protecting human rights, thereby greatly strengthening an international human rights norm.[22]

Many signs of growing openness were becoming evident at the everyday street level in Moscow, including arranging inexpensive tourist trips that brought Americans for brief visits. On one such trip that I took with my brother in 1975, we were approached a few times by individuals who wanted to discuss American writers and even Soviet living conditions. When we visited a Jewish synagogue, we were welcomed and discretely asked what religious items we had brought for them, as other visitors had done (we had not dared to bring any). And there was evidence of unofficial underground economic life, as individuals privately offered taxi services and purchased blue jeans.

FOREIGN INTERVENTIONS

Despite the improving bilateral U.S.-Soviet relations during the 1970s and 1980s, the United States intervened in many countries' domestic affairs because of their perceived relationship to the rivalry of the Cold War. The interventions included covert operations; for example, in Chile.[23] On September 4, 1970, Salvador Allende, the socialist candidate, won a plurality of the popular vote in a three-way race.

Nixon authorized efforts to ensure that the Chilean Congress did not designate Allende to be president, but those efforts failed and plans for a military coup were initiated. The CIA supported opposition groups and a punishing economic campaign was waged to undermine popular support for the democratically elected Chilean government. On September 11, 1973, a military coup was executed, led by the Chief of Staff of the Chilean Army, Augusto Pinochet. Allende committed suicide as military forces seized government offices. A bloody suppression followed, and then seventeen years of dictatorial rule by Pinochet. U.S. intervention was justified as necessary to avoid the establishment of a "Communist" government in Latin America. The costs to the Chilean people and to American standing and credibility in the world by the not-so-secret U.S. actions to overthrow the government and then to support Pinochet have been great.[24]

The region in which the American and Soviet governments particularly challenged each other was the Middle East, especially regarding the Israeli-Arab conflict. In the 1950s and 1960s, the Cold War was superimposed upon the Israeli-Arab conflict, with the United States supporting Israel and the Soviet Union assisting Egypt and Syria. In the 1970s, the structure of the Cold War underwent substantial changes, and the Arab-Israeli conflict for internal reasons and contextual reasons began to change.

MEDIATION OF ARAB-ISRAELI CONFLICT

Initially, Nixon did not seize the emerging opportunities for advancing peace in Israeli-Arab relations. One obstacle was Kissinger's rivalry with Secretary of State William Rogers. At the outset of his administration, Nixon wanted to keep Kissinger, his national security adviser, out of Middle East affairs because as a Jew Kissinger might be viewed as biased.[25] Consequently, Secretary of State Rogers had principal responsibility for handling the conflicts in the Middle East.

Fighting along the Suez Canal, which separated the Israeli-occupied Sinai from the rest of Egypt, broke out in March 1969. In April Nasser abrogated the cease-fire following the 1967 war, initiating the War of Attrition between Egypt and Israel.[26] Casualties in the war were heavy as a result of persistent shelling across the Suez Canal. In addition, the increasing Israeli bombing near Cairo threatened to bring substantial Soviet military personnel into air combat.

Rogers attempted to resolve the conflict, proposing a peace arrangement to be mediated by UN Ambassador Gunnar Jarrung.[27] The plan included setting a timetable for the withdrawal of Israeli military forces from Egyptian territory occupied after the 1967 war, measures of de-militarization, reopening of the Suez Canal to all shipping, and establishing recognized and secure borders. The plan was undermined by Kissinger and Nixon, whose actions contributed to the plan's abandonment following its vigorous rejection by the Egyptian and Israeli governments.[28] Kissinger in his back-channel meetings with Dobrynin linked progress in Vietnam with progress in the Middle East, indicating that American pressure on Israel to resolve the conflict with Egypt depended on Soviet aid in reaching an acceptable arrangement in Vietnam. This tough-minded approach and its focus on the Cold War appealed to Nixon, who sided with Kissinger rather than Rogers. This approach was another obstacle to effective U.S. peacemaking in the Middle East, but the change in Egypt's leadership opened new constructive possibilities.

Rogers had more success with a limited cease-fire initiative. The Israelis were concerned that the Egyptians would use the cease-fire to move up Soviet supplied anti-aircraft missiles that would intercept Israeli bombing sorties if combat recurred. Nixon assured the Israeli leaders that such violations would be monitored and if they occurred countered with additional superior aircraft. As recognized in analyses of mediation, a powerful mediator can add such sweeteners to help close a deal. Unfortunately, the Egyptians acted swiftly to do what the Israelis had warned about. U.S. monitoring did not prevent the violations and new aircraft would not entirely solve the new problem.

The structure of the Arab-Israeli conflict changed radically after Anwar El-Sadat, the vice president of Egypt, became president in October 1970 following Nasser's death. Sadat loosened Egypt's ties to the Soviet Union and began to change Egyptian domestic and foreign policies so they aligned Egypt with the United States. Sadat moved carefully, trying not to antagonize the Soviet Union or alarm the Egyptian officials closely associated with the Soviets. Sadat and other Egyptians believed that the Soviet leaders were not helpful enough and did not treat them with the proper respect, while Washington would be a better economic model and ally and provide a better route to Jerusalem.[29]

Sadat launched a public peace initiative on February 4, 1971, offering to re-open the Suez Canal, which was not usable following the June 1967 war, in exchange for a partial Israeli pullback of its occupation of the Sinai.[30] After some discussions, the Israeli government, headed by Golda Meier, decided not to enter negotiations on that premise. Nixon continued to view the Middle East primarily in terms of bilateral relations with the Soviet Union and viewed Israel as a regional power and a bulwark against the Soviets.

Disappointed at the lack of response to his peace initiative, Sadat began to threaten military action to regain the Sinai. The threat was discounted by Israel and the United States. However, Egypt and Syria did launch a powerful surprise attack on October 6, 1973, on the Jewish holy day, Yom Kippur which fell that year during the Muslim holy month, Ramadan. The Egyptians advanced swiftly across the Canal and the Sinai and the Syrians advanced from the north.

Kissinger had become secretary of state in September 1973 and retained the national security advisor office, while Nixon was already deep into countering the expanding revelations of the Watergate scandal. Kissinger had primary responsibility for U.S. policy in the Middle East. After driving into the Sinai, Egyptian forces halted their advances and by mid-October, Israeli forces began to push the Egyptian armies back, almost encircling the Egyptian Third Army. Kissinger flew to Moscow to negotiate with Leonid Brezhnev about the terms of a UN cease-fire resolution, which was passed by the UN Security Council on October 22. The Israeli army, however, continued to tighten the encirclement of the Egyptian Third Army. The Soviets indicated that they might intervene to preserve the Egyptian army, and in response U.S. forces were put on a nuclear alert. But both sides quickly backed away from the confrontation and the cease-fire took effect on October 25, 1973.

Kissinger arranged a Middle East peace conference in December 1973 in Geneva; it was co-chaired with the Soviet Union, thereby according some respect to the Soviet Union while he carried on his shuttle diplomacy. Kissinger went on to mediate two sequential disengagement agreements between Egypt and Israel, which entailed Israeli military withdrawal from a portion of the Sinai along the Suez Canal back into the Sinai Mountains. He also mediated a disengagement agreement between Israel and Syria. The negotiations were not conducted directly by the opposing sides; rather, Kissinger shuttled back and forth between the capitals of the adversary countries. This gave him great power to convey each side's concerns and preferences in a way that the other side could appreciate. It also allowed him to leak information and introduce possibilities that were given credence because of his skills and knowledge. Some critics, however, thought his mediation was manipulative and even deceptive.[31] Yet the terms were mutually advantageous for the opposing parties and were implemented.

Kissinger's apparent success contributed to public recognition of the possibilities of mediation in international conflicts. However, the mediation as practiced by Kissinger in these cases was inconsistent in many regards with the developing constructive conflict approach, as later assessed by several conflict resolution analysts.[32] While they generally acknowledged Kissinger's tactical skills and creativity in pursuing his step-by-step mediation approach, they noted that the high priority he gave to advancing U.S. interests and excluding the Soviets from the region sometimes had long-term adverse effects for the people in the region. He practiced mediation-with-muscle, both by dire warnings and by expanding the negotiation pie with offers of weapons, guarantees, and other benefits to each party to win its acceptance of a settlement deal. This was expensive for the United States, however, and also encouraged each side to raise demands of the United States as a price for a Kissinger success. At times, this unduly restricted future U.S. actions in the region. For example, to win Israeli agreement during the second Sinai negotiations, he promised U.S. toleration of Israeli retaliation for Palestinian attacks across the Lebanon cease-fire line as well as U.S. rejection of contacts with the PLO without Israeli concurrence.[33]

In Kissinger's eagerness to win agreements to drive the momentum for future agreements and to bolster his reputation, he may have chosen to mediate a problem more likely to succeed than undertake a more important problem, which would be more risky. This may have been the case in August 1974 when Kissinger chose to mediate the second Israeli withdrawal from the Sinai rather than seek an agreement between Jordan and Israel, which would have to deal with the West Bank under Israeli occupation. Of course, the choice may be interpreted as demonstrating the importance of recognizing the right time to undertake mediation. I. William Zartman and others have stressed the importance of intervening when the time is ripe.[34] A crucial component of a situation being ripe is when the adversaries believe they are in a hurting stalemate. The other component is the belief that there is an acceptable and feasible option to escape the stalemate—a belief that a mediator can help construct.

Each mediation undertaking will yield a variety of benefits and costs to each of the parties directly participating and to some degree to other stakeholders not a party to the undertaking. Adopting a conflict resolution approach, drawing from relevant research and experience, as discussed next, can help choose a combination of strategies that maximize benefits and minimize costs.

Growth of the Conflict Resolution Field, 1969–1980

Some of the persons discussed in the previous chapter, who had planted the seeds of the conflict resolution field, were disappointed at their limited achievements in theory and research.[35] In the 1970s, however, the size and range of the conflict resolution field suddenly began to grow, stimulated by an expansion of conflict resolution practices.[36] The rapid growth of the field of conflict resolution in the United States was in many ways a social movement, arising from the convergence of several other social movements of the 1960s and 1970s.[37]

Alternative dispute resolution (ADR) was an important component of the expanding conflict resolution movement. It entailed mediation by non-officials helping to settle local interpersonal disputes, deriving its energy from several sources. It was congruent with some of the sentiments of the 1960s; it offered an alternative to adversarial judicial proceedings and it empowered people to solve their own fights without relying on authorities. The frustrations of many people who had struggled in the 1960s to fundamentally transform American society propelled some of them into local community activism. In addition, the expansion of ADR was prompted by the expansion of the right for legal defense, the growth of the legal profession and litigation, and the ensuing congestion of the American court system. It was attractive to some lawyers and many non-lawyers as a way to reduce the burden on the courts.[38] Persons wishing to mediate in community dispute resolution centers receive training in mediation. Peer mediation has expanded greatly into many governmental and nongovernmental institutions, and consequently some basic insights of conflict analysis have been diffusing across the United States.

The mediation model associated with ADR tends to be facilitative, not directive. The mediator helps the parties find a mutually satisfactory agreement and strives to be neutral. In the interpersonal disputes between neighbors and between landlords and renters, which are the bulk of the disputes mediated, this model is appropriate. Mediators in larger-scale conflicts play much more varied roles, including contributing resources and introducing new options.

Conflict resolution as a social movement was also fostered by the peacemaking and mediation activities of religious organizations, particularly those associated with the Society of Friends (Quakers) and the Mennonites. Also, the field seemed to offer peace movement members, whose numbers soared in the early 1980s, a practical alternative to the nation's reliance on military options.[39] Finally, conflict resolution propositions arising from research and theory provided a theoretical basis and intellectual justification for its practices.

Problem-solving workshops were another growing sphere of conflict resolution practice in this period. In the previous chapter, I discussed the productive 1965 workshop with representatives from Malaysia, Indonesia, and Singapore that John Burton led. In 1966, he, Christopher Mitchell, John Groom, and other colleagues conducted a problem-solving workshop in Cyprus. Herbert Kelman joined as a member of the team of facilitators in the workshop between Greek and Turkish Cypriots, and realized that such workshops were a way to direct his interest in social psychology and international relations into practice.[40] He applied the method to the Israeli-Arab/Palestinian conflict, in which he had a long-standing interest. In 1971–72, he and Stephen P. Cohen taught a course at Harvard University that included a problem-solving workshop. Kelman, with colleagues and students, went on to do more than fifty workshops, some sustained, which included Palestinians and Israeli Jews who later became engaged in PLO-Israeli negotiations.

Informal intermediary channels also occurred more frequently and received greater attention. For example, Mike Yarrow edited a book containing accounts of Quaker intermediary efforts.[41] In addition, U.S. officials mediated major conflicts in the Middle East with apparent success, in the highly visible cases of Kissinger's shuttle diplomacy and President Carter's 1978 Camp David mediation, which is discussed in the next section of this chapter. The cases spurred public interest and academic analysis of various kinds of mediation.

Research and theorizing about conflict resolution expanded greatly during the 1970s, notably relating to a variety of negotiation forms, from tacit bargaining to face-face extended meetings. This flourishing field of endeavor drew much from the earlier work of Thomas Schelling, mathematical theories of games, social-psychological experimentation and empirical studies of particular negotiation cases.[42] In addition to analyses of various processes in negotiation, much research began to be focused on the impact of various strategies and tactics that affect outcomes of negotiation. This included studies of concession rates and reframing a conflict by breaking it up or by adding more issues for possible trade-offs. The repertoire of techniques quickly grew, based on discovering underlying interests and kinds of payoff matrices that contributed to creating new options.[43]

Another important proposition, which would have profound implications for the development of the constructive conflict approach, was given an empirical and theoretical grounding by the work of Gene Sharp. Nonviolent action to bring about desired social change or to resist undesired impositions has been used throughout human history, but its notable effectiveness in winning Indian independence and gaining denied civil rights for African Americans enhanced its salience. In explaining their application of nonviolent action, Mohandas Gandhi and Martin Luther King Jr. noted moral as well as practical considerations.

As a sociologist, Sharp based his analysis on the recognition that rulers' power depends upon the obedience and cooperation of their subjects or enough of them to control the others. He argues that nonviolent action can be more effective than reliance on violence, as a pragmatic matter. If the subjects withdraw their obedience, the rulers cease to have political power. In *The Politics of Nonviolent Action*, Sharp documents the many, many ways nonviolent action has been applied: by holding demonstrations, by not complying with particular laws, and by refusing to cooperate or by blocking economic and political activities.[44] He also laid out how to prepare for nonviolent action and ways of responding to repressive responses. To further this work he established the Albert Einstein Institution in 1983 (http://www.aeinstein.org).

In addition, numerous empirical analyses were done about international crises and how they do (and often do not) escalate into wars.[45] Other works analyzed conflicts more generally and how they can be conducted while minimizing destructive consequences and attaining transformations that have some mutually beneficial outcomes.[46] Some analysts had experience as active intermediaries, as Adam Curle had in the Nigeria-Biafra civil war of 1967–1970 and the 1971 Indo-Pakistan war.[47]

The demonstrations and analyses of effective ways to employ nonviolent strategies began to spread around the world. Gene Sharp's analyses were translated into many languages and widely read. He consulted with a broad range of governmental and nongovernmental organizations about nonviolent action. In the early 1970s, the International Fellowship of Reconciliation helped in the formation of Servicio para la Acción Liberadora en América Latina—Orientación No Violenta, which provided information and training about nonviolence.[48]

The number of workers in the field of conflict resolution, both practitioners and researchers, greatly increased in the 1970s. They provided the base and the stimulation for the institutionalization that occurred in the 1980s, discussed later in this chapter.

Renewed Cold-War Escalation, 1974–1980

During the détente period, many constructive conflict methods were used.[49] They were built on previous thought and practice and became part of the repertoire for government officials and private citizens. The methods include provisions to settle disagreements about interpreting agreements, procedures to monitor adherence to agreements, many negotiating and mediating techniques, and confidence-building measures. Those measures included exchanging information about planned military maneuvers by NATO and Warsaw Treaty forces and allowing each side to observe the other's large-scale military exercises.

When Gerald Ford succeeded Nixon in August 1974, he tried to continue Nixon's foreign policies in many ways, particularly regarding arms control efforts with the USSR. Leonid Brezhnev, although disappointed with the economic benefits that détente had yielded, wanted to continue it and pressed to meet with the new American president. Ford and Brezhnev met in Vladivostok in November 1974, and Brezhnev convincingly conveyed his profound desire for "friendly, stable, mutually advantageous relations with the United States."[50] They settled on the parameters for another SALT agreement, whereby each country would be allowed to have 2,400 strategic launchers, of which 1,320 missiles could have multiple warheads.

DÉTENTE TROUBLES

While détente was underway, however, American-Soviet rivalry also continued and confrontations sometimes erupted. These episodes related to external events challenged détente, weakened it, and ultimately contributed to its demise. In addition, domestic developments in the United States and the Soviet Union undermined support for détente.

The wars between Somalia and Ethiopia in the Horn of Africa, for example, pitted the United States and USSR against each other, damaging détente. In 1969, Major-General Mohamed Siad Barre took control of Somalia, installed a socialist regime, and established relations with the Soviet Union. Neighboring Ethiopia, under the rule of Emperor Haile Selassie, was receiving military assistance from the United States. However, a Marxist military group seized power in Ethiopia in 1974, and in 1976 Ethiopia signed a military assistance agreement with the USSR and expelled American military advisers. In 1977, Somali military forces invaded the Ogadan region of Ethiopia, inhabited largely by ethnic Somalis. The Soviet leadership switched to support Ethiopia and with Soviet aid and Cuban troops, the invasion was repelled. The United States then became Somalia's principle provider of military and economic aid.

During this period in post-colonial Africa, socialist ideology was attractive and aided Soviet influence, which the United States sought to counter. Invasions, separatist movements, and internal wars produced humanitarian disasters. That conceivably could have been an incentive for American and Soviet cooperation to stop supplying arms, strengthen UN peacekeeping operations, and provide humanitarian aid. Such a constructive approach was not considered by officials, and the legacy has been disorder, death, and havens for violent extremist groups.

Important changes within the United States also contributed to the deterioration of U.S.-Soviet détente. Ford experienced considerable pressure from Republican hawks who opposed détente and warned that the CIA was underestimating Soviet military power. In response, in May 1976 a "Team B" of hardliners was appointed to review intelligence data.[51] The report of "Team B," contrary to previous intelligence analyses (and later findings), concluded in late 1976 that the Soviet Union viewed détente as a means to gain military superiority.

Another matter impacting negatively on the détente relationship was the Soviet restriction on the rights of Jews to leave the USSR and the U.S. responses to that policy. American Jews and others mobilized in support of Soviet Jewry and helped obtain an amendment to the 1974 Trade Act that would pressure the Soviet Union to allow freer emigration.[52] The amendment, whose major co-sponsors were Senator Henry Jackson and Representative Charles Vanik, denied most favored nation trade terms to the USSR, unless freedom of emigration rights were implemented. The amendment was passed unanimously by both houses of Congress and signed by President Ford in January 1975. This reduced the possible benefits of détente for the Soviets, and the Soviet government responded initially by decreasing the number of exit visas.

AFGHANISTAN AND AMERICAN-SOVIET HOSTILITY

Jimmy Carter won the 1976 U.S. presidential election over Gerald Ford and was inaugurated in January 1977. Carter wished to be directly engaged in formulating and implementing his own foreign policy and preferred bold, comprehensive approaches. He chose Cyrus Vance, a lawyer with considerable government experience in defense matters during the Johnson administration, to be secretary of state. As his national security adviser he chose Zbigniew Brzezinski, a Polish-born international relations expert, whose writings and experience made him appear to be a dangerous Cold Warrior in the eyes of the Soviet leaders.[53]

The advancement of human rights was a central theme of Carter's foreign policy, and that was extended to the Soviet Union.[54] Soon after taking office, he wrote a letter to Andrei Sakharov, a leading Soviet dissident, and he received Vladimer Bukovsky, a dissident in exile, in the White House. Soviet leaders decried what they believed to be interference in the Soviet Union's internal affairs.

Carter also wanted to renew the negotiations regarding strategic arms control, following the SALT II understandings reached in Vladivostok by Ford and Brezhnev.[55] Numerous meetings were held in Washington regarding alternative U.S. positions to take on still-unresolved issues. The issues related to the number of launchers agreed upon at Vladivostok and whether the Soviet Backfire bomber and the U.S. long-range ground-launched cruise missiles (GLCM) should be counted as strategic launchers. Some officials favored remaining with the agreed-upon numbers and postponing additional cuts in the limits to launchers until future START III negotiations would begin, believing this would help maintain the cooperative Soviet-American relationship. Brzezinski and other officials favored a bolder approach that would reduce the levels and impede the modernization of Soviet ICBMs. Ultimately, on March 12, Carter chose the deep cuts approach.

The decision and its implementation may have been affected by domestic considerations, while possible Soviet responses were not given the proper weight. Some members of the new administration wanted to make a break from the past, to win a better deal than Kissinger had gotten, and to deflect right-wing pressure as manifested by the Committee on the Present Danger and by hardline Democrats led by Senator Henry Jackson. Members of the committee and their associates were the base for the neoconservatives who became so influential in George W. Bush's presidency.[56]

Putting the Vladivostok understandings aside greatly disappointed the Soviet leaders and raised their suspicions of U.S. intentions. SALT II negotiations were delayed and then progressed slowly; sometimes they were hampered by U.S. mistrust of stated Soviet positions, which was overcome when the underlying reason for the position was understood and then easily managed.[57] Unfortunately, by the time the treaty was signed in June 1979, it could not be ratified because the monitoring installations in Iran became unavailable after the revolution. Speedy negotiations are often crucial because they can be completed while the situation is favorable. For example, the Iranian Revolution in 1979 meant that Iran was no longer available to provide a site for monitoring Soviet missile testing, part of the methods agreed upon to verify compliance to the nuclear weapons testing agreements.

The 1979 Iranian Revolution was a transforming event in the Middle East, with profound implications for American policies in the region. Many sectors of Iranian society opposed Mohammad Reza Shah, viewing him as installed and propped up by the United States. As the revolutionary opposition grew, the gravely ill Shah and his wife left Iran in January; and in February, the regime fell. The Ayatollah Khomeini and his supporters gained control of the revolution and took power. To consolidate their rule, on November 4, 1979, student supporters of the Ayatollah seized the U.S. Embassy in Tehran and held the U.S. personnel in the Embassy hostage for 444 days. The ostensible catalyst for the seizure was to demand the Shah's return to Iran, after Carter allowed him to enter the United States for medical treatment of malignant lymphoma. Carter reported that he had informed Iranian officials that the Shah would visit the United States for medical care, and the response did not signal strong objection.[58]

An Algerian team, led by Foreign Minister Mohammad Benyahia, mediated the negotiations to arrange the freeing of the hostages in exchange for releasing the Iranian assets, which the United States had frozen. To further humiliate Carter, the hostages were released only on the day Reagan was inaugurated as president. The paucity of connections between Americans and Iranians, beyond the official relations between the Shah's government and the U.S. government, limited American understanding of the coming revolution or ability to influence its course.[59]

The Cold War sharply intensified after the Soviet invasion of Afghanistan in December 1979. This should not have been a total surprise. Back in April 1978, the Afghan Communist Party (the People's Democratic Party of Afghanistan, PDPA) had seized power from the government led by Prime Minister Mohammed Daoud. The Soviet leadership, however, had good relations with the Daoud government and had not sanctioned the coup. The PDPA was extremely doctrinaire and moved to impose a secular Marxist order; it also was divided into two antagonistic factions— the Khalq, led by Nur Mohammad Taraki, and the Parchams, led by Babrak Karmal. Taraki became head of the government and worked closely with another Khalq leader, Hafizullah Amin.

The Soviet government soon began to give assistance to the Afghan government and cautioned it to be less radical and repressive. Nevertheless, Taraki and Amin continued their ruthless policies and showed little regard for the Islamic concerns, local traditions, and ethnic identities of many Afghans. Resistance quickly grew, and a major uprising occurred in March 1979. Taraki and Amin rushed to Moscow, acknowledged the revolution was in danger and requested Soviet military assistance.[60] The Soviet Politburo discussed the situation and decided that the Soviet Union should not send troops into Afghanistan. They believed that the Afghan population was not ready for a Communist revolution and that Soviet military intervention would harm their efforts at détente and arms reduction and also arouse opposition of the nonaligned nations to the benefit of China. They reached this conclusion despite their belief that the U.S. government was directing the Afghan resistance. Taraki was told the decision and urged to win greater popular support from the Afghan people.

From the Politburo's viewpoint, the situation in Afghanistan continued to deteriorate. The Soviet leaders decided that Amin was conspiring against Taraki and was highly repressive toward Afghans; so in September they told Taraki to get rid of Amin. But the plot to do so was unsuccessful and instead Amin killed Taraki. The Soviet leaders mistrusted Amin and suspected he might become allied with the West and the United States would have a foothold in Afghanistan.

As already noted, during this time, Carter and Brezhnev continued some aspects of détente and made progress on the SALT II agreement, which they finally signed in June 1979. Carter faced domestic opposition to the treaty and he struggled to achieve ratification. It was thought that being tough with the Soviets might help win domestic support for ratification. On July 3, upon the recommendation of Brzezinski, Carter signed a presidential finding authorizing the CIA to begin providing radio equipment, medical supplies, and cash to the Afghan rebels.[61] This opportunity to inflict costs to the Soviet Union's international actions was attractive to many groups within and outside the U.S. government. At the same time, the Soviets openly reveled in their successes in Ethiopia, Nicaragua, Angola and elsewhere in the world. Thus, on September 13, Mikhail Suslov, the leading Soviet ideologue, proclaimed the growth of socialism and the "defeat of imperialist and neocolonialist forces."[62]

The wish and interest in fostering mutually agreeable accommodations and managing the arms race were not always strong enough to overcome seizing an opportunity for unilateral advantage or to hold back on actions that might be seen as threatening to the other side. Thus, on December 12, 1979, NATO leaders decided to continue their plans to deploy ground-launched Tomahawk cruise missiles and Pershing II intermediate-range ballistic missiles in Western Europe. Brezhnev had warned against this and proposed reducing Soviet SS-20s (intermediate-range ballistic missiles) if the West would hold off on that NATO escalation and conduct negotiations regarding these weapons systems.

Faced with a deteriorating situation in Afghanistan in late December, Politburo members again discussed intervening militarily. The possibilities of détente were attractive, promising greater trade, enhanced security by recognition of Soviet interests, and reduced military expenditures to better meet domestic Soviet needs. However, in reality, the possible benefits were not forthcoming and security threats were increasing. Soviet leaders worried that the United States would act militarily against Iran, where U.S. embassy personnel were held hostage. The trade benefits of détente were disappointing, partly as a result of the Jackson-Vanik amendment, and even SALT II was not going to be ratified.

KGB chief Yuri Andropov warned Politburo members that the Afghan government leader, Amin, was recruited by the CIA as part of a grand plot to create a new Ottoman Empire, which would incorporate southern republics of the USSR.[63] On November 26, 1979, Politburo members began preparations for a change in the Afghan government; Babrak Karmal, an exiled communist, was chosen to replace Amin. Covert attempts to kill Amin failed and an invasion was undertaken on December 25, 1979; KGB paramilitaries attacked and killed Amin and his aides. A new Afghan government was installed and a large-scale Soviet invasion was made to shore up the new government.

The U.S. government reacted fiercely. The invasion was perceived to threaten expanding Soviet power into the Middle East and Persian Gulf. Carter ordered cuts in trade and an embargo on grain sales to the Soviet Union; he increased U.S. military appropriations and military assistance to Pakistan and aid to the Afghan resistance to the Soviet invasion. Believing that the Senate would not ratify the SALT II agreement, he withdrew it from consideration.[64]

Destructively, the Soviet and U.S. leaders viewed each other as having more aggressive intentions than was warranted, which contributed to members in each side believing they faced severe immediate threats. In seeking to counter those dangers, and to mollify domestic hard-liners, each side took actions that punished the other side, thereby providing evidence of the presumed threats.

Proactive Peacemaking

Outside of the Cold War context, President Carter initiated an important peacemaking undertaking that is given too little attention. He averted a destructive conflict escalation with Panama that had erupted with violence in January 1964.[65] A 1903 treaty accorded a ten-mile-wide strip of Panamanian territory, from the Atlantic to the Pacific oceans, within which the Panama Canal was to be built and operated by the United States, in perpetuity. The Panamanians deeply resented this treaty, which they felt had been foisted upon them. Following the riots in 1964, President Johnson opened negotiations with the Panamanian government about the future status of the Canal Zone and the Panama Canal. In June 1967, new treaties had been agreed upon, but were not submitted for ratification due to the Senate's fierce opposition to them. Presidents Nixon and Ford pursued negotiations but did not complete them. Contrarily, Ronald Reagan ran in the presidential primaries, challenging Ford and asserting that the Panama Canal was ours and "we are going to keep it."

When Carter began his national election campaign, the Panama Canal issue was frequently brought to his attention. He learned about the history of the Canal and concluded after his election that negotiations should begin immediately and that an eventual agreement would have to acknowledge Panamanian sovereignty and schedule ending total U.S. control of the Canal. Despite anticipating strong congressional resistance, early in 1977 Carter opened negotiations with the Panamanian government, then headed by Omar Torrijos. The need for a new agreement was buttressed by military security considerations. U.S. military leaders argued that the Canal was in danger of attacks and sabotage and could most securely be operated with the cooperation of a friendly Panamanian government. However, the negotiations with the Panamanian government were difficult, and it took time to work out an agreement that would satisfy the basic interests of both governments.

The final agreement took the form of two treaties, which were signed on February 7, 1977. One treaty would return most of the Canal Zone territory to Panama. Panamanians would join the Americans in operating the Canal until the end of the century, when Panama would gain control of the Canal. The other treaty ensured the right of the United States to defend the canal from any external threat that might interfere with neutral service to ships of all nations. Carter, aware of evolving international standards regarding the rights of all nations and of the perceptions and needs of people impacted by U.S. power, risked challenging domestic resistance to "giving up the Panama Canal." To overcome opposition of arch-conservative senators such as Strom Thurmond and Jesse Helms, Carter mobilized former and current Republican and Democratic officials who understood the importance of ratifying the treaties. Carter also arranged for about forty-five senators to travel to Panama to meet Torrijos and appreciate the significance of the Canal's history for the Panamanians and also to examine the fragility of the Canal system.[66] The first treaty was ratified by the U.S. Senate in March 1978, and the second was ratified the next month. The treaties have been successful in securing the operations of the Canal and helped to avoid deteriorating relations between the United States and Panama.

Mediation of Israeli-Egyptian Conflict

Carter's mediation resulting in the Israeli-Egyptian peace treaty in 1979 was a major peacemaking contribution. When Carter took office he quickly moved to achieve a comprehensive Israeli-Arab peace agreement.[67] He wished to differentiate his policies from those of Nixon and Kissinger; while they took a step-by-step approach to resolving that complex conflict, Carter sought to resolve the interconnected set of bilateral conflicts that made up the Israeli-Arab conflict. Seeking a comprehensive settlement, Carter and Vance tried to convene a conference in Geneva, which would be co-chaired by the Soviet Union, as was the case in December 1973. It would include Israel, the major Arab states neighboring Israel, and the Palestinians.[68] Carter and Vance held many preparatory meetings with the leaders of Israel and of nearby Arab states. Initially, there were some indications that a generally acceptable settlement might be attainable, which included recognition of Israel within slightly adjusted borders along the former 1967 cease-fire line and the establishment of a national homeland for Palestinians in areas Israel still occupied after the 1967 war.

The situation changed when Menachem Begin became prime minister in June 1977, following the electoral victory of the Likud bloc, which was the first electoral win for this extreme nationalist party.[69] Begin made it clear that he favored the expansion of Jewish settlements in the occupied territories of the West Bank and Gaza, and they were. The representation of the Palestinians in any meeting with Israelis was a major issue, since the Israeli government would not meet with the PLO as long as it refused to recognize Israel. The inclusion of Palestinians as part of a unified Arab delegation was considered a possible solution, but that also raised many problems. The prospects of convening a general conference seemed increasingly dismal.

The Egyptian and Israeli governments began secret contacts, including a meeting in Morocco between Israeli Foreign Minister Moshe Dayan and an aide to Sadat, Hassan Touhamy, in mid-September 1977. In October, Carter, seeing his plans for a comprehensive conference stalled, encouraged Sadat to take some initiative. What Sadat did was astounding. To the surprise of Washington and the Arab world, on November 9 he announced his readiness to go to Jerusalem. The Israeli government invited Sadat to speak to the Knesset, and he did on November 20.[70] Israelis were ecstatic that peace might come. Sadat's actions, however, aroused the fury of the Arab League, which condemned the Egyptian betrayal at its summit meeting in Tripoli in December 1977. At that time the PLO also reaffirmed its rejection of UN Security Council Resolution 242.

The visit to Jerusalem was a grand gesture that resulted in transforming Israeli-Egyptian relations, as such conciliatory gestures can help accomplish.[71] It did not follow a GRIT scenario, which is undertaken unilaterally with an explanatory speech followed by a sequence of conciliatory initiatives. In this case, it was made possible and credible by prior direct and indirect informational exchanges and direct actions, including the full implementation of the prior Egyptian-Israeli disengagement agreements. Sadat hoped his dramatic act would provide a psychological breakthrough for Arabs and Israelis so that a comprehensive settlement would follow. But that was not to be.

The Israeli-Egyptian peace negotiations, which began after Sadat's visit to Jerusalem, soon appeared to be failing. The Egyptian and Israeli governments each sought U.S. government support and engagement in forging an agreement. Carter and his associates believed that no Israeli-Egyptian agreement could or should be reached without some agreement helping to resolve the Israeli-Palestinian conflict. Begin proposed autonomy for the Palestinians living in the West Bank and Gaza, which the PLO would certainly reject. Carter sought to convince Begin that adherence to Security Council Resolution 242 meant the withdrawal of Israeli forces from the West Bank and Gaza and not building Jewish settlements in those territories. Previous Israeli governments, led by the Labor Party, had interpreted the resolution to mean withdrawal for peace on all fronts. An Israeli peace movement organization, Peace Now, emerged and tried to push the Israeli government to take more accommodating positions in order to grasp the chance for peace that Sadat's visit to Jerusalem had presented.

The Americans worked hard to modify Begin's formulation so that substantive negotiations could be pursued. Carter finally proposed a summit meeting at Camp David with Sadat and Begin to forge an agreement. The summit lasted thirteen days, with a small team of Americans, Israelis, and Egyptians meeting in seclusion. After their first encounter, Sadat and Begin did not try to negotiate directly with each other. The American team shuttled back and forth between the two sides, working on a single-text draft agreement. During the day, they sought what changes each side wanted to make the agreement acceptable, and then during the night they revised the text, then followed the same process the next day. It is also worth noting that the Israeli and Egyptian teams each included one or two members who conveyed information and assurances from the other side to their own and sometimes came up with creative options, so they served as quasi-mediators.[72]

In the end, two agreements were reached: A Framework for Peace in the Middle East and the Framework for the Conclusion of a Peace Treaty between Egypt and Israel. The Framework for Peace in the Middle East was necessarily complex. It included provisions for Egypt, Israel, Jordan, and the representatives of the Palestinian people to negotiate a resolution of the Palestinian problem. It envisaged a transitional period of not more than five years following the establishment of a self-governing authority in the West Bank and Gaza. Israeli armed forces would withdraw into specified security locations, and no later than the third year, negotiations regarding the final status of the West Bank would occur between Israeli, Egyptian, Jordanian, and Palestinian representatives.

The Framework for the Conclusion of a Peace Treaty between Egypt and Israel was simpler. It included the total withdrawal of any Israeli presence in the Sinai, limitations on Egyptian military forces in areas of Sinai near Israel, and the establishment of full diplomatic relations between Egypt and Israel. The vexing issue was the linkage between the two agreements. Egypt wanted them to be linked in order to avoid signing a separate peace, but the Israelis successfully insisted that the peace treaty with Egypt could not be a hostage to other entities that were not signatories to the two Framework agreements.

Concluding the peace treaty between Egypt and Israel following the Camp David Summit proved to be extremely difficult, and personal mediation by Carter was again required. Carter had incorporated an important and not always recognized function: to draw attention to important stakeholders who are not themselves represented in the negotiations. Now he strove to persuade the leaders of Jordan, Saudi Arabia, and the PLO to consider participating in settling the Palestinian issue in the context of the Framework for Peace in the Middle East. Carter sent Assistant Secretary of State Harold H. Saunders to the region to exchange information and perspectives with Israeli, Jordanian and other leaders about building on the Framework. Saunders, however, received rough treatment in Israel as he conveyed Carter's answers to questions King Hussein had raised about the Framework.[73]

The peace treaty between Egypt and Israel was signed on March 26, 1979, but without any progress in advancing peace between Israelis and Palestinians. The terms of the Peace Treaty were speedily implemented, but the result was a cold peace for Israelis with Egyptians; thus, Israelis eagerly traveled to Egypt, but that was not reciprocated. There was no breakthrough for peace in the region. Indeed, the Arab League, meeting on March 31, 1979, denounced the signing of a peace treaty with "the Zionist enemy" and recommended the severance of political and diplomatic relations with Egypt.

Carter and the U.S. mediating team were skillful and extremely hard-working, and their effort was a necessary ingredient in achieving the treaty. However, the structure of the conflict was such that a separate peace between Egypt and Israel was likely, and it did not contribute to progress toward a peaceful, comprehensive resolution. In retrospect, if either the Israeli government or the PLO and some Arab states had demonstrated their readiness to accept the Framework for Peace in the

Middle East and add to its attractiveness to the other side, there might have been a response that would have enabled negotiations about a broader peace to begin. For that to have happened, major groups within each side would have had to overcome severe obstacles of fear, mistrust, and grief and open themselves up to negotiations.[74] But the U.S. government could not induce either side to follow that course. The U.S. mediation is widely regarded as remarkably successful, even if it failed to bring about a comprehensive resolution of the Israeli-Palestinian/Arab conflict. At times, the peace between Israel and Egypt has contributed to some subsequent moves toward a mutually acceptable accommodation between Israelis and Palestinians.

Escalations and De-escalations, 1981–1988

The Cold War severely intensified in the early 1980s, but then changed direction, and most remarkably it was peacefully transformed at the end of the 1980s. In accounting for this momentous change, I will discuss the notable roles of nonofficial actors as well as of leading officials in the United States, the Soviet Union, and elsewhere. Other foreign conflicts during this period when Ronald Reagan was president are also discussed.

COLD WAR ESCALATIONS

Ronald Reagan campaigned and was elected president as a conservative on domestic and international issues. Regarding foreign affairs he was a strong anti-Communist and a nationalist believing in America's exceptionalism. He believed that American military strength was paramount in the conduct of its foreign policy. After taking office, he quickly undertook a broad range of militant actions to coerce Soviet leaders to change their conduct at home and abroad. U.S. military expenditures rose, as did the anti-Soviet rhetoric. The covert assistance to the Afghan resistance fighting against both the Afghan government and Soviet forces supporting it was strengthened, including providing "stinger missiles," shoulder-held weapons that could destroy the helicopters being used by Soviet forces.

U.S. aid also was provided to create the Contras, a military force fighting the Sandinista government of Nicaragua, which came to power in July 1979. When the new Reagan administration helped escalate the civil wars in Central America, various American organizations acted in solidarity with groups in Central America opposing the governments or other organizations supported by the U.S. government.[75] Popular and congressional resistance to the Reagan administration's escalation of political and military interventions grew. This included reacting to the civil war in El

Salvador after Archbishop Oscar Romero was assassinated on March 24, 1980. In the three years he had been Archbishop, he worked with the exploited poor of El Salvador despite death threats, and his martyrdom attracted the attention of progressive Christians in the United States.[76] Then in December 1980, four American churchwomen working with refugees in El Salvador were raped and killed by Salvadoran National Guardsmen. In the United States, some Catholic and other religious activists regarded these events as confirming the extraordinary violence of the Salvadoran government, which nevertheless continued to have official U.S. support.

The Sanctuary movement was one form of opposition to the U.S. Central American policy. Beginning in 1982, churches across the United States provided safe havens for Central American refugees who were denied asylum by the U.S. government. In addition, the Democratic Congress challenged the Reagan administration's policy by blocking U.S. military aid to the Contras who were warring against the Sandinista government. The Reagan administration tried to circumvent this legislation by secretly selling arms to Iran in exchange for the release of American hostages in Lebanon and to obtain funding for the Contras. Afterward, this maneuver was revealed to the public in congressional hearings. This Iran-Contra scandal further raised broad opposition to U.S. Central American policy.[77]

Popular resistance to the Reagan administration's increased development and deployment of nuclear weapons also rapidly expanded. For example in 1980, the concept of a Nuclear Weapons Freeze Campaign was advanced by George Sammaripa and Randall Forsberg.[78] Many old and new peace organizations cooperated in the Freeze Campaign by organizing town meetings and demonstrations and gaining support from city councils, state legislatures, and members of Congress. A broad coalition mobilized a huge demonstration on June 12, 1982, in New York City.[79] By then, 169 U.S. representatives and 25 senators supported the nuclear weapons freeze.

Soviet leaders persisted in their own Cold War conduct. The war in Afghanistan to prop up the Afghan government continued, as did assistance to the Sandinista government in Nicaragua and other friendly governments and movements. The Politburo, however, seemed uncertain and was not innovative, as Brezhnev was becoming more ill and less able to provide energetic leadership. He died on November 10, 1982, and was succeeded by Yuri Andropov. Andropov was more energetic, but he also soon fell sick and died on February 9, 1984. The next leader, Konstantin Chernenko, was elderly and ill and he died on March 10, 1985.

The late 1970s and early 1980s were years of economic stagnation and even declining life expectancy, reasons enough for widespread dissatisfaction. The increasing openness of Soviet society enabled more signs of disaffection with the Soviet system to be expressed. Thus, underground newspapers began to circulate and dissidents began to be more visible in the Soviet Union. Beginning in the late 1980s, American Christian missionaries more frequently traveled to the Soviet Union to spread the gospel.[80] Jews in the USSR, who suffered discrimination and were hampered in practicing their religion, were refused the right to leave the country. But they were not isolated and contributed to the opening up of the Soviet Union. American Jews visited the Soviet Union and provided assistance to the "refuseniks." In 1988, I visited the crowded apartment of a refusenik in Moscow, at which Soviet and non-Soviet visiting scientists were holding an informal mini-conference on current scientific developments. Throughout the meeting, there were telephone calls from colleagues and supporters in other countries.

American intervention also was significant in Yugoslavia. Having broken free of Soviet domination in 1948, Yugoslavia created a unique socialist market system incorporating worker participation in management decision-making. The system was relatively successful until difficulties arose following the oil crisis of the 1970s and the large debts the Yugoslav government acquired. The International Monetary Fund managed the credit problem, but insisted on stringent austerity policies as a condition. As a result, economic conditions fell deeply in the 1980s, exacerbating ethnic and governance differences.

In March 1984, the Reagan administration issued the then-secret National Security Decision Directive (NSDD) 133, which highlighted U.S. policy "to promote the trend toward an effective, market-oriented Yugoslav economic structure."[81] The developments in Kosovo were especially destructive. Beginning in the late 1960s, Josip Broz Tito, the authoritarian president of Yugoslavia, implemented policies to improve the economic, political, and social status of the ethnic Albanians relative to the Serbs of Kosovo, who were a small but dominant minority there.[82] Consequently, the living conditions of the Kosovo Albanians improved, distressing some Serbs. Many Serbs began to move out of Kosovo, and Serb political and intellectual leaders roused Serbian ethno-nationalist sentiments, with terrible results (discussed in the next two chapters).

The United States provided assistance to organizations in many countries of Eastern Europe, which were undertaking nonviolent resistance to Soviet domination. A variety of external and internal forces and events fostered such resistance. For example, in 1979, Karol Józef Wojtyła, the former Cardinal from Cracow, made a remarkable return to Poland as Pope John Paul II. When his plane landed, church bells rang throughout the country. He delivered thirty-two sermons in nine days and was greeted by millions of Poles who saw they were not alone.

The next year, workers at the Gdansk shipyards went on strike, under the leadership of Lech Walesa. He also led Solidarity, a broad coalition of workers, intellectuals, and Catholic nationalists. It grew quickly and the government imposed martial law in 1981, imprisoning Walesa and many other Solidarity leaders. Martial law was lifted in 1983, but some degree of repression continued. In October 1984, Father Jerzy Popieluszko, a popular Catholic priest, was murdered by the police.

Nevertheless, Poles were behaving more and more freely. This was evident to me when I visited Poland in October 1985, and participated in a conference on social movements, including Solidarity, in Cracow.[83] The Polish participants discussed their differing positions about Solidarity and the Communist Party with directness and civility. In Warsaw, I visited the tiny urban cemetery where Jerzy Popieluszko was buried. The fence around the cemetery held floral displays and signs honoring Popieluszko, while union members with armbands protected the cemetery.

Finally, Poles, like other peoples in Eastern Europe, had relatives in the United States and other Western countries. The Poles settled in Western countries were sources of information about living conditions in the West, and also sources of support in many ways. For example, Poland had well-filled hard currency stores. The stores were crowded with Poles who had dollars and other hard currencies that had been sent them by relatives living outside Poland.

TERRORIST ESCALATIONS

Other foreign conflicts with only tangential relations to the Cold War also attracted considerable U.S. attention during the Reagan administration. Some adversaries in these conflicts employed methods that were regarded as terrorism by the United States.[84] The meaning of the word "terrorism," however, is widely debated. Since it denotes shameful conduct, each side in a conflict may refer to particular acts of the other side as terrorist, but does not so regard any of its own similar acts. Definitions of terrorism may focus on the intentions of the perpetrators, the targets of the actions, or characteristics of the act itself or their effects. Several of these characteristics are used in the definition guiding the U.S. intelligence community, in Title 22 of the U.S. Code. Section 2656f(d): "The term 'terrorism' means premeditated, politically motivated violence perpetrated against noncombatant targets by subnational groups or clandestine agents. The term 'international terrorism' means terrorism involving the citizens of more than one country. The term 'terrorist group' means any group that practices, or has significant subgroups that practice, international terrorism."[85]

By this definition, governments that overtly conduct bombings of cities or neighborhoods to terrify and intimidate people to gain their compliance are not committing terrorism. On the other hand, rebellious nongovernmental actors sometimes challenge the legitimacy of a state, and therefore regard the state's use of violence as illegitimate and sometimes a form of terrorism.

According to the U.S. definition, Muammar Gaddafi headed a terrorist group. He had seized control of Libya in 1969 and established a highly authoritarian political system. He supported violent organizations in the Palestinian territories and Syria and sent agents to assassinate Libyan dissidents outside of Libya, including in the United States. Shortly after taking office, Reagan was informed of credible evidence that Libyan hit squads had been sent to assassinate him and other high officials.[86] Several actions were taken to lessen the threats and to impose sanctions against Libya. The Libyan embassy office was ordered to be closed, U.S. citizens were told to leave Libya, and an embargo was placed on the importation of Libyan oil and the export of high technology to Libya.

In addition, deadly jabs began to be exchanged. Secretary of State Alexander M. Haig, Jr. and CIA Director Bill Casey acted to "bloody Qaddafi's nose," and secretly supported Chad to resist a Libyan invasion.[87] In August 1981, the U.S. Navy challenged Libya's extension of maritime claims to cover the Gulf of Sidra in the Mediterranean Sea, and when challenged by Libyan military airplanes shot down two.[88] Gaddafi retaliated for U.S. actions, with a bomb attack in April 1986 at a Berlin nightclub that killed two U.S. soldiers and injured seventy-nine servicemen. Thereupon, the United States retaliated with air attacks on targets around Benghazi and Tripoli, including the military barracks where Gaddafi resided. Gaddafi survived, but his two-year-old adopted daughter was killed.

Two years later, on December 21, 1988, a bomb secreted in stowed luggage destroyed Pan Am Flight 103 and killed the 259 people on board and 11 people on the ground in Lockerbie, Scotland, where the plane crashed. The persons responsible for this attack were not identified before Reagan completed his term in office. It was later determined that the perpetrator was a Libyan agent.

The U.S. program of violence against Gaddafi did not lead to his compliance. The United States might have more effectively mobilized UN or other multilateral sanctions to impose strong sanctions that contained violent Libyan adventurism.

INTERVENTIONS

In early 1982, Israeli officials visited Washington to discuss a plan: to crush the PLO then based in Lebanon and install Bashir Gemayel, a friendly Christian militia leader of the Phalangist Party, as president of Lebanon. They believed that Secretary of State Alexander M. Haig Jr. was not opposed.[89] On June 6, 1982, Israeli military forces began to fight their way up to Beirut, where they besieged Arafat and the PLO. As the military operations escalated, many associates of President Reagan, although not Haig, wanted to intervene to stop the fighting.[90] George P. Schultz replaced Haig as Secretary of State in July, and in August the United States helped to negotiate and implement the evacuation of the PLO from Beirut to Tunis. U.S., French, and Italian soldiers formed an international force to oversee the evacuation, and also to provide security for the Palestinian civilians left behind. The PLO departure was completed by September 1, 1982, and the international force was withdrawn by September 10, 1982.

On September 14, 1982, pro-Syrian elements assassinated Bashir Gemayel, who had been elected president. Then, on September 16, some members of a Phalangist militia massacred hundreds of Palestinians living in the Sabra and Shatila refugee camps, which were surrounded by Israeli Defense Forces (IDF). The U.S. military and other members of the international force had failed to protect the Palestinians and returned, but began to be seen in Lebanon as allied to Israel in the conflict there. On April 18, 1983, a suicide truck bombing of the U.S. embassy in Beirut killed 63 persons, including 17 Americans. U.S. officials believed that Hezbollah was responsible for the attack.[91] Hezbollah is a non-state actor whose members are Shi'a Lebanese; its spiritual leader was Sheik Mohammed Hussein Fadlallah. An even larger attack followed on October 23, 1983, when a suicide truck bombing destroyed the U.S. Marine barracks in Beirut, killing 241 marines. In response, President Reagan ordered the battleship *USS New Jersey* to shell the hills above Beirut, and he soon ordered U.S. marines to withdraw from Lebanon.

More attacks against Americans continued in Kuwait as well as in Lebanon, including suicide truck bombing of the U.S. embassy on December 12, 1983 in Kuwait. The Kuwaiti authorities quickly arrested, convicted, and imprisoned seventeen persons for the bombing; they were believed to be members of Al Dawa, an Iranian-backed Lebanese Shi'a group that was the forerunner of Hezbollah. Numerous American and other foreign nationals had been kidnapped and more were then taken hostage in Lebanon in order to win the release of the "Al Dawa 17." In January 1984, Malcom Kerr, president of AUB, was assassinated.[92] Overall, in the 1980s, fifteen Americans were taken hostage, as well as thirty-nine other foreign nationals; six were known to have been killed. In March 1984, CIA Beirut station chief William Buckley was kidnapped, tortured and killed. On September 20, 1984, a truck bombing of the U.S. embassy annex near Beirut killed twenty-four people, including two U.S. military personnel.

The CIA trained Lebanese and other foreign intelligence agents to strike at the presumed perpetrators.[93] On March 8, 1985, a truck bomb blew up the apartment building in Beirut where Sheik Fadlallah lived; over eighty people were killed, but not Fadlallah, who was not there. The militant Shia blamed the CIA, which denied responsibility for the operation. Finally, as a consequence of the many attacks and the lack of an effective counter-strategy, the U.S. government withdrew from and ended official activities in Lebanon.

Despite President Reagan's strong rhetoric about swift and effective retribution for terrorist attacks against Americans, that rarely occurred.[94] In part this was because Secretary of Defense Caspar Weinberger and most of the Joint Chiefs opposed using the military forces in counter-terrorism missions. More fundamentally, however, as with Libya, militant intervention and retribution against organizations conducting bombings and assassinations had little success. The withdrawal from Lebanon may have been the "least bad" option at the time. There might, however, have been more constructive alternatives. There might have been greater official recognition of the limits of violent retribution and discussion of longer-term strategies. Alternative strategies might have included greater cooperation with other governments and international organizations to impose sanctions on governments providing support to organizations carrying out bombings and assassinations. In addition, attention might have been given to the grievances the perpetrators are trying to overcome. Working with regional actors to find peaceful ways to address grievances might have yielded better results.

During the same time that various anti-American attacks were occurring, Iraq was waging a large-scale war against Iran. In September 1980, Saddam Hussein ordered a massive invasion of Iran, which initially advanced swiftly, but then the Iranian forces were able to resist effectively and the war went on and on with extremely heavy losses on both sides. Although Iraq had clearly committed a gross violation of international law, the United States was officially neutral and thereby weakened international law. The American antagonism toward the Iranian government because of the seizure of U.S. diplomats from the embassy in Tehran remained. Despite its official neutrality, the United States secretly provided Iraq with intelligence information and military assistance, and also openly contributed financial assistance. Moreover, the known use of chemical weapons against Iranian forces and Iraqi Kurds was not challenged by the United States.[95] Hussein could reasonably see that the U.S. government was not overly troubled at his violation of international law and treaties. The war went on until a cease-fire was finally reached in August 1988, aided by UN mediation.

The legacy of the Reagan administration included many problems in the Middle East that were exacerbated and would be highly troubling for presidential successors. However, progress was made in one regard that would be highly useful for President George H. W. Bush. In December 1988, Secretary of State Schultz opened a channel for direct communication with Arafat and the PLO, after extended indirect exchanges and with the assistance of nonofficial intermediaries.[96] This was accomplished a year after the Palestinian Intifada had begun; the Intifada was a largely non-violent, uprising by Palestinians living in the West Bank and Gaza against the Israeli occupation.[97] This popular resistance was in part a reaction to the lack of progress in their political and economic lives and to the Arab world's inattention as it focused on the Iraq-Iran war. This is another example of the complex ways many different conflicts are interlinked.

COLD WAR TURNING POINTS

The years 1983 and 1984 marked important constructive changes in the Cold War, after tensions between Soviet and U.S. leaders reached great heights.[98] On March 8, 1983, in a speech to evangelical Christians, Reagan called the Soviet Union an "evil empire." On March 23, 1983, he announced the Strategic Defense Initiative (SDI), which came to be called "Star Wars," and was viewed by Soviet leaders as a threatening move toward military dominance.

Within this context, a Korean Airlines 747 passenger plane flew over Soviet territory on September 1, 1983. Soviet commanders, believing the plane to be on a U.S. intelligence mission (indeed, a U.S. reconnaissance aircraft had been in the area about an hour before the airliner appeared there), ordered Soviet fighter planes to shoot the plane down, killing 269 people.[99] Reagan condemned shooting down the passenger plane as an act of barbarism, and the resulting controversy about the Soviet actions contributed to a major crisis. In November, U.S. ground-launched cruise missiles began arriving in Britain and Pershing II missiles in West Germany. Also during this time, U.S. military exercises probed and tested Soviet defensive systems. Warsaw Pact forces in East Germany, Poland, Czechoslovakia, and the Baltic republics were placed on alert.

President Reagan was briefed by CIA director William Casey that the Soviets feared that the United States might launch a surprise attack. Reagan grasped the dangerous implications of such a belief. Some analysts mark this as the turning point in Reagan's thinking. Reagan wrote in his memoirs that recognizing Soviet fears made him "even more anxious to get a top Soviet leader in a room alone and try to convince him we had no designs on the Soviet Union and the Russians had nothing to fear from us."[100]

Informal channels also provided Reagan with insights and understanding of Russian people and their aspirations. Suzanne Massie, who wrote about Russian culture and history, began meeting with Reagan in January 1984; she made several visits over the next four years, providing a view of Russians as humans and not simply robotic communists.[101] She also served as an informal channel for exchanges of information.[102] This influence coincided with Nancy Reagan's encouragement of an accommodation with the Soviets.

Furthermore, bonds that had been formed from earlier years of personal meetings between Soviet and American officials and private citizens were enduring enough that even with the intensification of the Cold War during Reagan's first administration, exchanges continued unofficially. Indeed, people-to-people exchanges flourished in the 1980s, and Reagan became an advocate of such programs.[103] On the Soviet side, the official Soviet Peace Committee helped organize many of the nonofficial as well as officially sponsored programs.

My experiences in Moscow in early 1985 revealed how American-Soviet exchanges contributed to the Soviet elites' interest in changing their society. I was in Moscow doing research on Soviet-American relations. Members of the Institute of U.S. and Canada Studies, whom I knew from their visits to the United States, invited me to speak at the Institute. Before my talk, I asked that copies be made of my handout. Assured there was "no problem," they took the paper. But the copies did not appear until halfway through my presentation when a secretary brought dozens of copies, which she had typed and retyped using carbon paper. I looked quizzically at my Soviet hosts, who informed me that the copier was broken that day. The actual problem was that using a copy machine required approval from upper levels of authority, presumably to avoid duplicating unauthorized materials. My hosts seemed embarrassed to view the situation through my American eyes. This is a micro example of soft power effects.

TRANSITION TO THE END OF THE COLD WAR

The crucial change producing the most profound turn in the Cold War was the Politburo's selection of Mikhail Gorbachev to be the new Soviet leader following Chernenko's death. Gorbachev was energetic and ambitious to make profound changes, which were desired by many Soviet leaders because they recognized the stagnation, backwardness, and rigidities of the Soviet system compared to the West. They wanted a change to invigorate their economy and to have more personal freedom.

Gorbachev initially did not change the policy direction of his predecessor and mentor, Andropov.[104] He sought to correct economic problems using new technologies and more discipline, and he tightened restrictions on drinking alcohol. He also believed that improving relations with the West and reducing the burdens of huge Soviet military expenditures were vital to reforming the Soviet system. However, he was slow to restructure Soviet society, linking that to the need for reducing military expenditures. By late 1988, Gorbachev's economic reforms were demonstrably unsuccessful and he and the foreign minister, Eduard Shevardnadze, increasingly made the argument to their associates that reducing military spending was necessary. That move required more conciliatory policies toward the West. The American public's opposition to Reagan's anti-Soviet militancy and Reagan's conciliatory gestures after 1983 helped make such a Soviet course of action plausible.

Gorbachev and his associates, through reading and meetings, had become familiar with the conceptions of security matters that were being developed by peace researchers in West Germany, Denmark, England, and elsewhere in Western Europe.[105] Their analyses indicated how security could be more assured by adopting military defense strategies that were not offensive rather than ones likely to be viewed as threatening. This went beyond agreeing upon confidence-building measures and providing procedures for mutual monitoring of adherence to past agreements. It included restructuring military forces so that they clearly were for defensive purposes, which the Soviets did undertake.

Gorbachev and Reagan energetically renewed arms control and arms reduction negotiations and quickly established good relations with each other. Reagan recognized that Gorbachev embodied a real change in Soviet policy and found it congruent with his growing sense of urgency to end the risk of a nuclear war. In many ways he was more pragmatic than his advisers and associates, believing as he did that change was possible with this Soviet partner.[106]

The congruence between Reagan and Gorbachev was particularly close regarding the perils of nuclear weapons and the desirability of reducing and ultimately abolishing them. This became apparent in their October 1986 meeting in Reykjavik. With little prior planning between the two governments, the two men were freer to explore an array of options about reducing the burdens and dangers of nuclear weapons. Gorbachev proposed cutting strategic weapons in half and withdrawing all Soviet and U.S. intermediate–range nuclear weapons in Europe. At one point in the negotiations, Reagan and Gorbachev both expressed the desire to eliminate all nuclear weapons. The obstacle to reaching such an agreement at that time was Reagan's insistence on proceeding with the SDI, while Gorbachev would not agree to reducing nuclear weapons unless SDI testing were restricted to laboratories. Nevertheless, Gorbachev subsequently agreed to the intermediate-range nuclear forces (INF) treaty to withdraw all such Soviet and U.S. weapons from Europe, which was signed in December 1987.

The inadequacies of the Soviet economy made improved relations with the West seem not only attractive but necessary to many Soviet leaders. Profound changes in Soviet ideology and practices, which brought them closer to American and West European patterns, also contributed to the transformation of Soviet-American relations. Gorbachev introduced what he called *peristroika*, a restructuring of the previous Soviet economic and social program. In accord with the policy of *glasnost*, or political openness, the Soviet government and the Communist Party no longer exercised total control of the media. He articulated the "new thinking" that was needed in the Soviet Union and also in the West. He believed that capitalism was changing and that imperialist militarism was not inherent in capitalism. Peaceful coexistence between different states was necessary in the integrated modern world. In his remarkable speech to the United Nations in December 1988, he said, "The de-ideologization of interstate relations has become a demand of the new stage. We are not giving up our convictions, philosophy, or traditions. Neither are we calling on anyone else to give up theirs. Yet we are not going to shut ourselves up within the range of our values." He went on to speak of the profound transformation underway within the Soviet Union, saying, "We have gone substantially and deeply into the business of constructing a socialist state based on the rule of law." Furthermore, he announced a unilateral cut of 500,000 persons in its armed forces and a withdrawal of 50,000 soldiers from Eastern Europe, with the remaining forces to be reorganized defensively.[107]

Respect for human rights was an integral element in the new thinking, and it was strengthened by U.S.-Soviet nongovernmental as well as governmental exchanges. For example, in December 1988, I participated in a Soviet-American Forum for Life with Human Rights, held in Moscow.[108] Soviet academics and officials spoke openly of creating a country of laws in which human rights would be protected, notions that would have been dismissed as unimportant bourgeois concerns in the past. They seemed naive in their assessment of how easily they could implement such a transformation of their country, but their contacts with people in the West had profoundly affected their sentiments and expectations.

During that visit, I also met several young men and women handing out leaflets calling on people to join what they called the Watch of Peace. I asked how I might help them. They responded that demonstrations were likely to break out in the Soviet Union and they added, "Teach us nonviolence." Indeed, training in nonviolence and in conflict resolution was already being conducted by Americans and others in several cities in the Soviet Union.[109]

Finally, Soviet withdrawal from Afghanistan and Soviet acquiescence in the fall of communist governments in Eastern Europe produced the final end of the Cold War. Soon after becoming general secretary, Gorbachev alerted Barak Karmal, the communist leader of the Afghan government, that Soviet troops would be withdrawn by the summer of 1986, and that he must broaden the social base of his government for it to survive.[110] As early as November 1985, Gorbachev proposed to Reagan that the United States assist in the Soviet withdrawal, agreeing to a nonaligned Afghanistan, return of refugees, and international guarantees of no interference from the outside. Reagan was not inclined to settle the war in Afghanistan and continued to support the Mujahedin attacking the government. Some U.S. diplomats in Afghanistan attempted to negotiate agreements with the Soviet government about an Afghan government, but for many CIA officers, killing Russians was more attractive, as payback for earlier Soviet aid to the North Vietnamese and the Viet Cong.[111]

In May 1986, the Soviets replaced Karmal with Muhammad Najibullah as head of what was to be a broad-based Afghan government. Then, in February 1988, Gorbachev announced that Soviet forces would be withdrawn from Afghanistan within a year. Representatives of the Soviet Union, the United States, Pakistan, and Afghanistan signed an agreement according to which the Soviets would withdraw militarily; Afghanistan would allow refugees to return; and Pakistan, the United States, and the USSR would not aid the fighters in Afghanistan. The Soviet Union complied, but the United States continued to provide the Mujahedin with military assistance, which was channeled to them by Pakistan. No U.S.-Soviet agreement was made to preserve a new Afghan government, which would have had highly constructive possibilities.

Soon after assuming leadership, Gorbachev and his close associates had concluded that Soviet military intervention to sustain the governments of the East European countries was untenable.[112] They recognized the great risk that those governments would not be able to transform themselves and win popular support, but the desired changes within the Soviet Union and in relations with the West required that the risk be taken. They encouraged the government leaders to make the liberalizing changes needed to survive. Within a few years, every Soviet-linked communist government in East Europe had ceased to be communist or had fallen nonviolently, except for the limited violence in Romania. Those changes in 1989 and their immediate aftermath will be discussed in the next chapter.

In the summer of 1988, as the Soviet forces pulled out of Afghanistan, a group of militant Islamic Arabs who had helped drive the Soviets out gathered in Peshawar, Pakistan to form al Qaeda. Two persons emerged as leaders of the group: Osama bin Laden and Ayman al-Zawahiri. Osama bin Laden was from a large prosperous family in Saudi Arabia and Zawahiri was a surgeon from Egypt.[113] Although fundamentalist in their religious views, both were knowledgeable about contemporary technology. At this time there was no agreement within al Qaeda about the next target in their struggle to advance their view of the true Islam,[114] and the United States was not on the list of possible targets.

Institutionalization of Conflict Resolution, 1981–1988

Despite the ongoing Cold War, associated local wars and covert interventions, the 1980s were years of major domestic developments that were consistent with pursuing foreign policy goals constructively. These included demographic, educational, normative, and institutional changes. For purposes of this book, I focus on the expansion of research and writing pertaining to contemporary conflict resolution as well as on its practice and on the establishment of an institutional infrastructure for its further development. The intensification of the Cold War in the early 1980s had worried many citizens, and that prompted the founding of new peace studies programs and interest in conflict resolution ideas.

Peace movement actions, as noted in the earlier discussion of resistance to Reagan's policies, sought to interrupt destructive U.S. foreign engagements. This was the case for the Sanctuary movement, which was a way to oppose and turn around U.S. military assistance to oppressive regimes in Central America. Much peace movement activity has been directed at opposing U.S. engagement in a particular war or opposing the development of weapons that were especially destructive when deployed or used in wars.[115]

Much American peace movement activity became proactive and devoted to the constructive waging of conflict. One form this has taken is in pursuing people-to-people contacts, even with countries whose governments may be in conflict with the U.S. government. This can take the form of sister cities' associations involving visitor exchanges, commercial ties, or country-to-country friendship associations.[116] Such associations may be based on ethnic bonds, shared ideology, or commercial interests.

Still other peace activism takes the form of direct nonviolent engagement in trying to lessen the destructiveness of ongoing conflicts.[117] One such undertaking was established in 1981 through the leadership of Quakers, the Peace Brigades International (PBI). Persons serving in the PBI accompany persons who are at risk of being killed or otherwise silenced in countries suffering from war or severe repression.[118] Such accompaniment is usually done by Americans and other persons from the Northern hemisphere in countries in the South. This can provide a significant level of security for the accompanied persons.

Some publications in the constructive conflict approach were influential beyond the conflict resolution field. Most notably, this was the case for Roger Fisher and William Ury's 1981 book *Getting to YES*.[119] Based on their experience teaching students and corporate executives how to negotiate, they clearly explained the defects of both hard-line and soft-line bargaining, the effectiveness of what they identified as principled bargaining, and what later came to be called interest-based negotiation. They identified a few basic aspects of such negotiation, including acting as problem solvers; focusing on interests, not on stated positions; separating the people from the problem; developing options for mutual gain; and insisting on the use of objective criteria. Many experimental and theorizing studies were also undertaken that buttressed and gave credibility to the training derived from *Getting to YES*.[120] The reasoning in the book was developed and effectively promoted by the Program on Negotiation, based in the Harvard University Law School and led by international law professor Roger Fisher.

Mediation research and practice in the context of the conflict resolution field also expanded greatly. This included research about varieties of mediation practiced in many different settings. For example, Deborah M. Kolb compared mediators in two government agencies dealing with labor-management relations: the Federal Mediation and Conciliation Service (FMCS) and a state board of conciliation.[121] The FMCS mediators acted as orchestrators, assisting the union and management to reach an agreement. The mediators on the state board acted as deal makers, constructing a package acceptable to both sides, and using persuasion and even manipulation to win acceptance. Furthermore, quantitative research assessing different kinds of mediation in various settings began to flourish.[122]

Research, practice, and theorizing about conflict resolution also expanded by increasing the variety of alternative strategies and the range of conflict stages given attention.[123] Thus, there was growing interest in getting adversaries to come to the negotiating table, recognizing the obstacles to that, and examining how those obstacles can be overcome.[124] There also was increased attention to the quality of the agreements reached and their durability, and the institutionalization of systems to handle recurrent disputes. This was becoming particularly evident in the mediation of public disputes, such as those that arise in conflicts relating to environmental issues.[125] Furthermore, during the 1980s, Alternative Dispute Resolution (ADR) processes were increasingly adopted in the activities of the U.S. Environmental Protection Agency.[126]

Interestingly, some former U.S. officials who were dissatisfied with the limitations of traditional diplomacy began advocating and practicing conflict resolution methods that helped develop important components of the field.[127] Their credentials and colleague networks helped gain credibility for their ideas and the conflict resolution field in general. This is notably the case for Track Two, or unofficial, diplomacy. Thus, Joseph V. Montville, while still a State Department official, became frustrated at the limits of official diplomacy in engaging reluctant adversaries. In 1979, working with the American Psychiatric Association Committee on Psychiatry and Foreign Affairs, he helped organize a series of workshops for a wide array of academics and retired officials pertaining to the Israeli-Palestinian conflict. They gave much attention to victimhood, dehumanization, and the trauma of loss, and Montville could see that normal diplomacy would not respond well to such matters. He retired from the State Department and has become an influential advocate, interpreter, and implementer of informal workshops and unofficial engagement between adversarial sides.[128]

Ambassador John W. McDonald is another State Department official who came to value the contribution that nonofficial diplomacy could make. In 1985, as a member of the Foreign Service, he gathered together cases of Track Two diplomacy for publication. But publication was blocked until a prominent State Department opponent retired in 1987.[129] After McDonald also retired, in 1987, he served as president of the Iowa Peace Institute. He developed the concept of multi-lateral diplomacy and founded the Institute for Multi-Track Diplomacy, which engages in peacemaking initiatives.[130]

During the 1980s, the CR field became firmly established within institutions of higher learning, and increasingly in other nongovernmental and governmental realms. In many ways, the conflict resolution approach was beginning to enter mainstream thinking and practice. The establishment of the United States Institute of Peace is an important and revealing part of that development. The concept of a National Peace Academy had been advocated and discussed many times in the history of the United States, but it was not until 1976 that a groundswell for its establishment emerged. In that bicentennial year of the Declaration of Independence, Democratic Senator Vance Hartke of Indiana and Republican Senator Mark Hatfield of Oregon introduced a bill to create the George Washington Peace Academy.[131]

Members of the peace and conflict resolution social movements mobilized to form the National Peace Academy Campaign, led by Milton Mapes and William Spencer. U.S. Senate hearings listened to diverse views, and it was decided that further study was necessary. A Commission on Proposals for the National Academy of Peace and Conflict Resolution was authorized by Congress and its members were appointed by President Jimmy Carter. The commission was chaired by Senator Spark Matsunaga of Hawaii, and included persons familiar with peace and conflict resolution theory and practice, notably Elise Boulding, James H. Laue, and William F. Lincoln.[132] The commission met with officials and educators and held public hearings across the country. Its final report was delivered to the Reagan administration in November 1981, after which Senator Matsunaga and Representative Glickman introduced bills to establish the United States Institute of Peace (USIP). The USIP would focus on international affairs and be governed by a bipartisan board of directors consisting of twelve persons appointed by the president and confirmed by the Senate. In addition, the Secretary of State, the Secretary of Defense, and the president of the National Defense University (or their designees) would be ex officio members, along with the nonvoting USIP president.

When it became evident that the USIP would be approved by Congress while Reagan was president, some supporters considered trying to stall it until a new president was in office, but congressional momentum was strong and the National Peace Academy Campaign supported a vote to establish the USIP. The United States Institute of Peace Act was passed and signed into law by President Ronald Reagan in 1984. But Reagan did not make appointments to the Board of Directors speedily, and the Institute was finally constituted in 1986. It has grown since its founding, and its work includes programs of education, research grants, fellowship awards, policy-related meetings, and reports and policy consultations.

Many political conservatives were opposed to the USIP, but it was also viewed with suspicion by some members of the peace and conflict resolution social movements, who thought it would simply serve as an agency of the U.S. government and might even be a cover for the CIA. The staff, including the first president, Ambassador Samuel Lewis, strove to demonstrate its independence and develop a broad constituency. It became an important bridge between traditional security thinkers in and outside the government, and academics and practitioners familiar with the conflict resolution approach. It would also become an important institution for peace and conflict resolution education as well as a provider of expert support for U.S. government security operations.

The Carter Center, based in Atlanta, Georgia, is an important example of the ways nongovernmental organizations doing conflict resolution work can at times complement official actions, at times compete with them, and at other times coordinate work by diverse actors. Former U.S. President Jimmy Carter and former First Lady Rosalynn Carter founded the Center in 1982. In addition to persons with official diplomatic experience, persons experienced in conflict resolution method joined the Center staff; Dayle E. Spencer, a lawyer/negotiator, was the founding Director of the Conflict Resolution Programs in the Center. The Carter Center's activities include mediating conflicts, overseeing elections, and fighting diseases worldwide.

Also in 1982, Search for Common Ground (SFCG) was founded in Washington, DC, by John Marks; it is funded by foundations and nongovernmental organizations. Initially, it focused on facilitating cooperation between the United States and the Soviet Union, and now conducts a wide range of activities to transform the manner in which conflicts are waged around the world, from adversarial ways to collaborative problem-solving methods. SFCG has expanded greatly and works in eighteen countries in Africa, Asia, the Middle East, and parts of Eastern Europe, with a staff of more than 300 throughout the world.

The William and Flora Hewlett Foundation contributed immensely to the development and institutionalization of the conflict resolution field. William Hewlett, the founding chairman of the Foundation, and Roger Heyns, who became its first president in 1977, strove to foster more constructive ways to resolve conflicts.[133] This was evident in the Foundation's early support for new decision-making models to resolve environmental issues. Then, in 1981, it joined with the Ford, MacArthur, and other foundations to establish the National Institute of Dispute Resolution. Importantly, in 1984, the Foundation launched a field-building strategy of providing long-term grants supporting centers for CR theory, practice, and infrastructure. Bob Barrett, the first program officer, began to implement the strategy, encouraging applications for grants. The first theory center grant was made in 1984 to the Harvard Program on Negotiation, a consortium of the Massachusetts Institute of Technology, Tufts University, and Harvard University. In the same year, it initiated publication of the *Negotiation Journal.*

In 1985, Hewlett grants were made to theory-building centers at the universities of Hawaii, Michigan, and Minnesota; in 1986 Hewlett-funded centers began at Northwestern, Rutgers, Syracuse, and Wisconsin universities, and then at George Mason University in 1987. By the end of 1994, eighteen centers were being funded, many of which established enduring graduate training programs. Practitioner organizations in the environment, community and many other sectors also began to receive grants. The infrastructure for the field was strengthened, primarily by supporting professional organizations. In 1985, Hewlett began contributing to funding the Society for Professionals in Dispute resolution (SPIDR) and the National Conference on Peacemaking and Conflict Resolution (NCPCR), and went on to support other professional conflict resolution associations.

The establishment of graduate programs in conflict resolution in the 1980s was also prompted by the rising student demand for training in the field. M.A. degree programs were instituted in several universities, including the Eastern Mennonite University, the University of Denver, the University of Notre Dame, and Wayne State University. Many universities began offering concentrations in conflict resolution, often issuing certificates in conjunction with Ph.D. or other graduate degrees. A major Ph.D. program in CR was established at George Mason University in 1987; but since then only three other Ph.D. programs have been instituted in the United States at Nova Southeastern University, the University of Massachusetts at Amherst, and Kennesaw University in Georgia.

The infrastructure for the continuing evolution and diffusion of conflict resolution theory and practice was firmly grounded by the end of the 1980s. The ideas and practices of the field were to be a relevant part of future American engagement in foreign conflicts, as discussed in subsequent chapters.

Conclusion

Conflicts have mixed constructive and destructive aspects. It is evident that in all kinds of foreign conflicts, they shift over time, becoming more and then less destructive. In many cases a destructive escalation on the part of some groups is countered by resistance and opposition by other groups. Relatively constructive policies may be pursued by leaders or by rank-and-file constituents at different times and places. Even the same persons or groups can be highly destructive in one set of circumstances and relations and highly constructive in other circumstances.

During the years covered in this chapter the United States was highly engaged in many foreign conflicts, often in contention with adversaries. They often involved resorting to deadly violence, with the exception of the years of Carter's presidency. U.S. interventions also often involved the use of armed force. The results of trying to coercively impose outcomes desired by the highest U.S. officials generally failed to accomplish their initial goals. The record of more constructive strategies is better. This is indicated by the mediations in the Arab-Israeli conflicts pursued by Kissinger and by Carter and by negotiating treaties between the United States and Panama regarding the status of the Panama Canal. More grandly, the transformation of the Cold War demonstrates the effectiveness of many constructive conflict strategies. This is analyzed further in the next chapter.

The evolution and institutionalization of the conflict resolution field means that there is a growing repertoire of tactics and strategies that can be used in taking a constructive conflict approach. This can offer more options than either doing nothing or resorting to violence.

4   Cold War Ends, New Conflicts Arise, 1989–1992

THE END OF the Cold War and the subsequent dissolution of the Soviet Union transformed the world in many ways. Numerous wonderful new opportunities for the people in the former Soviet Union, the United States, and around the world suddenly seemed to arise. But several terrible conflicts persisted and people everywhere were also confronted by serious new problems. Americans often responded to the opportunities and challenges in new constructive ways, but too frequently also in old destructive ways. The George H. W. Bush administration coincided with fundamental changes in U.S. relations with the Soviet Union and its successor states. The U.S. government reached many accommodative agreements with the Soviet leaders and then with the leaders of Russia and of the other new countries that had been part of the USSR. The agreements generally reflected the new realities. A world without a Soviet Union also presented new challenges and opportunities for Americans.

Five related overarching changes during this period dramatically affected the incidence and character of foreign conflicts and Americans' role in them. First, Soviet domination of Eastern Europe quickly ended and the power of the Soviet Union and then of Russia declined, as well as its control over many parts of what had been the Soviet Union. Consequently, the United States became the only superpower. Second, the global ideological struggle and great power rivalry was over, and therefore many wars in Central America and in Africa could be more easily settled. Third, at the same time, however, religious and ethnic identities and sentiments became much more salient. This contributed to the outbreak of violent conflicts, as erupted in Yugoslavia and elsewhere. Fourth, the UN became much more active and collective action was more readily undertaken; thus, UN peacekeeping operations sharply increased and expanded in the tasks they undertook. Finally, an international civil society grew greatly in prominence, evidenced by the expansion of international nongovernmental organizations and the acceptance of norms regarding human rights, both individual and collective.

In retrospect, although considerable gains were won by people in many countries more general and longer-lasting benefits might have been achieved as a result of the new realities. In this chapter, I discuss how some officials and non-officials conducted themselves in ways that were less constructive than they might have been, as well as how sometimes they behaved so that major constructive gains were won. These assessments provide further grounds to judge the usefulness of the constructive conflict approach.

The End of the Cold War, 1989

George H. W. Bush, who was vice president and had held many other major offices related to international affairs, began his presidency on January 20, 1989. He chose a team of persons with considerable government experience. James S. Baker III was secretary of state until he was succeeded by Lawrence Eagleburger in 1992; Dick Cheney was secretary of defense; and Brent Scowcroft was the national security advisor. Their experience was steeped in the decades-long militarized Cold War and its attendant hostility and mistrust.

Thus, in January 1990, when Bush submitted his budget for FY91, with a very small decrease in defense expenditures, Cheney testified in support of it and argued that past policies needed to be continued. Indeed, the uncertainty resulting from the decline in the Cold War meant that this was the "worst possible time to contemplate changes in defense strategy."[1] Many members of Congress reacted by drawing new budgets, with more substantial cuts in the defense budget. Some members of the administration also thought defense cuts and restructuring were appropriate and public opinion supported a peace dividend. Bush revised his budget, reflecting the new realities.

Although the political party controlling the executive branch of government had not changed, the new administration adopted a somewhat different approach in foreign affairs.[2] It generally sought to work better with Congress, and it functioned in a less-partisan manner than was the case during President Reagan's two terms in office. With the end of the Cold War it was able to act more multilaterally in international affairs, and was comfortable doing so. Most consequentially, however, members of the new administration initially were skeptical of Reagan's enthusiasm about changes in the Soviet Union and favored cautious policymaking.[3] At the outset, they were actually satisfied with the status quo in Europe and did not seek any major transformations. This even pertained to the idea of Germany remaining divided, but that quickly changed.

Despite the great changes in the world, U.S. goals and policies in foreign affairs had considerable continuity. They remained narrowly focused on advancing U.S. economic, military, and political power. As Baker reminisces, "The stronger West-West ties were, the more leverage this would put on Moscow to adapt peacefully to the realities of its decline. And the more we could move the Soviet Union toward our interests and values, the better."[4] While the Cold War was ending and when the Soviet Union was breaking up, Bush and his associates often seemed to take one-sided advantage of the Soviet Union and its successor state, Russia. More fundamentally, the policies often seemed driven by events outside American control rather than by any precise plan.

When the Bush administration took office, the Soviet Union was accelerating its remarkable transformation, spurred by Gorbachev's policies of *peristroika* and *glasnost* and his advocacy of New Thinking. In March 1989, free elections were held for a new Congress of People's Deputies. A free media carried news about many severe problems in the Soviet society and economy. Social movement organizations began to flourish and they prompted rallies advocating various new social and political policies.[5] Many of these changes brought Soviet society into much more congruence with American society. The ideals of protecting human rights, of free expression of views and of rights to move about and to organize were widely espoused.

In foreign policy, Gorbachev unmistakably conveyed to the governments and Communist Party leaders in the Eastern European countries that the Soviet Union would not prop them up.[6] They would have to appeal to and serve the needs of their own countries' citizens to survive in office. Gorbachev clearly asserted his belief in the right of self-determination and his desire that the Soviet Union be part of a common European home. He held out the vision of one European system stretching from the Atlantic Ocean to the Ural Mountains.

Progress in arms control agreements continued to be made.[7] This included the negotiations limiting nuclear weapons, resulting in signing the Strategic Arms Reduction Treaty. It included a prohibition of chemical weapons and the treaty on Conventional Armed Forces in Europe, which was signed in November 1990.

In the context of rapidly changing relations between the United States and the Soviet Union, the many periods of immense turmoil within the countries of Eastern Europe and within the Soviet Union and its successor states posed great challenges for managing the changes constructively. However, the transformations within the societies formerly ruled by communist parties greatly increased the asymmetries between Western and Eastern countries, which would hamper reaching mutually beneficial accommodations and agreements. This is illustrated by the increased economic weakness of the formerly Communist-ruled countries.

REVOLUTIONARY CHANGES IN EASTERN EUROPE

In 1989, Soviet and American government leaders concentrated their attention on the tumultuous events in Eastern Europe. They did not foresee nor control the sudden and yet fundamental transformation, driven from below, within all the countries that had been dominated by the Soviet Union. Indeed, the speed and totality of the changes in these countries were astonishing even to the people making them happen.[8] Conflicts that had seemed frozen revealed underlying dynamism and erupted, then quickly moved through the major stages of conflicts.

In February 1989, Polish government leaders began roundtable talks with Solidarity leaders and soon agreed to hold free elections, which were held in June. Solidarity won an overwhelmingly large electoral victory.[9] Gorbachev informed the Polish Communist leaders that the USSR would accept a non-Communist government; the people's choice was not to be denied and Tadeusz Mazowiecki, associated with Solidarity, became prime minister. In July, Bush visited Warsaw to lend support and encouragement for reform.

Hungary had achieved significant economic reforms and limited political liberalization during the 1980s, but full democracy was not established until 1989. In July 1989, Bush visited Hungary following his visit to Poland and offered Most Favored Nation trading status to Hungary. In October 1989, the Communist Party convened its last congress and re-created itself as the Hungarian Socialist Party. Also in October, the parliament adopted legislation providing for multi-party parliamentary and direct presidential elections.

In Czechoslovakia, the Communist government was driven from power in what was called the Velvet Revolution. On November 17, 1989, riot police tried to suppress a peaceful student demonstration in Prague, which resulted in increasingly large demonstrations. Finally, a two-hour general strike was held throughout Czechoslovakia on November 27, and the next day, the Communist Party announced that it relinquished power. On December 10, President Gustáv Husák appointed the first largely non-Communist government in Czechoslovakia since 1948, and immediately resigned. Václav Havel was elected President of Czechoslovakia on December 29, 1989.

An escalating series of popular events in the autumn of 1989 brought about particularly consequential changes in the German Democratic Republic (GDR).

They resulted in the fall of the Berlin Wall, the subsequent re-unification of Germany, and the absorption of the GDR into West Germany, the Federal Republic of Germany (FRG).[10] As people in Poland, Czechoslovakia, Hungary, and other East European countries began to break loose from Soviet control, East German citizens also began to demonstrate and many voted with their feet by leaving the GDR and crossing into Czechoslovakia and Hungary, hoping to move further west. When 10,000 East Germans were housed in the FRG Embassy and in camps in Budapest, the situation became unsustainable. The Hungarian foreign minister discussed the matter with Soviet Foreign Minister Eduard Shevardnadze, who said the East Germans should be allowed to leave.[11] On September 11, the Hungarian border with Austria was opened for East Germans, who began entering West Germany.

On October 7, Gorbachev came to Berlin to celebrate the 40th anniversary of the GDR, although there was little to celebrate.[12] Opposition to the hardline leader of the GDR, Eric Honecker, was apparent in street demonstrations throughout the GDR. Younger leaders of the ruling Socialist Unity Party secretly discussed ousting the intransigent Honecker, and Gorbachev conveyed his conviction that fundamental changes in Germany were needed. After mass demonstrations broke out in Berlin, on November 7, the East German politburo resigned. Honecker was ousted by the party leaders and replaced by Egon Krenz, who quickly began to make concessions to public demands.

The Berlin Wall fell due to the conjuncture of East German officials' misunderstandings and the direct actions of excited East Berlin crowds wanting to enter West Berlin.[13] Without clarity about new travel laws for East Germans wishing to travel outside of East Germany, the spokesman of the central committee of the ruling party held a press conference on November 9 to announce the new Politburo's composition. Asked about the travel laws, the spokesperson mistakenly stated that GDR citizens could travel abroad at the border crossings, starting immediately. This incorrect news spread quickly and East Germans rushed to the Berlin Wall. Television showed the gathering crowds, prompting more East Germans to go to the crossing points and shout for the gates to be opened. The East German border guards had no specific responsive orders and opened the gates. There was no violence. East and West Berliners danced, sang, and drank together. The Cold War was no more.

The future of Germany raised grave issues. Would Germany be unified and if so, would it be a neutral country or an ally of the West and a member of NATO? Or would two states be continued in some new configuration? Every possible solution posed new problems for some stakeholders.[14] Gorbachev was alarmed at the prospect of a unified Germany in NATO and he promptly conveyed to Bush that the Soviet Union had vital interests in the future of Germany and that the Soviet Union, the United States, Britain and France as the World War II victors had responsibilities regarding Germany.[15] British Prime Minister Margaret Thatcher and French President François Mitterrand had serious reservations about a unified Germany. Bush and Baker welcomed German unification if it also meant its inclusion in NATO, but they recognized that reassurances were needed to win Soviet acquiescence.

The people of West and East Germany began acting as if unification was underway. Helmut Kohl, the German chancellor and leader of the Christian Democratic Union, initiated public discussions about the future of Germany by proposing several joint FRG-GDR commissions relating to economic, cultural, and political matters leading to some confederated arrangement.[16] But the continuing movement of East Germans into West Germany and other events increased the momentum toward German unification. Kohl and Foreign Minister Hans-Dietrich Genscher made it clear that West Germany would be centrally engaged in deciding the future of the two Germanys.

In February 1990, Baker discussed with Gorbachev the proposal that NATO "jurisdiction" would not be extended to the GDR territory, but this formula was soon rephrased to state that eastern Germany would have a "special military status" within NATO. In early February, Gorbachev informed Kohl that he accepted the unification of Germany in the immediate future.[17] The results of the March 12 election in the GDR gave incontrovertible evidence that German unification was certain and imminent. The West German Christian Democratic Union and its allies, favoring speedy unification, won 50% of the vote; while the West German Social-Democratic Party, favoring a slower pace for unification, won only 21%.

The Soviet leaders did not present a coherent plan to slow German unification or even to prevent NATO membership.[18] Differences among Soviet government factions produced ambiguous and shifting positions. Ongoing moves of unification spurred negotiations. Formal negotiations about the future of Germany were conducted by the two Germanys and the USSR, the United States, Britain, and France.[19] Very quickly, on September 12, 1990, the Treaty on the Final Settlement with Respect to Germany was signed. The treaty was part of a complex set of trade-offs among the German, Soviet, American, British, and French governments, a basic negotiation technique. Among the treaty provisions: Germany was united, fully sovereign and free to choose an alliance; it renounced atomic, biological, and chemical weapons; and it was assured that all Soviet troops would be withdrawn by the end of 1994.[20]

Treaty negotiations were conducted in the context of the accelerating changes in Soviet society, which preoccupied Gorbachev. Along with the negotiations, positive inducements were used. Verbal assurances were made by the Western powers that NATO would not be extended eastward, but no agreements were put in writing.[21]

West Germany offered noncoercive inducements to win Soviet agreement to the treaty, in the form of significant side payments. In early February, Kohl assured Gorbachev that Germany would assume all the economic and financial obligations that the GDR had with the USSR.[22] The German government granted economic assistance for the withdrawal of the 380,000 Soviet military personnel based in East Germany and the construction of new housing for them in the Soviet Union.

In a very short time, Europe was dramatically new. Germany was reunited. The Communist parties in all East European countries were gone by the end of 1991. The growing civil society organizations, often aided by transnational linkages, had the ideas and organizational resources to bring down Communist rule and to institute democratic systems of governance.[23] The powerful popular movements in each Eastern European country had produced revolutionary changes even in the face of totalitarian rulers. The movements in each country had their own dynamics, but they reinforced each other and on the whole achieved fundamental changes nonviolently. These mass movements became another set of examples illustrating the power of nonviolent action and its ability to shape the direction of institutional transformations. The revolutionary changes followed years of popular movements to bring about reforms in Hungary, Czechoslovakia, and Poland that had "failed." But movement leaders and their supporters learned from the failures, and those failures paved the way for later triumphs. Again, ideas were powerful tools to bring about major social changes.

There is much to celebrate about the Cold War's ending, but the immediate outcome also contributed to new problems. Reflecting on plausible alternative policies for managing the end of the Cold War is worthwhile because it can help infer valid lessons for other conflict transformations. The unification of Germany is especially pertinent. In retrospect, it may seem that the rapid flow of events could follow only one course, but even at the time, some alternative directions were noted.

In February 1990, Kohl and Genscher spent a weekend at Camp David with Bush and Baker.[24] Kohl and Genscher introduced a package of incentives to ensure Soviet acceptance of unification, including using the Conference on Security and Cooperation in Europe (CSCE) to bring the Soviet Union into the new Europe. Bush and Baker were perturbed about that idea, concerned that the Germans might try to build up the CSCE as an alternative to NATO. They did not want to restructure NATO or diminish its primacy, ensuring as it did U.S. preeminence in Europe. The end of the Cold War might reasonably have been the occasion for a fundamental change in the significance and structure of NATO, an essentially military alliance.

Without a Soviet threat, the central mission for NATO was gone. Its survival required a new mission, which was deemed to be extending stability throughout Europe. To fulfill that mission, NATO did undergo several changes that would help speed German unification and assuage Soviet concerns.[25] The changes included reducing personnel at headquarters and lessening reliance on nuclear weapons. It included expanding exchanges with senior leaders from former Warsaw Pact military forces by creating the North Atlantic Cooperation Council to provide a forum for discussions about defense and other issues and included all former Warsaw Pact states. The Partnership for Peace Plan was established in 1994 to expand military coordination and exercises on a bilateral basis with individual non-NATO states. In the future, however, the primary change was to be the expansion of NATO membership eastward toward Russia's borders.[26]

Given the new circumstances and mission, a more fundamental change may well have reduced the primacy of military organizations and methods to provide stability and security. That probably would have required the creation of a new regional organization focusing on economic, social, and political cooperation. Another possibility would have been to expand the CSCE's authority, functions, and level of activity.[27] This would have more effectively assisted in transforming the Soviet Union and its successor states, as well as the transformation of the former Communist states of Eastern Europe. Indeed, Soviet leaders did express ideas about strengthening the CSCE to include conflict resolution centers.[28]

Another way to enhance security and stability after the end of the Cold War would have been to expand the UN's capabilities in these areas. One possibility would have been to enhance the role of the UN so that it could set parameters for NATO actions, since the UN could function better when the USSR was not likely to use its veto to consistently oppose the United States. More specifically, the UN could expand its peacekeeping, peacemaking, and peacebuilding interventions, which did happen to an important degree, as discussed later. The end of the Cold War presented the opportunity to significantly develop UN capabilities in these regards; for example, by creating a UN rapid deployment force to intervene in destructive conflicts when there was agreement to do so.

There was little public attention paid in the United States or elsewhere, however, to any of these options. Instead, Americans generally celebrated the U.S. victory in the Cold War and viewed the victory as attributable to American power and to NATO, which it led. Even if NATO was no longer needed and was ill-designed for the new problems, suggestions to dismantle or transform it were generally ignored.

If alternative policies for managing relations with the new Russia and for German unification with its incorporation into NATO had been seriously considered, however, the aftermath might have been better in important ways. Alternative arrangements might have enhanced Gorbachev's reputation and given him more cover for his other political and economic reforms, weakened the Soviet hard-liner resistance to him, and provided institutional support for the societal transformations that were needed within the Soviet Union and its successor states. The growth of NATO has contributed to the powerful U.S. capability for global military influence and actions. However, the implementation of particular alternative policies might have had other greater long-term benefits for the United States. The subsequent expansion of NATO to countries that had been part of the Soviet Union was to have injurious consequences for U.S.-Russian relations. Giving serious consideration to how this would be viewed by Russian leaders would have been beneficial.

It is worth noting that the conflict resolution and peace studies communities failed to provide detailed options of creative new structures applicable to the opportunities that the end of the Cold War presented. That would have required preexisting large centers or institutes with staff members developing plans for future contingencies. But they did not exist in the United States. Such centers did exist for national security studies, but their contingency planning was within the Cold War paradigm.

EXPLAINING THE END OF THE COLD WAR

Numerous competing explanations have been made for the Cold War's demise, often selecting ones that support preferred policies in a current conflict.[29] Some people argue that it was Reagan's strategy of coercive confrontation that defeated the Soviet Union. In the first Reagan administration, U.S. military activities were intensified, including assisting the groups attacking Soviet forces in Afghanistan, as well as Soviet-supported governments and movements in Central America and Africa. U.S. military expenditures increased and work on the Strategic Defense Initiative (SDI) was begun.[30] In short, the U.S. government raised the costs to the Soviet leadership of maintaining its empire and competing with the United States. By this account, the Soviet leadership was forced to yield to U.S. wishes.

Some analysts add another dimension to this perspective. Reagan articulated the importance of advancing freedom and democracy against the "evil" Soviet system. This moral imperative not only helped mobilize Americans and the West, but also aroused and aided dissidents within the Soviet Union and the countries of Eastern Europe that it dominated. This muscular idealism was part of the Cold War from the outset, but was elaborated in the writings of analysts and officials who became identified as neoconservatives.[31]

Other analysts and political leaders stress the inherent weaknesses of the Soviet system. A frequently recognized problem relates to its state-directed economy. The centrally planned Soviet system had been effective in raising industrial production in earlier decades, but it increasingly failed in developing newer, fast-changing technologies and in satisfying more than basic consumer needs. Another widely noted weakness was its authoritarian and often repressive political system, limiting freedom of expression. The very success of the Soviet system in providing educational and basic material needs made the lack of freedom more intolerable. This effect was amplified by Communist ideology that promised to deliver a good life to the workers—to the "common people."

In addition, the Soviet Union inherited the Russian Empire, with its numerous nationalities over whom Soviet leaders sought to retain control. They tried to create a new Soviet identity, under Russian leadership, and yet allow for some cultural autonomy for the constituent republics. This mixture was not to endure, as analysts of ethno-nationalism and geopolitical overextension anticipated.[32]

Some observers stress the importance of beliefs and values, emphasizing that the way people think about their social relations strongly affect their actions. Since the Russian Revolution of October 1917, believers in Soviet Communism and believers in democracy-capitalism each proclaimed that their values and beliefs had universal validity and were not only to be defended, but would defeat the mistaken thinking of the other. The Cold War was in large degree an ideological struggle, which began to end as leaders and others in the Soviet Union began to lose their faith in the Soviet ideology. Former believers in the Soviet ideology doubted that it correctly explained and guided political and economic conduct. The democratic-capitalist ideology became more attractive and provided a superior interpretation of the world.

Other political figures and scholars stress that the long-term American strategy of containment, pursued for decades, prevented disastrous escalations while the Soviet system stagnated and then imploded. That the United States and the Soviet Union, despite their great rivalry, avoided direct military engagements is a remarkable achievement, identified by some analysts as a long peace.[33] Many persons give credit to the nuclear standoff, and the threat of mutually assured destruction, for the absence of a direct war between the United States and the Soviet Union. Some analysts and officials credit the skills of political leaders for carefully managing the Cold War and stopping crises from escalating into warfare. In time, shared understandings and patterns of conduct developed that helped transform the conflict.

The underlying structure of the conflict between the United States and the Soviet Union is stressed by still other writers. Despite the great power rivalry and the ideological contest, the two countries had no territorial dispute between them, and such disputes are a major cause of wars. They actually did not militarily threaten each other's existence, although at times some people on each side suspected or even believed that the other side did.[34]

Still other analysts stress the important roles played by private citizens acting in many different ways within and among the countries engaged in the Cold War.

Peace movement organizations pressured government leaders, transnational organizations complemented official transactions, and people-to-people exchanges fostered mutual understanding.[35] Moreover, at critical times, mass movements adopted nonviolent actions that withdrew the authority they had previously given to heads of government.

In addition, the work of various nonofficial channels of diplomacy contributed ideas and information that helped bring about the transformations within the Soviet Union and in conducting the Cold War. The particular analyses by peace and conflict researchers in Western Europe and the United States provided attractive alternatives to the Cold War's adversarial conduct.

Other observers emphasize the workings of the global system, which is becoming increasingly integrated and interdependent. Economic production, investment, and trade bind groups and peoples together, so that even large economies cannot be wholly independent. The intensification of international communications also reduces the degree to which any country can be controlled by its government and increases the degree to which people in each society are influenced by developments elsewhere.

Finally, many people emphasize the major roles played by particular individuals. The personality and convictions of Gorbachev and Reagan are most often stressed.[36] Certainly Gorbachev's recognition of the need for fundamental changes in Soviet policies was well-grounded. And his commitment to undertaking transformational policies was thoughtful and courageous. The remarkable changes in Reagan's views of relations with the Soviet Union, as discussed in the previous chapter, began in 1983 and 1984, even before Gorbachev began to lead the Soviet Union. They prepared him to recognize the significance and reality of a fundamental change within the Soviet Union and in its relationship with the United States.

At many other periods of the Cold War, specific persons are recognized as contributing significantly to the transformation, even if they sometimes also acted in ways that actually retarded the transformation for a time. These personalities include Nikita Khrushchev, John F. Kennedy, Willy Brandt, Leonid Brezhnev, Andrei Sakharov, Joseph Rotblatt, Margaret Thatcher, Richard Nixon, Randall Forsberg, Suzanne Massie, Pope John Paul II, and Henry Kissinger.

There is some merit to each of these explanations, and no single one is sufficient to account for all aspects of the transformation. They combined over different time periods and affected diverse groups in each camp to varying extents in accounting for particular changes.[37] The achievement of bringing about such a world-changing phenomenon is to be acclaimed, particularly since so little violence occurred during the final months of the Cold War. Nevertheless, the many years getting to those final months were terribly costly in lives lost and damaged as well as wasted and devastated human infrastructure and environment.[38] The burdens of nuclear weapons development, testing, and maintenance have been immense; furthermore, the legacy of nuclear weapons proliferation continues to threaten humanity. The many regional wars were costly in American and Soviet lives and the lives of Koreans, Vietnamese, Afghans, and people of many other countries.

In retrospect, it is evident that the Cold War could have been waged more constructively if either side had less grandiose aspirations and more modest methods of struggle. Major groups within the Soviet and American societies had vested interests in waging the struggle by credibly threatening to defeat the other side militarily, even at the risk of immense civilian deaths resulting from nuclear warfare. Furthermore, to win support for the immense burdens of preparing for such a war and of waging proxy wars around the world, the other side was depicted as powerful, growing stronger, seeking total victory, and looking for weaknesses to exploit. Many times each side overestimated the other's strength and its threatening intentions. More accurate knowledge by members of each side about the other, helped by more transparency and transnational interactions would have helped lessen mutual fears. On several occasions, better analyses, more nuanced policies, and more skilled application of conflict resolution perspectives might well have averted episodes of destructive escalation.

There are, nevertheless, positive legacies resulting from the way the Cold War was transformed. Primarily, it demonstrates that constructive benefits can result from multidimensional engagement between adversaries, public participation, and problem-solving thinking. The reality that internal Soviet changes were crucial to the transformation contributed greatly to the durability of the new relations in Europe.

The transformation of the U.S.-Soviet relationship might be viewed as confirming the effectiveness of the GRIT strategy, in which one of the parties in a conflict unilaterally initiates a series of cooperative moves; these are announced and reciprocity is invited, but the conciliatory moves continue for an extended period, whether or not there is immediate reciprocity. A comparative analysis indicated that the GRIT strategy fit the change in U.S.-Soviet relations better than did the tit-for-tat strategy, discussed in Chapter 2.[39] GRIT had been urged in the early 1960s as a strategy for the United States to employ so as to induce reciprocation from the Soviet Union and break out of the Cold War. Ironically, it was a Soviet leader who undertook GRIT's most spectacular and extreme enactment. However, the entire process might be viewed as documenting that GRIT fails to produce symmetrical cooperation and instead simply manages a unilateral defeat or decline.[40]

The ending of the Cold War cannot be explained by Soviet policy as shaped only by Gorbachev. Changes within and between the Soviet Union and the United States for over thirty years had brought Gorbachev to power and affected his thinking.

The transformation resulted from a multilevel, interconnected series of interactions. Developments within and among European countries and their relations with the Soviet Union and the United States were also important in bringing about the transformation.[41] Critically, the Soviet leaders came to recognize that ultimately, the United States did not seek to forcibly overthrow the Soviet system, as Reagan made evident after 1983 and in his relations with Gorbachev. That recognition freed the Soviet leaders to risk great internal changes.

Many of the factors and processes stressed within the constructive conflict approach and the realities upon which it is based are clearly relevant in accounting for the Cold War's ending. The idea that conflicts are dynamic and become transformed over extended time periods is central in the approach and for understanding this case. Workers in the conflict resolution field recognize the importance of nonviolent inducements in waging conflicts; they include nonviolent coercive action, persuasive arguments, and the promise of positive benefits. Certainly, America's social, political and economic attractiveness, its soft power, was highly important in the transformation of the Soviet Union and provided inducements that were used with great effect in the struggles that ended the Cold War.

The Soviet Union Dissolves, New Conflicts Emerge, 1990–1992

Soon after the Cold War ended, the forces that undermined Soviet domination in Eastern Europe contributed to the collapse of the Soviet Union itself. Soviet leaders gave popular self-determination legitimacy in Eastern Europe. That became attractive within the Soviet Union, as the Communist ideology and Soviet identity withered. That thinking converged with the rising salience of dormant national and ethnic identities, which fatally undercut the USSR. The breakup of the Soviet Union was accomplished by a remarkably peaceful transfer of power to the constituent republics making up the Union of Soviet Socialist Republics. This constructive transformation was assisted by the Organization on Security and Cooperation in Europe and the European Union (EU).[42]

THE DISSOLUTION OF THE USSR

The Soviet breakup resulted from the convergence of many long-term social trends, prior events and structures, and the interactions of many individuals and groups. The actions of some people who tried to avert the disintegration of the Soviet Union actually hastened it. America's role in affecting the course of the Soviet Union's break-up was modest, but it played significant roles in shaping some consequences of the Soviet Union's disappearance.

The Soviet leaders' moves toward political reform, the protection of human rights, and a relatively unregulated market economy took on a momentum of their own. New organizations, claims, and beliefs undermined the power and the legitimacy of authoritarian rule by the Communist Party. In the summer of 1989, coal miners went out on strike in Siberia and then across the breadth of the Soviet Union.[43] They had lived and worked in miserable conditions; food was in short supply and medical care inadequate. Now the miners declared these conditions unacceptable; large-scale strikes spread, making powerful television images of masses of protesting workers. As David Remnick concluded: "After July 1989, the illusion of a gradual, Gorbachev-directed 'revolution from above' was over."[44] A revolution from below had begun.

The possibility that Gorbachev's reform efforts might lead to the dissolution of the Soviet Union was signaled by events in the Baltic countries: Estonia, Latvia and Lithuania.[45] Those countries had been forcibly incorporated into the Soviet Union in 1940, in the context of the 1939 pact between Hitler and Stalin that unleashed World War II.[46] The changes introduced by Gorbachev opened a path for the independence of the Baltic countries. He and his associates spoke favorably of popular self-determination and acknowledged the illegitimacy of the Soviet absorption of the Baltic countries.

The struggle to restore the independence of the three countries was conducted by nonviolent means, often novel and creative ones. For example, in Estonia, starting in May 1988, patriotic Estonian songs were performed and collectively sung in a series of music festivals. Then in November 1988, the Estonian legislative body proclaimed the Estonian Sovereignty Declaration, which was followed by various acts of protest, defiance, and noncompliance with Soviet laws.

In Latvia, in the summer of 1988, major social movement organizations began to emerge, which shared the goal of restoring democracy and independence. In March 1990, supporters of independence won the election for a new legislature and they declared Latvian independence on May 4, 1990.

In Lithuania as well, a mass movement emerged in 1988 to win democratic and national rights. Consequently, the Lithuanian Supreme Soviet amended the constitution to assert the supremacy of Lithuanian laws over Soviet legislation and to establish a multi-party electoral system. On March 11, 1990, the Supreme Council of Lithuania proclaimed the restitution of Lithuanian independence.[47]

During 1990, steps toward breaking up the USSR were taking place in many other parts of the Soviet Union. On October 28, 1990, democratic parliamentary elections were held in Georgia, and it declared its independence on April 9, 1991. However, this was not recognized by the Soviet government before it collapsed in December 1991.

The Russian Soviet Federation declared its sovereignty on June 12, 1990, and limited the application of many Soviet laws on Russian territory. In June 1991, Boris Yeltsin was popularly elected president of the Russian Federation. Gorbachev had dismissed Yeltsin as the Communist Party leader of Moscow in 1987 because he called for overly radical reforms, and their intense rivalry contributed to the Soviet Union's dissolution.

Clearly, Gorbachev and his close associates faced severe challenges within the Communist Party and within the Soviet Union as they sought to advance reforms. Their policies were resisted by hardline military, Communist Party, government, and KGB leaders, who believed the changes were undermining their power and the Soviet Union itself. Rumors of a likely coup grew. U.S. officials learned that senior Soviet officials had plans to overthrow Gorbachev, and they carefully warned him of the danger. Gorbachev defeated challenges in the Parliament and was confident that he was in a secure political position. In December 1990, Shevardnadze shockingly resigned as foreign minister, warning that a dictatorship was coming.[48]

At the same time, Gorbachev and the policies he pursued were increasingly supported by workers, intellectuals, political office holders, and many others seeking to create a liberal democratic society. Indeed, many groups were critical of Gorbachev and his circle, charging they were taking only half-measures and moving too slowly.[49]

Separatist movements erupted within several Soviet Republics and economic problems grew, manifested in shortages of almost all products. Gorbachev and other Soviet leaders planned for a new, looser Union, which was widely supported in a referendum in March 1991. A treaty implementing elements of the new federation was to be signed by Gorbachev, Yeltsin, and the Kazakh president, Nursultan Nazarbayev, in Moscow on August 20, 1991. On August 4, Gorbachev went for a vacation at his luxurious dacha in the Crimea, planning to return to Moscow on August 20.

Numerous senior Soviet officials who rejected Gorbachev's policies conspired to prevent the signing.[50] On August 18, a few of the conspirators flew to the Crimea to confront Gorbachev; they held him captive and demanded that he either declare a state of emergency or resign and name Vice President Gennady Yanayev as acting president, requiring the conspirators "to restore order" in the country. Gorbachev vehemently refused to cooperate.

Rebuffed by Gorbachev, the delegation returned to Moscow. After hurried discussion and some drinking, the conspirators decided to act, but the actions were not carefully planned. Early in the morning of August 19, they announced a state of emergency and that Gennady Yanayev was acting president. However, Yanayev was bewildered about what he was supposed to do.

Yeltsin immediately condemned the coup attempt and established his base of operations in the Russian Parliament building, the White House. It was soon encircled by army tanks, under command of the coup leaders, but thousands of people gathered around the White House to nonviolently demonstrate against the coup and to block any military action against Yeltsin. The inept putsch rapidly unraveled and the junta recognized they had failed. On August 21, the tanks turned around and jubilant soldiers went back to their barracks amidst applauding crowds. An airplane with Yeltsin's representatives along with Russian troops flew to the Crimea to free Gorbachev. Upon Gorbachev's return to Moscow, he initially tried to continue as before, not recognizing that the Communist Party had self-destructed. But Gorbachev soon accepted the new realities; on August 24, he resigned as general secretary of the Communist Party and dissolved the Party's Central Committee.

Bush preferred Gorbachev to Yeltsin as a partner and was worried about the breakup of the Soviet Union, beyond the independence of the Baltic countries. Indeed, there was reason to be concerned about widespread violent disorder. However, the United States could not have averted the shattering of the USSR. The events producing that radical change were driven by prior developments and the conduct of leading groups within the far from homogenous Soviet Union.

The successor state, the Russian Federation, faced immense economic crises, which the United States might have helped it to overcome but did not.[51] Changing from a command economy with state-owned production capabilities to a free market economy with privatized ownership of the means of production was hugely challenging. At the same time, the price of petroleum, the leading export commodity, had greatly declined. Large-scale Western aid, as was provided to Poland, was needed but was not provided to Russia.

Following the dissolution of the Soviet Union in December 1991, Yeltsin undertook to transform Russia's socialist command economy into a free market economy and initiated price liberalization and privatization programs. These policies were consistent with the neoliberal policies urged by the International Monetary Fund (IMF), the World Bank, the U.S. Treasury Department, and several American academic economists.[52] Unfortunately, however, these policies to remake Russia in America's image had harmful consequences. For example, due to the method of privatization, a relatively small number of people took ownership of a considerable amount of the national wealth and a powerful economic oligarchy soon emerged.

The breakup of the Soviet Union and the end of Soviet control of Eastern Europe unleashed numerous conflicts, most of them related in some degree to ethnic identities. The former Soviet Republics were not ethnically homogenous, but generally had non-Russian majorities and minorities with the same (or similar) identities in now-bordering countries. Some of those conflicts escalated into violent wars of secession or expansion. As the constructive conflict approach emphasizes, profound contentious changes often occur without recourse to destructive wars. Regional international governmental organizations were very effective in preventing long-lasting violent conflicts and oppressive treatment of minorities. For example, the EU insisted upon basic citizen rights for ethnic Russians in the territories of the three Baltic countries, if they were to be considered for membership in the EU. The governments of the Baltic countries generally complied. Thus, too, the Organization for Security and Cooperation in Europe (OSCE), the successor to the CSCE discussed in Chapter 3, provided important services to foster peace and protect minority rights. The OSCE has a High Commissioner on National Minorities (HCNM) with the authority to intervene in response to a crisis related to national minority issues that threaten international peace. Max van der Stoel, during his tenure as the first HCNM, 1993–2001, helped avert destructively escalating conflicts by his quiet mediation regarding the language and education rights of the Hungarian minority in Romania and the citizenship rights of ethnic Russians in Estonia.

As these startling events were happening within the Soviet Union and in Eastern Europe, international relationships were reframed and transformed so old conflicts were settled but new major conflicts erupted. Possibly, greater U.S. restraint and regard for the concerns of the Soviet Union and its successor states and their peoples would have better served Americans' long-term interest. In any case, the end of the Cold War and of the Soviet Union enabled constructive conflict transformations to be realized in many parts of the world, aided by constructive official and non-official American actions.

LESSENING REGIONAL CONFLICTS

Wars in Africa and Central America declined as the Cold War no longer sustained them. For example, the civil wars in Central America were ended by negotiations. The agreements did not occur automatically, but partly resulted from negotiating a new American-Soviet/Russian relationship, even if impaired sometimes by contentious issues.

At the outset of the Bush administration, some American officials were skeptical that the changes being wrought by Gorbachev would be enduring. The idea of "testing" the Soviet Union, as a way to appear proactive while not initiating any reciprocal cooperative actions, was applied.[53] Baker and other officials sought changes in Soviet conduct to test the Soviet leaders' adherence to the new thinking advocated by Gorbachev. Understandably, this was not well received by Soviet officials, feeling that they were being asked to jump through hoops for the Americans. As Shevardnadze said irritably to his aides, "Are the Americans willing to do nothing to help us? . . . We take these huge steps and all we hear from Washington is, '*More! More!*

You must do more!'" Rather than "testing," with its connotations of superiority, mutual exploration of options probably would have been less offensive and more likely to be effective.

Sometimes, however, U.S. actions that might have been presented as fostering mutual interests were not so portrayed. For example, in the early 1990s, President Bush undertook major policy changes in the Asia-Pacific region, in conjunction with the closing of the Clark air and the Subic naval bases, after the U.S. and the Philippine governments failed to agree to extend the leases. U.S. troops were reduced in number and distributed more widely in Southeast Asia. In 1991, Bush announced that the United States "would remove, for destruction or storage, all tactical nuclear weapons from U.S. ships, submarines and land-based air squadrons."[54] This could have been presented as a non-provocative defense policy and so reassure China and other Asian countries.[55] Rather, it was presented as strengthening America's role as a regional balancer in managing crises.

The negotiation processes that yielded agreements ending the civil wars in Nicaragua, El Salvador, and Guatemala were begun and facilitated by the mediation efforts of the former Costa Rican president Oscar Arias, the UN, and the Organization of American States. With the collapse of presumed threats that Soviet-supported governments would be sustained in Central America, the U.S. government felt little need to protect oligarchic governments resisting popular challenges in El Salvador, Honduras, and Guatemala or to support the militant challenge to the left-leaning government of Nicaragua. Peace agreements were negotiated in those countries with the mediation assistance of regional and international leaders. The peace agreements, however, generally did not change the structural inequities in those countries.[56]

AFGHANISTAN AND LINGERING CONFLICTS

The violent conflicts in Afghanistan in which the United States and the Soviet Union were engaged during the last decade of the Cold War did not disappear with the Cold War's cessation. They persisted in a different form, but were not given fresh attention by U.S. officials once the Soviet Union had withdrawn its military forces. The likelihood that the radical Islamic militias, which had been supported by the United States in their fight against the Soviet occupation, would become a threat for the United States was largely ignored. Keeping in mind how conflicts persist, even as they are radically transformed and change their form and manner, would have been beneficial.

After the Soviet military forces completed their withdrawal from Afghanistan in February 1989, U.S. involvement with Afghanistan largely ended. Many persons in the CIA had regarded U.S. intervention in the war in Afghanistan as payback for the Soviet role in the Vietnam War.[57] Persisting with a Cold War framing, once the Soviets had withdrawn from Afghanistan its future mattered much less. State Department officials engaged in Afghan affairs did see some value in curtailing assistance to the Afghan mujahedeen fighting the Afghan government headed by Najibullah, who had been supported by the Soviet military forces. But Ronald Reagan determined that the CIA could help supply the rebels as long as the Soviets provided aid to their allies in Kabul.[58]

As the fighting raged, the Afghan government headed by Najibullah unexpectedly survived after the withdrawal of Soviet forces. He had put aside secularism and Communist ideology and become the leader of a nationalist coalition. The government defeated attacks by various militia groups, in part due to the severe fighting among them. That might have been an opportunity for re-framing the conflict and for U.S.-Soviet cooperation to establish a broad coalition government that would have settled the civil war and prevented the Taliban from taking power in Afghanistan.

President George H. W. Bush and his administration were understandably preoccupied with the tumultuous changes in Eastern Europe as the Cold War ended. Moreover, some members of the administration initially were uncertain of Gorbachev's commitment to the new thinking he promoted. In May 1989, Baker and Shevardnadze met in Moscow and discussed the many contentious issues between their countries and explored possible collaborative solutions. Baker was delighted that Shevardnadze discussed Afghanistan without linking U.S. support of the mujahedeen there to Soviet military assistance to the Sandinista government of Nicaragua. Indeed, Shevardnadze even indicated a Soviet willingness not to insist that Najibullah be part of a coalition government in Kabul.[59] But it did not happen.

Early in 1992, a Communist commander of an Uzbek militia, Abdul Rashid Dostum, defected and joined forces with Ahmad Shah Massoud's mujahedin. Najibullah recognized his desperate situation and, in March 1992, at the urging of a UN mediator, announced his readiness to resign the presidency when a successor government was established with UN assistance. But it was too late. The militias of Massoud and Dostum took control of Kabul, and Najibullah found sanctuary in the UN compound. Fierce fighting among the militias continued, including intense shelling of Kabul by the forces of Gulbuddin Hekmattyar. In September 1992, Kabul fell and Najibullah was seized and killed. Following more fighting, the Taliban arose in 1994, took Kabul in 1996, and then dominated most of Afghanistan.

In retrospect, the United States and the Afghans would have been better served by reaching a diplomatic solution and incorporating diplomatic efforts to sustain an Afghan government that was not dominated by extreme Islamic militias Instead, contending militias created conditions that enabled the Taliban to seize the government and provide a haven for al Qaeda.[60] Furthermore, relying on covert operations contributed to channeling assistance to Afghan resistance groups through Pakistan's Inter-Services Intelligence (ISI), which continued to favor some militant jihadist militias.[61] This contributed to the developments in Afghanistan that helped make possible the tragic September 11, 2001, attacks in the United States.

Intervention in the Gulf War, 1990–1991

The Middle East was not quiet during the great transformation of East-West relations in Europe. A terrible war was initiated in 1980 by Iraq against Iran and waged with a huge loss of lives, until it was ended in 1988 with the assistance of UN mediation. Saddam Hussein, despite the great human and material costs of that war, soon began making demands on Kuwait.[62] Iraqi officials claimed that Kuwait was pumping oil from Iraqi petroleum fields and demanded $2.4 billion as partial compensation. Iraq also claimed that Kuwait was exceeding Organization of the Petroleum Exporting Countries (OPEC) oil production quotas. In early July, Kuwait agreed to abide by the quotas, and the crisis seemed to abate. Nevertheless, by the end of July 1990, one hundred thousand Iraqi troops were massed on the Kuwaiti border.

The U.S. government did take some measures that bolstered Kuwait's military defenses. It sold two KC-135 aerial-refueling tankers to Kuwait and announced joint military maneuvers with the United Arab Emirates in the Persian Gulf. U.S. public and private statements, however, left some ambiguity about U.S. actions in the event of Iraqi military operations against Kuwait.[63]

The U.S. and the Iraqi governments were each sending mixed signals about their views and plans regarding the other's policies. Each side misjudged what the other would do. Hussein, given the favorable conduct of the United States during Iraq's aggressive war against Iran, may have believed that it would not strongly oppose Iraq's absorption of Kuwait.[64] U.S. officials thought Hussein was bluffing and even if he used military force it would be for very limited purposes. A more consistent U.S. policy presentation, in coordination with other governments, that Iraqi military attacks against Kuwait were unacceptable might have prevented the Iraqi invasion.[65]

On August 2, 1990, Iraqi forces invaded and swiftly occupied and then incorporated Kuwait. Bush declared the invasion would not stand and rallied a global coalition to militarily liberate Kuwait. Russia, demonstrating its new relationship with the United States, joined in supporting strong UN and U.S. actions to undo the invasion.[66]

Saudi Arabia and other Arab countries were alarmed at Hussein's likely expansion of power and ambitions if the independence of Kuwait was not restored.

The U.S. government quickly mobilized an international response to the invasion: UN condemnation of the invasion and imposition of sanctions to force Iraqi withdrawal. On August 6, the UN Security Council resolved to impose economic sanctions against Iraq. The U.S. government regarded the mediating efforts of King Hussein of Jordan and the Arab League as unrealistic. While the sanctions were being implemented, preparations for a military campaign were set in motion.

The American public was divided about the U.S. undertaking a large-scale military intervention in the Gulf. Major efforts to rally public support for such an action were undertaken by the Kuwaiti government as well as by the U.S. government. The government of Kuwait spent many millions of dollars to establish Citizens for a Free Kuwait, which hired Hill & Knowlton, at the time the largest public relations firm in the United States, to conduct a broad campaign to convince Americans to liberate Kuwait.[67] Saddam Hussein's long history of brutality within Iraq and the extremely harsh occupation of Kuwait made him an easy target for demonization. The public relations campaign to intensify and spread this view of Saddam also included considerable disinformation. A notable example of this was the tearful account by a 15-year-old Kuwaiti girl of witnessing Iraqi soldiers enter a hospital and remove the incubators from 312 infants, leaving the infants on the floor to die. This report was given great publicity and cited by President Bush and other officials as illustrative of the horrors of the Iraqi occupation of Kuwait. After the war, investigations revealed that this event had not happened.

Besides pointing to the atrocities perpetrated by Saddam Hussein and his regime, many other reasons were put forward in support of U.S. military intervention. Intervention could not be justified in terms of waging the Cold War. Immediately after the Iraqi invasion of Kuwait, the urgent need to prevent Iraqi aggression against Saudi Arabia was stressed, even in a face-to-face meeting between U.S. Secretary of Defense Cheney and his advisers with the Saudi royal family.[68] Evidence of this threat was crucial in convincing the Saudi leaders to invite U.S. military forces into Saudi territory to defend their country and to prepare for militarily liberating Kuwait. Cheney pledged that the troops would not stay after the Iraqi threat ended or the king said they should leave, but the troops came and remained after the war.

These events fatefully contributed to Osama bin Laden's grievances against the United States. After leaving Afghanistan in 1989, Osama bin Laden returned to his home in Saudi Arabia as a popular person, celebrated for his fight to drive the Soviet communists out of Afghanistan. When he learned that U.S. soldiers were coming to protect Saudi Arabia, he was appalled.[69] He unsuccessfully argued against non-Muslims doing that and proposed to Prince Sultan, the minister of defense, that he could organize a mujahedeen army that would defeat the threat, with faith. His hostility toward American crusaders increased and his relations with the royal family deteriorated, as is discussed in later chapters.

In any case, Iraq's gross violation of international law was almost universally condemned and the American public believed some kind of action to restore Kuwaiti independence was appropriate. But more was needed to achieve consensus supporting military action. Baker and others pointed to the economic damages that would follow from Saddam's increased control of petroleum; intervention was needed to protect American "jobs, jobs, jobs."[70] This argument seemed to have little weight in the public mind. The assertion that Saddam Hussein was developing nuclear weapons, however, did seem to be a powerful argument.

At the same time, some critics of the relentless movement to use ground troops to expel the Iraqi forces from Kuwait argued that real diplomatic negotiations might still avert a ground war.[71] Suggestions about possible negotiation strategies that might have succeeded in achieving an Iraqi withdrawal without war were made by several advocates of the conflict resolution approach. For example, Roger Fisher and some associates at the Program on Negotiation at Harvard University, argued that negotiations with Saddam Hussein might well bring about an Iraqi withdrawal if the United States considered the choices that Hussein perceived he had and presented him with options that made withdrawal acceptable to him, yet did not give up what was essential to the United States and other defenders of Kuwaiti independence.[72] They reasoned that Hussein saw the choices he faced at that time such that the consequences of withdrawing were all dangerous for him while the consequences of refusing to do so were actually more attractive.[73]

Remarkably, this interpretation of Hussein's view of his circumstances is supported by firsthand evidence. On October 28, 1990, Yevgeni Primakov, the director of the Soviet Institute for World Economy and International Relations, went to Baghdad to meet with Hussein and discuss Iraqi withdrawal. He later reported,

Saddam asked, "How can I announce the withdrawal of troops if I am not informed how the question of the removal of U.S. forces from Saudi Arabia will be resolved? Would the UN sanctions against Iraq be lifted, or would they remain in force? How would my country's desire for an outlet to the sea be ensured? Would there be some sort of linkage between an Iraqi withdrawal and solution of the Palestine problem?" Without knowing the answers to these questions, he said, he could not relax his position: "For me, that would be suicidal."[74]

Such questions suggest options that were not discussed.

By the end of October, Bush had already decided that military force would be necessary. The alternative of containing Iraq from further aggression and imposing strict sanctions that would strangle the Iraqi society was raised by Secretary of Defense Powell, but never seriously debated.[75]

The various reasons for intervention and the wide range of goals to be achieved contributed to a lack of coherence between means and ends. If simply restoring Kuwaiti sovereignty were the goal, military action might not be necessary. If overthrowing Saddam were the goal, then a large-scale military operation going on to Baghdad might be required. The agreement of a wide variety of constituents, allies and other actors also would affect the implementation of any chosen U.S. government policy.

President Bush and his primary advisers decided that a U.S.-led military coalition was necessary to expel Iraqi forces from Kuwait. Furthermore, this could be done with minimal coalition deaths and casualties. In addition, a humiliating defeat of the Iraqi forces would probably shatter his ability to remain in power.

Bush announced on November 9 that U.S. military forces would begin to be greatly increased in the region. On November 29, the Security Council authorized member-states to use all necessary means after January 15, 1991, to enforce previous resolutions. An intense and sustained bombing campaign was begun immediately after the deadline passed. The bombing continued day after day, week after week, greatly damaging Iraq's infrastructure, but without bringing about a withdrawal from Kuwait.

During this time, no significant effort to mediate or negotiate an end to the Iraqi incorporation of Kuwait was undertaken. Bush was clear that Hussein's aggression should not be rewarded and his policy was to insist upon unconditional withdrawal without any concession or face-saving measure. However, to win domestic support and to demonstrate that the Bush administration did all it could to avoid war, President Bush proposed a high level bilateral meeting with the Iraqi government.[76] Indeed, Baker met with the Iraqi Foreign Minister Tariq Aziz in Geneva on January 8, 1991. He simply informed Aziz that the coalition forces would quickly demolish the Iraqi military organization.

U.S. government leaders had more aspirations than simply restoring Kuwait independence. They included demonstrating U.S. military capabilities, effectively destroying Iraqi military power, ending any development of weapons of mass destruction, and ideally, overthrowing Saddam. Ending Saddam's dictatorial rule might liberate the Iraqi people and create the possibility of creating a friendly democratic state in the Arab world. Waging a war seemed to promise to achieve at least some of these broad aspirations.[77]

The U.S.-led ground campaign was launched on February 22, 1991. The ground forces quickly drove the Iraqi soldiers back into Iraq. The fleeing Iraqi soldiers were attacked from the air and destroyed. On March 3, Iraq accepted the terms of cease-fire. The U.S. and coalition forces suffered light casualties.

Bush was realistically careful not to expand the stated objectives of the operation: coalition military forces did not march on to Baghdad and impose a new govern-ment. The international coalition mobilized to liberate Kuwait could not have been held together for such an expanded goal. This restraint also avoided the overreach-ing that would likely have had even more disastrous consequences than those that did occur, as his son's embrace of neo-con goals later demonstrated.

In any case, the humiliating defeat of Saddam and his military forces might be expected to result in the end of his rule in Iraq. Indeed, massive uprisings against the Iraqi government erupted in the north among the Kurds and in the south among the Shia. But they were ruthlessly repressed by Saddam's army. The resulting human disasters were somewhat mitigated by life-saving assistance by the United States, particularly for the Kurds in the north.

The U.S. government leaders could and did claim that a great victory had been achieved and a new world order seemed to have been established. Kuwait was liber-ated and some of the broader U.S. aspirations appeared to be realized. The actions demonstrated the immense military power and reach of the U.S. government and its ability to mobilize global support for its policies. U.S. global leadership seemed unchallenged by other governments.

Not all the hopes of the Bush administration, however, came to fruition. Most fundamentally, Saddam remained in power. To mobilize support for going to war against Iraq, Bush had demonized Hussein, depicting him as evil incarnate.[78] To then make any compromises with him would be difficult and could be seen as a grave failure. The most extreme actions can be justified to end evil. Such views and rhetoric contribute to misperceptions and to conflicts being waged destructively.

Ironically, the goals that Iraq cease to possess weapons of mass destruction or the capacity to produce them and also to end its program to develop nuclear weapons were achieved, but not recognized or claimed at the time. In 2004, a definitive report by Charles A. Duelfer, commissioned by President George W. Bush, con-cluded what earlier reports had indicated; that is, in the 1991 Persian Gulf War and in the subsequent UN inspections, Iraq's weapons of mass destruction and capacity to produce them were destroyed. In 1991 Saddam Hussein ordered the destruction of chemical and biological weapons and ended his nuclear program.[79] After Saddam Hussein was captured, he was interrogated by FBI agent George L. Piro from Febru-ary 7 to June 28, 2004.[80] Hussein explained that he had feared making this evident because he believed that would make him vulnerable to Iranian aggression.

Ominously, U.S. military bases in Saudi Arabia, which were to be temporary, remained. They became one of the primary grievances of Osama bin Laden when he began his program to drive the United States out of the Middle East.

The human and material costs of the war and of its devastating consequences might be seen as a very heavy price for the Iraqi withdrawal, which might have been achieved more constructively by relying on intermediaries and negotiations to a greater degree. More constructive policies would have required persistent strong sanctions, threatening military action, and some escape for Saddam.

The policy pursued had some constructive qualities. The war was fought with the authorization of the United Nations Security Council and by a broad coalition of countries. This could be seen as a strengthening of the international norms against aggression and of international organizations. Moreover, it was conducted without an overreaching march on Baghdad. The episode was viewed by many American leaders as a sign of an emerging new world order with global norms and institutions playing an ever-growing role, correctly led by the United States. But some highly nationalistic Americans were appalled, claiming that this new world order was part of a conspiracy to extinguish American sovereignty and forcefully impose UN controls over the United States.[81]

Intervention in Yugoslavia and in Somalia

The outbreak of terrible wars in the former Yugoslavia posed great challenges regarding possible American intervention. Soon after Yugoslav President Josip Broz Tito died, in May 1980, ethnic strife within and between the constituent republics of Yugoslavia began to escalate.[82] Ethnic tensions were exacerbated by a spiraling downward economy, as noted in the previous chapter. Before its breakup, Yugoslavia had consisted of six republics and two autonomous provinces, roughly divided along ethnic lines. The six republics were Serbia, Croatia, Bosnia and Herzegovina, Slovenia, Macedonia, and Montenegro, and the two autonomous regions were within Serbia: Vojvodina and Kosovo. Many political and religious leaders and many intellectuals emphasized the past and present grievances of their particular ethnicity within Yugoslavia. Despite decades of integration and many close inter-ethnic ties, mutual recriminations escalated and resulted in nonviolent and violent secessions and in aggressive seizures of territory.

In 1988, Serbs led by Slobodan Milošević, an extreme ethno-nationalist Serb, took control of Vojvodina and Kosovo, which was followed by ending their autonomy.

On June 28, 1989, Milošević, then president of Serbia, gave a major speech at the field where the Battle of Kosovo had been fought 600 years earlier. At that battle, the medieval Serbian kingdom was defeated and then annexed into the Ottoman Empire. The speech celebrated the battle's significance for Serbian identity, but the population of the province of Kosovo had become overwhelmingly ethnic Albanian. The loss of autonomy was accompanied by discrimination against and resistance by ethnic Albanians. It is noteworthy that the Albanians' resistance at the end of 1990 was clearly nonviolent.[83] They drew nonviolent ideas and practices from old traditions and from the recent nonviolent movements in Eastern Europe. Early manifestations of this nonviolent approach included large-scale demonstrations by miners in November 1988 and February 1989. As discussed in the next chapter, the nonviolent movement grew and received some international attention, but became overshadowed by an armed struggle.

In January 1989, protesters allied with Milošević forced a new government leadership in Montenegro. These changes effectively meant that Serbia had four of the eight votes constituting the presidency of Yugoslavia. Spurred by a Serbian crackdown in Kosovo, Slovenia declared its independence June 25, 1991, and after several days of fighting Yugoslavia accepted the secession. Few Serbs lived in Slovenia and Milošević and his associates calculated that without Slovenia in Yugoslavia, Serbian domination of Yugoslavia and the country's military forces would be strengthened.

The U.S. government was determined not to become entangled in what was deemed to be a place with enduring hatreds that America could not fix. The Bush administration denied that there was a threat to American interests that warranted military intervention. Bush and his advisers, notably Acting Secretary of State Lawrence Eagleburger and General Colin Powell, Chairman of the Joint Chiefs of Staff, opposed military intervention, being greatly concerned about becoming mired in a set of intractable ethno-nationalist wars.[84]

Intervention, however, can take many forms and need not necessarily involve military engagement. More options exist at the early stages of a conflict's emergence and escalation than when terrible violence has been unleashed. The destruction of Yugoslavia was beginning when Baker left a CSCE meeting in Berlin for a one-day trip to Belgrade, Yugoslavia.[85] On June 21, 1991, Baker met in separate rooms with Bosnian President Alija Izetbegovic, Macedonian President Vladimir Gligorov, Slovenian President Milan Kučan, as well as Milošević. He stressed to each that the CSCE and the United States opposed the use of force to resolve political differences, and while supporting Yugoslav territorial integrity, would recognize border changes if made by peaceful, consensual means. He urgently raised the issue of protecting human rights for various ethnic groups in Yugoslavia. He warned of the dire consequences of violent disruptions upon the already poor economic situation, promising CSCE and U.S. economic assistance if political changes were made peacefully.

Such declarations, warnings, and promises, if made dramatically, persistently, and in close coordination with and among European states, years earlier might have been effective in averting the vicious wars that destroyed many lives in Yugoslavia. Considering a broader range of strategies involving more stakeholders might have revealed alternatives to choosing either diplomatic urgings or military intervention. For example, economic policies by the IMF and other financial institutions might have been changed to lessen the severe economic hardships that their insistence on austerity had generated.[86] In 1990 Ante Marković was the prime minister of Yugoslavia and was well regarded throughout the federation. He solicited economic relief from the Bush administration, such as postponing debt payments, but that was not granted. Such support would have helped overcome the economic crisis and strengthened Marković relative to Milošević. By dealing with an underlying reason for the escalating conflicts, such external financial assistance might well have prevented the destruction of Yugoslavia.[87]

In addition, engaging with Serb, Croat, and other Yugoslav ethnic groups in America might have helped calm rising antagonism in Yugoslavia and help create new political options there. Insistence on reforms of the Yugoslav federal system and slowing or avoiding its breakup may have been plausible. Reliance on international law would have meant withholding support for secession by segments of Yugoslavia.

With German initiation, European governments soon recognized the new countries breaking out of the former Yugoslavia. The anti-Communist sentiment in the West and prejudice against the Milošević-led Serbia contributed to the Western readiness to accept the secession of the constituent republics of Yugoslavia.[88]

In mid-summer 1991, violence erupted in many areas of Yugoslavia, particularly between Serbs and Croats. At this time, substantial international intervention finally began. Britain, France, and Germany wanted the European Community (EC) to keep the diplomatic lead and keep NATO on the sidelines. The United States was initially comfortable with that policy, but there were differences among the European governments about how to proceed. Mediation efforts were undertaken by the former British foreign secretary Peter Carrington, who was soon joined by former Secretary of State Cyrus Vance. The UN imposed an embargo against sending arms to any party in the fighting, presumably to block possible Russian arms being sent to Serbia. Economic sanctions were also imposed against Yugoslavia.

Nevertheless, relations among the constituent republics and ethnicities continued to deteriorate. In 1991, Croatia declared its independence, under leadership of another ethno-nationalist figure, Franjo Tudjman. The Serbs in the eastern region of

Croatia, Krajina, declared their independence, which Croatia sought to suppress. Serb militia forces in Krajina were supported by the Serb-controlled Yugoslav People's Army to join those areas to Serbia. In the spring of 1992, Bosnia-Herzegovina was torn by fighting between local Serbs joined by Yugoslav army forces against Bosnian Croats and Muslims, and Serbs laid siege to Sarajevo. The UN Security Council authorized a peacekeeping force, United Nations Protection Force (UNPROFOR), which began operations in February 1992, initially in Croatia. The subsequent calamities are discussed in the next chapter.

President Bush and his advisers also were concerned about intervening in Somalia, where a civil war had erupted and now was causing a humanitarian disaster. Small UN peacekeeping missions were proving inadequate to halt the disaster and were having difficulties in distributing material aid. Nevertheless, the Bush administration clearly stated that U.S. military intervention would be very risky and vital U.S. interests were not threatened, and so determined to avoid military intervention.

Domestic considerations, however, raised the salience of the violent conflict in Somalia. In the summer of 1992, American public attention was aroused by disclosures of Serb-controlled concentration camps in Bosnia and also by the growing humanitarian disaster in Somalia.[89] Liberal humanitarians increased the pressure for U.S. intervention. During his 1992 presidential election campaign, Bill Clinton urged more active humanitarian intervention in Bosnia and in Somalia. Following Clinton's victory and further reports of failing UN missions in Somalia, Bush concluded that a more forceful intervention was advisable, and U.S. military leaders thought that Somalia was more doable than Bosnia. The plan for intervention, approved by UN Secretary General, Boutros Boutros-Ghali, was to deploy 30,000 troops (from the United States and other countries) and secure key airports, ports, roads, and aid centers in central and southern Somalia. The deployment would be under U.S. command and presumably for a limited time.[90] In December 1992, U.S. military forces began landing in Mogadishu to protect the delivery of humanitarian supplies. However, there were some unresolved differences between U.S. and UN Secretariat officials about the duration and scope of the U.S. deployment. Subsequent events are discussed in the next chapter.

Mediation of Israeli-Palestinian Conflict

Before discussing the important mediation efforts undertaken by the Bush administration to achieve Israeli-Palestinian peace, the non-official American endeavors to help resolve the conflict should be noted. To illustrate the complexities and dilemmas of such efforts, I call attention to the American Friends Service Committee (AFSC).[91]

Elmore Jackson, director of the Quaker United Nations Office, conducted mediation between Egyptian and Israeli government leaders before the 1956 Suez war,
which was described in Chapter 2. In later years, however, the Friends did not undertake mediation at the high official level. The AFSC had been engaged in helping
Jewish refugees from the Nazis and Palestinian refugees after the war that led to the
establishment of Israel.

Following the war, the AFSC began carrying out many kinds of projects in Gaza,
the West Bank and Israel, including providing schooling and medical care for Palestinians. In 1973 it established the Quaker Legal Aid and Information Center in East
Jerusalem. Associated volunteers monitored Palestinian conditions and published
reports of their findings. They also facilitated dialogue between Palestinians and
Israeli Jews and participated in nonviolent actions against the Israeli occupation of
the territories seized in the 1967 war. In 1970, the AFSC published *Search for Peace
in the Middle East*, and in 1982, *A Compassionate Peace: A Future for the Middle
East*, presenting a vision of what a just peace would be for Jews and Palestinians.[92]

These actions and writings made the Quakers unacceptable mediators in the eyes
of the Israeli government. In a larger perspective, however, their work can be viewed
as contributing to constructive conflict escalation, by stressing concerns for justice
for all major stakeholders. The activities were directed at reducing some of the asymmetry of the Israeli-Palestinian relationship and recognized the needs of both
peoples.

Many other American and international NGOs were engaged in matters related
to resolving the Israeli-Palestinian conflict. Many acted in solidarity with nongovernmental and official Israeli or Palestinian organizations. Others directed their
activities toward the American public or the U.S. government, providing information or urging one or another government policy. Still others engaged in Track Two
diplomacy to help overcome the obstacles to resolving the conflict between Israeli
Jews and Palestinians. Specific examples of such engagements are noted at various
points in this book.

From the perspective of the constructive conflict approach, the many Track Two
diplomacy endeavors in the Israeli-Palestinian conflict deserve special attention.[93]
They vary in the social/political level of the participants, from high, semi-official
elites to grassroots youth. They have been conducted without outside facilitation or
convened and facilitated by outside academics, institutes, or governments. They
tend to either emphasize process and the building of relations and understanding or
to emphasize outcome and the generation of ideas for agreements.[94]

Interactive problem-solving workshops are a major kind of nongovernmental
peace endeavor, which have been frequently undertaken in the Israeli-Palestinian
conflict. One of the most prominent scholar/practitioners of this work is Herbert

C. Kelman, long-time professor at Harvard University. Drawing on his experience with John Burton and his expertise in social psychology, in the early 1970s, he began organizing and facilitating a series of problem-solving workshops for Israelis and Palestinians. Nadim Rouhana worked with Kelman in developing a continuing workshop, which began in 1990 and continued until 1993 when the Oslo process began.

The workshops, bringing together politically influential Israelis and Palestinian, were designed to encourage sharing perspectives and joint thinking.[95] They made three kinds of contributions to the initiation of direct negotiations between Israeli and Palestinian officials in the Oslo peace process, discussed in the next chapter. First, dozens of Israelis and Palestinians over the years had participated in these workshops, learning how people on the other side felt and thought about the national relationship. They learned how to better communicate with each other. Many of them moved into negotiating and advisory positions when official negotiations began, using what they had learned. Second, substantive matters were discussed in the workshops and formulations and shared ideas could be used in negotiations.[96] Third, the very existence of such meetings, and the many other interactions between members of the two communities, helped create an atmosphere that made plausible the belief that a peaceful solution to the Israeli-Palestinian conflict could be constructed.

Such Track Two diplomacy was particularly useful prior to official direct negotiations getting underway. Once official negotiations are being conducted or could be readily undertaken, Track Two meetings dealing with substantive and technical issues are likely and useful.

The Bush administration, following the war to liberate Kuwait, undertook a major mediation endeavor to open direct Israeli-Palestinian negotiations to settle their conflict. Several background developments converged to make a breakthrough in Israeli-Palestinian relations seem feasible. The end of the Cold War meant that Soviet support for the PLO, Syria, and Iraq was less significant and the value of Israel to the United States was lessened. This might have made the Palestinian and Israeli leadership more interested in exploring the possibility of resolving their conflict. The Palestinian Intifada, which began in December 1987, also contributed to the readiness of Palestinians and Israelis to seriously consider a settlement of their conflict.

More immediately, the U.S. success in forming the broad coalition, including nearly all Arab countries, to drive Iraqi forces out of Kuwait enabled and seemed to require a major effort by the U.S. government to resolve the Israeli-Palestinian conflict. The U.S. assurance that such an effort would follow the military action against Saddam was a commitment that was expected to be honored. Its capability to make progress on an Israeli-Palestinian accommodation seemed to be demonstrated by the effectiveness of the U.S.-led military operations and of its diplomacy, which prevented Saddam from provoking an Israel-Arab confrontation and thereby diverting the actions against him.

Secretary of State Baker, with high energy and skill, orchestrated a conference in Madrid that included leaders from Israel, Egypt, Syria, and Jordan.[97] Palestinians were included as part of the Jordanian delegation, but functioned independently. Their selection, however, was circumscribed: Israel required that they not be members of the Palestine Liberation Organization (PLO). However, Jordanian authorities obtained approval from the PLO leadership of the Palestinians (who were not PLO members) joining the delegation. Three arenas of negotiation were devised: a general brief conference, bilateral meetings between Israel and each neighboring country, and regional meetings on issues of common concern such as water, refugees, and security.[98]

The Israeli-Palestinian negotiations were the primary one, but they soon became stalemated.[99] The Israeli government, controlled by the Likud Party led by Yitzhak Shamir, ensured there would be no agreement. When the Labor Party defeated Likud, however, progress still was not made. Without Yasser Arafat and the PLO publicly directing the negotiations, an agreement was not possible. Furthermore, the PLO leaders believed the United States opposed Palestinian statehood for them and did not want to deal with them.[100] In any case, the Palestinians insisted on statehood and the Israelis offered only autonomy. Finally, the news leaks and press conferences associated with the negotiations hampered considering creative options.

The felt need for reaching some kind of settlement, however, remained. An alternative channel and a more realistic composition of the negotiation teams was constructed to forge a peace agreement between Palestinians and Israeli Jews. That was the Oslo peace process, which began secretly between PLO officials and non-official Israeli representatives, and was facilitated by the Norwegian government. Its course is examined in the next chapter.

Broadening the Conflict Resolution Field, 1989–1992

This concluding section focuses on the increasing differentiation in the conflict resolution field and its expansion into new realms of action, viewed in the context of the new global circumstances at the end of the twentieth century. This section pertains particularly to the period of George H. W. Bush's presidency but also to some extent in the period when Bill Clinton was president.

The profound changes in the world system beginning in 1989 necessarily influenced the practice and theorizing of the conflict resolution field. I cite four dramatic changes related to the end of the Cold War and of the Soviet Union, which affected American engagement in foreign conflicts and the constructive conflict approach.

First, with the end of the Cold War, the UN was more likely to take actions to stop large-scale violence threatening international peace. UN peacekeeping operations immediately expanded greatly: the number of missions increased from 5 in 1988 to 11 in 1992, with troops coming from 26 countries in 1988 and 56 countries in 1992.[101] During the Cold War, the peacekeeping missions consisted of lightly armed troops, usually from small neutral countries, deployed to monitor borders after cease-fires had been reached. This was the first generation of UN peacekeeping. After the Cold War, the tasks expanded to include humanitarian, political, and security functions and the missions were more diverse, including civilians as well as military personnel from a greater range of countries.[102] This came to be called the second generation of peacekeeping, or multifunctional peacekeeping.[103]

Second, the Cold War's ending meant that proxy wars could be more readily concluded and new ones avoided. This produced not only reductions in armed violence but settlements reached by negotiation rather than imposed by one side; and imposed endings are associated with greater deaths than are negotiated endings. However, negotiated endings are more likely to erupt in wars again within five years.[104] These realities have contributed to the increased attention to building enduring peaceful arrangements, and helping people to recover from the traumas, dislocations, fears, and hatreds felt after mass violence has ceased. On the other hand, the dominant power in each bloc during the Cold War could and did sometimes suppress violent conflicts within the bloc.

Third, instead of the ideologically related wars of the Cold War years, violent conflicts associated with religious and ethnic identities became much more common. This is related to the increase in religious militancy within Islam, Hinduism, Judaism, and Christianity. Very destructive conflicts also erupted along ethnic lines, in many cases when the mantle of authoritarian Communism weakened and disappeared.

Fourth, the preeminence of United States militarily, ideologically, economically, and culturally delivered considerable authority to decisions made by American leaders. Major collective international actions were not made without a significant American role, or at the very least acquiescence.

All these developments made it more likely that external interventions in violent conflicts would occur. Those interventions would tend to be multilateral, conducted by governments, international governmental organizations, and nongovernmental organizations. The interventions were likely to be couched in terms of protecting human rights and spreading democracy. On at least some occasions, these developments helped open up space for enhanced constructive conflict practice and ideas.

EXTENDING THE CONFLICT RESOLUTION FIELD

The conflict resolution field was deeply affected by these many developments. It has become more highly differentiated and extended its range of endeavors. The field, through research and applications by persons who considered themselves as workers in the field and by those who did not so identify themselves, affected the way various conflicts were conducted and contributed to the increase in peaceful accommodations in the 1990s and subsequently. This was noted in the earlier discussions of the transformation of Eastern Europe and the new countries established after the dissolution of the Soviet Union. It was also evident in the ending of apartheid in South Africa. There was increasing interaction and cooperation between self-identified conflict-resolvers employed in the academy or in NGOs with government officials engaged in international affairs. The United States Institute of Peace was important in building links among these kinds of workers.

During the early 1990s, the practice of conflict resolution grew in its previously established arenas, but it also expanded into several new spheres of work. More specialized applications and research activities became evident, related to the previously noted changes in the world. Three new domains of research and practice are particularly noteworthy during this time period: communal identities, the terms of negotiated agreements, and external intervention.

First, the reality of recurrent destructive escalations of long-lasting conflicts, often related to ethnic, religious, and other communal identities, drew attention to protracted or intractable conflicts.[105] This was apparent in a surge in research and theorizing about the role of identities in social conflicts, and particularly discussions and debates about ethno-nationalism.[106] Some analysts argued that ethnicity is a primordial phenomenon, relatively permanent and unchanging.[107] Many other analysts stressed that it is socially constructed, with people choosing a history and common ancestry and creating, as much as discovering, differences from others. Still others viewed identity from an instrumentalist vantage point, arguing that group identity is often nourished by elites in the pursuit of political objectives.[108] I take the approach that most aspects of ethnicity are socially constructed and vulnerable to instrumental manipulation, but some traits of ethnicity are not easily modifiable by such social processes.

Nationalism combines ethnic and other communal identities with political claims, including having an independent state, and nationalism has long been an important component in formulating contentious goals. National pride, however, is not necessarily ethnocentric. Casual observations and social psychological research indicate that positive attachment to one's country—patriotism—can be separate from feelings of national superiority—nationalism.[109]

Second, more attention began to be given to research about the effects of different terms of negotiated agreements. Simply reaching an agreement was rarely enough for most conflict protagonists or for conflict analysts. Consequently, there was a growing literature debating the relative durability and equity of different settlements. One such issue is power sharing, a governance system that ensures representation of diverse groups in policymaking and in administrative institutions, particularly in the police and military services.[110] For example, in South Africa in 1994, major opposition parties were guaranteed that they would have a seat in the government and in the cabinet for a transitional period, and would hold parliament seats proportional to their numbers in the population.

Many other aspects of governance and conflict management began to be examined as possible aids to constructive conflict transformation.[111] They pertained to the timing of elections as well as the structure of electoral systems, to judicial institutions, to constitutions, to the composition and authority of military forces, and to the organization of the economy. The results of the research were not always consistent, since the effectiveness of any particular institution or strategy is contingent on the particular circumstances of a conflict.

One empirical finding received a great deal of attention outside as well as inside the academy. The finding was that democratic countries did not make war against each other.[112] This robust finding was dubbed the democratic peace. Considerable research and theorizing ensued to account for this relationship, including demonstrating mutual regard, experience with compromise, and popular engagement in governance. Of course, the transition to democracy in authoritarian-ruled countries is often marked by considerable violence over many years.

Finally, research and analyses regarding external interventions proliferated. External interventions included military operations by UN peacekeeping forces, but also increased mediation undertakings. This was highlighted in the 1992 report, "An Agenda for Peace," by UN Secretary-General Boutros Boutros-Ghali.[113] Even after violence was stopped or a negotiated agreement was reached, the frequent recurrence of wars made evident the need for external intervention to sustain agreements. Governments and international governmental organizations were not fully prepared and lacked the capacity to manage the multitude of problems that followed the end of hostilities. They increasingly employed nongovernmental organizations to carry out some of the needed work of humanitarian relief, institution building, protection of human rights, and training in conflict resolution skills. The number and scope of NGOs working on such matters grew quickly, many of them applying conflict resolution methods.

Some of the methods, which had been developed years before to help prepare adversaries for de-escalating steps, began to be employed at the later phases of conflicts as well as in peacebuilding. These included small workshops, dialogue circles, and training of protagonists to improve their capacities to negotiate and use mediation. Such practices helped avert a renewal of vicious fights by fostering accommodations, and even reconciliation at various levels of the antagonistic sides. Furthermore, these activities began to be viewed in the context of each conflict's long-term transformation, rather than as independent episodes.

In some cases intervention yielded significant success, as in preventing a renewed outbreak of civil wars in Namibia and Mozambique. In other cases, intervention froze a conflict so that violence was ended, but no mutually acceptable accommodation was reached for a very long time, as in Cyprus. In still other cases, renewed war quickly followed peacebuilding intervention efforts, as in Angola and Rwanda. As will be discussed in later chapters, the number and scope of external interventions in violent societal and international conflicts have grown, but also have become highly controversial.

This large and growing body of literature has drawn from and contributed to the work done in the fields of conflict resolution and peace studies, particularly regarding conflict transformation, which would be more inclusive of all actors and more enduring. The idea of conflict transformation means that intractable conflicts could be overcome: the conflict might continue but in a relatively legitimate, constructive manner. Thus, the Program on the Analysis and Resolution of Conflicts published its initial collectively written book, *Intractable Conflicts and Their Transformation,* in 1989.[114]

DIFFUSION OF CONFLICT RESOLUTION WORK

A great expansion of the concepts, research findings, and actual practices of conflict resolution began in the late 1980s. Certainly the growth of the field in the United States meant that America was a center from which many beliefs and experiences flowed. The diffusion, however, was not only in one direction; ideas and practices from each part of the world more and more influenced the ideas and practices in other regions. Analyses and reports about peace and conflict research, methods, and approaches flourished in Western Europe and grew in African, Asian, Latin American and Arab societies.[115] Some traditional ways of thinking about conflicts in those societies cast light upon conventional conflict management methods in the United States and other Western countries. For example, the idea that conflicts are a rupture of social relationships and those relations need to be restored in order to overcome the conflict is widespread in traditional societies and can provide useful insights about resolving conflicts in the more individualistic Western societies.

This also meant that conflict resolution practitioners from the United States and similar Western European countries would do better work by attending to local cultural means of managing conflicts. They should intervene carefully and elicit aspects of those methods as they try to apply the methods with which they are familiar.[116]

In addition, the conflict resolution approach was taken up in countries where great struggles for human rights, freedom, and justice were underway and in countries recovering from long periods of authoritarian rule and oppression. In those settings, conflict resolution thinking was adapted and new experiences, practices, and thinking generated that flowed back to influence American conflict resolution work. For example, this was true of the struggle against apartheid in South Africa, as may be seen in the work and writings of Hendrik van der Merwe.[117] Such usages and elaborations contributed to developing the constructive conflict approach.

The sweeping changes in Eastern Europe drew attention to the importance of nongovernmental social movements and social movement organizations in bringing about and sustaining societal change. For decades earlier, social scientists and conflict resolvers had studied and written about the importance of these phenomena. The value of various groups with a stake in a conflict participating in resolving a conflict was examined and stressed. The importance of such broad engagement to sustain democratic governance was increasingly recognized.

In 1989, Raymond Shonholtz founded Partners for Democratic Change, drawing on his experience with Community Boards of San Francisco, one of the first neighborhood and school mediation programs in the United States. Partners for Democratic Change started as an association of conflict resolution centers newly established in Poland, Lithuania, Hungary, Czechoslovakia and Bulgaria. It was created to advance civil society and the culture of nonviolent dispute resolution. It continues, having established centers in 20 countries around the globe, which are run by local nationals.

In addition to the work of international governmental organizations, such as the OSCE discussed earlier, transnational NGOs and scholar/practitioners provided mediation and conflict resolution training in conflict-torn areas of the former Soviet Union. For example, Susan Allen Nan, from George Mason University, and colleagues from fifteen different universities in the United States and Europe engaged in conflict resolution work since 1992 in Georgia and the regions of Abkhaz and of South Ossetia.[118] They provided training and engaged in scholar/ practitioner work such as advising conflict protagonists, performing conflict resolution tasks, and influencing international policy regarding those regional conflicts.

Similarly, Paula Garb, from the University of California–Irvine, helped establish dialogue meetings among academics, journalists, and others from opposing sides in Abkhazia after the fighting had subsided. She went on to help organize conferences to compare cases of conflict resolution efforts assisting citizen peacebuilding in conflicts undergoing transformations.

Academics in the conflict resolution field tended to emphasize particular processes that self-identified workers in the field advocated and practiced. How officials and non-officials applied, misapplied, or failed to apply the constructive conflict approach was not fully examined. Furthermore, the goals and institutional structures to be favored received less attention. Therefore, people working in the field were not well prepared to actively engage in advocating for particular national or international institutional arrangements.

On the whole, the evolving field of conflict resolution and the emerging constructive conflict approach were congruent with the new developments in the world system. The growing world integration and interdependence made the constructive conflict approach quite appropriate.

Conclusions

The end of the Cold War and the dissolution of the Soviet Union were the most important events affecting American engagement in foreign conflicts during the period covered in this chapter. How Americans viewed and reacted to these events in this period are critically important. For many Americans in government and outside, they marked a great victory for the United States and a total defeat for the Soviet Union and Communism. It is suggestive to broadly compare this ending with the aftermaths of World War I and World War II.

After World War I, defeated Germany was humiliated and harshly treated, which contributed to the Nazi rise to power there. The defeat and breakup of the Ottoman Empire and the establishment of new borders and protectorates by the victorious British and French contributed to decades of authoritarianism and disorders in the Middle East. After World War II, the defeated Germany and Japan suffered severe losses resulting from the military devastation inflicted upon them. But the general populations in both countries were then aided in recovery and in some degree were regarded as liberated allies. At least this was true for West Germany. Overall, profound resentments and revenge-seeking political movements have not occurred.

After the end of the Cold War, as discussed in this chapter, Russians had generally participated in ending the old Soviet system and sought to be part of a greater

European system. But some of the indignities and economic troubles many people experienced generated grounds for later resentments. More attention to such possible reactions to American post–Cold War conduct would have been beneficial.

The developments in the ideas and practices of the conflict resolution field and its growing influence did make some contributions to managing American engagement in foreign conflicts. These contributions, however, were limited and did not relate much to the larger issues from the United States being the world's only superpower.

5   America in a Globalizing World, 1993–2000

IN THE 1990S, the people of the world were reaching ever-greater integration and interdependence. Since the Cold War ended, new terms have been used to characterize the evolving world system. However, the multitude of changes cannot be captured in a single word or phrase such as globalization or information age. Such names suggest more coherence than is warranted. In reality, many diverse and in some ways contradictory developments have long been underway transforming the world. Changes move at different speeds and in different directions, with varying implications for international conflicts.[1] The major global developments are discussed, before analyzing important episodes of American engagements in foreign conflicts between 1993 and 2000.

Major World Developments

Eight global developments significantly affect American participation in foreign conflicts: (1) intensifying transnational communication, (2) increasing worldwide economic integration, (3) expanding variety of global actors, (4) shifting global class relations, (5) the rising status of women, (6) changing global norms, (7) growing world population and environmental pressures, and (8) an increasing repertoire of ways to conduct conflicts.

INTENSIFYING TRANSNATIONAL COMMUNICATION

Technological innovations have been made and continue to be made at an ever-increasing rate.[2] By the end of the twentieth century, several major innovations had been combined to enable information to be stored, retrieved, and transmitted in more and more compact forms and with increasing speed and economy via the Internet. People and material goods also were transported more swiftly and at decreasing cost by air. Technological advances enabled more and more people in the world to quickly exchange images and words with each other. These advances also enabled people to experience and react to the same events at the same time, as they were conveyed on television, in films, and through the internet. Terrible conflicts, disasters, and perceived abhorrent practices anywhere in the world became increasingly difficult to ignore.

The new forms of communication magnified the extent to which people could communicate easily over great distances and increase the capability for one sender to reach many people at one time. Scattered persons and groups could more readily coalesce and pursue their specific solutions to the problems they experience.

INCREASING WORLDWIDE ECONOMIC INTEGRATION

As the world's economy became increasingly integrated, people in different parts of the world became more interdependent. The new information technologies and reduced transaction costs for communication make possible global financial markets operating twenty-four hours a day, seven days a week, as well as global markets for the production and distribution of material products and even the provision of some services. The expanding forms of outsourcing exemplify another kind of transnational economic engagement. For example, not only are manufactured goods produced in foreign countries under contract to U.S. clothing company specifications, but technical assistance for customers is also provided overseas.[3]

These developments generate more issues of possible contention and the dependencies make people in various countries more vulnerable to economic sanctions and boycotts as forms of coercion as well as more susceptible to proffers of economic benefits.

EXPANDING VARIETY OF GLOBAL ACTORS

As the new millennium began, the governments of the world remained major actors in international affairs. However, a great variety of relatively autonomous organizations acting beyond any one country's borders have proliferated. Increasingly, transnational actors participate in international and national affairs, and expand in scope.[4] More and more they affect the actions of every state, and to that extent they lessen each state's sovereignty.

Transnational actors include international governmental organizations (IGOs) working on economic, political, military, and social matters, such as the UN, the World Bank, the IMF, the EU, NATO, and the OSCE. Although member-states collectively determine the policy of the IGOs to which they belong, the result is often a collective decision that may differ considerably from the initial preferences of individual governments. Furthermore, to varying degrees, IGO executives and staff influence the decisions that are made and how they are implemented.

The number and scope of international nongovernmental organizations (INGOs) have grown greatly since the 1960s.[5] In addition to organizations based on occupational or religious affiliations, a newer variety of organizations began to flourish, concerned with humanitarian crises and issues related to human rights, development, women, and the environment. INGOs relating to peace existed from the early years of INGO formation, but expanded into conflict resolution work in the field's growth surge in the 1980s.

INGOs provide avenues for grassroots organizations and sub-elites to influence and counter powerful IGOs and transnational corporations. This is institutionalized in the UN, which accords many INGOs a consultative status. This is true for organizations seeking to advance human rights, to protect the environment, to raise the status of women, or to protect low-paid workers. It is also true for organizations that have contrary effects as they promote expansion of particular industries, religious beliefs, or economic ideologies.

International conflicts have traditionally been thought of in terms of state-to-state affairs, but non-state actors have always played important roles in transnational contentions. They include religious organizations, business corporations, ideological movement organizations, and ethnic identity groups. States may engage in conflicts with one or more such organizations, and two or more INGOs may be in conflict with each other. They have been particularly salient in national independence struggles and in struggles to establish particular forms of political or religious systems. They may conduct guerrilla wars or campaigns resorting to terrorist attacks.

Finally, non-state actors also notably include business corporations based in one country and operating in several other countries. They have been a feature of capitalism from its beginning and exercise great influence on matters that concern their managers. Many of them are immense in size and their size has also increased, but not relative to the increasing size of national economies.[6]

SHIFTING GLOBAL CLASS RELATIONS

The economic ranking of persons and organizations within countries, and the ranking of countries and regions within the world system could not be static with so many far-reaching global changes. For two hundred years since the late 1700s, the distribution of economic and political resources became, despite some backsliding, more equal in increasing number of countries in the world. Living standards generally rose for the lowest ranking persons and more categories of people won greater political power.[7] However, beginning in the mid-1970s, in the United States and many other countries, income and wealth inequalities have significantly increased.[8] The wealth of the very rich is increasingly used to gain political influence, which results in decisions and legislation favorable to the rich and the corporations from which they derive their wealth.[9]

Globally, living conditions in the world have improved on the average, particularly for the very poor. But the gap between the world's richest persons and the poorest greatly increased in the 1990s.[10] The UN's human development report, combining income, life expectancy, and literacy, reports that human development actually fell in twenty-one countries in the 1990s, but fell in only four countries in the 1980s.[11] Patterns of investment and trade unequally benefit the persons and organizations that guide those patterns.

Global economic inequalities are also manifested in the way some countries lag far behind the highly developed countries of North America, Western Europe, and Japan. For example, consider the economic and social circumstances of the Arab countries. Despite the great petroleum reserves in several Arab countries, economic growth in the region had been extremely weak during the 1990s, even compared to the developing world as a whole. and social–political conditions were stifling.[12]

The growing inequalities breed resentment among people in many countries of the world, making them susceptible to the rhetoric of leaders who arouse anger at persons and groups they hold responsible for their distress. Sometimes the rhetoric is dangerous scapegoating along ethnic or religious lines.

RISING STATUS OF WOMEN AND FEMINISM

The enhanced status of women seemed secure in economically advanced countries. Women increasingly moved toward greater equality in the work force, political life, civil rights, and personal security. These developments were related to changes in the character of economic activity and in ways of thinking about gender.

The increasing participation of women in the political institutions of the countries in which they live can be expected to contribute to less violent ways of dealing with international conflicts.[13] Marshall and Ramsey found that societies in which women are relatively empowered are less likely to use force in international relations. Consistent with those findings, Caprioli and Boyer found, in their quantitative analysis of international crises from 1945 to 1994, that as domestic gender equality increases, a state's use of violence in international crises significantly decreases.

Concomitant with women's rising status, feminist ideas have been developed in recent decades, which have growing worldwide influence. They enshrine the claim that women have rights equal to those of men, but also pertain to certain beliefs about the workings of any social order. The traditional masculine approach to social relations, stressing hierarchy, hiding feelings, and relying on coercion is contrasted and sometimes regarded as inferior to the feminist approach emphasizing the importance of building social relations, working cooperatively, and reaching decisions consensually. Many men adopt elements of the feminist orientation, but some react against the feminist perspective and against women assuming roles that had been exclusively filled by men. They view these developments as threats to traditional religious values and practices and to their interests.

CHANGING GLOBAL NORMS AND VIEWS

There has been a remarkable expansion in norms and views that are conducive to applying the constructive conflict approach. The extreme horrors of World War II spurred the formulation and widespread governmental agreement to the standards set forth in the 1948 United Nations Universal Declaration of Human Rights and the additional later covenants proclaiming economic and social rights.[14] INGOs have contributed to arousing public support for human rights and pressure governments to honor and protect them. There has been a growth of international laws defining gross human rights violations that are enforced by international courts and international tribunals.[15]

Many indicators reveal declining support for going to war, preparing for war, or justifications for war, since the end of World War II.[16] For example, the number of months of military conscription declined, the idea of changing borders between countries by war was increasingly viewed as unacceptable, anti-war convictions were commonly expressed in popular culture.

Democratic ways of thinking and associated norms and institutions became increasingly influential throughout the world. The wave of de-colonization struggles fostered efforts at establishing democratic forms of government especially in Africa and the end of the Cold War resulted in another great wave of democratization in Eastern Europe and in other regions.

GROWING WORLD POPULATION AND ENVIRONMENTAL CHALLENGES

The world's population has been growing rapidly and will continue to increase, even if the rate of growth is slowing down. From 1950 to 2000, the world population grew from 2.5 to 6.1 billion. Projections of future growth vary, with a medium projection, most often used, of 8.9 billion people in 2039 and then beginning to decline as birth rates decrease. Population growth coupled with increasing production and consumption means much more environmental degradation, which stresses humans. That combination also intensifies competition for essential resources including water, arable land, and sources of energy. Environmental degradation and population increases place people under pressure and intensify competition that can generate severe conflicts.[17] This becomes manifest in struggles over access to resources such as water and petroleum and destructive conflicts may erupt within as well as between countries.

Climate change is a pressing global problem that is already stressing many people in areas that are increasingly impacted adversely. Local environmental injuries contribute to pressures underlying conflicts. Responding to this immense challenge calls for global collective action. That should be a superordinate goal to unite humankind, and yet that is rarely very high on anyone's agenda.

GROWING REPERTOIRE OF WAYS TO CONDUCT CONFLICTS

The final development I discuss is the increasing repertoire of ways to fight and to settle conflicts. The expanding variety of conflict methods derives from the changes previously discussed. Thus, some technological developments contributed to creating innovative weapons, normative developments affect strategies for their use, and intensifying communication and integration increase their diffusion and impact. Advances in military technology garner most popular, academic, and governmental attention. Indeed, the advances in destructive capacity and in the precision of such weapons as well as in their safety for those employing them are spectacular.

Important advances, however, have also been made in nonviolent coercive methods and in noncoercive methods as well. The success of nonviolent action in bringing about regime changes and in averting coups, and the increased sophistication in the strategy and tactics of nonviolent action increases its credibility as a method of struggle. The expansion of the means of communication and the greater use of television and the internet increases the possibility of outsider intervention, and hence affects the conduct of partisans who seek external support, or at least to deny support to the adversary. American NGOs have helped develop and promulgate ways of conducting struggles that tend to avert their destructive escalation. This is notable in the cases using nonviolent methods of conflict transformation, which are discussed in this and subsequent chapters.

These eight trends in many ways are conducive to applications of the constructive conflict approach. However, there are also aspects of many of them that tend to yield destructive conflicts. For example, the speed and magnitude of the changes can disrupt established social conventions, producing distress, anger, and destructive contention. They neither ensure progress toward constructive conflict management nor condemn humanity to increasingly destructive conflicts.

Perspectives of Clinton Administration and of American Public

Some observations are warranted about the Clinton administration's foreign affairs perspectives and the American public's foreign policy orientations. They are the setting for Americans' engagement in foreign conflicts in the last years of the twentieth century.

CLINTON ADMINISTRATION'S INTERNATIONAL PERSPECTIVES

George H. W. Bush had been president in the few years of transition from a bipolar to a unipolar world. Bill Clinton became president in a world in which the United States was the only superpower and the world system shaped by the Cold War was gone. His administration would have to help determine what the U.S. role should be in the emerging new global system.

The Clinton administration's international actions were in many ways aligned with the many long-term global developments discussed earlier. Bill Clinton and members of his administration embraced the centrality of global economic affairs, and specifically favoring freer foreign trade as well as expanding American foreign investments. Thus, they energetically and successfully won public and congressional support for the North American Free Trade Agreement with Canada and Mexico.[18] Clinton's victories were achieved with Republican support, while many Democrats opposed the treaty. Opposition was based on trade union concerns about threats to American jobs and working conditions and also on public concerns about damaging the environment.

The new president faced human-rights tragedies in Somalia, Rwanda, Haiti and Yugoslavia. In the election campaign and in his selection of foreign policy officials, Clinton emphasized the American role in the world to advocate for democracy and human rights.[19] In this regard, he distinguished his approach from his predecessor,

George H. W. Bush, who adhered to a more traditional realist approach. Clinton also distinguished his approach from that of some Left segments of the Democratic Party by emphasizing security in a military sense and signaling an assertive American role in the world.

His initial foreign policy appointments were largely drawn from the Carter administration, but not its highest ranking members. For secretary of state, Clinton chose Warren Christopher, who had served as deputy to Carter's secretary of state, Cyrus Vance. Madeline Albright was chosen to be ambassador to the UN (upgraded to cabinet rank) and she went on to serve as secretary of state in Clinton's second term. Other major appointments were made from other arenas of experience and links to Clinton. Les Aspin, chairman of the House Armed Services Committee, was chosen to serve as secretary of defense, but was replaced within a year by his deputy, William Perry, who also had served in the Carter administration. Several members of the executive branch favored humanitarian intervention; they included National Security adviser Anthony Lake, and in the State Department, Albright and Richard Holbrooke.

There is evidence that elite civilians without military experience tend to be more hawkish in the use of military force, including more supportive of humanitarian interventionist foreign policy goals, compared to elite military officers or civilians with military experience.[20] This is dramatically illustrated by General Colin Powell's exchange with Albright when he was Chairman of the Joint Chiefs of Staff during Clinton's first year as president. When he was explaining to civilian leaders his views on when and how to use military force, Albright asked in frustration, "What is the point of this superb military that you're always talking about if we can't use it?"[21]

On the whole, there were considerable continuities in the foreign policies preferred by the Clinton administration with those of George H. W. Bush. From the outset, Clinton and his foreign policy team were strongly inclined to work with and through IGOs, notably NATO. Efforts to work internationally through the UN were often thwarted by Republican distrust and lack of confidence in the UN, most prominently by Senator Jesse Helms.

Clinton's commitment to international norms relating to human rights was exemplified by expressions of regret regarding previous U.S. foreign policy actions. For example, on a visit to Guatemala in March 1999, he said, "For the United States, it is important that I state clearly that support for military forces and intelligence units which engaged in violence and widespread repression was wrong, and the United States must not repeat that mistake."[22]

Clinton, as a Democrat, wanted to avoid appearing weak on national security issues, since Republicans often made that charge. He wanted to demonstrate that he was willing to use military force and he stood with the troops.[23] Significantly, Clinton had no precise foreign policy program or doctrine, as he was focused on domestic and particularly economic concerns. In these regards, he had a sympathetic American public.

At the same time, U.S. military power remained immense, and after the Cold War, relatively stronger than ever. One indicator of this is the size of its military expenditures; in 1993 it was $463,504 million, in constant 2011 U.S. dollars.[24] No other country spent anything close to that amount. Russia's spending had fallen to only $63,822 million; and China's spending was still small, only $23,454 million; France's expenditures were $67,991 million; and the United Kingdom expended $53,046 million, all in constant 2011 U.S. dollars.

AMERICAN PUBLIC'S FOREIGN POLICY VIEWS

In general, the American public had favorable views of the UN and supported cooperating with it. In June 1995, 66% of the public viewed it favorably. This is a higher percentage favorable than of the U.S. Congress (53%) or of NATO (61%).[25] Interestingly, there was some volatility in the favorability percentage; for example, 76% favored the UN in July 1994. Differences among self-identified political party adherents were not as great as might be expected by attending to political party leaders. In June 1995, 75% of the Democrats viewed the UN favorably, compared to 63% of Republicans and 66% of Independents. Importantly, it has generally been the case that the American public wanted U.S. foreign policy to strengthen the American economy and gave low priority to promoting democracy abroad.[26]

GROWTH OF THE NEOCONSERVATIVE PERSPECTIVE

The American foreign policy consensus that characterized much of the early periods of the Cold War was challenged, however, by influential Democrats and Republicans who urged greater militancy against the Soviet Union and then greater American assertiveness in the world after its demise. They came to be called neoconservatives, or neocons.[27] Many neocons had direct and indirect connections with Senator Henry "Scoop" Jackson, a strongly anti-Communist Democrat. They were more radical than most Republicans in over-estimating Soviet military capabilities, opposing arms control agreements, and advocating large increases in U.S. military spending.[28] Many of them became Reagan Republicans, some serving in his administration while others were employed by conservative think tanks and journals.

Soon, neocons included the next generation of militant conservative Republicans who never had been Democrats. They favored remaking the world in America's image, and might be better designated as "democratic imperialists."[29] The end of the cold war, which the neocons regarded as a defeat of the Soviet Union due to the hardline policies that they had advocated, prompted them to set new goals for the United States. Again, these exceeded what many other Republicans, including president George H. W. Bush, thought were realistic. Many conservatives tend to be traditional "realists," believing in the importance of power relations, particularly military power, and eschewing idealistic concerns. Some of them may be termed assertive nationalists, wishing to use American power to maintain American preeminence. They tend to view the world from a narrow U.S-centric point of view, according primacy to American interests and values. This is associated with a belief in American exceptionalism, which holds that its special nature gives it a privileged role in the world.

In 1990, Richard Cheney, then the secretary of defense, set up a group to draft a post–Cold War strategy; the group consisted of Paul Wolfowitz, the deputy secretary of defense; Lewis Libby, Cheney's chief of staff, and Eric Edelman, a foreign policy adviser to Cheney.[30] A draft was leaked to the *New York Times* in March 1992, and the subsequent controversy resulted in a more moderate version.[31] The earlier draft proposed a new order based on "convincing potential competitors that they need not aspire to a greater role or pursue a more aggressive posture to protect their legitimate interests." The new draft reflected much less sense of threat from other powers and envisaged more international cooperation with other countries.

In 1997, some members of the neocon network formed a new advocacy group, the Project for the New American Century. William Kristol chaired the project, with Robert Kagan, Devon Gaffney Cross, Bruce P. Jackson, and John R. Bolton serving as directors. In September 2000, it released a report, "Rebuilding America's Defenses," maintaining that the basic tenets of the earlier Pentagon draft were sound.[32] U.S. global dominance should be so great that it could not be challenged by other powers. It laid out a doctrine that could be drawn upon by a new Republican administration with sympathetic leaders, under the right circumstances. Those leaders and circumstances arose after September 11, 2001 (as examined in the next chapter).

Several conservative think tanks had growing influence in the second half of the twentieth century. In the mid-1950s, the American Enterprise Institute for Public Policy Research began its expansion into a highly influential center where conservative intellectuals and political leaders could gather and produce books and op-ed pieces advocating limiting the U.S. government and other conservative concerns. The Heritage Foundation was founded in 1973 by persons dissatisfied with Richard Nixon's embrace of the "liberal consensus" and the non-polemical, cautious nature of existing think tanks. These conservative think tanks operate with very large budgets; for example, the Heritage Foundation had an operating budget of $32.5 million in 2000.[33]

Unlike more traditional research and policy centers, these conservative think tanks concentrate on the dissemination of a point of view. They produce policy-oriented op-ed pieces, magazine articles, appearances on television, and well publicized books. Some groups of Democrats have founded policy centers that are intended to counter the activities of the predominately conservative centers. The Progressive Policy Institute, affiliated with the Democratic Leadership Council (DLC), is one example.[34] The DLC was founded in 1985 and promotes the "Third Way," for governance in the networked new economy of the twenty-first century. Bill Clinton has been highly identified with the DLC, which he chaired, as has Senator Joseph Lieberman, former House Democratic leader Richard Gephardt of Missouri, and Senator Evan Bayh of Indiana.

American Intervention Challenges

This section centers on American engagements that were characterized by U.S. officials as largely humanitarian interventions in contested circumstances. Unlike interventions in the Cold War, the interventions were generally justified in terms of countering large-scale violations of human rights, mass violence, or political oppression. In some such cases, it would seem necessary to threaten or to employ U.S. military force. In these circumstances, the furtherance of American values and interests is likely to be an important concern for many Americans supporting the intervention, but sometimes little acknowledged.

SOMALIA INTERVENTION

In December 1992, George H. W. Bush had ordered U.S. military forces to land in Mogadishu to protect the delivery of humanitarian supplies. Bill Clinton had campaigned emphasizing humanitarian concerns, multilateralism and peacemaking and after his election he seemed prepared to be more assertive.[35] Increased fighting among Somali factions suggested to Clinton administration officials that the previous U.S. plan was too limited to be effective. This resulted in the UN Security Council passing Resolution 814 in March 1993, which expanded UN responsibilities in Somalia. U.S. Ambassador to the UN Albright proclaimed, "We will embark on the unprecedented enterprise aimed at nothing less than the restoration of an entire country as a proud, functioning and viable member of the community of nations."[36]

Although progress was made in distributing humanitarian aid, UN and U.S. peacekeepers experienced more military clashes with Somali militias, particularly one led by Mohammed Farrah Aidid, the dominant figure in Mogadishu. Momentously, on June 5, 1993, Aidid's forces attacked a UN unit of Pakistani soldiers, killing 23 of them. This was vehemently condemned by the UN Security Council and Clinton. The commander of the UN forces, Jonathan Howe, a retired U.S. admiral, issued an order to arrest Aidid, and a campaign to capture Aidid was undertaken by UN and U.S. forces.

By now, dissent was growing in the United States. Notably, Democratic Senator Robert Byrd said it was time for Americans to come home. Former president Jimmy Carter warned that some reconciliation with Aidid was necessary to end the U.S. mission in Somalia. Furthermore, Clinton himself was finding the foreign policy matters were a diversion and hindered advancing his domestic agenda.[37]

On the ground in Somalia, however, the fighting escalated. On October 3, an airborne U.S. Army force in Mogadishu attempted to seize two of Aidid's high-ranking officers. Somali militia and armed civilian fighters shot down two Black Hawk helicopters. The subsequent rescue operation to secure and recover the crews of both helicopters resulted in a battle with 18 U.S. deaths and 80 wounded. Most vividly, CNN recorded Somalis cheering as the body of a marine was dragged through the streets. There was no outcry for retaliation, but there were calls for the United States to withdraw from Somalia. Clinton proposed a more forceful protection of assistance for six months, to be followed by a stronger UN intervention. He also said it was not America's job to rebuild Somalia society.[38]

In retrospect, the UN and the United States had misdiagnosed the situation on the ground and had expanded the goals of the intervention without having the requisite capabilities and commitment to achieve them. Although thousands of lives were saved by the intervention, the failure of achieving its expanded goals impacted future U.S. responses to humanitarian crises.

Many Republicans and particularly the neocons charged that Clinton's assertive multilateralism was misguided. They also condemned his efforts at nation-building in Somali and pointed to his failure, perhaps inconsistently, as vindication of their own views. Intense Republican partisanship hampered constructive decision-making, as discussed later. The problems with the U.S. intervention in Somalia contributed to Clinton's decision not to intervene a year later to halt the genocide in Rwanda.

RWANDAN GENOCIDE

The United States did not intervene significantly as conditions in Rwanda deteriorated and descended into a massive genocide. Contention in Rwanda between the majority Hutus and the minority Tutsis goes back to the arbitrary ethnic classification instituted during German and then Belgian colonial rule. Ethnic strife grew in struggles for political control between Hutus and Tutsis exacerbated by their fight for independence. Following Rwanda's independence in 1962, there were massacres in 1973, 1991, and 1992.

In 1992, the Organization of African Unity (OAU) managed to mediate a ceasefire between the Rwandan government and the Rwandan Patriotic Front (RPF), which was based in Uganda and consisting largely of descendants of the Tutsis who had been driven from Rwanda. After more fighting in early 1993, the presidents of Rwanda and Uganda requested that the UN Security Council authorize the U.N. Observer Mission Uganda-Rwanda. Its mandate was to serve along their common border and halt military assistance to Rwanda. A more ambitious peace effort was undertaken by the OAU.[39] France, Germany, Belgium, and the United States had observer status. After thirteen months of negotiations, the Rwandan government and the RPF signed the Arusha Accords in August 1993. They agreed to form a transitional government, including the RPF; Tutsi and Hutu military forces would be integrated; refugees would be able to return; and a UN peacekeeping force would be established

Many Hutu political and economic leaders, however, opposed this plan and tried to ensure its failure. For example, some of them supported a new radio station, which in June 1993 began broadcasting programs inciting hate and violence against Tutsis. When the genocide began, the station gave instructions on whom and how to kill Tutsis and moderate Hutus.[40]

The UN Assistance Mission in Rwanda was authorized by the Security Council on October 5, 1993. The mission, totaling 2,500 soldiers and military observers, was deployed in Rwanda on November 1, 1993. But the political leaders failed to progress in implementing the Arusha Accords. On April 6, 1994, the presidents of Rwanda, Juvénal Habyarimana, and of Burindi, Cyprien Ntaryamira, were killed when the plane they were on was shot down as it prepared to land in Kigali, Rwanda.[41]

Almost immediately after the assassination, anti-Tutsi militias, notably the Interahamwe, began killing Tutsi and moderate Hutus with machetes and other simple weapons. The killing escalated and lasted one hundred days, during which somewhere between 800,000 and 1,000,000 Tutsis and moderate Hutus were murdered. The killings stopped when the Tutsi-led RPF rebel movement, headed by Paul Kagame, captured Rwanda's capital, Kigali.[42]

Could the United States have prevented the genocide or helped end it earlier? Most discussions of this question focus on U.S. military intervention to stop the killing and the great political obstacles to any such undertaking. I think attention also should be given to possible earlier actions by the U.S. and other external actors.

When implementation of the Arusha Accords stalled, immediate strong and creative engagement by the United States and the UN might have forestalled the assassinations and genocide. The UN assistance mission might have been greatly
strengthened and pressure might have been brought against the would-be spoilers of
the Accord. The rising anti-Tutsi hate campaign might have been countered, as local
organizations asked, by condemnations and warnings.[43] Working more closely with
the RPF might have conveyed that spoilers would lose more by failing to agree with
the proposed transition than they would by going along with it. Promises of economic benefits and warnings of economic costs might have influenced some of the
wealthier Hutu extremists.

Once killings started, various other actions might have had some impact on reducing and ending the killing. The radio programs inciting the genocide could have
been jammed. Warnings of forthcoming international trials for perpetrators of the
genocide might have been issued. The military campaign of the RPF would not have
been hampered, and even might have been assisted under appropriate conditions. In
general, finding local people and organizations that opposed the genocide might
have avoided or at least reduced the great tragedy that befell Rwanda.

HAITI INTERVENTION

Haiti posed another pressing foreign crisis for Clinton. After decades of tyrannical rule,
a relatively free presidential election had been held in December 1990 and a populist
Catholic priest, Jean-Bertrand Aristide, won. But he was soon overthrown by a military
junta. The Bush administration had failed to restore Aristide to the presidency, and
Clinton had campaigned that he would. As president, Clinton led in imposing severe
economic sanctions against Haiti's ruling junta. Simply blocking the ongoing flow of
Haitian refugees was morally and politically difficult to sustain after campaigning to
end it. The Congressional Black Caucus and members of Clinton's National Security
Council believed restoring Aristide would be highly desirable for America's interests.[44]

Clinton obtained UN assistance in pressuring the Haitian junta to yield, and the
UN named Dante Caputo its special envoy. To further demonstrate his resolve,
Clinton invited Aristide to the White House in March 1993. A few days afterward,
Caputo went to Haiti and the junta leaders agreed "in principle" to yield power, but
only Junta stonewalling followed. In May, the United States obtained support for a
Security Council resolution ordering an oil embargo, which resulted in meetings in
July that included General Raul Cedras, the coup leader. After very tough negotia-
tions, the Governors Island Accord was agreed upon, which Aristide accepted. Aristide would return to power, in steps, and Cedras would resign but not be brought
to trial.

Instead of implementing the Accord, however, the regime renewed acts of terror in Haiti. In October, when a shipload of American and Canadian military engineers attempted to land, they were prevented from coming ashore by mobs shouting "Somalia! Somalia!" Rather than taking military action, president Clinton sought and obtained a UN Security Council resolution tightening the embargo of Haiti. After months of debates within the administration, on September 15, 1994, Clinton issued a public warning to the military regime to leave or be forced from power. As the U.S. invasion force was dispatched to transfer power from the Haitian military rulers, Jimmy Carter went to Haiti and met with Cedras to obtain his resignation. Carter was joined by Senator Sam Nunn and former chairman of the Joint Chiefs of Staff Colin Powell, and they successfully arranged a transfer of power. The Haitian military leadership went into exile.[45] American troops landed unopposed and Aristide returned in triumph.

Aristide was restored as president by a credible threat of force and an escape route for the dictatorial regime leaders. American troops remained in Haiti until April 1996. This did not end the tragic political problems and natural disasters the Haitian people have suffered. But within the constraints of the circumstances, Americans could claim some benefits from the intervention for both countries.

WARS IN YUGOSLAVIA

While these American engagements in Somalia and Haiti were underway, terrible wars and large-scale atrocities were occurring among the peoples of the former Yugoslavia. The early stages of these tragedies were noted in Chapter 4. The immediate matter confronting Clinton was the terrible situation in Bosnia and Herzegovina, a former constituent republic of Yugoslavia with Serb, Croat and Muslim populations. Bosnian Serbs had taken military control of 70% of the country, accompanied by ethnic cleansing in that territory. A new mediation effort had begun, under Cyrus Vance, appointed by the UN, and former British foreign secretary David Lord Owen, replacing Peter Carrington, representing the European Community (EC). They proposed a peace settlement dividing Bosnia into ten cantons under a nominal central government in Sarajevo.[46] Initially, it seemed that leaders of the different ethnic communities in Bosnia thought the plan was acceptable. But it was not supported by the Clinton administration, claiming that it rewarded Serb aggression. The division actually assigned the relatively more valuable territory to predominantly Muslim cantons. It appeared that Clinton preferred an American solution to one sponsored by the EC and the UN. Better terms for Muslims and Croats in Bosnia, however, would not seem possible without significant military intervention on the ground, for which there was very little American support.

In early January 1993, Alija Izetbegovic, leader of the Bosnian Muslims, after visiting with officials of the incoming Clinton administration, thought that the United States would provide troops and gain better terms, so he raised his requirements to accept the Vance-Owen plan.[47] Granting his wishes then made the plan unacceptable to the Bosnian Serbs and the plan failed. Richard Holbrooke, in a memorandum to Christopher and Lake, on January 13, 1993, argued: "If the Vance-Owen plan is rejected, we must face the fact that the negotiating track is effectively dead – and using it as an excuse for inaction or insufficient action is no longer acceptable."[48]

Members of the Clinton administration discussed alternative policies, with little enthusiasm for any of them. One possibility was to lift the arms embargo against Bosnia and "threaten NATO air strikes against Serbian forces."[49] Unconvincingly put forward for support from European allies, the plan was not supported and was soon discarded. Alternative strategies seemed constrained by focusing on different ways of intervening militarily or to be largely unengaged. American leadership might have been more effective by having been more supportive of a regional solution than striving for greater U.S. prominence.

Gradually, in early 1995, a new strategy emerged. The United States would help the Croatian and Bosnian Muslim forces obtain more arms, which enabled the better equipped and trained Croatian forces to begin driving Serb forces from the Croatian territory they had seized earlier. In July 1995, the horrendous massacre in Srebrenica, Bosnia outraged the American public, demonstrated the failure of past international policies, and increased the conviction of Clinton advisers that forceful U.S. intervention was necessary. In April 1993, the UN had declared a few Bosnian locations, including Srebrenica, "safe areas" under UN protection against Bosnian Serb attack. The United Nations Protection Force (UNPROFOR) was inadequate for the task, but it was the best that could be agreed upon. Furthermore, over time, Bosnian Muslims used Srebrenica as a base from which they launched attacks against Serbs. In July 1995, a contingent of 400 lightly armed Dutch peacekeepers, part of UNPROFOR, was unable to prevent the town's capture, and a grotesque massacre took place which saw the killing over 8,000 men and boys.

Widespread revulsion to the massacre strengthened the views of U.S. officials who had favored military intervention. The United States supported the Croatian large-scale military offensive, begun August 4, 1995, to capture the Serb-controlled Krajina area within Croatia. They were brutally effective, and then joined with Bosnian forces to advance further. Beginning on August 30 and continuing for two weeks, NATO launched an extensive air campaign against Serb military positions in Bosnia. The campaign was clearly U.S. dominated, and was not brought to the UN Security Council for authorization. American leadership and NATO relevance was forcefully demonstrated.

There is evidence that U.S. leaders pushed for bombing Serb positions as a way to make evident NATO's relevance even after the Cold War had ended.[50] This was particularly important at a time when the European Community/European Union was showing an inclination to act independently. Moreover, the newly unified Germany had joined France in encouraging more independence for the EU. Indeed, the EU began adopting measures to implement the Common Foreign and Security Policy. This could be seen in Washington as a challenge to the dominance of NATO, and a reason for U.S. leaders wishing to retain primacy in European and world affairs to demonstrate the importance of NATO.[51]

In the context of the advances on the ground and the bombings, the U.S. undertook a diplomatic effort to reach a comprehensive peace settlement among Croatia, the Federal Republic of Yugoslavia (Serbia and Montenegro) and Bosnia-Herzegovina, including its three communities: Bosnian Muslims, Bosnian Croats, and Bosnian Serbs. The U.S. negotiating team was led by Richard Holbrooke. For all of the coercive power that the United States might exercise it could not impose a settlement. As is generally true, the leaders of the antagonistic sides had to agree to the same settlement if one was to be reached. Mediators, as discussed in Chapter 1, may provide a wide variety of services that assist adversaries to discover, construct, or accept a negotiated settlement to a conflict. The services include facilitation, such as assisting each side to better understand the concerns and underlying needs that drive their adversaries' actions and discovering trade-offs that make a deal mutually acceptable. Other services may be adding resources to make a deal more attractive and likely to be honored, or pointing to losses and hardships if a deal is not reached.

In this case, after years of terrible warfare, the failure of the U.S. mediating effort would most likely mean continuing warfare and great suffering for many people on each side. More particularly, the tide of the ongoing fighting had turned against the Bosnian Serbs and of Serbia so that a likely peace settlement would require some territorial concession by them since they had previously violently extended their borders. Furthermore, the more powerful Serbia, led by Milošević, had interests distinct from those of the Bosnian Serbs and ensured their concession for his interests as head of Serbia. These interests including ending the severe economic sanctions imposed upon Serbia. Holbrooke and the U.S. team applied many of these mediation practices and took advantage of the structural conditions to work for cease-fires first and then a peace settlement that all sides accepted. Although Holbrooke and the team did not impose a settlement, there was strong guidance reflecting their ideas of what was fair and durable, and not inconsistent with U.S. interests.[52]

Beginning in late August, the U.S. team began to shuttle among the leaders of the three Bosnian communities, Milošević, and other major stakeholders. With the NATO bombing continuing, they prepared a statement to be signed by the Bosnian

Serb leaders declaring a cease-fire and the lifting of the siege of Sarajevo. Milošević helped convince the Bosnian Serb leaders to sign it on September 14. With additional shuttle diplomacy, a comprehensive cease-fire agreement was announced by Clinton on October 5, 1995.

Finally, the primary leaders of the contending Balkan entities were brought together for face-to-face negotiations to reach a final peace settlement, meeting at the Wright-Patterson Air Force Base in Dayton, Ohio, on November 1, 1995. Holbrooke led the U.S. delegation and directed the negotiations; UN officials were not present and European representatives attended, but did not have a substantive role. The negotiators remained in isolation for three weeks, climaxed by a U.S. ultimatum that the settlement be signed by all parties or the United States would end its mediation. It was signed by the delegation leaders on November 21.

The peace agreement established the Federation of Bosnia-Herzegovina and of the Republika Srpska. The Federation is highly decentralized, but it retains a central government, with a rotating state presidency. The Republika Srpska's population is largely Serbian; overall, the Serbs were allocated 49% of Bosnia, compared to 43% in the 1992 Vance-Owen plan.[53] A multinational Implementation Force (IFOR) was established under NATO, not UN, direction, and with a substantial U.S. contingent. Following the settlement, large-scale violence did not recur, but little reconciliation and unity was achieved and U.S. troops remained with the IFOR in Bosnia. The years of brutal warfare after the failure to reach a settlement in 1992 probably have contributed to the hatreds and mistrust obstructing reconciliation and collaboration. A less-coercive and more balanced U.S. intervention, which was more multilaterally shaped and implemented, might have produced an earlier peace that did not require an ongoing external military presence. Of course, the greatest responsibility for the prolonged warfare and the gross human rights violations in the wars falls to many of the leaders on the different sides in the fighting. This was attested to at the trials conducted in The Hague by the International Criminal Tribunal for the Former Yugoslavia.

Soon after the fighting in the former Yugoslavia had subsided, the long-standing conflict relating to Kosovo began to escalate. As noted in Chapter 4, in 1989 ethnic Albanians began a nonviolent resistance struggle against the Serbian government's effort to assimilate them into Serbia. The leading organization in the struggle was the Democratic League of Kosovo (LDK), led by Ibrahim Rugova. Their strategy was designed to achieve four goals: to contest the legitimacy of Serb Institutions in Kosovo, maintain Albanian community life in Kosovo, avoid provoking Serb repression or being provoked into violence, and mobilize international support. As a result, in the future Kosovo would become independent.[54]

International attention was soon gained, but proved misleading. No significant support was received from the United States. The LDK actions were impressively effective in maintaining Albanian community life; for example, by sustaining their own educational system. By 1996, however, there was increasing criticism among some Kosovo Albanians of Rogova and his patient, prudent approach. The Dayton conference had ignored Kosovo and it seemed his nonviolent approach would not succeed.

Greater attention and authority accorded earlier to the nonviolent LDK by the United States, European countries, and international organizations might have averted the destructive escalation that happened. Instead, a rival approach and organization emerged in Kosovo, the Kosovo Liberation Army (KLA). It began to launch attacks on Serb civilians that would provoke Serb repression, and in that it was successful. Initially, the U.S. government identified the KLA as a terrorist organization, but soon also objected to the Serbian government's repression. That changed to a censuring of Serbia, as it waged counter-insurgency attacks against the KLA.

In October 1998, Clinton sent Holbrooke to meet with Milošević and arrange a cease-fire of the escalating fighting.[55] Holbrooke insisted that Milošević stop offensive actions in Kosovo and pull back his forces, under international supervision, or Serbia would be bombed. Milošević agreed to the pullback and did comply. However, the KLA seized this opportunity to launch a new offensive, which had some NATO and OSCE assistance.[56] Serbia undertook a counteroffensive. As a result of this surge in fighting, the Albanian civilians in Kosovo suffered greatly.

To halt the fighting, the Contact Group (the United States, the United Kingdom, France, Italy, Germany, and Russia) organized a peace conference, which was held at Rambouillet, near Paris, in February 1999. The U.S. negotiators made it clear that if Serbia refused an agreement the United States deemed acceptable, Serbia would be bombed. Serbian negotiators accepted most of the proposed political elements of an agreement, including regional autonomy for Kosovo and the end of repression there. On February 23, the Contact mediators delivered the full text of the proposed agreement. It included a Military Annex, according to which NATO personnel would have unrestricted access not only to Kosovo but the entire Federal Republic of Yugoslavia.[57] Not surprisingly, that was rejected by the Serbian negotiators. There is evidence that the U.S. government wanted a Serbian rejection so that NATO military action could ensue, demonstrating the capacity and value of NATO.[58]

On March 24, 1999, NATO planes, 70% of which were U.S. aircraft, began bombing operations in Serbia and Kosovo. This was justified as responsive to a humanitarian emergency, but it was undertaken without UN authority and the result was a humanitarian calamity. Serbian repression and ethnic cleansing of ethnic Albanians in Kosovo was unleashed; in the course of the war, 850,000 ethnic Albanians (half of the population) were driven out of Kosovo. What was supposed to be a short war to bring peace went on with escalating bombing until June 10. The terms of the eventual settlement to end them were hardly different than those Serbia was ready to accept at the conference in Rambouillet. It differed in that NATO would not have the authority to move anywhere in Serbia.[59]

This interpretation of U.S. policies in addressing the challenges of the breakup of Yugoslavia suggests that the policies were often significantly directed to enhance the role of NATO and of the United States in Europe. Of course, the many people involved in deciding and implementing U.S. actions regarding Yugoslavia differed in their judgments and they changed over time. Usually, they were justified by the protagonists as advancing humanitarian considerations and the alternative was disastrous inaction. This account suggests more constructive alternative actions that might have resulted in averting or shortening the Yugoslav wars and reducing the deaths and displacements related to them. The value of bolstering NATO and American dominance as a U.S. goal also should be considered. Interestingly, that has not been part of the public debate. Neither Republican nor Democratic political leaders would claim such reasons to justify the actions taken. Universal humanitarian reasons were emphasized to justify military intervention.

In any case, even if the goal of advancing U.S. primacy were appropriately salient, the actions taken probably served them less well than would the application of more constructive alternatives. Earlier reliance on nonmilitary options and collective actions with other governments and international organizations might have better served long-term, broad American interests. The independent countries after the breakup of Yugoslavia may have become more successfully multiethnic than they became after the long brutal wars that did occur. In the case of Serbia, the American bombing that killed and frightened civilians probably set back the growing opposition to Milošević. It contributed to the estrangement from the United States among many Serbs, who viewed the United States as having attacked a sovereign country and intervened in its domestic political affairs.[60] Finally, more constructive policies would have provided less precedent for resorting to unilateral military action, which eased the ill-fated path to the invasion of Iraq during George W. Bush's presidency.

As it was, relatively constructive U.S. policies sometimes were pursued in the former Yugoslavia. For example, the United States aided local groups to oust Milošević from power by contributing to his electoral defeat in September 2000 and his resignation.[61] Political opposition to Milošević had been widespread in Serbia, but it was highly fragmented, offering no programmatic alternative.[62]

In 1998, university students, disgusted with Milošević and past failures to mobilize against him, adopted a new strategy. They relied on a nonhierarchical structure to evade governmental repression or co-optation. They conducted well-planned performances mocking the government; mobilized people throughout the countryside, not focusing on Belgrade; and maintained nonviolent discipline.[63] They operated with the name Otpor, meaning "resistance." Otpor insisted that the opposition parties agree on a single candidate to oppose Milošević in national elections that Milošević was sure he could control. Members of Otpor improvised their strategy and many tactics, but were delighted to discover that the core ideas of nonviolent action had been written by Gene Sharp (discussed in Chapter 3).[64]

The U.S. and other Western governments aided many local initiatives to increase the capacity of citizens to hold valid democratic elections in Serbia.[65] The U.S. government was the largest funder of these initiatives, largely through the U.S. Agency for International Development and the State Department. American support also was provided through the National Endowment for Democracy and many nongovernmental organizations.[66] For example, from mid-1999 to late 2000, approximately $40 million was spent by the American public and private groups on democracy-promoting programs in Serbia.

Opposition political parties united in choosing Vojislav Kostunica to run against Milošević in the national elections on September 24, 2000. The polling stations were carefully monitored by opposition observers and the voting results were quickly sent to a central location so the outcome of the election would be immediately announced. Kostunica decisively defeated Milošević, but Milošević refused to accept the results. On October 5, protestors from across Serbia drove and marched to join together in Belgrade. The massive nonviolent protests overwhelmed the government forces blocking highways into Belgrade and they went on to seize the parliament building. Milošević resigned two days later.

Obviously, the overthrow of Milošević and the establishment of democratic electoral procedures were the work of the Democratic Opposition of Serbia, civil society organizations, and of many university students, workers, and other people throughout Serbia. It followed years of wars and terrible losses by the Serbian people. But the assistance from the United States and other Western countries contributed to channeling dissatisfactions regarding Milošević's rule into a nonviolent struggle for a democratic transformation. Several features of this intervention help explain its effectiveness. The providers of assistance worked closely with local organizations, giving money directly to locals and functioning in a decentralized manner. Furthermore, the scale of assistance was relatively large and sustained and the actions of diverse providers were well coordinated.

Adversarial Relations

The chapter now turns to conflicts where the U.S. government confronted entities it regarded primarily as adversaries. It is also noteworthy that these were all asymmetrical conflicts, in which the United States was the more powerful party. America faced no enemy that posed an existential threat to it. There were some adversaries in the 1990s, however, that were viewed as damaging or threatening important American interests in the Middle East or elsewhere. This analysis focuses on America's emerging conflict with al Qaeda and other militant Islamic groups that perpetrated violent attacks on Americans. I also discuss the conflicts that continued when Clinton took office as president, between the United States and Iran, Iraq, and North Korea.

During Clinton's terms as president, Americans suffered several deadly attacks, which were officially regarded as terrorist attacks. As discussed in Chapter 3, the meaning of the word "terrorism" is problematic and lacks universal agreement. Nevertheless, generally I will use the term as it is applied by U.S. officials. My discussion centers on attacks upon American citizens and interests, particularly in the Middle East or by groups largely based there between 1993 and 2000.

During the 1990s such attacks between the United States and transnational non-state organizations were increasing, particularly by militant Islamic organizations acting covertly. As discussed at the outset of this chapter, transnational nongovernmental organizations are not territorially bounded, but their members reside within and move across territories over which governments claim to exercise legitimate control.

Covert violent attacks were also conducted by agents or organizations controlled by governments. Some governments executed such activities in association with non-state actors operating in other countries against the governments there. When the targets of such operations are officials or non-combatants and the purpose is regarded to be frightening or intimidating people or governments, the actions tend to be regarded by the U.S. government as state-supported terrorism.

TRANSFORMING LIBYAN RELATIONS

When Clinton took office in January 1993, the U.S. government was engaged in procedures to bring to justice the persons responsible for blowing up Pan Am 103 on December 21, 1988. The plane was flying from London to New York and crashed in Lockerbie, Scotland.

An intensive international police investigation was made during the presidency of George H. W. Bush. It yielded evidence implicating two agents of the Libyan government, Abdelbaset Ali Mohmed a1 Megrahi and Al Amin Khalifa Fhimah. In November 1991, the U.S. and British governments charged them with the Pan Am 103 bombing and sought their extradition. In October 1991, a French court had issued warrants to arrest the Libyan agents charged with the 1989 bombing of a French airliner, UTA 772. In January 1992, the American, British, and French governments obtained UN Security Council Resolution 731 calling for Libyan cooperation with investigations of the bombings.

In February, Libyan president Muammar Gaddafi, to avoid his country receiving sanctions, offered to turn over the UTA suspects to a French court and the Lockerbie suspects to an international tribunal. The U.S. and British governments insisted that the Lockerbie suspects be tried in U.S. or British courts. Gaddafi then offered to yield the suspects to the Arab League, which was also rejected by the American and British governments. On March 31, 1992, the UN Security Council adopted Resolution 748, imposing limited sanctions on Libya, including embargos on air travel and of sales of aircraft and of arms.

Under pressure from the families of the victims of Pan Am 103's destruction, the Clinton administration pressed for progress in bringing the alleged perpetrators of the bombing to justice.[67] On November 11, 1993, the UN Security Council adopted Resolution 883, which tightened aviation sanctions, froze Libyan government assets, and banned some oil-transporting equipment.

Nelson Mandela, president of South Africa, later helped advance negotiations to lift the sanctions against Libya.[68] In October 1997, Mandela went to Libya and expressed gratitude for the Libyan support in the South African anti-apartheid struggle. In visits to Washington, London, and Tripoli, he conveyed the views of Gaddafi to American and British officials and theirs to him, communicating his own recognition of each side's sense of morality regarding the Lockerbie case. This helped create a moral space for Gaddafi to negotiate and enabled Mandela to strongly urge Gaddafi to speak respectfully of the United Nations, as well as to work for all sides' compliance to the agreements that were reached. Mandela effectively used his resources of stature, moral authority, and independence.

Gaddafi acted more respectably, not supporting terrorism and improving his relations with Arab and African governments. This reduced the chances of renewing Resolution 883, which required review every four months. Therefore, the U.S government came up with a new option. The trial would be held in the Netherlands before a Scottish judge and under Scottish law. After more negotiations, in March 1999 Gaddafi agreed to surrender the two suspects and UN sanctions would be suspended (but not lifted). The trial was held in January 2001 and the defendant Megrahi was found guilty of murder and sentenced to prison for life, while his co-defendant was not found guilty and was freed. Subsequently, as discussed in Chapter 6, Libya took further steps and restored normal relations with the United States.

ATTACKS BY AL QAEDA, 1993–1996

During Clinton's presidency, America was struck by a variety of bombing attacks, by domestic and foreign actors and by state and non-state entities. I give special attention here to al Qaeda attacks and to attacks attempted, conducted, or supported by it and by the Iranian or the Iraqi governments.

On February 26, 1993, a truck bomb exploded in the garage of the World Trade Center in New York, killing six people and injuring 1,042 people.[69] Within a few days, the FBI had amazingly retrieved the serial number of the rented truck and arrested Mohammed A. Salameh when he returned to the rental agency to collect his deposit for the truck, which he had reported was stolen. Three others involved in the attack were soon arrested, and they were tried and found guilty on March 4, 1994. One of the leaders of the attack, Ramsi Yousef, a Pakistani, had escaped and left the United States.

The FBI investigation after the attack uncovered a network in the New York metropolitan area that centered on Omar Abdel Rahman, a blind Egyptian religious leader who Egyptian authorities had sentenced for terrorism in absentia.[70] Tracking him led to a cell that was planning bombings of the Lincoln and Holland tunnels and other landmarks in the New York area. Arrests, trials, and convictions followed.

In January 1995, Manila police fortuitously located Yousef in Manila.[71] Although he escaped, his plan to place bombs in eleven 747 airliners taking off from Asia was discovered. All U.S. flights from Asia were halted for a day and searched for explosives involving contact lens cleaning fluid as well as batteries and a watch, but no bombs were found. A month later, Pakistani authorities located and arrested Yousef. He was extradited to the United States, where he was tried and found guilty in January 1998.

Unrecognized at the time, some of those linked to these attacks were connected to bin Laden and the emerging al Qaeda. Bin Laden financed the Afghan Services Bureau, which paid bills and financed activities of some of the people involved in the attacks. For example, Sheik Omar Abdel Rahman was a member of the Egyptian Islamic Jihad organization that helped form al Qaeda, and he spent time in Afghanistan with bin Laden.[72]

In addition to these legal proceedings, the Clinton administration took several measures to counter future terror attacks. Richard A. Clark was the national coordinator for counterterrorism on the National Security Council and worked intensively and skillfully to bring all relevant governmental capabilities to bear on this task.[73] Federal funding for counterterrorism rose from $5.7 billion in 1995 to $11.1 billion in 2000.[74] The FBI had increased authority to counter terrorist activities; for example, funding of terrorist groups was made a felony and wiretap rules were expanded.

By 1994, there was growing evidence in the U.S. counterterrorism community that an organization existed, associated with someone that had been identified only as a financer of terrorism, Osama bin Laden. Al Qaeda had begun to emerge in Afghanistan among a small group of Arabs who had fought alongside the Afghan mujahedeen, seeking to drive the Soviets out of Afghanistan. When the Soviets withdrew in 1989, the major Afghan mujahedeen leaders fought among themselves to form a new government in Afghanistan. The Saudi, Egyptian, Palestinian and other Arab fighters looked for other struggles to enter. Their differences in religious thinking and preferences about where to go next contributed to rivalries and factional disputes among them.[75]

When the Arab fighters dispersed from Afghanistan, bin Laden returned to Saudi Arabia and was warmly received by the public for his role in Afghanistan. But he soon became estranged from the royal family, initially because he opposed the Saudi invitation for U.S. troops to enter the country and confront the Iraqi threat. His criticism of the ruling family led to his banishment from Saudi Arabia in 1992. He was courted by the government of Sudan and formed a close relationship with Hasan al-Turabi, a major political and religious leader in Sudan. Bin Laden made large financial investments and established bases for his activities in Sudan. In April 1996 international sanctions were imposed against Sudan for its complicity in the attempted assassination of Hosni Mubarak and in terror attacks elsewhere. In response to the sanctions, the Sudanese government forced bin Laden to leave and in May he flew to Afghanistan, having lost his investments and many of his al Qaeda fighters.[76]

AL QAEDA ATTACKS, 1996–2000

After being forced out of the Sudan, bin Laden found a safe haven in Afghanistan, which in 1962, was largely controlled by the Taliban led by Mullah Mohammed Omar. Osama bin Laden and his associates interpreted elements of the Islamic tradition and circumstances to specify grievances, set corrective goals, and construct strategies to reach them that would appeal to Muslims to mobilize money and personnel to establish a transnational organization that could conduct large-scale violent activities. In August 1996, bin Laden issued a 30-page-long "Declaration of War against the Americans Occupying the Land of the Two Holy Places," published in London's *Al Quds al Arabi*. He declared:

[T]he people of Islam had suffered from aggression, iniquity and injustice imposed on them by the Zionist Crusaders alliance and their collaborators. Their blood was spilled in Palestine and Iraq.

The latest and the greatest of these aggressions . . . is the occupation of the land of the two holy Places . . . by the American Crusaders and their allies.

Death is better than life in humiliation! Some scandals and shames will never be otherwise eradicated.[77]

On February 23, 1998, bin Laden was joined by Ayman al Zawahiri and other associates in publishing the "Jihad Against Jews and Crusaders" in London's *Al Quds al Arabi*. They condemned the wrongs committed by the United States against Muslims, including:

First, that for over seven years the United States has been occupying the lands of Islam in the holiest of places, the Arabian Peninsula, plundering its riches. . . humiliating its people. . . . Second, . . . the great devastation inflicted on the Iraqi people by the crusader-Zionist alliance. . . . Third, if the Americans' aims behind these wars are religious and economic, the aim is also to serve the Jews' petty state and divert attention from its occupation of Jerusalem and murder of Muslims there. . . .

The statement continued:

On that basis, and in compliance with God's order, we issue the following fatwa to all Muslims: The ruling to kill the Americans and their allies –civilians and military – is an individual duty for every Muslim who can do it in any country in which it is possible to do it.

The recourse to violently attacking Americans reflects the limitations of the network, but was undertaken with the faith that it would provoke reactions that would win more adherents.

Following the fatwa, bin Laden gave interviews and held press conferences in Afghanistan, which gained him fame, money, and recruits from many countries. Then, a major attack was carried out: on August 7, 1998, the U.S. embassies in Kenya and Tanzania were bombed by trucks loaded with explosives. The embassy in Tanzania was severely damaged and 11 persons were killed and 85 wounded, all Africans. In Kenya, 257 persons died, including 12 Americans and some 5,000 people were injured.[78] The bombings were widely viewed by Muslims with dismay and incomprehension, since the purpose seemed unclear and would likely provoke a dreadful response. Yet that seemed to be the point: to lure the United States into Afghanistan.[79]

Again, several kinds of actions were taken by the U.S. government to counter such attacks. First, evidence was quickly marshaled that identified al Qaeda as the perpetrator and President Clinton decided that more than retaliation, the destruction of al Qaeda was the U.S. objective.

The CIA reported that a source in Afghanistan provided information of the place bin Laden and his top associates were to meet on August 20. National Security Advisor Sandy Berger was tasked to coordinate measures to launch a military attack on that date. In addition to the al Qaeda camp where the meeting was to take place, other targets were al Qaeda camps in Afghanistan; and a pharmaceutical plant in Sudan, which was suspected of being owned by bin Laden; and a chemical weapons facility.[80]

As planned, seventy-five cruise missiles were launched, but their effects on the ground were limited. The facility in the Sudan was actually a pharmaceutical plant. Bin Laden and leading al Qaeda figures were not at the camp they were expected to be. Some cruise missiles failed to detonate and some landed in Pakistan. Berger said that twenty or thirty al Qaeda men were killed, but other observers report even fewer deaths.[81]

At the time, the scandal surrounding Clinton's relationship with Monica Lewinsky was a complicating matter insofar as any military action might be viewed as driven by the desire to distract attention from the scandal. Clinton and the national security team tried to avoid letting such concerns affect the choice or timing of any actions taken. Nevertheless, many opponents of Clinton did charge the missile attacks were intended to divert attention from the scandal. On the other hand, bin Laden celebrated his survival and won more attention and admiration in some parts of the world.

Other U.S. policies were undertaken that would prove more effective in countering al Qaeda. A survey of U.S. embassies around the world was undertaken. The most vulnerable to violent attack were moved or rebuilt. Extensive operations were made within the United States and in other countries to block the flow of money to al Qaeda. This required overcoming resistance from some other governments and parts of the U.S. government and overcoming ignorance about the ways in which funds could be transferred from one place to another in the world.

These strategies recognized that the adversary was not a single person or a unitary entity. In included a core leadership group, camps and cells with fighters of varying ethnicities and interests, supporters who contributed funds and other resources, and passive admirers who might become more or less engaged. In addition, various governments, religious organizations, corporations, and advocacy groups would have their own reasons to cooperate with or to oppose al Qaeda. Each such entity might be susceptible to particular American policies. The U.S. government diplomatically conveyed an array of inducements in seeking cooperation from other governments. Much less was done however to try to influence the various publics and possible constituent parts of the al Qaeda movement. I think it is also noteworthy that relatively little was done in this period by nongovernmental religious and nonreligious organizations to reduce support for the al Qaeda movement or to propose other policies for the U.S. government to pursue to counter al Qaeda.

U.S. counterterrorism officials thought it likely that al Qaeda was planning attacks around the onset of the new millennium, and warnings of possible attacks were sent out to U.S. embassies and military bases and to all levels of law enforcement agencies in the United States.[82] A U.S. customs officer, Diane Dean, at the border between British Columbia and Washington State noticed one person in line fidgeting strangely, and when she approached him he started to run away. The man, Ahmed Ressam, was quickly apprehended. His parked car contained explosives and a map of the Los Angeles International Airport.[83] The FBI followed many leads flowing from Ressam's arrest. This included a sleeper cell in Montreal, which led to others in Boston and New York. No attacks were carried out around the turning of the millennium, despite the plots.

Law enforcement personnel were able to be effective, sometimes assisted by the not-so-skilled would-be perpetrators. However, barriers to full cooperation among the many agencies engaged in preventing terror attacks and bringing perpetrators to justice continued to exist.

In the closing months of President Clinton's second term in office, on October 12, 2000, at Aden, Yemen the *USS Cole* was rammed by two suicide attackers in a boat carrying explosives, killing seventeen U.S. sailors. Without agreement on who did it no new retaliatory action was taken.

COUNTERTERRORISM STRATEGIES

The Clinton administration's approach to countering terror attacks encompassed many inter-related strategies to prevent and to minimize the effects of such attacks. To fashion effective ways to prevent terror attacks, valid analyses of the reasons that some people undertake or support terror attacks against the United States are necessary. Of course, there are a variety of explanations, such as the grievances that some people feel and how they identify the persons responsible for their grievances. The explanations also have to do with the methods those people believe can be used to redress and reduce their grievances.

For al Qaeda leaders, fighters, donors, or fans, the grievances vary, but included a generalized sense of humiliation they attributed to American disrespect, a calculation that the U.S. protected oppressive, un-Islamic regimes such as in Egypt or Saudi Arabia, or a belief that America cooperated with Israel in denying Palestinians their rights. The recourse to violent attacks, even resulting in suicide, may flow from lack of perceived alternatives, religious beliefs, desire for revenge, payments to self, or benefits for a martyr's family.

In the longer term, American efforts to reduce the grievances and the incentives to resort to violence can be important. For example, there might have been support for schools in Pakistan that were oriented more secularly or more moderately Islamic than the schools supported by Saudi funds for teaching the strict Islam they favored. There may also have been more attention and responsiveness to moderate Islamic voices. American policy toward the Israeli-Palestinian conflict might have been more attentive to Palestinian interests and yet considerate of long-term Israeli interests. On the whole, there was relatively little attention to undertaking American policies that might undermine the attractions of al Qaeda in the Islamic world.

The greatest attention was given to intelligence and police work at the local, national, and international levels in order to interdict terror plots and to find and put on trial perpetrators of terror attacks. This improved in the course of time during Clinton's presidency. In the later years, more success was also had in cutting off donations to organizations supporting al Qaeda. Another strategy was to harden potential targets, which included making embassy buildings, large public events, and air travel more secure. An additional strategy was to inflict damage on facilities and resources of governments or localities that were havens or supports for groups that had committed terror attacks. The strategies constrained al Qaeda and did not overreact in ways that were counterproductive. On the other hand, the strategies did not yet incapacitate or gravely weaken al Qaeda.

IRANIAN RELATIONS

At the outset of president Clinton's administration, Secretary of State Christopher branded Iran an outlaw nation.[84] Improving relations was encumbered by the U.S. role in the 1953 overthrow of Iranian Prime Minister Mohammed Mossadegh, and the Iranian seizure of the U.S. embassy in 1979. More immediately, Iran aided Lebanon's Hezbollah, which had attacked Americans in the 1980s and engaged in clashes with Israeli forces in Lebanon. In May 1993, a "dual containment" policy in the Gulf was announced to limit the threats posed by both Iran and Iraq to U.S. interests.[85] The strategy incorporated various tactics to deal with each country. Iran would be contained by military deterrence, economic sanctions to discourage foreign investment in Iran, and rallying other countries to discourage Iranian support for terrorism and pursuit of a nuclear capability.

Actually, a dual containment policy threatened to reduce the effectiveness against either one, particularly since the EU sought to engage Iran and expand trade and investment.[86] Nevertheless, U. S. efforts to use economic sanctions to influence Iranian policy about the development of nuclear weapons and interfering with the Israeli-Palestinian peace process continued. Accusations of Hezbollah bomb attacks on Jewish and Israeli targets in Argentina and elsewhere lent support to the sanctions policies. In 1995, the U.S. government took additional actions against Iran, including blocking an Iran-Conoco oil deal and banning all trade and investment with Iran.[87] Then in December 1995, Congress passed legislation incorporating $20 million for CIA operations against Iran. Covert and overt exchanges of retaliatory actions were underway between the U.S. and Iranian governments.

U.S. government actions against Iran were vigorously promoted by influential American NGOs. They included the American Israel Public Affairs Committee (AIPAC), which contributed to congressional legislative measures aimed at changing Iranian conduct. However, there were also signs in 1996 of the Clinton administration considering a new approach toward Iran. In January, James Steinberg, Director of Policy Planning, gave a speech about containment without referencing Iran in that context.[88] The potential for establishing better relations with Iran began to be considered as the prospect of changes within Iran seemed more likely.

On June 25, 1996, the U.S. Air Force facility in Khobar, Saudi Arabia, was destroyed by a truck bomb, killing 19 Americans and wounding over 350 Americans, Saudis, and other nationals. Early investigation indicated that Hezbollah al Hijaz, a Saudi Shiite group with close links to Iran's Revolutionary Guards and Lebanon's Hezbollah, was implicated. But the intelligence was unclear about the involvement of Iranian senior leadership.

Clinton and his national security team considered a massive military retaliation against Iran, but quickly recognized such operations could escalate quickly and seriously.[89] Like president Kennedy's policy during the Cuban Missile Crisis, a more measured tit-for-tat response was pursued, coupled with communications with the adversary. The White House warned Iran to desist from further attacks. In addition, American installations in the Gulf region were hardened and U.S. warplanes were deployed to a remote air base in the Saudi desert. The Clinton administration also conducted intelligence operations targeted against the Revolutionary Guards and Iranian intelligence personnel around the world. Iran never acknowledged its role in Khobar, but terror attacks were stopped and the Hezbollah al Hijaz organization was dismantled in the late 1990s.[90]

In November 1996, Clinton was re-elected. With greater self-confidence and a new foreign policy team a rethinking of Iranian relations appeared possible.[91] Then, American-Iranian relations actually began to be transformed following the August 1997 Iranian presidential elections, when a reformist Islamic cleric, Sayyid Moham-mad Khatami, was victorious. He indicated, in a 1998 CNN interview, that he was open to a new relationship with the United States and wanted to bring down the "wall of mistrust" with the American people.[92] This statement and the domestic governance reforms he introduced won support internationally and reduced sup-port for the U.S. dual containment policy.

The Council on Foreign Relations had sponsored a task force on U.S. policy toward Iran and Iraq in 1996–1997 and the Independent Study Group reviewed policy relating to the Persian Gulf region.[93] Nearly all members of the task force and most members of the Study Group were former government officials. They largely concurred with the Clinton administration's goals and called for more moderated policies and possible accommodations with Iran.

Official efforts to engage the Islamic Republic began after the Iranian overtures. Clinton sent a series of public messages affirming his interest in improving people-to-people relations.[94] On the Eid al Fitr (end of Ramadan feast) in January 1998, Clinton said in a videotaped message that the United States "regrets the estrange-ment of our two nations . . . and I hope that the day will soon come when we can enjoy once again good relations with Iran." U.S.-Iran sports exchanges received high-level attention at the White House.

Clinton made several efforts toward direct diplomatic relations with Tehran. In October 1997, the administration sent one message through the Swiss Embassy in Tehran, inviting Iranian officials to meet without pre-conditions with three high-level U.S. officials at a location chosen by Iran. But Iran did not respond positively. In May 1998 Vice president Al Gore, while visiting Saudi Arabia, asked Crown Prince Abdul-lah to arrange direct talks between Washington and Tehran. Again the Iranians de-ferred and asked that people-to-people dialogue occur before official talks were begun.

The U.S and Iranian governments, however, did interact directly in multilateral settings. The most active discussions were at the UN, pertaining to Afghanistan and the Taliban. Shiite Iran had its own differences with Sunni Taliban controlling Afghanistan. The talks were held in the context of a 6-plus-2 dialogue, which in-cluded Afghanistan's six regional neighbors, the United States and Russia. Secretary of State Albright attended one meeting after the UN pledged to persuade her Ira-nian counterpart to attend, but he did not come.

In March 2000, the U.S. government undertook a broader effort to begin direct talks, which included Albright's public acknowledgement of intervening im-prproperrly in Iran,

In 1953, the United States played a significant role in the overthrow of Iran's popular prime minister, Mohammed Mossadegh . . . the coup was clearly a setback for Iran's political development and it is easy to see why so many Iranians continue to resent this intervention by America in their internal affairs.[95]

Albright also announced the beginning of a process to return millions of dollars in frozen Iranian assets. The money had been held since 1980 after Iranian militants seized the U.S. embassy and kept its personnel hostage. The changes also included lifting an import ban on several Iranian luxury goods such as pistachios and caviar, and relaxing entry restrictions for Iranian scholars and athletes to visit the United States.

These efforts failed to produce direct negotiations to resolve differences between the two countries. Iranian Supreme Leader Ayatollah Ali Khamenei and more hardline elements in Iran opposed such talks as well as the domestic reforms.[96] But step-by-step mutually accommodative interactions were occurring as Clinton's presidency came to an end.

One side benefit of the more conciliatory U.S. policies toward Iran was that it won Saudi cooperation in sharing intelligence relating to terror attacks on U.S. personnel in Saudi Arabia.[97] Saudi officials had refused to share such intelligence because they thought that revealing Iranian involvement might result in the United States making war on Iran, which would be disastrous for the region. When it seemed the United States would not be going to war against Iran, they became cooperative on intelligence matters.

The management of the terrorist attacks in a measured, positive and negative tit-for-tat manner avoided a destructive escalation and probably contributed to a stabilized relationship. A fundamental and enduring transformation might have come with the implementation of a GRIT strategy by the U.S. government. But even the persistence in deeds as well as words required by GRIT might not have been adequate to be successful.

IRAQI RELATIONS

President George H. W. Bush left office when relations with Iraq were quite hostile.[98] Hussein, for his part, mistakenly contributed to this continuing by acting provocatively hoping that Clinton would change U.S. policy. Hussein refused to allow UN aircraft to enter Iraqi airspace in the southern Iraqi no-fly zone, which stymied UN weapons inspections. In response, Bush had ordered air attacks on Iraqi targets on January 15 and 16, 1993.

The case against Hussein was further bolstered by the Iraqi attempt to assassinate former president George H.W. Bush when he visited Kuwait in April 1993.[99]

The Kuwaiti police arrested the persons plotting the assassination, thus preventing it. The plotters admitted that the Iraqi intelligence service recruited them and provided the vehicle and explosives for the planned attack. Clinton and his foreign policy team decided to retaliate by striking the Iraqi intelligence headquarters. On June 26, 1993, more than twenty cruise missiles were fired against the headquarters. The Iraqis were warned of dire consequences if any terrorist attack against the United States was attempted by them again. There were none.

During the eight years of Clinton's presidency, severe economic sanctions against Iraq were continued with slight modifications. In addition, with some interruptions, UN inspections were conducted to discover and destroy Iraq's chemical and biological weapons and end any program to build nuclear weapons. As noted in the last chapter this was actually already achieved, but the search for evidence that such weapons and plans did exist continued. The publically stated goal of the U.S. government was to "contain" Iraq, but for many persons with official and non-official experience with Hussein such coercive action would be necessary as long as Hussein remained in power. As the Council of Foreign Relations' Independent Task Force asserted in 1997, "The continued rule of Saddam Hussein poses a danger to the stability and security in the region . . . . It is difficult to see how any policy in the military sphere other than continued containment can be adopted so long as Saddam remains in power."[100]

When Clinton became president, a plan to overthrow Saddam was being urged by Ahmed Chalabi, a leading Iraqi exile. The plan, called "End Game," envisioned revolts by the Iraqi Kurds in the north and Iraqi Shi'a in the south that would result in an insurrection by the Iraqi military forces and the end of Saddam's rule. This might seem completely unrealistic, since such revolts had been brutally suppressed by the Iraqi military forces immediately after they were driven out of Kuwait. Nevertheless, the desire to believe that an internal revolution could be instigated by exiles like Chalabi and the Iraqi National Congress was strong enough for neocons to urge support for such a revolution and for the CIA to dispatch agents to the Kurdish area of Iraq.

The Kurds in the north functioned with considerable autonomy under the protection of the U.S. no-fly zone, but the Kurds were deeply divided.[101] The U.S. government favored the faction led by Massoud Barzani, the Kurdish Democratic Party. The second largest faction, the Patriotic Union of Kurdistan, was headed by Salal Talabani and was believed to be supported by Iran. In August 1996, Barzani's forces attacked the Talabani faction, surprisingly with support from Saddam. The U.S. government regarded Saddam's actions as an invasion of Kurdistan, launched two cruise missiles against Iraq, and demanded that Iraq withdraw from the Kurdish area. Barzani explained he had been attacked by Talabani and invited Saddam to help block Iranian influence. In any case, the U.S. agents in the Kurdish area quickly left.

In the next years, Saddam halted U.S. personnel participating in the inspection teams and then negotiated their return, with Russian mediation. The U.S. policy of endless sanctions had decreasing support from other governments. As French president Jacques Chirac observed, the Iraqi leaders had to be offered a solution that would end the sanctions—a light at the end of the tunnel.[102] Instead, and despite the serious 1996 setback in the Kurdish region of Iraq, a program to overthrow the Iraqi government became official U.S. policy.

The Iraq Liberation Bill was overwhelmingly passed by Congress and signed into law on October 31, 1998. President Clinton also signed an appropriations bill including $8 million for assistance to the Iraqi democratic opposition, at least $3 million of which would be a grant to the INC.

Many Americans in religious and humanitarian organizations, as well as participants in the peace studies and conflict resolution fields, were highly critical of the harsh sanctions imposed upon the Iraqi people. Many reports detailed the suffering and loss of life of Iraqi civilians. A program allowing Iraqi oil sales to pay for importing food was introduced, but this had limited benefits for the general population. Despite widespread recognition of the devastation caused by the sanctions and their failure to produce the desired changes in the Iraqi government policies, alternative approaches were not widely discussed in the United States, except to support attempts to overthrow the Iraqi government.

An alternative approach might have ruled out external efforts to destroy the ruling regime of Iraq. The shift in relations with Iran in Clinton's second term could have helped assure Hussein against Iranian attack if he were more accommodating toward the United States. Assurances of survival might have resulted in Saddam acknowledging that, in actuality, his country's weapons of mass destruction and the capacity to produce them had been abandoned. Presenting the possibility of a political solution in the future might also have facilitated engagement with the Iraqi people and enabled them to have more direct communication.

NORTH KOREAN RELATIONS

Finally, U.S.–North Korean relations deserve attention. The U.S. government had become deeply concerned about North Korea's developing nuclear weapons program and sought United Nations approval for strong economic sanctions.[103] By June 1994, U.S. plans to attack North Korea's nuclear facilities were being prepared. The danger of a war was averted when former president Jimmy Carter went to North Korea and persuaded Kim Il Sung, North Korea's leader, to dismantle its graphite nuclear reactors under certain conditions. The U.S. and North Korean governments then conducted negotiations leading to the October 1994 Agreed Framework, according to which North Korea would roll back its nuclear arms program and the United States would gradually normalize political and economic relations, help replace the graphite reactors with two light water nuclear reactors, and supply heavy fuel oil on an interim basis until the new reactors were on line.[104]

The Agreed Framework was achieved in the context of other bilateral negotiations and agreements. From the North Korean perspective, the main goal was normalization of political and economic relations, but the United States often viewed the Framework as a nonproliferation tool.[105] Another source of misunderstanding was the failure to implement one element of an agreement in order to put leverage on the other side for it to implement another element it had agreed to do. A failure to implement an element, then, was taken as a rejection of the agreement, not as a bargaining ploy.

Implementation of the agreement did not occur in a timely fashion and each side became suspicious of the other. North Korea's launch of a medium-range missile over Japanese territory in August 1998 further undermined the agreement. Nevertheless, Clinton and Albright took constructive steps that were to lead to agreements that would resolve serious issues between the two countries. They asked former defense secretary William Perry to head a review of U.S. policies regarding North Korea. The group doing the review consulted widely in the United States and in Asia and Europe. They recommended a comprehensive step-by-step initiative, offering North Korea the choice between improving relations or confrontation.

In accord with the constructive conflict approach, the promise of benefits was presented; offering to improve relations was critical. That would follow from agreements about supervising nuclear activities and ending destabilizing missile development programs. In May 1999 this was communicated in Pyongyang by Perry and Wendy Sherman, counselor to the State Department.[106] Several steps demonstrating mutual goodwill soon followed. The South Korean president, Kim Dae-jung, had already begun his "sunshine policy," trying to warm relations with North Korea. In June 2000 he was welcomed in Pyongyang by the North Korean president, Kim Jong-Il, a strikingly amicable event, followed by family visits across the previously closed border. In October 2000, Vice Marshall Jo Myong Rok, the second highest military figure in North Korea, was sent to Washington to invite President Clinton to come to Pyongyang. He also conveyed constructive proposals relating to the missile programs. Later that month, Albright traveled to Pyongyang to advance negotiations and prepare for a summit meeting. Preparations for Clinton to travel to Pyongyang were begun, but this was put on hold when Bush was declared to be the next U.S. president. When Bush chose Powell to be the next Secretary of State, he was updated on the progress that had been made. Powell gave assurances that he would continue the work underway. As discussed in Chapter 6, Bush had something else in mind.

POST–COLD WAR RELATIONS WITH THE RUSSIAN FEDERATION

It is a premise of the constructive conflict approach that conflicts may be positively transformed and appear to be ended, but they rarely completely disappear. Great attention is properly given to peacebuilding after a high level of violence or threat of violence has ended. The Soviet Union is gone, but its successor state continues to have relations with the United States, which are likely to have some matters of contention. Many Soviet reformers wanted cooperative relations with the West and admired aspects of the political and economic systems there. The transition, however, was profoundly difficult. A large amount of financial assistance would be needed for the Russian government. Some grants were awarded beginning in 1992 and continued into the early years of president Clinton's administration. Many grants were given to the Harvard Institute for International Development, and its professors of economics urged rapid privatization and free-market policies.[107] Such policies were readily used by local enterprising insiders and an oligarchical system resulted, leaving many vulnerable Russians in dire straits.

Russian military and economic power had greatly diminished as the Soviet Union dissolved. It was not regarded as a likely rival in the near future. However, as it regained its economic footing, the possibility of its leaders seeking to regain its past stature and overcome what some Russians would have experienced as humiliation could not be dismissed. That course became more likely when Vladimir Putin joined president Boris Yeltsin's administration and then became acting president on December 31, 1999, when Yeltsin resigned unexpectedly. Putin went on to win the subsequent 2000 presidential election.

During this period NATO expanded eastward. In June 1993 the Clinton administration approved a plan regarding NATO, which included opening membership to Central and East European countries, "provided they met the same political and military standards as other members."[108] Many governments desired such membership, and the prospect of membership was to be an inducement for economic liberalization, respect for minorities, and civilian control of military forces. Enlargement was to occur gradually, which "would help reassure Moscow that NATO's enlargement . . . would be a step toward Russia, not against it."[109]

Understandably, however, Russian leaders were not reassured.[110] They could well ask, against whom was security being provided? The Russian establishment was concerned not so much about the countries of Eastern Europe but about the enlargement that included the countries that had long been part of the USSR, and especially opposed to expansion into the Ukraine. The United States' setting a limit to NATO expansion to exclude the Ukraine and other former parts of the Soviet Union might have provided the bases for sustained cooperation. Increasing reliance on the EU and the OSCE might have had more chances of avoiding nationalist forces in Russia. These options were not a significant part of the official discussions.[111] However, the costs and dangers of NATO enlargement were raised and better alternatives were proposed, for example in a book published by the Cato Institute.[112]

Mediation of Israeli-Palestinian Conflict

During president Clinton's administration, Americans contributed to the mediation, most notably, of the Israeli-Palestinian conflict.[113] The mediation efforts taken by U.S. officials and private citizens were extensive, yet ultimately were unsuccessful.[114]

Bill Clinton was the beneficiary of an astounding breakthrough in relations between Israeli Jews and Palestinians. Secret negotiations, facilitated by Norwegian officials, had been conducted between PLO officials and Israeli non-officials, and then by official Israeli representatives. Starting in December 1992, they negotiated for months to reach agreement on a Declaration of Principles (DOP).[115] The agreement was signed in Washington, DC, in September 1993 by Shimon Peres for the government of Israel and by Mahmoud Abbas, also known as Abu Mazen, for the PLO. Warren Christopher witnessed the signing for the United States of America and Andrei Kozyrev for the Russian Federation. In a carefully choreographed encounter, Rabin and Arafat shook hands before a wide television audience.[116]

The mutual recognition so demonstrated dissolved a fundamental grievance on each side. The Palestinians could believe that Israeli Jews finally recognized them as a people and the Israeli Jews could believe that the Palestinians at last accepted their Jewish state. The DOP spelled out a framework for an interim period not to exceed five years in which progress toward peace would move step-by-step to build mutual confidence.[117] This seemed reasonable given the deep mistrust between Palestinians and Israeli Jews.

The signing of the DOP was widely greeted with joy and hope, but not by everyone. In December 1993, I traveled with an interreligious group of Muslims, Christians, and Jews to Jerusalem, Cairo, Amman, and Damascus. We often discussed with the people we met whether or not the agreement was irreversible. Some of the Arabs and many of the Palestinians in the diaspora were skeptical and thought it could and even should be reversed. The critics saw the agreement as a deal for the benefit of Israel and of Arafat and the PLO, but not serving the interests of Palestinians in the diaspora as well as in the occupied territories.

Most Palestinians in the occupied territories and most Israeli Jews sought their own countries, independent of each other. Therefore each side's leaders did not believe they needed to appeal to the other side's constituency. The leaders were primarily interested in maintaining the support of their own constituents. Consequently, bad behavior by some members from the other side would be denounced and used to mobilize against the other side. Moreover, some Jewish extremists viewed the conflict in terms of religious nationalism; all the land of Israel had been given to them irrevocably by God, while some Islamic activists and ethno-nationalist Palestinians regarded the existence of a Jewish state on their ancestral land as an unacceptable Western intrusion. This made the Oslo process vulnerable to disruption by spoilers from each side.[118]

Clinton set out to assist the Israeli and PLO leadership in implementing and advancing what came to be called the Oslo Peace Process. Dennis Ross, who had served as director of the State Department's policy planning staff during George H. W. Bush's administration, was appointed by Clinton to be the special Middle East coordinator to lead U.S. mediation efforts.[119] He and his deputy Aaron David Miller worked assiduously to bring about the numerous agreements in the Oslo Peace Process, but they did tend to see the Israeli-Palestinian relationship more from the Israeli than the Palestinian perspective.[120]

Initial moves seemed auspicious. In September 1995, Israeli-Palestinian negotiations led by Prime Minister Rabin and Chairman of the PLO Arafat produced the Interim Accord that established the Palestinian Authority (PA). It set forth how and when the redeployment of Israeli military forces and the transfer of Israeli control in the West Bank and Gaza to the PA would be implemented. Three areas were distinguished. Area "A" included six cities (Jenin, Nablus, Tulkarem, Kalkilya, Ramallah, and Bethlehem, with special arrangements in Hebron). The Palestinian Council would have full responsibility for civil matters, internal security, and public order. Area "B" comprised the towns and villages of the West Bank, where the Palestinian Council was granted full civil authority, while Israel would have overall security authority. In area "C," comprising the unpopulated areas, areas of strategic importance to Israel, and Jewish settlements, Israel would keep responsibility for security and public order.

In addition, from July to October 1995, a secret Stockholm channel functioned in a hybrid Track Two and back-channel fashion.[121] Israeli and Palestinian academics under the supervision of Yossi Beilin and Mahmoud Abbas met regularly to create a draft of a framework for concluding a final status agreement.[122] They actually succeeded in fashioning a draft that they presented to Beilin and Abbas, who proposed some adjustments in the document, which were accepted. Abbas set out to persuade Arafat that this was a solid basis for negotiations and Beilen was to bring it to Rabin, but Rabin was assassinated before he could do so. The draft was not officially adopted, but many of its provisions were used in subsequent documents.

The peace process begun by the Oslo Accords was opposed by some Israeli Jews, and a few extremists took violent actions to stop the progress. On February 25, 1994, Baruch Goldstein, an Israeli settler and member of the far-right Israeli Kach movement, fired on unarmed Palestinian Muslims praying inside a site holy to Muslims and Jews, the Ibrahim Mosque or the Cave of the Patriarchs in Hebron. Twenty-nine worshippers were killed and 125 wounded. The attack ended after Goldstein was beaten to death by survivors. The attack set off riots and protests throughout the West Bank. Prime Minister Rabin condemned the attack and Goldstein was widely denounced by the Jews in Israel, but venerated by some of the Jewish settlers in Hebron.

On November 4, 1995, Yitzhak Rabin participated in a huge peace rally in Tel Aviv. But when the rally concluded, Rabin was assassinated by Yigal Amir, an Israeli law student and right-wing extremist who opposed the Rabin-led peace accords with the Palestinians.[123] Many world leaders came for Rabin's funeral, including U.S. presidents Clinton, Bush, and Carter, King Hussein of Jordan, and president Mubarak of Egypt. Clinton and Ross tried to ensure that Rabin's commitments would be sustained and implemented.[124] Nevertheless, the assassination did lasting damage to the peace process.

Shimon Peres, who succeeded Rabin as prime minister and leader of the Labor Party, undertook to fulfill the policies Rabin had begun. He chose not to hold immediate elections, wanting to serve as prime minister and be elected on his own record. Some elements of the Interim Accords were implemented. Notably, Palestinian elections in the West Bank and Gaza were held on January 20, 1996, which elected Arafat as president. Many of the PA leaders were from the PLO and had been with Arafat in Tunis after leaving Lebanon in 1982.

Although there was some further progress, serious obstacles appeared. Peres, perhaps to show that he could be tough in fighting terrorism, ordered the assassination of Yahya Ayyash, a Hamas leader known as a bomb maker.[125] Hamas launched a devastating series of suicide bomb attacks in Tel Aviv and Jerusalem, killing over fifty Israelis. In addition, Peres ordered a large-scale attack against Hezbollah forces in southern Lebanon in the context of a series of retaliatory attacks with them. Unfortunately, a UN refugee camp was hit by Israeli fire, killing over one hundred civilians. All this played into the hands of the hardline Likud Party led by Benjamin Netanyahu.

In the May 1996 Israeli elections, Netanyahu and the Likud Party narrowly defeated Peres and the Labor Party. The new Likud-led coalition government greatly slowed the peace process by failing to implement the agreement the Israeli government had reached with the PLO to withdraw Israeli security forces from Hebron.[126] Further interim steps were stalemated, despite some back-channel talks.[127] By the fall of 1998, Clinton and Albright were sufficiently frustrated by the many months of deadlocked negotiations to try a summit conference. The conference was held near Wye River, Maryland, mediated by Clinton, Albright, Berger, and Ross. Netanyahu and his new defense minister, Ariel Sharon, were there for Israel and Arafat for the PA. The meeting did not go well at the outset but Clinton, who was away some of the time, returned and worked intensively on October 22–23 to salvage an agreement. The agreement was to implement the somewhat modified earlier Interim Agreement of September 28, 1995. However, no substantive progress was actually made. On the contrary, Jewish settlements in the disputed Palestinian territories continued to grow and the PA increased the military capabilities of its security forces. Officially, statements from both sides set forth their own narratives with little recognition of the other side's concerns. Unofficially, bi-national dialogue meetings were held and Track Two policy meetings were conducted.

The end of the Cold War lessened Soviet and then Russian support for the Palestinians and reduced U.S. fears that the Israeli-Palestinian conflict would escalate into a U.S.-Soviet confrontation, reducing the urgency of dealing with that conflict.[128] All this might have been seen as weakening the bargaining strength of the Israelis and Palestinians and making both sides more ready to conclude a peace deal. But it did not, and the U.S. leadership was increasingly critical of both sides. The lack of progress with interim measures contributed to thinking in the United States and in Israel that a shift to final status negotiations might be more productive.[129] The major issues in dispute would be negotiated in order to end the conflict with a comprehensive peace agreement.

In the Israeli elections on May 17, 1999, Ehud Barak, leader of the Labor Party, won a landslide victory. He had promised to move quickly to negotiate a comprehensive peace with the Palestinians. To the consternation of the Palestinians, however, Barak brusquely publicly announced that the implementation of the Wye agreement would become part of those negotiations.[130] He reasoned that additional Israeli territorial concessions would reduce the incentives for the Palestinians to make concessions on important issues such as the Palestinian refugees' right of return. This tough negotiating policy is generally not a good way of overcoming mistrust from one's negotiating partner. Nevertheless, Barak won Clinton's agreement and ultimately Arafat's acquiescence.

Full-scale negotiations were begun in Jerusalem on July 29, 1999, between Israeli and Palestinian negotiation teams led by Gilead Sher and Saeb Erekat, respectively.[131] Severe differences quickly appeared, but persistent negotiations, aided by high-level mediation by Egyptian and American officials, did yield a foundational agreement. The Framework Agreement on Permanent Status was signed on September 4, 1999, at Sharm A-Sheikh, Egypt. The negotiations to fill in the broad framework, however, made little progress, revealing great differences on crucial elements of a peace agreement, including the Palestinian refugees' Right to Return, arrangements for control of Jerusalem, and the borders between the two states. Recourse to a Swedish-facilitated channel of high-level negotiations was tried but also proved ineffective. Barak urged resorting to a U.S.–sponsored summit meeting and Clinton agreed, despite Arafat's reluctance.[132] With limited confidence of success, Clinton invited the Israeli and Palestinian leaders to join him at Camp David beginning on July 11, 2000.[133] Initially, Barak and Arafat each waited for the other to offer concessions; when this led nowhere, the U.S. team presented some proposals for an agreement and they too were simply opposed. Only gradually were some Israeli offers made, contingent on Palestinian concessions from their initial claims. Mistrust persisted, but the gaps in what Arafat and Barak each insisted upon seemed to have narrowed some. To avoid an admission of failure, Clinton proposed parameters for an agreement, but that also failed to result in an agreement and after two weeks Camp David II ended.

Clinton blamed Arafat for the failure, rather than praising the accomplishments made and correcting some of the reasons an agreement was not reached.[134] Indeed, issues essential to a final status agreement, which had not been subjects of negotiation earlier, were now on the table. Some members of each side believed a peace agreement could yet be salvaged.[135] Mubarak renewed active mediation efforts. Arafat visited Arab capitals to maintain support for standing firm and holding out for Palestinian claims. Barak consulted widely, particularly to explore creative and practical ways of overcoming the more emotional and symbolic differences regarding the future of Jerusalem.

In August, bilateral Palestinian-Israeli negotiations were renewed, focusing particularly on Jerusalem. The idea of a meeting among Barak, Arafat, and Clinton in conjunction with the UN General Assembly meetings in September was discussed, but was not to be realized. Nevertheless, bilateral negotiations on all the core issues continued and the terms for a permanent status agreement were close enough for Barak and Arafat to meet. Their meeting at Barak's home on September 25 was cordial.[136] The next day their representatives departed for Washington and U.S.-mediated negotiations. Hopes were high.

The high hopes were soon dashed. On September 28, Ariel Sharon, leader of the opposition Likud Party, visited the Temple Mount/Haram al-Sharif area, accompanied by Israeli police.[137] Israeli officials had advance knowledge of the plan, but did not think that it could or should be disallowed. The police shot at protesters and large-scale protests the next day produced a rapid escalation of violence; the second

Intifada was underway. The subsequent violence spread quickly, with no clear condemnation of the violence by PA leaders. Indeed, Palestinians who had been jailed for violence against Jews were released, and more rejectionist Palestinian groups such as Hamas conducted suicide bombings. Palestinian confrontations and attacks initially targeting Jewish settlements in the West Bank and the Gaza Strip were then extended into cities within the 1967 Israeli borders. The Israeli government conducted many air strikes on Palestinian targets and imposed closure on the Palestinians, denying them employment in Israel and preventing their movement from one population center to another.

On December 9, 2000, Barak announced he was resigning as prime minister, and in accord with electoral rules would remain in office until he would face elections on February 6, 2001, when he was likely to be opposed by Sharon. He could reasonably expect that if a permanent status agreement were attained, he would be re-elected and if it was not reached, he would be defeated. Failing efforts were made to reach an agreement in the waning days of Clinton's presidency, and even continued into January 2001.

The disastrous end to the peace process has produced innumerable explanations of "what went wrong."[138] In discussing explanations, it should be recognized that the heaviest responsibility lies with the primary adversaries. However, given the focus of this book on American involvement in foreign conflicts, I give more attention to American intermediary actions.

I comment on three phases: the stagnation in the peace process when Netanyahu was prime minister, the final status negotiations mediated by the United States and the violence of the second Intifada. Although progress was significant initially, it became markedly stuck during the years that Netanyahu was the Israeli prime minister. Even when agreements were reached, they were not implemented and the Israeli government and the Palestinian leadership pursued policies that made a mutual accommodation between them more rather than less difficult. On the Israeli side, Jewish settlements were expanding mostly close to Jerusalem, but also elsewhere in the occupied territories, and Palestinians collectively were not treated as peers. On the other side, the PA leadership did not counter the inflammatory language in schools and the press about Israeli Jews, and did not foster an open democratic political system or equitably develop the Palestinian economy. Neither side's leaders helped prepare their respective constituencies to accept what would be realistically needed to achieve a mutually acceptable sustainable peace agreement.[139]

The Clinton administration officials dealing with Israeli-Palestinian relations might have done more to overcome the obstacles to advancing peace. They were not sufficiently insistent about timely implementation of agreements that had been made. Furthermore, they failed to strongly counter constituency policies of leaders on both sides that were obstacles to a peace agreement. They might have encouraged each side to do better by helping them coordinate conciliatory steps. The asymmetries in Israeli-Palestinian resources and capabilities hampered reaching an equitable accommodation. The United States might have done more to help redress the imbalances, including giving more attention to the Palestinians, providing them more assistance for negotiations and recognizing the relevance of their moral and legal claims. Having high-ranking members of the U.S. mediation team who were comfortable with and insightful about the Palestinian leadership would have been extremely valuable.[140]

Of course, many other governments might have acted in ways that would have contributed to equitable progress toward Israeli-Palestinian peace. Arab countries with large numbers of Palestinian refugees and their descendants might have done more to normalize their lives. Arab governments might have established more accommodative relations with Israel as it progressed in implementing agreements with the PA, as Jordan had. They might also have given more assistance in developing the Palestinian economy and encouraged the Palestinians to construct reasonable compromises with Israel.

Many nongovernmental organizations conducted important work building mutual understandings and creating new solutions to the many problems in Israeli-Palestinian relations. Even more such work was needed, particularly to reduce and marginalize the efforts of groups on both sides to undermine and disrupt a peaceful accommodation.

Once the permanent status negotiations had begun, the mediator role for the U.S. government was greatly enlarged and required even greater engagement as issues that had not been well discussed between the Israeli and Palestinian leadership were now on the table. This was particularly important in working with the Palestinian leadership, which had done little preparatory work. Barak's notion of reaching an agreement by placing Arafat in a pressure cooker was not likely to succeed. The mediators needed to help each side understand the other and help them provide important reassurances. Not to do so can be devastating. For example, the Israelis were stunned by Arafat's dismissal of the fundamental Jewish belief that the Jewish Temple that the Romans destroyed had been located on the Temple Mount.

The mediation by Carter's team at the first Camp David summit may be usefully compared to the methods at the second Camp David summit.[141] After the opening statements by Menachem Begin and Anwar al-Sadat, they did not try to negotiate directly with each other. Carter's team worked with a single text for a possible agreement, shuttling back and forth each day to get corrections to the text, which they revised each night. At the second Camp David, president Clinton deferred to Barak's thinking about the needed negotiation format, and only as the summit was coming to an end did Clinton offer his sense of the parameters for an end-of conflict agreement.[142] In addition, the issues in dispute between Egypt and Israel were less complex and essential for the parties than was the case for the Israelis and Palestinians, and Sadat and Begin were in stronger domestic circumstances than were Arafat and Barak.

Finally, the initial acts of violence associated with Sharon's visit to the Temple Mount/Haram al-Sharif were excessive.[143] Their intensity quickly led to even greater exchanges of violence, including attacks upon Israeli soldiers by Palestinian police and by the Tanzim, the armed wing of Arafat's party, Fatah. If the leadership on both sides had demonstrated effective action to reign in the violence, it is even imaginable that that would have had a salutary effect on the negotiations. It would have demonstrated the real desire to live in peace together and the capability to make it happen. Instead, people on each side had reason to believe that the other had no desire or capability to make peace happen.

Evolving Constructive Conflict Ideas and Practices

In the 1990s, the fields of peace studies and of conflict resolution had become well established in the United States and in many other countries. They were taught in many colleges and universities and they were increasingly utilized in practice by persons who identified themselves as workers in these fields and also by others who did not so regard themselves. Key words in the fields had gained wide currency. Thus, Google Scholar searches of publications with the words "conflict resolution" rose from 7,910 in 1980 to 15,600 in 1990 and then jumped to 47,300 in 2000. Similarly, the words "conflict mediation" rose from 1,080 to 2,830 and then to 9,130 over those twenty years.[144] Of course, the usages of these words were certainly not always congruent with their meaning in the fields and the constructive conflict approach's syntheses of the fields.

For all this growth, the fields' relevance for American foreign policy was quite circumscribed. Foreign policy discussion and application remained largely within varieties of traditional international relations thinking. Indeed, a particularly U.S.-centric perspective had become salient, as indicated by the neoconservative thinking. I therefore emphasize three developments in the constructive conflict approach that are particularly relevant for American engagement in foreign conflicts: constructive conflict escalation, peacebuilding after mass violence and oppression, and the expansion in assessing applications of the approach.

CONSTRUCTIVE CONFLICT ESCALATION

How conflicts can be nondestructively escalated to advance freedom, justice, and other widely shared values is the central hallmark of the constructive conflict approach. I focus here on two kinds of strategies: nonviolent action and conflict intervention.

Many kinds of nonviolent resistance in the form of noncooperation, disobedience, and protest demonstrations have always been part of human history. The use of nonviolent methods, influenced by research and theoretical analysis as well as by prior example, is relatively new in foreign conflicts. The systematic attention to nonviolent action entered the emerging constructive conflict approach in 1973 with the publication of Gene Sharp's book, *The Politics of Nonviolent Action*.

The recourse to nonviolent struggle contributed greatly to the end of the Cold War and the dissolution of the Soviet Union as well as to the establishment of more democratic forms of governance. Those experiences contributed to increased analysis and attention to the constructive potentialities of nonviolent struggle. Nonviolent action was successfully applied in Serbia as previously discussed. In addition, in the years from 1993 through 2000, there were nonviolent struggles in eight other countries: Egypt, Croatia, Senegal, Tanzania, Peru, Indonesia, Nigeria, and Ghana; all were successful or, in two cases, partial successes.[145]

In the 1990s, many of Sharp's writings, including brief pamphlets, not only had been translated into many languages, but had become available for downloading at his and other websites. Other authors also analyzed nonviolent actions inferring principles for effective practice. For example, Peter Ackerman and Christopher Kruegler published *Strategic Nonviolent Conflict* in 1994.[146] A film documenting the effectiveness of nonviolent action in overthrowing oppression and authoritarian rule all over the world, *A Force More Powerful* was shown on PBS in 2000 and was made widely available for viewing in many languages. Jack DuVall was the executive producer of the television program, and co-authored a companion book (with Peter Ackerman) of the same name.[147]

The end of the Cold War and the increasing integration of the world enhanced America's capability and interest in intervening in foreign conflicts. The reasons often given by American leaders pertained to stopping large-scale violence, ending autocratic and oppressive rule, and safeguarding democracy and human rights. Other reasons were also discernible as important or even more important by observers from the United States and other countries. They include responsiveness to domestic popular concerns, desires to secure economic interests, and the wish to demonstrate U.S. dominance. As indicated by the analyses of U.S. interventions in this chapter, the interventions often failed to be effective and were sometimes counterproductive, at least in part due to the multiplicity of purposes and the limited range of alternative ways of intervening considered.

Some advocates of the constructive conflict approach did attempt to examine and propose relatively constructive interventions. For example, economic sanctions had begun to be taken up as nonviolent ways to coerce governments to behave more in congruence with international human rights standards. However, as in Iraq, they can impose severe hardships on the people in the countries being sanctioned, without bringing about the changes being sought. One effort to remedy this problem was to specify and impose smart sanctions, which would target the leaders of the government directly, impose arms embargoes, or boycott particular commodities such as oil or diamonds.[148] With greater precision and improved administration such sanctions result in greater effectiveness for particular policy goals.

A great deal of attention was given to early warning and possible preventive actions. For example, the Carnegie Commission on Preventing Deadly Conflicts issued a report on these matters in 1997.[149] After great attention to developing signs of destructive conflicts in order to spur preventive actions, it became apparent that failing to foresee bad circumstances was not the great barrier to preventive efforts. Government leaders often had warnings of emerging destructive problems, but intervention usually did not seem politically feasible prior to extremely severe conditions. Furthermore, if prevention action was taken successfully, political leaders would find it difficult to claim credit for averting the disaster. More fundamentally, government officials typically do not know what actions would actually be effective. Their repertoire of policies is too limited and often very costly. Finally, warnings of unusual events may simply be discounted by high-ranking decision-makers whose judgment is limited by their preexisting beliefs.

One of the advantages of the constructive conflict approach is that it widens the range of policies that may be considered. It draws attention to diverse actors and policies at various conflict stages. For the United States, the paramount figure in making and executing U.S. foreign policy is the president, but in many realms other government officials and nongovernmental actors do conduct and influence foreign affairs in conjunction with actors in other governments and multinational organizations. Working collaboratively with other governmental and nongovernmental organizations can help avoid the pitfalls and risks of unilateral undertakings.

The emphasis on conflict transformation in the constructive conflict approach helps avoid grandiose expectations of establishing harmonious relations that are without major conflicts. Instead it focuses attention on how conflicts can be reframed or re-defined to be more constructively managed. This may be aided by active mediation, Track Two undertakings, people-to-people diplomacy, and altering the context for the conflict. Such activities can incorporate a wide variety of strategies. They can help reduce the salience of a deteriorating conflict by raising the salience of other antagonists that the opposing sides in the conflict share. They can help make less contentious arrangements become more attractive or plausible by adding resources or giving political cover to antagonists accepting a deal. The small steps in averting the deterioration of U.S.-Iranian relations, discussed earlier, are illustrative of the possibilities and the limitations of such efforts.

PEACEBUILDING AFTER MASS VIOLENCE AND OPPRESSION

The engagement of international governmental and nongovernmental organizations in peacebuilding after wars or oppressive rule greatly expanded in the 1990s. Increasingly, organizations sought to provide humanitarian relief, assistance in building political and social institutions, economic development assistance, and reconciliation among former enemies. This resulted in numerous publications analyzing such undertakings and proposing better ways to provide such services from a constructive conflict perspective.

Much of the thinking and practice in the fields of peace studies and conflict resolution were readily adaptable in work fostering reconciliation across ethnic, religious, or other communal differences after mass violence or authoritarian rule. They also resonated with issues integral to a broad conception of reconciliation that encompasses truth, security, mutual regard, and justice.[150] Certain political, economic, and cultural developments were also recognized as important in building enduring peaceful relations. Considerable attention also was given to various political institutions and their likely contributions to equity and stability; for example much attention was given to electoral and political party systems.[151] The difficulties in transitioning to a democratic order after authoritarian rule or bitter wars were examined and possible ways of overcoming the difficulties were increasingly investigated.[152] Finally, attention also was given to major social structural features of countries and their place in a global context.

ASSESSING PRACTICE

With the increased interventions and self-conscious thought by people engaged in conflicts about their policy choices, a great deal of research was undertaken to evaluate applications of conflict resolution and peace studies ideas.[153] Often, evaluation research was required by agencies contracting out the work; such evaluations tended to be specific to particular projects. Such evaluations are difficult since so many other factors shape outcomes. However, broad assessments of economic policies of the IMF and other international governmental organizations also began to be made.[154]

Such analyses and assessments indicate that U.S. interventions to mitigate foreign conflicts have had limited constructive effects. I will consider more recent efforts in the next two chapters and offer suggestions for reforming the infrastructure shaping American engagement in foreign conflicts so as to improve the results in the concluding chapter.

Conclusion

The world has undergone immense changes in the last few decades and the rate of change is increasing. Therefore, Americans should face foreign conflicts with fresh eyes, discerning what is new. Ways of dealing with conflicts that seemed sensible in the past must be revised and novel approaches should be developed to improve results.

Many of the developments discussed in this chapter interact and reinforce each other's contributions to the constructive waging of conflicts. However, they do not always combine to foster a peaceful and just world; rather, sometimes several of them interact and jointly enhance the likelihood that particular conflicts will be waged destructively. Certain developments combine to evoke resentment against Americans among people in many parts of the world. American failure to recognize the bases for such resentments exacerbates hostile feelings.

Other combinations of developments, however, may nullify adverse consequences each would have alone. Contradictory consequences create opportunities for Americans to affect the course of a conflict. How peaceful and just the emerging global society will be depends in good measure on the actions that individuals and groups take in the conflicts they fight. Furthermore, it should be stressed that these developments vary in their aspects and relative significance in different regions of the world. Their impact in South Asia is not the same as in the Middle East or in Central America. Americans' policies must be shaped for a particular time and place, for and by particular actors, within the context of these broad historical changes.

The ongoing global developments are far-reaching and profound and the United States is an integral part of them. Americans are necessarily linked in innumerable ways to the rest of the world. Powerful as the United States may be, it cannot alone shape the world and its many conflicts. Americans should view the foreign conflicts that the United States faces in the context of these developments, contradictory as their implications may be. Taking them into account and working in tune with the changes underway will make engagement in foreign conflicts more likely to be successful than if Americans ignore or dismiss them.

The high degree of global interdependence and the contradictory character of many developments in it prevent any single governmental or nongovernmental actor from directing future developments. Attempts to implement unilaterally designed grandiose plans to change, fix, or even help other countries or peoples will have unintended consequences. Indeed, the results may be severely counterproductive. The risks of such unwanted results are reduced if elements of all the stakeholders in a conflict participate in trying to resolve it.

Many of the global developments discussed here should contribute to the constructive waging of conflicts. Yet, the United States has too often engaged in international conflicts in ways that have contributed to their destructiveness. The U.S. government's manner of conduct, based on assumptions of America's supremacy in power and virtue, has understandably appeared as unwarranted arrogance to many people elsewhere in the world and to many Americans as well. To understand how this could have happened requires an examination of developments within the United States and its relations with peoples and governments around the world. In the next chapters, I continue to discuss features of American society and of the U.S. government that affect how Americans deal with terrorist attacks and attempts to transform Afghanistan and Iraq.

6 The War on Terrorism and Other Foreign Conflicts, 2001–2008

THE PREVIOUS CHAPTERS have portrayed considerable, if uneven, progress in developing the ideas and practices of the constructive conflict approach and also in their applications. That progress, however, was contested and remained marginal to a significant degree in U.S. foreign policies in the years 2001 through 2008. Many of the major U.S. foreign policy decisions made during the presidential administration of George W. Bush were incongruent with the constructive conflict approach.[1] They were also often contrary to the traditional realist approach.[2] In this chapter explanations for the strategies chosen are discussed, their consequences assessed, and alternatives suggested.

Domestic Setting and Bush Administration's Approach

The major global trends and basic features of the American society as they relate to foreign affairs, discussed in Chapter 5, continued during the first years of the new millennium. Of course, the attacks of September 11, 2001, had profound impacts on Americans' engagements in foreign conflicts. They reinforced some trends and features and countered others, at least for a time. The strength and nature of the impacts, however, were themselves shaped by the country and the world in which the attacks happened.

The fierce Republican attacks against Clinton and his associates indicated a growing political polarization and the increasing role of the extreme right wing within the

Republican Party and among its supporters. The partisanship diminished in some ways following the attacks of September 11, 2001. However, the domestic and foreign policies pursued by Gearge W. Bush's administration deepened the partisanship.

The intensifying polarization was due to many factors. Fundamentally, political polarization was highly associated with the sharply increasing income and wealth inequalities in the United States that began in the mid-1970s.[3] The rich could use their wealth to gain political power so as to enrich themselves further. Ideological differences became more firmly attached to political party designations. The increasing political and ideological polarization was also fueled by changes in the mass media and the public's reliance on them as sources of information. The information channels proliferated, and some became highly ideologically partisan. People increasingly chose to get news and other information from sources that gave them the opinionated information they wanted to receive.

Television news programs, the primary source of news,[4] included more and more human-interest stories and entertainment material. Radio call-in shows were predominately hosted by commentators who were nationalistic, sometimes to the point of jingoism; they were often highly emotional and lacked civility. They certainly did not model how conflicts could be handled constructively, with attentive and respectful listening and a search for integrative solutions.

Information and interpretations were increasingly generated by influential conservative think tanks that were supported by very wealthy persons. The ideology, if implemented, often would yield tax and other monetary benefits for such sponsors. They were less engaged on foreign policy issues than domestic matters, but their ties were with the Republicans.

The foreign policy establishment that had articulated and helped guide the bipartisan foreign policy consensus in the early years of the Cold War had long been absent. Efforts to forge bipartisan agreements on some matters of foreign policy, such as foreign trade, were sustained. However, the shift to the right of large segments of the Republican Party made even ad hoc agreements or international cooperation very difficult.

Political polarization was also intensified in some ways by the presidential race between Vice President Al Gore and Governor George W. Bush. The election campaign was marked by personal attacks and domestic ideological differences, but foreign policy issues were not highly salient. Bush did not propose a radical imperial foreign policy. In his October 11 debate with Gore, when asked by Jim Lehrer how he would project the United States around the world, Bush asserted, "If we're an arrogant nation, they'll resent us. If we're a humble nation, but strong, they'll welcome us. And our nation stands alone right now in terms of power. And that's why we've got to be humble and yet project strength in a way that promotes freedom."[5]

He went on to say, "We can build coalitions, but we can't put our troops all around the world." At the time these words appeared surprising, and later actions might indicate they were spoken to win votes. Possibly, however, they derive from Bush's lack of familiarity with foreign affairs and the absence of a clear comprehensive view regarding U.S. foreign policy.

The election results generated great political bitterness. Gore won the popular vote, but the electoral vote was not clear because the vote tally in Florida was in dispute. Bush's victory was decided by a five to four Supreme Court decision that awarded the decisive Florida electoral votes to Bush. The Court's decision seemed blatantly political in the eyes of Democrats and therefore Bush's election, even if Gore acquiesced, was viewed as lacking legitimacy. Under such circumstances, one might have expected Bush to try to win over Democrats and unify the country by his administration appointments and initial policies. On the contrary, he acted as if he had won a landslide endorsement.

An indication of how ideologically militant Bush's appointments were likely to be was his selection of Richard Cheney to be his vice-presidential running mate and then to oversee his transition team and interview candidates for cabinet posts. In 1990, Cheney, then the secretary of defense, established a group to draft a post–Cold War strategy; the group included Paul Wolfowitz, the deputy secretary of defense; Lewis Libby, Cheney's chief of staff; and Eric Edelman, a foreign policy adviser to Cheney.[6] The leaked draft strategy generated great controversy, and a somewhat moderated version became the official public report. In 1997, some members of the neocon network formed a new advocacy group, the Project for the New American Century, which released a report in September 2000, "Rebuilding America's Defenses," which reaffirmed the basic tenet of the earlier Pentagon draft regarding unchallengeable dominance.[7]

Several other members of the neocon network were chosen to fill many senior positions in the new Bush administration. Donald Rumsfeld was chosen to be secretary of defense and Paul Wolfowitz was appointed deputy secretary of defense. John R. Bolton was under secretary of state for arms control and international security. Lewis Libby was Cheney's chief of staff (again). Many of these men had worked together in past Republican administrations.[8] Other major appointments related to defense, foreign relations, and intelligence included retired General Colin Powell as secretary of state and Condoleezza Rice as national security advisor, a scholar of the Soviet Union and also a close confidant of Bush. George J. Tenent continued to serve as director of the CIA. John Ashcroft was appointed to head the Department of Justice.

In the eight months of Bush's presidency prior to 9/11, he did not act to increase defense spending or to begin building an anti-ballistic weapons system, as might have been expected from what he said during the campaign.[9] He did nonetheless promptly take many foreign policy actions demonstrating that he was pursuing a very different approach than Clinton had. For example, Clinton's support for the South Korean president Kim Dae-jung's policy of dialogue and reconciliation with North Korea was abruptly ended when the South Korean president came to Washington in March to see the new American president.[10] Bush made clear in July that the Kyoto Protocol, an international agreement to respond to global climate change, was "dead." He went on to oppose a new protocol to the Biological Weapons Convention, the Comprehensive Test Ban Treaty, and the International Criminal Court (ICC). He also put on hold U.S. engagement in the Middle East peace process, which was at a perilous point as he took office.

War on Al Qaeda, Terrorism, and the Taliban

Surprisingly, the Bush administration upon taking office did not give high priority to countering the threat of terrorist attacks in the United States or against American interests elsewhere. This is indicated by the general lack of interest or responsiveness to the warnings about the al Qaeda threat. Continuing or even intensifying intelligence operations against al Qaeda during the spring and summer of 2001 may not have uncovered the plot to conduct the September 11 attacks, but taking more seriously the alarm of Richard Clarke and others who had been working on these matters in Clinton's administration might have spurred a heightened alertness, which might have resulted in connecting some dots of information and disrupting a piece of the complex plot.

The 9/11 Commission Report concluded that "In the spring of 2011, the level of reporting on terrorist threats increased dramatically . . . ."[11] As reports of threats increased, the FBI sent out messages to all field offices tasking them to use all resources to obtain more information. The U.S. Central Command raised the force protection for U.S. troops in six countries to its highest level. Clarke, the national coordinator for counterterrorism, submitted to national security advisor Rice intelligence memos with increasingly alarming reports of plans for a spectacular attack within the United States. The August 6 Presidential Daily Brief included an article prepared by the CIA for the president entitled "Bin Laden Determined to Strike in the US." However, no National Security Council or other high-level meetings on the threats were held before the September 11th attacks.

Recognizing the potential value of early warnings in avoiding destructive escalations, obstacles to taking appropriate preventive actions must be overcome. In this case, a major terror attack within the United States executed by a small nongovernmental organization based in the Middle East seemed very improbable and readily ignored. Indeed, Cheney and Wolfowitz indicated their belief that Iraq in some way was the real source of terror threats.[12] Perhaps leaders of the new administration felt that trying to deal with the al Qaeda threat when it was so unlikely, would interfere with progress on their high priority domestic and international interests.

BUSH ADMINISTRATION'S RESPONSES TO SEPTEMBER 11TH ATTACKS

The horrifying attacks on September 11th were immensely shocking to President Bush, his associates, and the American people. Governments and peoples around the world expressed their outrage at the act and solidarity with the United States. Responding to those attacks became the central galvanizing feature of the Bush administration's foreign policy. As Bush quickly said and reiterated, "We have to think of this as an opportunity."[13] The response was to wage a comprehensive Global War on Terrorism (GWOT), which was interpreted in terms of the ideology of key foreign policy figures in the new administration. It also had a transforming effect on domestic policies, resulting in the creation of the Department of Homeland Security.

This framing of the response had many skeptics from the outset.[14] Critics argued that a war against terrorism had no clear limits or ending, since terrorism had always been a part of human history. Furthermore, a more constructive approach would seek to circumscribe the enemy, limiting the conflict while isolating the adversary. In this case, al Qaeda was clearly the perpetrator of the attacks, and the attacks could widely be recognized as criminal. That narrower focus would avoid linking the perpetrators to every other group identified as terrorist by other governments. On the other hand, the framing of the response as a war would be complicated by legal processes, as became evident in taking and holding of prisoners. Finally, using the term "war" could stifle dissent and the serious discussion of alternative policies.

From the perspective of various Bush administration members, the assertion that the country was fighting a global war on terrorism had many benefits. It would facilitate mobilizing Americans to undertake severe measures to prevent future terrorist attacks. It would induce people to rally around the flag and support the president in wartime. It would enable taking military actions against other possible antagonists by linking them to the terrorist enemy. It could support larger objectives that would then further justify the recourse to war. Indeed, going after the states that harbor terrorists by overthrowing their governments was attractive to many on the team, who saw this as a pathway to changing the Middle East and the world. Different members of the Bush foreign policy team were more attracted by one or another of these political, bureaucratic, or moral concerns.

The one strong voice within the Bush foreign policy group opposing the overambitious goals implicit in a global war against terrorism was secretary of state Powell. He urged limiting the war to one against al Qaeda. He argued against trying to change regimes that may harbor terrorists, thereby creating new client states. Rather, he favored seeking to change their policy of providing safe havens for terrorists by using persuasion and other means. That approach would be cheaper in lives and money and be more sustainable in the long run.[15]

A response framed as a global war against terrorism was congenial to the neoconservative network and a conventional popular way of thinking, but did not fit so well within other approaches, including the constructive conflict approach. The war framing lent itself to demonizing the enemy, referring to it as evil. That understanding of the enemy did not require serious attention to what the evildoers say their reasons are. Reasons attributed to the enemy could be chosen that would serve one's own interests. For example, Bush asserted that al Qaeda attacked the United States because they thought the country was weak, so if America is strong al Qaeda would not attack it.[16] That is not convincing. Bin Laden and other al Qaeda leaders clearly stated that the U.S. dominance and offensive meddling in the Middle East was to be fought; if they wanted to attack weak powers, many were available. The trouble with misunderstanding the concerns that drive an adversary's conduct is that efforts to isolate it and to win over allies are likely to fail. This was part of the reason that the public diplomacy efforts of the Bush administration were so unsuccessful, as recognized in official commission reports.[17]

In reality, a global military war was not the only way in which al Qaeda and the threat of terrorism were countered by the United States. Various legal methods were relied upon to stop attacks and bring perpetrators to justice. Efforts were made to cut off funding to al Qaaeda. Many methods of persuasion were deployed through public diplomacy to isolate al Qaeda and induce its supporters to withdraw. Positive inducements were offered to win over allies to assist in isolating al Qaeda and defeating it. This multiplicity of efforts necessarily sometimes resulted in competitive and contradictory actions.[18] For example, the work of the FBI and the CIA were not always complementary.

The primary immediate response to the attacks was to launch a military invasion of Afghanistan to destroy al Qaeda and overthrow the ruling Taliban regime. On September 20, 2001, Bush addressed a joint session of Congress, issuing an ultimatum demanding that the Afghan government turn over bin Laden and other al Qaeda leaders to the United States. Mullah Mohammed Omar, leader of the Taliban government, asked that evidence of al Qaeda's guilt be presented. No real negotiations ensued and extensive bombing of the al Qaeda camps and other targets in Afghanistan began on October 7 and continued for weeks. The Northern Alliance, an anti-Taliban Afghan militia, began to advance against them. U.S. ground forces were introduced, but they were small, 316 Special Forces troops and 110 CIA agents; and initially progress was slow.[19] Administration leaders feared that very large forces would be needed and a quagmire would result.

Then, in early November, the tide of the war changed. Smart bombs and drones, targeted by the forces on the ground, gravely damaged the Taliban, and the Northern Alliance forces quickly advanced to enter Kabul on November 13. Rumsfeld and the neocon officials and intellectuals were triumphant. The easy victory contributed to the confidence that overthrowing Saddam Hussein could also be readily accomplished. One of the caveats the constructive conflict approach stresses is that a success can result in overreaching, in leaping forward in what turns out to be reckless and misguided conduct.

Indeed, the victory in Afghanistan was not complete and the costs were just beginning. Significantly, the task of pursuing and destroying al Qaeda was not accomplished. The forces needed to close the Afghan-Pakistan border were not put in place. Despite the intense fighting during December in the Tora Bora Mountains extending along the border area, Bin Laden and his associates escaped into the tribal region of Pakistan.

Interestingly, when it came to stabilizing Afghanistan and forming a government there, the UN largely handled the initial tasks. The UN Security Council acted quickly to mandate the International Security Assistance Force, with Turkey taking the lead (UNSC Resolution 1386, December 20, 2001), and a UN Assistance Mission in Afghanistan was established to coordinate humanitarian and reconstruction aid for the Afghan people (UNSC Resolution 1401, March 28, 2002).

In late 2001, members of many Afghan ethnic and civic groups and representatives of the United States, Iran, Russia, India, and Germany were brought together under UN auspices at a conference held in Bonn, Germany, to discuss the future government of Afghanistan. For days the conferees argued over how to develop acceptable working relationships among the country's many ethnic groups (Pashtun, Tajik, Hazara, Uzbek, Turkmen, and others). Finally, with crucial Iranian assistance, an agreement was reached for provisional arrangements in Afghanistan.[20] It was signed on December 5, 2001, pending the re-establishment of permanent government institutions. It endorsed the 1964 Afghan Constitution, except for the provisions relating to the monarchy.

A prominent Pashtun Afghan leader from the Kandahar region, Hamid Karzai, was appointed chairman of the Interim Authority. Karzai had opposed the Soviet occupation from 1979 to 1989 and served briefly in the mujahedeen cabinet in 1992–94. After 1994, Karzai had organized fighters against the Taliban while based in Quetta, Pakistan, and at the same time became known to U.S. officials and business interests through consulting projects for a possible natural gas pipelines through Afghanistan. In October 2001, he led an armed Pashtun militia offensive against the Taliban in the Kandahar region. Being a visible force against the Taliban among the Pashtun, Karzai was a natural for selection as interim leader by the Bonn conference.

In June 2002, former King Mohammed Zaher, also a Pashtun, opened an emergency Afghan grand council, or *Loya Jirga*, which was convened to determine how to form a permanent government. Hamid Karzai was elected president of the Transitional Authority, the interim government for the period while a new constitution was drafted and approved. Elections were scheduled for two years later. Following President Karzai's inauguration in June 2002, Afghan citizens had high expectations for quickly achieving stability and economic health. However, those hopes slowly eroded as Afghans suffered frequent violent attacks, continued insecurity throughout the country (except in Kabul), and the lack of secure and adequate transportation, employment, education, and medical care.[21] Building an Afghan national army proved to be extremely difficult. One problem was that national soldiers with good skills tended to leave and join militias where they could get better wages. Other problems related to the role of Pakistan and the actions of its military intelligence agency, the Inter-Services Intelligence (ISI), which was interested in supporting militant Islamic groups to counter India's rule in Kashmir.

In the months after the September 11th attacks, Bush set forth his administration's overall foreign policy approach. In his September 20, 2001, speech to Congress, he said, "Our forces will be strong enough to dissuade potential adversaries from pursuing a military build-up in hopes of surpassing, or equaling, the power of the United States." In his June 1, 2002 speech at West Point he went further, warning of the threats the United States now faced and declared, "To forestall or prevent such hostile acts by our adversaries, the United States will, if necessary, act preemptively." In September 2002, the government issued a comprehensive 2002 National Security Strategy of the United States, consisting of several post 9/11 presidential speeches. The doctrine set forth in these speeches drew in part on the September 2000 report of the Project for the New American Century, entitled, "Rebuilding America's Defenses."

One other set of ideas became important in the foreign policy orientation of the Bush administration. They related to the importance of having moral clarity and rejecting notions of moral relativism usually attributed to the Clinton administration and Democrats in general. This meant that "good" and "bad" people can and should be clearly distinguished from each other; indeed, some people are categorically evil and compromise with them is unacceptable. Such simplification can guide decisive action, but not wise policy.[22]

A unilateralist, militant, and morally clear foreign policy orientation was congenial to Bush for many reasons. It resonated with his religiosity and with his desire for a simple, forceful line, which projected strength. The policy orientation appears to be consonant to many elements of his political base: the religious right, the neoconservatives, corporate executives, and the wealthy. It also would appear to have popular appeal, being bold and tough in the face of external threat and an expression of American self-assurance and can-do confidence.

AMERICAN PUBLIC'S RESPONSES

There was only a muted critique of the Bush administration's doctrines and conduct in waging the GWOT. An alternative approach did not gain public attention. Yet there is evidence that the American public's opinions were in alignment with a more multilateral and less militant and grandiose U.S. foreign policy orientation. The goals of American international involvement as viewed by the American public are varied and often in dispute. One important variation is the relative emphasis on humanitarian concerns for other peoples versus the advancement of narrow self-interests of Americans. Admittedly, this distinction is sometimes difficult to make. For example, the goal of promoting democracy in another country may be urged not for the sake of a people subjected to tyranny but to make the United States safer from attack or to serve other American interests. Nevertheless, people frame and claim goals in terms of one or the other end of this policy dimension.

Public opinion surveys conducted by the Chicago Council on Foreign Relations provide information about Americans' foreign policy views.[23] In a survey done about a year after September 11, 2001, respondents were asked the importance of twenty possible foreign policy goals. Not surprisingly, 91% considered "Combating international terrorism" to be very important. In general, the foreign policy goals that the American people regarded as very important tend to be defensive and neither imperialist nor unselfishly humanitarian. The public seems cautious and does not give high importance to goals that are hugely ambitious. A few of the goals that are deemed to be highly important to leaders in the Bush administration were not so regarded by most Americans, for example, "Helping to bring a democratic form of government to other nations," was regarded as very important by only 34% of the respondents. Many other goals widely thought to be very important seemed to be of relatively low priority to neocons, for example, "Protecting jobs of American workers," was regarded as very important by 85% of the respondents.

The means the public believed should be used to advance American foreign policy goals were varied. These methods are often discussed in terms of acting multilaterally in cooperation with allies or else acting unilaterally. The other dimension often discussed is the degree of reliance on military force versus diplomatic and other nonmilitary methods of coercion and persuasion. In these matters, too, some strong divergences appeared between the general public and the leaders in the Bush administration.

Public opinion surveys consistently show that most respondents favored the U.S. acting multilaterally in international affairs. One question asked over time is: "What kind of leadership role should the United States play in the world? Should it be the single world leader, or should it play a shared role, or should it not play any role at all?" In September 1993, 10% chose the first option, 81% the second, and 7% chose the third option.[24] The responses varied only slightly in subsequent years and in October 2001, the proportion of respondents choosing each of the three options was 12%, 79%, and 3%, respectively (the balance did not answer or said they did not know).

A year after the September 11, 2001 attacks, survey respondents were asked to choose the statement closest to their view, with the following results: "As the sole remaining superpower, the U.S. should continue to be the preeminent world leader in solving international problems," 17%; "The U.S. should do its share in efforts to solve international problems together with other countries," 71%; and "The U.S. should withdraw from most efforts to solve international problems," 9%. In the same survey conducted for the Chicago Council on Foreign Relations, respondents were asked whether, in responding to an international crisis, the United States should or should not take action alone if it does not have support of its allies. The responses were 31% said the U.S. should act alone, and 61% the U.S. should not act alone.[25]

Finally, the American public's preference for multilateralism is also demonstrated by the widespread support for major international treaties and agreements. Respondents in the same survey were asked if they thought that the United States should or should not participate in each of the following proposals. The percentage supporting participation in each case was very high.

1. The treaty that would prohibit nuclear weapon test explosions world-wide, 81% should participate and 14% should not participate.
2. The treaty that bans all use of landmines, 75% should participate and 19% should not participate.
3. The agreement to establish an International Criminal Court that would try individuals for war crimes, genocide, or crimes against humanity, if their own countries won't try them, 71% participate and 22% should not participate.
4. The Kyoto agreement to reduce global warming, 64% participate and 21% should not participate.

These findings are particularly striking given the clear opposition to American participation in these treaties and agreements by Bush and his administration.

The American public has also generally been supportive of the UN since its establishment. Moreover, public support for cooperating with the UN rose following the terrorist attacks of September 11, 2001. In early September prior to the attacks, 58% of the public thought the United States should cooperate fully with the UN, and that increased to 67% a year later.[26]

Many respondents may not be well informed about the particularities of these diverse issues and may vary in their responses depending on question wording. However, there is a striking consistency in responding to a great variety of questions about preferences regarding America's goals and whether those should be pursued unilaterally or in concert with other countries. The sentiment for being engaged in international affairs and working with other countries seems stable and widespread.

The public's multilateral preferences are more congruent with a constructive conflict approach than was the unilateralism of the Bush administration. First, strategies utilizing a multilateral approach tend to isolate the adversary and lessen the support it might otherwise win, which would make its leaders less likely to insist on objectives that would be regarded as unacceptable. Second, multilateral strategies tend to gain supporters, which would mean increased resources so that resistance can be strengthened while costs are more widely borne. Significantly too, working with allies and supporters tends to provide more information and perspectives, which should enable wiser strategies to be developed than otherwise would be done.

Finally, the American public's preferences regarding the use of military and non-military means of achieving U.S. objectives must be considered. Americans' readiness to resort to military force varies greatly with likely casualties, the ends being served, the scale and costs, and the alternatives deemed available. Thus, in June 2002, the percentage favoring military operations in the war on terrorism varied with the operations proposed. For example, 92% responded they would "Approve the use of U.S. troops to destroy a terrorist camp," 84% would "Favor attacks by ground troops against terrorist camps and other facilities to combat terrorism," 73% would "Favor toppling unfriendly regimes that support terrorist groups threatening the U.S.," and 54% would "Favor the use of U.S. troops if the government of Saudi Arabia requested our help against an attempt to overthrow it."[27]

Very large proportions of Americans also favored various nonmilitary means to fight terrorism. They did not want to rely exclusively on military force, but saw the value of diplomatic instruments, economic sanctions, foreign aid, and programs to promote democracy in other countries. The percentage of respondents expressing approval for the use of various diplomatic tools to fight terrorism include: (1) Diplomatic efforts to apprehend suspects and dismantle terrorist training camps, 89%;

(2) Setting up an international system to cut off funding for terrorism, 89%; (3) Working through the UN to strengthen international laws against terrorism and to make sure UN members enforce them, 88%; (4) Trial of suspected terrorists in an International Criminal Court, 83%; (5) Diplomatic efforts to improve U.S. relations with potential adversary countries, 80%; and (6) Helping poor countries develop their economies, 78%.

Americans did seem to value nonmilitary means, even in fighting terrorism. Their views indicated an appreciation of the many new conditions and possibilities resulting from globalization. Interestingly, the survey questions did not include other options related to public diplomacy or support of nonviolent direct action operations.

Despite the general preference to utilize diplomatic and other nonviolent methods, there is sufficient support for the use of military force in different circumstances that government leaders have great leeway in obtaining license to employ military force.[28] Framing the threats to the United States to be extremely grave yet susceptible to defeat by armed forces at not too high a cost can gain widespread acceptance of military options. But other frames could win support for strategies that embed military means within a broad political, social, and economic program over the long term. After all, the public's recognition of the importance of nonmilitary methods of dealing with foreign conflicts suggests that comprehensive strategies to prevent conflicts from escalating in ways that threaten the United States will win sustained public support.

The Bush administration's policies obviously were not derived from the results of public opinion surveys. Indeed, in many ways they were at variance with the preferences expressed by Americans shortly after the September 11, 2001 attacks. Yet, considerable public support, or at least popular acquiescence, to the Bush administration policies developed as the U.S. government advanced along the road to war in Iraq.

One intriguing element in accounting for this phenomenon is the belief of many Americans that other Americans are more unilateralist than they actually are. This misperception contributes to public support of the United States acting unilaterally, as indicated by an analysis of a national survey conducted in February 2003.[29] When asked about the proper role of the United States in the world, 16% chose the unilateralist response that "the U.S. should continue to be the preeminent world leader," 71% chose the multilateral choice that "the U.S. should do its fair share," and 13% chose the isolationist, "the U.S. should withdraw from most efforts to solve international problems." The respondents were then also asked which option they thought would be chosen by other Americans; 35% thought the unilateral response would be chosen, and only 45% believed the multilateral option would be preferred.[30]

Furthermore, persons who incorrectly thought the unilateral views were the majority views were almost twice as likely to endorse a presidential decision to invade

Iraq even if the UN Security Council did not support it. Believing the American public was supportive of a unilateralist approach gave legitimacy to carrying out such policies. Another question arises. Why did the American public so overestimate the public's unilateralist tendencies? Perhaps they inferred this from the way the matters were presented in news media. Or, perhaps for some the unilateral acts of the president's people were assumed to reflect popular sentiment in order to preserve their faith in the American political system.

Invading Iraq

The idea that the United States should invade Iraq and replace Saddam Hussein with a democratic system of government had been in the minds of some members of the neocon network for many years. Immediately after the al Qaeda attacks of September 11, Bush and some officials of his administration began acting to wage a preemptive war on Iraq.[31] The president seemed to view the al Qaeda attacks as the opportunity to make it happen. For several months, he conveyed that no decision to invade Iraq had been made. However, actions were taken to gain support for the invasion, and by November 2002 the big decision was evidently made.

GOING TO WAR IN IRAQ

I will not present the extensive evidence available then or available since that the decision to invade Iraq was misguided. Choosing a preemptive war to overthrow the Saddam Hussein regime has been widely recognized as a dreadful mistake for the United States, and it has had disastrous consequences.[32] I do examine how such a bad decision and the subsequent poor implementations happened, and consider more constructive alternative policies.

The processes of decision-making used by Bush and his close associates for the big decision to go to war and for many subsidiary decisions were contrary to the realities emphasized in the constructive conflict approach. I cite six characteristics of the processes that were used, noting the resulting difficulties for making good decisions regarding interactions with an adversary. First, the decision to go to war and many related decisions were made by a very small group, rather than by a diverse group of relevant and knowledgeable persons engaging in a deliberate discussion of what the problem was and what the alternative ways of solving it were.[33] Such broad discussions are likely to maximize choosing the best path forward, as was illustrated by the calculated U.S. response to the Soviet placement of missiles in Cuba in 1962.

Second, the objective to be achieved by going to war was not clearly articulated. It seems the president decided to go to war, but the reasons he gave were numerous and shifting, including: Saddam Hussein poisoned his own people, he has weapons of mass destruction, he is planning to produce weapons of mass destruction, he is a dictator, he cooperated with al Qaeda, he "tried to kill my dad," he failed to comply with Security Council resolutions, and he did not cooperate with UN inspectors.[34] This multitude of reasons resulted in many people wondering, "Why did Bush really decide to go to war?" Many of the reasons given would not warrant an invasion. The plethora of reasons made it difficult to think about which strategies would best satisfy them, but ultimately many of them came to be listed as objectives for the war, as set forth in National Security Presidential Directive #24, which the president signed on January 20, 2003.

Third, little attention was given to thinking about the conflict as it might be viewed by the adversary. Deeming Hussein to be a bad guy, even the embodiment of evil, his point of view was not worthy of attention. But failing to consider the enemy's concerns can result in grave misunderstandings. In this case, Saddam Hussein was reasonably worried that Iran and other enemies constituted serious threats to his regime and that possessing weapons of mass destruction (WMD) could deter them from attacking him. Therefore, he might want to preserve some ambiguity even after he had abandoned possessing or producing such weapons. As noted in the last chapter, that turns out to have been true.

Fourth, having decided that waging war against Iraq was correct, Bush, Cheney, Rumsfeld, Wolfowitz, and their associates focused on how to get the American people to support the decision. They sought to stifle doubters in authority and induce them to stay in line. They readily exaggerated the evidence that did exist and ignored the caveats that often accompanied the possible evidence of the threats that Saddam posed. For example, they gave undue credence to the Iraqi exile Ahmed Chalabi, who warned of the threat posed by Saddam and of his vulnerability to being overthrown.[35] And very importantly, many people, out of loyalty, concern about their careers, timidity, and various other reasons did just go along.

Fifth, Bush, Cheney and others downplayed the risks of waging war to remake Iraq and stressed the threats that Saddam presented to the United States. They tried to create a sense of imminent danger, a feeling of urgency that would induce people to put aside their doubts and not take the time for the situation to become clearer. This was the case, for example, starting in September 2002, with the effort to have Congress pass a resolution authorizing military action before the November midterm elections.

Sixth and fundamentally, they failed to seriously consider alternative options and the potential balance of costs and benefits of different options. The possible undesired political and social consequences within Iraq and the Middle East resulting from an invasion were not debated. Instead, they assumed that the consequences they desired would result from their actions; for example, the democratic majority role of the Iraqi Shi'a would be a model for Iranians to follow in a post-Khomeini Iran.[36] A review of various nonmilitary strategies was reduced to what had been done previously, which was disparaged as a failure. The military option was accorded a privileged primacy.

Bad as this process for making the decision to wage a preemptive war was, the American system of government would seem designed to prevent such seriously mistaken decisions from being made and so poorly implemented.[37] The various institutional and public constraints existed to some degree, but they were overwhelmed. To begin, within the executive branch itself several major departments and agencies with their own interests, expert knowledge, and constituencies might be expected to have played a larger role than they did in shaping the big decision and related subsidiary ones. After all, they swear an oath to defend the constitution, not the decisions of a president.

The failure to engage in collaborative decision-making, which would entail respectful exchanges among diverse stakeholders on the same side in the conflict with Iraq, had tragic consequences. One element in this failure was the overly militarized view of the conflict by Bush and his neoconservative associates. War was viewed as a military matter, waged by members of the armed forces. Nevertheless, secretary of state Powell ordered a detailed study of the "Future of Iraq." It reviewed past efforts on nation-building and policies regarding the many contingencies that the United States would face in a post-Saddam Iraq. When the Pentagon established the Office of Reconstruction and Humanitarian Assistance in January 2002, Powell sent the names of State Department Arab experts who could join the vanguard entering Iraq.[38] He named Thomas Warrick and Meghan O'Sullivan to head the group. Rumsfeld, however, rejected them. Powell immediately called Rumsfeld, asking "What the hell is going on?" Rumsfeld explained that postwar planning had to be done by supporters of the change, not those who had opposed it. The row was settled by higher authority in the White House, keeping O'Sullivan on the task but not Warrick. In the end, the Americans in charge of postwar management had little knowledge or direction about what to do and the reconstruction work went very badly.[39]

Powell was not part of an open-ended, serious discussion about going to war or pursuing other courses of action. He thought his job was to pursue a diplomatic strategy, but to ultimately support the president's decision, even if it was to go to war, unless he thought the arguments for war were 100% wrong, and ultimately he thought they were not.[40]

A few officials in the Department of State did resign in protest of the decision to wage a preemptive war. Thus, on February 13, 2003, Ambassador Joseph Wilson, former chargé d'affaires in Baghdad, publicly questioned the need for waging war in Iraq and resigned from the Foreign Service. On February 27, John Brady Kiesling, another career diplomat, resigned on similar grounds in a *New York Times* letter. On March 10, John H. Brown, a career diplomat with twenty-two years of service, resigned; he was followed on March 19 by the resignation of Mary Ann Wright, a diplomat with fifteen years of service in the State Department.

Several high-ranking military officers publicly disagreed with the judgments and decisions of Rumsfeld and Wolfowitz about waging a war to overthrow the Iraqi government.[41] Top levels of the army particularly disagreed with the Pentagon civilians' ideas about the size of the military force needed to occupy Iraq. Most famously, General Eric Shinseki, the Army chief of staff, went public with the Army's calculations while appearing at a Senate Armed Services Committee hearing, on February 25, 2003.[42] When asked directly by Senator Carl Leven what the magnitude of the Army's force requirement to occupy Iraq would be, he replied, "on the order of several hundred thousand soldiers." Wolfowitz had been telling senior army officers that he thought within a few months after the invasion the military force would be only thirty-four thousand. Two days after General Shinseki's testimony, Wolfowitz told the House Budget Committee that such predictions "were wildly off the mark."[43]

Brent Scowcroft, who served as national security advisor to President George H.W. Bush was an early critic. He wrote an August 15, 2002 op-ed in *The Wall Street Journal* entitled "Don't Attack Saddam," arguing that the war would distract from the broader fight against terrorism and the Israeli-Palestinian conflict, which should be the U.S.'s highest priority in the Middle East. In September, former chairman of the Joint Chiefs of Staff Hugh Shelton agreed that war in Iraq would distract from fighting terrorism. Retired Marine General Anthony Zinni, former head of Central Command for U.S. forces in the Middle East, vigorously expressed his concerns in an October 2002 speech at the Middle East Institute. In a follow-up interview with *Salon*, Zinni said he was "not convinced we need to do this now," arguing that deposing Saddam Hussein was only the sixth or seventh top priority in the Middle East, behind the Middle East peace process, reforming Iran, our commitments in Afghanistan, and several others.[44]

In the months before the invasion of Iraq, Congress held many hearings with distinguished former members of the military and national security communities, including many who favored a more realistic approach to international relations and who were critical of the decision to invade Iraq and the planning for it. For example, General Joseph P. Hoar (Ret.) warned the Senate Foreign Relations Committee that the invasion was risky and perhaps unnecessary. Morton Halperin, associated with the Council on Foreign Relations and the Center for American Progress, warned that an invasion would increase the terrorist threat.[45]

I well remember that during the build-up to starting the war in Iraq, I expressed my belief that this was a bad idea to government office holders, would-be office holders and others wanting to be in the good graces of the government. They usually did not really argue with me, but neither would they agree. They said, "It's going to happen." I replied, "I expect so, but it is wrong and it is urgent to say that." The response was often a shrug.[46]

A free press should be a guardian against the way the Bush administrations was making decisions and mobilizing support for going to war. Cultural, political, and organizational features of the news media, however, tended to produce news reports congruent with the government officials' preferences. Even reporters, who tried to be objective, faced difficulties in reporting information that officials might regard as critical of them or as undermining their policies. Critical reporting may be punished by loss of access or even worse. The George W. Bush White House was viewed as particularly ready to punish those they regarded as adversaries.[47] Moreover, commentators based in conservative think tanks and ideologically conservative media outlets vehemently attacked critics, particularly if the dissenters previously had been associated with the administration.[48] This served to isolate critics and intimidate would-be dissenters.

Some long-standing procedures also tended to produce reports in the mainstream media that were congruent with official sources. Reporters, commentators, and other communicators of information depended on officials as their sources and cultivated relations with them; therefore, many communicators were careful to avoid offending their sources. Furthermore, in matters of foreign relations many American reporters and commentators felt it their duty to regard American official sources as issuing solid news and information.

Thus in early 2003, as the U.S. government moved to make war against the Iraqi government, the news media generally conveyed the official belief that Iraq possessed biological and chemical weapons and was close to developing nuclear weapons. But the UN inspectors in Iraq found no evidence of that and there was disagreement within the American intelligence community about the correctness of the belief.

After the fall of the Saddam Hussein regime, when no WMDs were found, a few writers examined the failure of the news media to report reasonable doubts about the existence of WMD in Iraq before the war.[49] The editors of the *New York Times* undertook an investigation of their own coverage and on May 26, 2004, they admitted that, "In some cases, information that was controversial then, and seems questionable now, was insufficiently qualified or allowed to stand unchallenged."[50]

The political polarization of American society also contributed to the polarization of the media, which in turn reinforced the societal divisions with dreadful consequences. A comprehensive study of how and why Americans held misperceptions relating to the reasons for the United States going to war in Iraq was done by the Program on International Policy Attitudes at the University of Maryland, and the Knowledge Networks based in California.[51] In analyzing three surveys conducted from June to September 2003, questions about three misperceptions were posed: (1) clear evidence "that Saddam Hussein was working closely with the al Qaeda terrorist organization," (2) since the war with Iraq ended, "Iraqi weapons of mass destruction" were found, and (3) the majority of the people in the world "favor the U.S. having gone to war." One or more misperception was held by 60% of the respondents, with 20% having two of these misperceptions and 8% having all three.

Significantly, the number of misperceptions the respondents held was associated with the source they primarily relied upon for news. Thus, the percentage with one or more misperception ranged from 80% for those who relied primarily on Fox, to 71% for CBS, 61% for ABC, 55% for NBC, 55% for CNN, 47% for print media, and 23% for PBS-NPR. Further analysis demonstrates that these variations cannot wholly be explained by respondent characteristics such as education or political party identification. The source of news clearly affected beliefs that would justify the Bush policy toward Iraq.

Some developments did counter the growing influence of extremist conservative thought in the news and opinion media. The rapid growth of the Internet enabled private citizens and small groups to distribute and share information through listservs and websites. They also enabled citizens to readily access newspapers and other information sources from all over the world as well as reports from American research institutions. However, citizens must reach out to access such sources, and that kind of reaching out is most likely done to sources that will fit the searchers' predispositions.

Groups of liberals and progressives began trying to compete with the influential conservative radio talk shows and other media outlets. These attempts, however, had relatively little success, but the efforts were increasing.[52]

Some television programs and radio programs, notably on PBS and NPR, produced programs in which discussions were generally carried on with civility and issues explored in a collegial manner, conducive to constructive dialogue. The nongovernmental organization Search for Common Ground arranged for the production of a ten-part series for television, showing facilitated discussions between persons holding different views regarding abortion or gun control as they sought for possible common ground.[53] The series was aired on 110 public television stations in 1989–1990.

Finally, general information about conflicts and how to wage them was conveyed in films, television dramas, theatrical plays, comedians, novels, and many other sources of both popular culture and of "high" culture. Much of this glamorizes violent combat, making it seem essential to manhood.[54] Of course, the horror and futility of war was also sometimes depicted. What was relatively absent was the depiction of heroic peacemakers, struggling nonviolently, mediating skillfully, or interceding without escalating violence.

Despite the Bush administration's efforts to mobilize support to militarily overthrow Saddam Hussein, considerable popular opposition to invading Iraq was manifested during the months leading up to the war. There were demonstrations across the United States; the largest, involving about 300,000 to 400,000 protesters, was held on February 15, 2003, in New York City while smaller demonstrations occurred in Seattle, San Francisco, Chicago, and other cities.

Consistent with the antiwar sentiment of the protests, prior to going to war in March 2003, American public opinion generally favored a diplomatic solution over military intervention.[55] A January 2003 CBS News/*New York Times* poll found that 63% of Americans wanted President Bush to find a diplomatic solution to the Iraq situation, compared with 31% who favored immediate military intervention. That poll also found, however, that if diplomacy failed, support for military action to remove Saddam Hussein was above 60%. Other polls found that majorities of the public believed that Iraq posed threats that were good enough reasons for the United States to take military action. Considering the elite and media leaning in favor of military action, the level of public opposition may be puzzling. One explanation is public attention to the strength of foreign views against an invasion.[56]

Days before the beginning of the war on March 20, a *USA TODAY*/CNN/Gallup Poll found support for the war was related to UN approval. Nearly six in ten said they were ready for such an invasion "in the next week or two." But that support dropped off if UN backing was not first obtained. If the UN Security Council were to reject a resolution paving the way for military action, only 54% of Americans favored a U.S. invasion. And if the Bush administration did not seek a final Security Council vote, support for a war dropped to 47%.[57]

The American political institutions should have provided a deliberative process by which the American public would be represented in any decision to undertake a preemptive war. The U.S. Constitution states that Congress has the power to declare war. However, U.S. presidents acting in their capacity as commander of chief sometimes have taken war actions without such declarations. In 1973, Congress passed the War Powers Resolution, overriding President Richard Nixon's veto. It provides that the president can send armed forces into action only if authorized by Congress or in case of an attack upon the United States. Furthermore, the president must notify Congress within forty-eight hours of committing armed forces and forbids the troops remaining more than sixty days without authorization.

Bush wanted some kind of congressional resolution that could be interpreted as authorizing him to order military actions against Iraq. He was also convinced that a UN Security Council resolution that could be understood to authorize military force was necessary to win support from Congress and from other countries. Until September 2002, Bush repeatedly said he had not decided to militarily overthrow Saddam Hussein. However, as early as February 2002, Bush had ordered General Tommy Franks of the Central Command to begin moving military forces out of Afghanistan to the Gulf.[58] The military buildup near Iraq was preparatory for a war if it was ordered and itself became a driver for war.

Then, on September 3, Andrew H. Card, White House chief of staff, gathered senior White House staffers together to coordinate efforts to obtain a congressional vote authorizing military force in Iraq before the November 5 midterm elections. In an interview that got much attention, Card explained the sudden flurry of activity that followed, "From a marketing point of view, you don't introduce new products in August."[59] Bush administration leaders were attentive to public opinion and thought they could lead it.[60]

The timing of the campaign helped convey a sense of urgency. On September 4, Bush invited eighteen congressional members to the White House, reminding them that back in 1998 Congress had voted overwhelming for regime change in Iraq. He said that he embraced that policy and sought suggestions and thoughts about deciding what actions should be taken. Briefings of members of Congress followed, making the case for going to war. Many Democrats felt that their opposition to the Gulf War in 1991 had harmed them politically and they could not advance their political career if they opposed going to war against Saddam Hussein's regime.[61]

The resolution that authorized Bush to take the country into war was sponsored by Dennis Hastert, speaker of the House of Representatives, and House minority leader Richard A. Gephardt. Many Democrats were dismayed at Gephardt's cooperation with Bush.[62] Significantly, the resolution did not precisely authorize going to war. Rather, it stated, "The President is authorized to use the Armed Forces of the United States as he determines to be necessary and appropriate . . . " This allowed some members of Congress to vote yes, but claim that they meant only to strengthen the president's diplomatic efforts.

The resolution was passed by the House of Representatives on October 10, 2002, by a vote of 296–133, and passed by the Senate early the following morning, by a vote of 77–23. In the House, 82 Democrats voted yes and 126 voted no; but in the Senate, 29 Democrats voted yes and only 21 voted no. Senators seriously considering running for the presidency voted yes, including John Edwards, Joseph Biden, and Hillary Clinton.[63]

The United Nations remained as a possible restraint on going to war. Bush and his senior advisers believed that to sustain domestic and international support for a military invasion to overthrow Saddam Hussein's rule they needed a UN Security Council resolution that would provide some degree of authorization. On September 12, 2002, Bush addressed the General Assembly and lodged many complaints about Iraq's violations of previous UN resolutions, production of weapons of mass destruction, grave human rights violations, and refusal to cooperate with UN inspections. The speech was followed by U.S. negotiations for a new resolution authorizing military action against Iraq, with particular attention given to obtaining support from Security Council members France, China, and Russia. The Iraqi government announced that it would allow the reentry of UN arms inspectors, but this was dismissed by the United States as a ploy.

After almost two months of negotiations Resolution 1441 was agreed upon by the Security Council members, and it was passed unanimously on November 8, 2002. But the governments voting for the resolution critically disagreed about its meaning. John Negroponte, representing the United States, forthrightly declared, "If the Security Council failed to act decisively in the event of further Iraqi violation, the resolution did not constrain any Member State from acting to defend itself against the threat posed by that country, or to enforce relevant United Nations resolutions and protect peace and security in the region."[64] Other government representatives, including those from France, China, Russia, and Syria, said that there were no hidden triggers or automaticity with the use of force in the resolution. UN authorization for the use of force would require another resolution.

Although the Bush administrations did not believe that it was constrained from going to war to disarm Iraq by SC Resolution 1441, British Prime Minister Tony Blair, facing fierce opposition in England for supporting Bush and war, wanted to go back to the UN and have a resolution authorizing war.[65] No such resolution, however, could be approved and none was put up for a vote.

On January 25, 2003, Bush asked Powell to make the case at the UN that Saddam had WMD and was in violation of UN resolutions. Bush asked Powell because he thought Powell had the credibility to do it effectively. Powell agreed, but brushed aside the case as prepared by Lewis Libby, Cheney's chief of staff, believing it incorporated much misinformation. Powell sought to make his own determination by going over relevant material and speaking with CIA officials who were working on Iraqi possession of WMD and possible links to terrorism. He accepted some evidence that was considered suspect or clearly inaccurate by other analysts and prepared his presentation.[66] His presentation to the Security Council on February 5, 2003, received great attention and was deemed have made a convincing case against Saddam, as judged by the American public, the *New York Times*, and others who had been in doubt previously. Bush, Cheney, Rumsfeld, and others in the administration were overjoyed.[67]

Meanwhile, UN inspections were underway in Iraq, fulfilling the provisions of SC Resolution 1441.[68] Hans Blix, executive chairman of the United Nations Monitoring, Verification and Inspection Commission (UNMOVIC), presented an update on inspections to the Security Council on February 14, 2003:

> In my 27 January update to the Council, I said that it seemed from our experience that Iraq had decided in principle to provide cooperation on process, most importantly prompt access to all sites and assistance to UNMOVIC in the establishment of the necessary infrastructure. This impression remains, and we note that access to sites has so far been without problems, including those that had never been declared or inspected . . .
>
> How much, if any, is left of Iraq's weapons of mass destruction and related proscribed items and programmes? So far, UNMOVIC has not found any such weapons, only a small number of empty chemical munitions, which should have been declared and destroyed. Another matter — and one of great significance—is that many proscribed weapons and items are not accounted for. . . .One must not jump to the conclusion that they exist. However, that possibility is also not excluded.

Additional reports were made to the Security Council on March 7; they clearly stated that Iraq was complying with SC Resolution 1441. The reports indicated that the resolution could be claimed to have succeeded, making war unnecessary. One report was made by Blix, who said,

> Inspections in Iraq resumed on 27 November 2002. In matters relating to process, notably prompt access to sites, we have faced relatively few difficulties. . . . This may well be due to the strong outside pressure . . .
>
> This is not to say that the operation of inspections is free from frictions, but at this juncture we are able to perform professional no-notice inspections all over Iraq and to increase aerial surveillance . . .
>
> While cooperation can and is to be immediate, disarmament and at any rate the verification of it cannot be instant. Even with a proactive Iraqi attitude, induced by continued outside pressure, it would still take some time to verify sites and items, analyse documents, interview relevant persons, and draw conclusions. It would not take years, nor weeks, but months. Neither governments nor inspectors would want disarmament inspection to go on forever. However, it must be remembered that in accordance with the governing

resolutions, a sustained inspection and monitoring system is to remain in place after verified disarmament to give confidence and to strike an alarm, if signs were seen of the revival of any proscribed weapons programmes.[69]

The other report was made by Mohamed El Baradei, director general of the International Atomic Energy Agency. He also reported Iraqi compliance, saying:

> After three months of intrusive inspections, we have to date found no evidence or plausible indication of the revival of a nuclear weapon program in Iraq...
>
> I should note that in the past three weeks, possibly as a result of ever-increasing pressure by the international community, Iraq has been forthcoming in its cooperation, particularly with regard to the conduct of private interviews and in making available evidence that could contribute to the resolution of matters of IAEA concern...
>
> The detailed knowledge of Iraq capabilities that IAEA experts have accumulated since 1991, combined with the extended rights provided by Resolution 1441, the active commitment by all states to help us fulfill our mandate and the recently increased level of Iraqi cooperation should enable us in the near future to provide the Security Council with an objective and thorough assessment of Iraq's nuclear-related capabilities.[70]

These statements unfortunately received little attention in the United States. Powell's analysis was widely viewed in the United States as convincing that Iraq had not been in compliance with previous resolutions and military action was needed. Elements of Powell's report were disputed and refuted, but they too received little attention.[71] The countdown to the start of hostilities had begun.

In short, a few persons in powerful positions believing, for various reasons, that going to war against Iraq was a good idea were able to marshal American support for doing so. Many possible opponents lacked the strong conviction that such a war would be a mistake. Of course the target of the war, Saddam Hussein, was indefensible as a ruler, and little attention was given to the Iraqi people. What a war might unleash within Iraq was not seriously considered.[72] Administration leaders seemed ready to believe that superior new military technology could somehow bring a new political order into existence. The illusion that Ahmed Chalabi would be a major figure in the new Iraq obviated the need for great preparation to bring about an immense transformation of the country.[73]

In retrospect, it is hard to imagine what might have been done to prevent the U.S. invasion. Still, reflecting on what various Americans might have done differently can be a useful exercise. I note how greater understanding of and reliance on the constructive conflict approach might have yielded viable alternatives. Crucially, alternative strategies that might effectively have responded to the problems posed by the realities of Iraq were needed to avert the march to war. Elements of such alternatives were proposed and promoted by prominent opponents to war.[74] Various components of alternative strategies, deriving from a constructive conflict approach, warrant attention. One set of elements in formulating an alternative strategy would have been to examine the conflict with Iraq in the context of interlocking conflicts. Some critics of the preemptive war did this by emphasizing the priority of the struggle against al Qaeda in Afghanistan. Other critics pointed to the centrality of the Israeli-Palestinian conflict for U.S.-Arab relations: positive U.S. efforts to advance peace in that conflict would weaken Saddam Hussein relative to the United States.

Clear attention to the relative importance of various goals the United States had regarding Iraq would have helped select appropriate strategies to attain each. If the primary goal were that Iraq not have weapons of mass destruction or be producing them, the goal was certainly already largely achieved and probably fully achieved by the end of 2002. The inability of UN inspectors to discover them, the knowledge that the Iraqi officials did undertake a program to demolish them, the severe sanctions, and the extensive bombing of Iraq in the past all had contributed to this result.

Scott Ritter, a leading former UN arms inspector who resigned in 1998, had become convinced that Iraq no longer had weapons of mass destruction and that the members of the Bush administration were marketing unsubstantiated allegations asserting Iraq had WMD and was connected with al Qaeda.[75] Convinced that it would be a tragic mistake for the United States to invade Iraq, he began appearing on television and radio programs and giving lectures to influence public opinion to oppose invading Iraq. In January 2003, in desperation, he thought President Bush might change his mind if Iraq could be said to be undergoing a regime change. He joined efforts for a delegation to go to Baghdad where he believed it would be possible that Iraqi government leaders would set forth their policy to cooperate fully with the UN, to implement domestic policies that are consistent with UN obligations, and to begin working with outside agencies to create the conditions for free elections. The trip, however, was not undertaken.

The possibility of a mediated agreement avoiding an invasion and satisfying many American goals is imaginable. Iraqi compliance might be stabilized by linking other changes related to human rights and democratization to lessening of UN sanctions and establishing diplomatic relations with the United States. It might seem impossible that Saddam, an autocrat who directed many atrocities, would ever allow domestic changes that would place him and his regime at great risk. But over time, domestic opposition can evolve that leads to transitions, and the egoism of an autocrat leads him to hold elections he believes he will win. The earlier account of the electoral ousting of Milošević in Serbia in September 2000 is illustrative.

U.S. OPERATIONS IN IRAQ AND AFGHANISTAN AND THE AMERICAN PUBLIC'S RESPONSES

Initially, the early U.S.-led military campaign against Iraqi forces seemed successful. But U.S. attempts to oversee a transition to a democratic Iraqi political system were inadequate and mistaken. The Iraqi army was dismissed and U.S. military forces were inadequate to maintain order. Much of the U.S. personnel undertaking to create a democracy were inexperienced and knew little about Iraq.[76] The Kurds managed to gain considerable autonomy, but the struggle between Sunni and Shi'a was complicated by the reality that the more numerous Shi'a were gaining political power after being subordinated to the Sunni. Very soon widespread sectarian violence between Sunni and Shi'a militia arose and an insurgency against the U.S. forces emerged, aided by an influx of Islamic militants from other countries.

U.S. leaders in Washington were slow in recognizing the realties with which they were confronted in Iraq and then slow to adopt new strategies. Gradually, the Iraqis themselves began to work out some accommodations. Shi'a and Sunni were driven to live in more ethnically distinct neighborhoods. Very importantly, many Iraqis turned against those who viciously bombed civilians, many of the perpetrators being seen as foreign zealots. Sunni Iraqis then began to cooperate more broadly with the U.S. military in countering the foreign fanatics. This was significant in making "the surge" have some positive results.

Similar sectarian problems existed in Afghanistan and the U.S. and allied forces became mired in fighting among different ethnic and ideological groups as they sought to defeat the Taliban. The wars in Afghanistan and in Iraq each drained resources and attention from the other and from dealing with al Qaeda.

As the wars dragged on and American casualties rose without good prospects of ending, let alone winning, the wars, the American public turned against the wars. Immediately after the 2003 invasion most public opinion surveys within the United States showed a substantial majority of Americans supporting war, but that began to fall less than a year after the war started. Support for war fell as problems rose. The leadership of al Qaeda had been greatly weakened, but local Islamic extremists had been aroused and independently conducted terror attacks, such as the bombing attacks in Madrid, on March 11, 2004.[77]

Peace movement organizations, such as the American Friends Service Committee, the Fellowship of Reconciliation, Pax Christi, and Peace Action, maintained their opposition to the wars, but they were careful to express support for the troops, having learned that it was counterproductive to seem to be criticizing U.S. soldiers while opposing the Vietnam War.[78] Significantly, in addition, the Internet had become a source of alternative information from what the mass media provided and a safe way to exchange views that helped to mobilize activism.[79]

Notable individuals with considerable government experience spoke out critically about the waging of the war in Iraq. For example, Clarke, in his 2004 book *Against All Enemies* and during his testimony before the 9/11 Commission, criticized the U.S. war in Iraq because it diverted resources from the fight against al Qaeda. Furthermore, he argued that the invasion of Iraq would actually enhance the efforts of Osama bin Laden and other Islamic radicals, who had long predicted that the United States planned to invade an oil-rich Middle Eastern country. Lt. Gen. William Odom, former director of the National Security Agency, made similar arguments in a May 2004 interview.[80]

Some critics of the Bush administration's foreign policies, particularly waging the war in Iraq, offered alternative policies. For example, in 2004, a diverse group of persons who had held positions of high responsibility for the planning and execution of American foreign and defense policy formed an organization to seek a change in U.S. leadership, "Diplomats and Military Commanders for Change." On June 16, 2004, the group issued a statement decrying the policies being pursued by the Bush administration in Iraq. The failure by the Bush administration to deal with the grievances and mistrust of many people in the Islamic world was the major reason for the failures of its public diplomacy efforts.

The presidential election of 2004 might be viewed as a popular referendum regarding Bush's foreign policy and his invasion of Iraq, but his Democratic opponent, Senator John Kerry, did not propose a fundamentally different approach.[81] Kerry was a heroic Vietnam veteran who had become an active leader in the movement to end U.S. engagement in that war. He was critical of the way the wars in Afghanistan and Iraq were being waged and argued that he would be a better war president, working better with allies and reducing troops in Iraq. The reality that there were no weapons of mass destruction in Iraq was clear, but Bush brushed that aside and the public appeared to be unconcerned.[82] The Republicans called Kerry a flip-flopper who readily changed positions. Bush insisted that Kerry say, knowing what was now known in 2004, whether he would have voted yes in October 2002 for the congressional resolution authorizing the president to use military force if he deemed it necessary. Kerry said he would still have voted yes, undermining his arguments that Bush wrongly took the country into a war.[83] The Democrats seemed afraid to say they had fallen for the bad evidence supplied them. The ground had not been prepared for a fundamental challenge to the Bush administration's reckless conduct.

If Kerry had clearly argued that the invasion was wrong and that his own vote, which Bush used to claim authority to go to war, was a mistake, perhaps it would have made him seem more authentic and courageous. Undoubtedly, given his years of warning about the threats posed by Saddam Hussein, it would have been difficult for him to credibly say that.[84] However, if he did choose such a strategy, even if he were defeated, the realities of the war would have been better discussed. As it was the American electorate did not have clearly different approaches to foreign policy to choose between.

After the election, the wars continued going badly and criticism grew. Beginning in December 2004, polls consistently showed a majority of the American public thinking the invasion of Iraq was a mistake. As of 2006, opinion on what the United States should do in Iraq was split, with a slight majority favoring a timetable for withdrawal but against withdrawing immediately. However, in this area responses varied widely with the exact wording of the question.[85]

An improvement in the Iraqi situation has popularly been attributed to a surge in the number of U.S. troops deployed in Iraq, announced by Bush in January 2007. This increase along with a more comprehensive counter-insurgency strategy had been urged by widely acclaimed General David Petraeus and by General Raymond Odierno.[86] Important changes, however, had occurred earlier among Iraqis, which complemented the surge and may account for its apparent success. In July 2005, it was recognized that the vast majority of the numerous suicide attackers in Iraq were foreigners, mostly Sunni Arabs from the Persian Gulf countries.[87] By early 2006, these extremists, who had been viewed by local Sunni tribes as allies against the Americans, were now viewed as dangerous threats.[88] Some of these foreign fighters belonged to al Qaeda in Iraq; they overreached, killing innocent Iraqis and imposing themselves. The local Sunni tribal leaders began to cooperate with U.S. forces against these extremists. Gradually, the local people began to accommodate their differences without violence and use new and old institutions. Recovering from the immense destruction of lives, infrastructure, and trust resulting from decades of sanctions and years of war and occupation would take a very long time. Having contributed so much to the destruction, constructive American policies would be difficult, limited, and risky.

Contentions with North Korea and Iran

In George W. Bush's first State of the Union address in January 2002, he spoke of an "Axis of Evil," referring to Iraq, Iran, and North Korea. Even if this term was meant to refer to the axis between WMD and supporting terror, it would have insidious implications.[89] The government leaders in Iran and North Korea, seeing the emerging steps to invade Iraq, could reasonably anticipate that their countries would be next, which was more likely to produce resistance rather than surrender. It is a premise of the constructive conflict approach, and conventional realist thinking, to divide and isolate an antagonist, not broaden and bind together adversaries. Reaching out to elements within the enemy camp avoids dehumanizing large swaths of people and of counterproductive overreaching. Failing to do so can be self-defeating.

CONFRONTING NORTH KOREA

Upon taking office as president, George W. Bush had made it clear that he would not continue Bill Clinton's policies regarding North Korea (Democratic People's Republic of Korea, DPRK). He would take a tougher, uncompromising approach. Thus, Clinton's support for South Korean president Kim Dae-jung's policy of dialogue and reconciliation with North Korea was abruptly and publically ended when the South Korean president came to Washington in March to see the new American president.[90] Kim Dae-jung first met with Colin Powell, who assured him of continuing U.S. negotiations with North Korea, which were described in the previous chapter. Bush's radical change in U.S. policy obviously had not been discussed with the secretary of state.[91] Actually, the North Koreans had already gotten the message. In January 2001, the North Korean ambassador to the UN, Li Hyong Chol, went to Washington to convey North Korean interest in continuing to improve relations with the United States. He met with Thomas Hubbard, the acting assistant secretary of state for East Asia, in his office and was informed only that a review process was underway. There was no follow-up.[92]

Americans knowledgeable about North Korea recognized that it wanted closer relations with the United States. The North Koreans felt they had been victimized by their powerful neighbors for centuries. Thus, a North Korean official is quoted as recalling a Chinese saying, "Keep those far away close, and those close to you keep at a distance."[93] However, Bush and his team did not want to seriously negotiate with North Korea's leaders. The regime was demonized, and it provided a reason to develop an anti-ballistic weapons system, which in itself was desired.[94] Stopping nuclear weapons development became the key U.S. objective in relations with the DPRK.

North Korea had responded to the attacks of September 11, 2001, with expressions of condolences and propositions to cooperate in countering terrorist attacks. However, the North Korean gestures received little attention, and instead the threat of North Korea's nuclear program was raised as a source of possible terrorist attacks.[95] In actuality, Kim Jong Il, the president of the DPRK, began a process of economic reforms in North Korea and improvement of relations with Japan and with South Korea.

These developments were not taken as signs of North Korean changes upon which further progress might be based. Rather, the U.S. government threatened North Korea, as demonstrated by Bush's inclusion of North Korea in the Axis of Evil in his 2002 State of the Union address. He proclaimed the propriety of the United States acting preemptively to prevent hostile acts in speeches and in the National Security Strategy issued in September 2002.

U.S. hardliners, such as Bolton, argued that North Korea was pursuing a highly enriched uranium program and violating the Framework Agreement. That became the focus of U.S. concerns related to the DPRK. Nevertheless, formal negotiations were undertaken with the DPRK, at which U.S. conditions would be presented but no dialogue would occur.

In October 2002, James A. Kelly, the assistant secretary of state for East Asia and the Pacific, went to Pyongyang with the intelligence reports of the clandestine enrichment of uranium.[96] The North Korean delegation presented many initiatives sought by the United States, but the U.S. delegation said there would be no negotiations until enrichment programs were halted. In a fateful follow-up with Kang Sok Ju, senior deputy of Kim Jong Il, the U.S. delegation members understood Kang's assertion that the North had a "right" to nuclear weapons as an admission of engaging in nuclear enrichment. No clarifications were sought. The message went out that the North Koreans defiantly admit they had a highly enriched uranium program.[97]

To avert a complete breakdown of the Framework Agreement, former ambassador Donald Gregg, journalist and professor Don Oberdorfer, and Korea Society vice president Fred Carriere went to Pyongyang one month later. They met with the same officials Kelly had, including Kang Sok Ju, and discussed what had happened at the meeting with Kelly.[98] The North Koreans said that they had made no such admission and they were still trying to find a way to preserve the Framework Agreement. As they had said earlier, they would clear the U.S. concerns in return for recognition of their sovereignty, the ending of sanctions, and a non-aggression treaty. They obtained a message from Kim Jong Il to George Bush saying the nuclear issue could be resolved if North Korean sovereignty was recognized and firm assurances of non-aggression were made. The message was delivered to Steve Hadley, deputy national security council advisor, who quickly and definitively said, "We don't reward bad behavior."[99]

The neocon foreign policy approach, relying heavily on the use of military power, was recognized by neocons in the Bush administration as not workable against North Korea.[100] Militarily attacking North Korea would not have the potential gains they could envisage for Iraq and the cost would likely be the devastation of Seoul, the capital of the Republic of Korea. There would be no support regionally, particularly given the high costs of providing for the people of North Korea.

Furthermore, China would hardly passively accept a U.S. military intervention. To manage the situation, the Bush administration chose to avoid acting as if North Korea's actions created a crisis, even while claiming Iraq's possible plans for weapons of mass destruction constituted a crisis. Some recourse to diplomatic actions would have to be made, even as the continuing tough talk about the evilness of the North Korean regime would hamper diplomacy.

The problems grew with the collapse of the Framework Agreement. In South Korea's elections on December 19, 2002, Roh Moo-Hyun, who campaigned to continue Kim Dae-jung's reconciliation policies, was elected president. The Bush administration, citing its unwillingness to "reward bad behavior," largely sustained its hardline rhetoric and positions and reliance on coercive sanctions. The U.S. efforts to make the North Korean government stop developing a nuclear weapons program failed, even after resorting to sanctions, tough talk, and threatening actions. The latter included joint U.S.-ROK military exercises and the ROK's fortification of islands close to the DPRK coastline. The problems persisted because, since the mid-1990s, no one playing a guiding role in Washington about forming North Korean policy had asked the most fundamental question: Why do the North Koreans want nuclear weapons? If the question were asked, a diplomatic solution might have been found.

In the second term of Bush's presidency, the U.S. renewed some diplomatic meetings, in the form of six-party multilateral proceedings, which engaged the United States, South and North Korea, Japan, China, and Russia. In this context, in July 2003, Roh asked the Chinese government to mediate between the United States and the DPRK, to keep the North Koreans in the six-party meetings. Indeed, China sometimes did seem to pressure the North Koreans to moderate what the United States regarded as provocative actions.[101] But Kim Jong Il had his own domestic as well as security reasons for acting as he did.[102]

One of many escalating episodes occurred in October 2006, when the North Koreans staged their first nuclear test. This followed an intensification of the sanctions directed at the DPRK.[103] In September 2005, the Bush administration had increased financial sanctions by freezing North Korean accounts at the Banco Delta Asia (BDA). This was announced a day after assistant secretary of state Christopher Hill, the U.S. envoy to the six-party talks, and the North Koreans had reached agreement on principles for rolling back DPRK's nuclear program. Hill was concerned that the North Koreans would then react by walking away from the agreement and from further participation in the six-party talks. Pyongyang indeed made it clear it would not return to six-party negotiations until the United States freed the North Korean BDA accounts and met for bilateral talks. Finally, on October 31, 2006, at a meeting arranged by the Chinese, Hill stretched his instructions (with secretary of state Condoleezza Rice's support) and he met North Korean official Kim Gye Gwan bilaterally.[104] They arranged for a bilateral group to address the BDA issue. The North Koreans agreed to return to the six-party talks, and after four months an agreement was reached to return the frozen North Korean money and to return International Atomic Energy Agency inspectors to North Korea. In June 2007 the money was returned, in October 2008, the United States took North Korea off the state sponsors of terrorism list (but sanctions were reinstated later by executive order) and the IAEA inspectors re-entered the DPRK's nuclear facilities. The respect of bilateral talks and the removal of sanctions was more effective than the imposition of more sanctions.[105]

In short, the Bush approach was unlike the one that over the years resulted in the transformation of the Soviet Union and the end of the Cold War. At the completion of Bush's eight years of a generally hardline, coercive policy, the autocratic Communist North Korean rulers were still in power and internal repression remained strong. Most significant for U.S. policy goals, North Korea had emerged as a declared nuclear power. A more consistent U.S. multilateral, diplomatic strategy with fewer threats might also have failed to prevent this development, but it would have better served U.S. relations with other countries in the region and it very well may have produced greater constraints of and cooperation with North Korea regarding its military posture.

Two other constructive options deserved attention. First was the possible use of official and non-official mediation. In the previous chapter, former president Carter's mediation during Clinton's presidency was noted and during Bush's presidency, some elements of mediation between the United States and North Korea were sometimes provided by Chinese officials. More use of formally recognized mediation by the UN or regional international organizations would probably have been useful. Informal, non-official channels might also have been developed even further, perhaps with judicious acknowledgment and open reporting.

Second, nongovernmental exchanges and cooperative civic events may have helped produce a context in which political relations could be more productively pursued in a longer time frame. One such program is the regular non-official visits between Syracuse University and Kim Chaek University of Technology in Pyongyang that began in 2002.[106] The program was initiated by Stuart J. Thorson, professor of political science and international relations, with assistance from The Korea Society based in New York. During the period examined in this chapter, North Korean scientists visited Syracuse University seven times to collaborate on information technology, and a Syracuse University team met six times with their North Korean counterparts in North Korea or China. In August 2005 a Regional Scholars and Leaders Seminar program was begun, with South Korean and Chinese participation. In 2007 the

U.S.-DPRK Scientific Engagement Consortium was established to explore possible academic scientific activities. These exchanges of scientists have allowed them and their associates to understand their unique and shared technical problems as well as their cultural and social circumstances. Such understandings, developed over time, reduce misunderstandings and bolster political cooperation.

In addition, some people-to-people events occurred. In October 2007 the first group of North Koreans toured the United States in an exhibition of Tae Kwon Do, a popular Korean form of martial arts. The North Korean team appeared in California, Iowa, Kentucky, and Georgia. The trip was led by George Vitale, a Tae Kwon Do senior master, who also headed the New York State Police security detail in New York City for New York governors George Pataki and Mario Cuomo.[107] In 1989 he took the USA Tae Kwon Do team to Pyongyang to compete in the first Tae Kwon Do tournament hosted by the DPRK.

Finally, another people-to-people contact was carried out in February 2008, when the New York Philharmonic performed in Pyongyang. The concert was enthusiastically welcomed by an audience that included high government officials.[108] The White House chose to minimize the importance of the event, not saying anything about its significance for relations between the two peoples. The U.S. government refused to grant visas for a reciprocal visit by the DPRK State Symphony.

CONFRONTING IRAN

Branding Iran as evil and joined in an axis with Iraq was strange since the United States was on the road to war against Iraq. Iran and Iraq had been intense antagonists and were unlikely allies. Moreover, as discussed in the previous chapter, the new president of Iran was a moderate with whom some movement toward accommodation had been made by the Clinton administration. The antagonism directed at Iran is even more striking in the light of Iran's conduct after the September 11, 2001 attacks. The Iranian government immediately had held the "terrorist Taliban" responsible and permitted Iranians to hold street vigils expressing sympathy for Americans.[109] Powell told the press that Iran would be included in the coalition against terrorism. Significantly, Iranian officials said they were willing to reestablish diplomatic relations with the United States.

When the U.S. military forces invaded Afghanistan to overthrow the Taliban and were in pursuit of al Qaeda, Iran offered and provided considerable assistance: opening ports for transiting humanitarian aid, rescuing stranded U.S. pilots, and urging the anti-Taliban Northern Alliance forces, which it had helped arm, to cooperate with the U.S. forces. In addition, Iran helped in brokering the selection of Hamid Karzai, the U.S.-favored candidate, to be president of Afghanistan.[110] Furthermore,

Iran, with its largely Shi'a population and clerical regime, was likely to have great influence in Iraq after the fall of Saddam, and the coming to power of the Shi'a majority. Threatening Iran on the assumption that the regime in Iran would be overthrown following a new secular-democratic Iraq resulting from the U.S. invasion of Iraq was not a likely scenario, despite neocon expectations.

Persisting in treating Iran as part of the Axis of Evil might seem odd under these circumstances. Indeed, although Condoleezza Rice and her deputy, Stephen J. Hadley, had initially suggested Iran be so identified in the January 2002 speech, they then had second thoughts because they viewed Iran as having some democratic elements in its political structure and an emerging democracy movement.[111] But Bush wanted to include Iran, and it would strengthen Iranian hardliners who had argued against president Khatami's détente policy toward the West. Significantly, even before the U.S. military invasion of Afghanistan, the United States had adopted the rule proposed by Hadley that tactical collaboration with rogue states like Iran was possible in the GWOT, but not any strategic change in relations.[112] Many members of the neocon network and other right-wing Republicans felt strongly antagonistic to the Iranian government following its establishment after the 1979 revolution. They included Michael Ledeen of the American Enterprise Institute, Zalmay Khalilzad, William Kristol, Richard Perle, and others who called for regime change in Iran.[113]

Remarkably, shortly after the fall of Baghdad to U.S. military forces, the Iranian government proposed comprehensive negotiations with the United States to resolve the major issues of contention between them.[114] The offer was brought to Washington in May 2003 by the Swiss ambassador to Iran, who functioned as the caretaker for American interests in Iran. The offer had the approval of Iran's Supreme Leader, Ayatollah Ali Khamenei, and proposed to answer nearly every American wish. The proposal included, in a dialogue of mutual respect, to end Iranian support to Hamas and Islamic Jihad and to pressure them to stop attacks on Israel. It offered to support Hezbollah's transformation to a purely political party in Lebanon. It offered to place Iran's nuclear program under international inspection. Finally, Iran offered to accept the Saudi peace plan announced in March 2002, recognizing Israel if it withdrew from all occupied territories and accepted an independent Palestine.

Iran sought in return the ending of U.S. sanctions; respecting Iran's right to access to nuclear, biological, and chemical technology; and supporting Iranian demands for war reparations from Iraq and acknowledging its national interests in Iraq. Furthermore, it wanted members of the Mujahedin-e Khalq Organization (MEK) based in Iraq to be given to Iran in exchange for al Qaeda operatives captured in Iran. (The MEK was a U.S.-designated terrorist organization of Iranian origin.) Step-by-step negotiations were proposed to reach a mutually acceptable agreement and a transformed relationship.

Secretary of State Powell and his deputy, Richard Armitage, saw this as an opportunity and favored a positive response. However, this was blocked by the opposition of Dick Cheney and Donald Rumsfeld, who saw the proposal as a sign of weakness and thought the United States could get everything that it wanted by dictating the terms of agreement or changing the regime. No interagency meeting was held to discuss the proposal and a response to Iran was not even made. The seemingly easy military victories by the United States in Afghanistan and Iraq were a basis for self-destructive overreaching. Soon thereafter insurgency warfare erupted in Iraq and the U.S. position relative to Iran became much weaker, as Iranian influence in Iraq increased.[115]

Stephen J. Hadley, in reviewing the George W. Bush administration's Iran policies in 2010, celebrated the early cooperation between the U.S. and Iranian governments in fighting terrorism, and he attributed its brevity to "Iran's growing support for extremist groups and new revelations about its secret nuclear facilities."[116] He did not mention Iran's May 2003 offer for comprehensive negotiations to transform the U.S.-Iranian relationship. In regard to Iran's nuclear program, the United States offered Iran a choice between verifiably abandoning its pursuit of nuclear weapons capability, which would produce a relaxation of sanctions and support for a civilian nuclear program, or if that choice were rejected, suffering greater international sanctions and the risk of military action.

That process certainly does not fit the model for negotiations that are intended to produce a constructive, mutually agreeable settlement. The kind of negotiation undertaken by the Bush administration appears to be coercively imposing its desired outcome. The Bush administration strategy was to slow Iranian progress to gain nuclear weapons and to hasten the time when public pressure would cause the regime to change its policy or to be transformed into a government that would make that choice.

Another major issue of contention, from the U.S point of view, was the Iranian support of terrorism. As discussed in the preceding chapters, this pertained particularly to support of Hezbollah, but insofar as direct attacks on U.S. interests are concerned that ceased in the 1990s. Hadley acknowledges that Hezbollah did not undertake terror attacks against Americans during Bush's presidency. The global war on terror blurs distinctions about who is committing terror attacks against whom. Hezbollah, Hamas, and Islamic Jihad are militant antagonists of Israel, but the ways for U.S. officials to counter such attacks are not likely to be the same as if the attackers were targeting Americans.

An additional major U.S. goal was to improve the human rights of the Iranian people, which suffered under what is reasonably viewed by Americans as a highly autocratic regime. That would more likely occur slowly and from the inside, however, than be forced by U.S. insistence.

Mahmoud Ahmadinejad succeeded Khatami to become president of Iran in August 2005. He was generally regarded domestically and internationally as advancing more hardline policies and speaking more intemperately, which diminished the possibilities of ameliorating the hostile relations between Iran and the United States. During the remaining years of Bush's presidency, international and national sanctions were intensified to induce Iran to curtail its progress toward developing the capability of producing nuclear weapons.

At the end of Bush's presidency, its supporters claimed some gains in relations with Iran. For example, Hadley argued that a framework for international governmental and banking cooperation to impose economic sanctions was enhanced and that U.S. military power against Iran was strengthened in the region.[117] Furthermore, he pointed to increased Iranian debate about the foreign and domestic policies of the hardline Iranian regime. However, the lack of success is even more evident. Iran had made considerable progress in developing nuclear capabilities for purposes of energy or of weapons. Mistrust between the governments had increased. The Iranian government could rally domestic support by blaming U.S. sanctions for its economic problems and sustain nationalist Islamic fervor to resist American threats.

Various alternative approaches might be considered. Some supporters of the Bush administration's general approach toward Iran advocated bigger "carrots" and bigger "sticks" to achieve a grand bargain.[118] However, the proposed grand bargain could reasonably be viewed as giving the United States what it wants from Iran, including Iran's ceasing to develop nuclear capabilities, while Iran would get what the United States thinks Iran needs, including reducing sanctions and improving Iranian economic conditions by foreign trade and investment.

Research indicates that when sacred values are a component of a conflict, the offer of material benefits alone can be counterproductive.[119] In such circumstances, if one side also makes some concessions to the other side regarding what is sacred, it will improve the likelihood that its proposed deal will be accepted. The frequency with which Iranian officials expressed the desire for respect suggests that they felt they were not treated with the respect they deserved. Accepting material benefits to buy off sacred values then would be dishonorable.

Additionally, the constructive conflict approach suggests that a grand bargain would be fashioned from mutually respectful dialogue and attentive negotiations. In this case, U.S. efforts at reaching a grand bargain would begin with responding seriously to the Iranian proposal of May 2003.

Moreover, reflecting on the constructive conflict approach would suggest looking at the way accommodations in one conflict can contribute to de-escalating conflicts that are linked to it. In this case, many analysts have stressed that the Israeli-Palestinian conflict and the U.S. government's involvement in it is a source of widespread Arab and Islamic antagonism toward the United States.[120] Management of relations with Iran would be eased if U.S. engagement in the Israeli-Palestinian conflict was seen as more even-handed and the plight of the Palestinians was given greater priority. The Bush administration's role in the Israel-Palestinian conflict is examined in the next section of this chapter.

There was a paucity of nongovernmental organizations and initiatives bridging the contentious relations between the U.S. and Iranian governments. One basis for significant bridging conduct was the significant Iranian diaspora in the United States. Family ties were a channel for an exchange of information that could then diffuse in many circles. An important organizational manifestation of this is the National Iranian American Council (NIAC), founded in 2002. It has become effectively active in representing Iranian American views to members of Congress, striving to ensure that human rights are upheld in Iran and civil rights of Moslems are protected in the United States.

Before concluding this section, it is worth noting that the Bush administration's policy toward Libya did not follow the same hardline neoconservative approach used toward North Korea and Iran. Rather, Bush continued the path followed by his predecessors, as described in earlier chapters.[121] Perhaps the step-by-step progress initiated by his father, George H. W. Bush, had gone so far that it was unstoppable. In 2003, Libya reached an agreement regarding compensation with the Pan Am families and accepted responsibility for its officials' actions; with that, the UN sanctions were removed. Finally, negotiations yielded an agreement for both the ending of U.S. economic sanctions and the verifiable dismantlement of its programs to develop chemical, biological, and nuclear weapons. Thus, American-Libyan relations were transformed and their economic ties were renewed.[122]

Accounts for this transformation are controversial because different parties defend or criticize past policies and use their explanation to argue about future policies.[123] I believe that the early unilateral U.S. economic sanctions may have had little effect, but the targeted multilateral sanctions proved to be effective. They isolated Libyan officials and also hampered the maintenance of oil drilling and the exploration for new oil fields. Moreover, after the Reagan administration, the U.S. efforts to overthrow the Gaddafi regime were put aside. This meant that if Gaddafi met specific requirements, his regime could survive and economic benefits would result for U.S. and Libyan companies.

Mediation of Israel-Palestinian Conflict

When Bush took office, Israeli-Palestinian relations could hardly be worse. The Oslo peace process was dying amid the violent second Intifada and its violent suppression. Nevertheless, Israeli and Palestinian negotiators met in Taba, Israel, in

January 2000. The negotiations inched forward, but not to Arafat's liking, and Barak had already resigned as prime minister. On February 6, 2001, Ariel Sharon, leader of Likud, overwhelmingly defeated Barak. I was visiting Israel at the time of the election, and found that Israeli friends who had devoted themselves to working for a peaceful accommodation between Jews and Palestinians in two states were devastated, some vowing to give up their activist struggle for peace. Labor Party supporters had abandoned Barak and could not abide the idea that Sharon would be the prime minister.

Before becoming president, Bush had little experience outside of North America, but he had visited Israel in December 1998 with three other governors.[124] The trip included a helicopter tour of Israel, conducted by Ariel Sharon, then the Israeli foreign minister. Bush was struck by Israel's security challenges and very impressed by Sharon.

Upon taking office as president, Bush in effect brought U.S. policy into greater alignment with those of the hardline Israeli government.[125] Short-term official Israeli policies were generally supported and relatively little was done to support democratic Palestinian state-building. This tendency was buttressed after the 9/11 attacks and the response was the global war on terrorism framing. Israel's long experience with attacks on civilians, sometimes by suicide bombers, made its enemies terrorists, and its ways of countering them models of U.S. counterterrorism conduct.

Despite Bush's preference to disengage from the Israeli-Palestinian conflict, early in his administration Secretary of State Powell sought to end the ongoing violence in Israel and the occupied territories and to reopen paths for a mutually acceptable accommodation.[126] Powell drew upon the report issued in April 2001 by George Mitchell and other dignitaries, which assessed the reasons for the violent breakdown of the peace process and made some policy suggestions, as had been commissioned by President Clinton. It provided a balanced critical view of what had happened.[127] The authors concluded that Arafat was not responsible for starting the violent Intifada but had done too little to stop it. They also concluded that Sharon's walk on Haram al-Sharif/Temple Mount, in September 2000, accompanied by hundreds of Israeli police, contributed to spiraling contention, as did the continuing Israeli settlement growth.

The report proposed ways to end the violence, which Bush accepted and won seeming agreement from the opposing sides. Bush requested CIA Director George Tenent propose a plan to restructure PLO security forces. Slowly, during the summer of 2001, some progress was made to curb the violence. Then came the September 11, 2001 al Qaeda attacks. Powell saw this as a reason to build a broad coalition, including Islamic allies, and actively strive for progress toward peace between Israelis and Palestinians.

The neocons in the administration, on the other hand, brushed that aside and wanted to move quickly for military action in Afghanistan and then in Iraq.

Bush allowed Powell to explore diplomatic possibilities, while the invasion in Afghanistan was immediately undertaken and plans for mobilizing support to invade Iraq were being considered. In a November 2001 speech at the United Nations, Bush did present his vision of a Jewish state and a Palestinian state, existing side-by-side, living in peace. Sharon himself, on September 23, 2001, spoke of offering the Palestinians a state of their own, which had not previously been officially proffered.[128] However, little action was then taken to help make that a reality.

Early in January 2002, the Israeli navy intercepted a vessel with fifty tons of weapons and produced evidence, convincing to Washington officials, that the weapons were from Iran and destined for the PLO.[129] For Sharon, Arafat had no credibility and discussions of expelling or even killing him began among some leading Israelis. Bush reasoned with Sharon against killing or expelling Arafat, noting that isolating him in his office compound would be more effective. In the spring of 2002, violence escalated again with a suicide bombing in Netanya, Israel, killing twenty-nine people, and the Israeli's reaction entailed severe attacks in Jenin in the West Bank. Bush declared that the Israelis had the right to defend themselves against terrorism. Israeli military operations intensified, reoccupying most of the West Bank, confining Arafat to his compound in Ramallah, and so ending the Intifada.

As the plans to invade Iraq matured, Bush felt pressure from Saudi Arabia and other Arab countries, important allies in attacking Iraq, to do something to assist the suffering Palestinians. On June 24, 2002, Bush delivered a major statement regarding U.S. policy relating to the Israeli-Palestinian conflict. The preparation of the speech was difficult because of the disagreements among the leading figures in the administration.[130] Colin Powell and others in the State Department still sought serious engagement in Israeli-Palestinian progress toward a final status agreement; but Cheney, Rumsfeld, and others in the White House believed that the United States could no longer try to work with Arafat.[131] Condoleezza Rice drafted a speech that seemed to satisfy these concerns and those of Israel and the Saudis. Bush declared that the United States would support the establishment of a Palestinian state when new Palestinian leaders fight against terrorism and destroy its infrastructure.

To make progress on the reform and democratization of the Palestinians, Powell began to work multilaterally with the UN, the European Union, and Russia, forming the Quartet. In the fall of 2002, the Quartet drafted a road map for steps to achieve peace between a Jewish state and a Palestinian state, which was discussed with the Israeli government.[132] Soon after the invasion of Iraq, in March 2003, the text of the road map was announced. In the first phase of the road map, a cease-fire would be established, Israeli settlement activity would be frozen, and Israeli military forces would withdraw to their positions in September 2000. The release of the road map also followed the election of Mahmoud Abbas as prime minister of the Palestinian Authority (PA). He pledged to end terror and to work for a negotiated peace, which indeed he had done for many years in both secret and open channels.[133]

Little progress, however, was made in implementing even the first phase of the road map. Israeli targeted killing of Hamas leaders, and Hamas's deadly attacks on Israeli civilians constituted ongoing violence. The Quartet failed to oversee the implementation, a critical aspect of mediation in this case, and by January 2004, the road map plan was abandoned.

Sharon had a new way to overcome the intolerable circumstances—by unilateral Israeli actions.[134] He accelerated the building of a wall separating the Jewish and Palestinian populations in the West Bank and he would remove the Jewish settlements within the Gaza strip, which was already enclosed by such a barrier. He also considered the future consolidation of the settlement blocs, leaving a half or a little more of the West Bank for a Palestinian state. He gained President Bush's support for this unilateral plan.

The potentiality of new constructive developments clearly arose after Arafat died in November 2004, and Mahmoud Abbas succeeded him as president of the PA. American hopes for Palestinian political reform and democratic progress grew after the free and well-run election in January 2005 confirming his presidency.

Important changes were developing in Israeli society regarding support for a two-state solution. Many Israeli Jews began discussing the demographic problem that made it impossible for Israel to be a Jewish state, and a democratic state, and incorporate all the occupied territories. A two-state solution was needed to be both a Jewish and a democratic state. Many leading members of the nationalist Likud Party came to this opinion, including Sharon, and for some of them, unilateral disengagement could be the way to that solution. Consequently, a new political party, Kadima, was established in November 2005 by moderates from the Likud Party, joined by some political figures from the Labor Party. It became the largest party in the Knesset after the 2006 elections.

The Bush administration became more consensually focused regarding the Middle East when Rice succeeded Powell as secretary of state in January 2005, following Bush's re-election. With Arafat gone and Abbas as president of the PA, the possibility of negotiating a two-state solution would seem feasible. Significantly, however, no one in the White House brought up any idea of deviating from Sharon's disengagement plan, even when the primary reason for it was gone.[135] In Jerusalem as well, the disengagement path continued to be followed and was not reconsidered. Sharon fought for and won Cabinet votes approving Israeli withdrawal from Gaza and the removal of the Jewish settlers there.

This was carried out in August 2005. Americans hoped that economic and political developments in Gaza would be a model of what Palestinians could accomplish and encouraged and warned the PA to prepare for the departure of Israeli military forces. Abbas assured the United States that the PA was prepared to control developments in Gaza. However, Hamas and other armed militia groups had been well established in Gaza, and the PA had limited security capability in the Gaza Strip.

The unfortunate handling of the many prosperous greenhouses owned by Jewish settlers exemplified the disorders following the Israeli withdrawal. No cooperative plans were made by the PA and the Israeli government about the disposition of the greenhouses. James Wolfensohn, former World Bank president and special envoy for the Quartet, raised $14 million from private donors to purchase the greenhouses and transfer them to the PA.[136] However, extensive looting of the greenhouses occurred by local Palestinians. Then, as some production was renewed, marketing was severely hampered by the Israeli prevention of reliable export channels.

The withdrawal from Gaza happened while Palestinian elections in the West Bank and Gaza were being planned. Abbas wanted Hamas to participate electorally and so avoid a civil war among Palestinians. However, the United States and Israel regarded Hamas to be a terrorist organization and did not think a political party with its own armed forces should compete in democratic elections. They had long encouraged the PA to use force if necessary to disarm what they regarded as the infrastructure for terrorist attacks. Nevertheless, the United States deferred to Abbas's decision, anticipating that the Fatah Party and others making up the PLO would defeat Hamas in the elections.[137]

U.S. mediation certainly was hampered by the complexities of Palestinian politics, but the realities should have been taken seriously and more efforts made to deal with them. Too often, Israeli government views were accepted as policy guides. Hamas was denied engagement, yet its capabilities needed more recognition, and Palestinian weariness with Fatah's corruption and incompetence was not responded to adequately. The United States and the other mediators might have tried to monitor all the parties' conduct and insist on fulfilling the commitments of the Roadmap. Wishing that an election would fix matters was not wise.

In the January 2006 elections for the Palestinian Legislative Council, Hamas won a surprising victory. It won enough seats to form a majority government on their own. The victory was partly due to a badly run campaign in which Fatah candidates ran against each other for some of the same seats, but it was also due to being viewed as corrupt and as failing to accomplish much. Hamas may also have won support from appearing to be fresh, more militant, and more Islamic, which had increasing appeal. In any case, neither the Bush administration nor the Fatah or the Israeli leaders had plans about what to do if Fatah were defeated.

The Hamas triumph posed an immense challenge to reaching a two-state solution to the Israeli-Palestinian conflict. On January 30, the Quartet acted to overcome this challenge. It declared that "future assistance to any new government would be reviewed by donors against that government's commitment to the principles of nonviolence, recognition of Israel, and acceptance of previous agreements and obligations. . . ."[138] U.S. lawyers reasoned that the U.S. government could not give any funds to a terrorist organization, which ruled out giving money to Hamas or entities it controlled. This was understood by the United States Agency for International Development, however, as permitting contact with the Palestinian presidency and PA entities that are independent of the prime minister and cabinet ministers.

On February 8, 2006, Khaled Meshal, a high Hamas leader asserted that Hamas would not change, but also offered a long-time cease-fire if Israel withdrew to the 1967 borders.[139] Neither the United States nor Israel treated this as a possible bargaining position that might be explored. On March 29, a Hamas government was sworn in, with Ismail Haniyeh as prime minister and Hamas members filled almost all cabinet positions. The United States then ceased contact with the new government and suspended aid to it.

In January 2006, Sharon had suffered a severe stroke that left him in a coma until he died in 2014. Ehud Olmert immediately began exercising the powers of the prime minister's office and led Kadima to a victory in the March 2006 elections, becoming prime minister of the new government on May 4.[140] Olmert had been a Likud leader, more nationalist than the pragmatic Sharon, but transformed by the demographic considerations to join in forming Kadima.

On the Palestinian side, Fatah and Hamas leaders unsuccessfully tried to form a sustained unified Palestinian government, but there was sporadic violent fighting and then a territorial split. In December 2006, fighting broke out in the West Bank after Palestinian National Security Forces fired on a Hamas rally in Ramallah and intense fighting continued into January 2007 in the Gaza Strip. In February 2007, Khaled Meshal of Hamas and Mahmoud Abbas, the PA president and leader of Fatah, met in Mecca and signed a Saudi-brokered power-sharing deal.[141] However, in May 2007, deadly clashes erupted again in Gaza. Leaders of both parties called numerous cease-fires, but none lasted. In June, Hamas took control of the Gaza Strip from Fatah after deadly battles and President Abbas dismissed the Palestinian government. He appointed an independent, experienced economist, Salam Fayyad, as prime minister. The United States welcomed the appointment and lifted a ban on aid to the new Palestinian government.[142]

Also during these years, Israel battled Hamas in Gaza and Hezbollah in Lebanon, exacerbating the spoiler effects of provocative actions. On June 25, 2006,

Hamas militants launched a raid into Israel from Gaza, killing two soldiers and capturing an Israeli conscript, Gilad Shalit. Israel then invaded Gaza to suppress the firing of Qassam rockets from Gaza and to secure Shalit's freedom. Large-scale incursions and bombardments ensued, but Shalit was not released and Israeli military operations continued during the summer of 2006.

In July 2006 a Hezbollah ground contingent crossed into Israel and attacked a squad of Israeli soldiers; they killed eight soldiers and captured two others.[143] Olmert reacted with large-scale attacks by land, sea, and air striking at targets that included the Hezbollah headquarters, the major TV station and radio station, and the International Airport in Beirut. Hezbollah responded by firing around 4,000 rockets; however, about three-fourths of them hit open areas. Hezbollah engaged in guerrilla warfare with the Israeli Defense Force (IDF), sustaining greater casualties than the IDF. However, the IDF was not winning a decisive victory over Hezbollah and the international pressure grew to stop the fighting.

Condoleezza Rice worked with Fouad Siniora, prime minister of Lebanon, and with Omert to obtain a Security Council resolution that would not have Hezbollah return to its prewar status nor have it claim victory.[144] On August 11, 2006, the UN Security Council unanimously approved Security Council Resolution 1701, which was accepted by the Lebanese government, Hezbollah, and the Israeli government and ended the hostilities. However, although the text stated that the Lebanese army should control all Lebanese territory, Hezbollah actually controlled more territory than ever before.[145] Also, while the text required the disarmament of Hezbollah, it soon rearmed and was stronger than ever.

In Israel, the war was regarded as a mistaken, badly waged overreaction to the Hezbollah raids. Olmert, already weakened by charges of corruption, lost considerable public confidence, which was a reason to try for progress with Abbas. Rice had also lost confidence that Olmert could make progress in bilateral Israeli-Palestinian negotiations, given the internal problems leaders on each side faced. Rice drew from the conflict resolution toolbox the idea to place that bilateral relationship in the context of regional and global concerns, thereby reframing elements of the bilateral conflict. She arranged a large international conference including governments that could help give cover to Olmert and Abbas to make concessions that could help negotiations. This participation was largely absent in the failed Camp David negotiations.

The conference came together on November 27, 2007, at the U.S. Naval Academy at Annapolis to witness Olmert and Abbas announce a renewal of negotiations. Remarkably, intensive Israeli-Palestinian negotiations, already begun, continued between Olmert and Abbas until September 16, 2008, when the last meeting was held. Persons involved or familiar with the negotiations report that Olmert and

Abbas were very close to a comprehensive agreement, each having made important concessions and agreed on solutions to difficult issues relating to Jerusalem and the monitoring of the Jordanian border with a Palestinian state.[146] Some issues remained, but there were no further meetings and nothing was signed.[147]

Many events hampered completing a two-state peace agreement, which both leaders believed was possible until the window of opportunity closed. Olmert was attacked on charges of corruption, challenged by rivals as his coalition had defections, and reviled by right-wing political leaders in Israel and some members of the Jewish diaspora in America. At the end of July, Olmert announced he would resign when a new leader of the Kadima Party was chosen in elections at the end of September. Abbas also was concerned about challenges from Hamas and other would-be spoilers. He wanted a full agreement to put before the Palestinians and thought he had until January to continue and complete negotiations with Olmert or even continue negotiations with a successor government. However, Tzipi Livni won the Kadima Party leadership, and was unable to form a coalition government, resulting in national elections in February 2009. Although Kadima remained the largest party in the Knesset, Likud's Netanyahu was asked to form a government by President Peres, which he did. It was Netanyahu's Likud-led government that president Obama faced as he started a new mediation effort.

Although the Bush administration failed to mediate a peace agreement between Palestinians and Israelis, some policies of the Bush administration directed to strengthen and democratize the Palestinian society were successful. They could contribute to a constructive path to a mutually negotiated accommodation between Israelis and Palestinians. Reforming the PA was a way of increasing support from the Palestinian people and also to reassure the Israelis that a Palestinian state could be an economic and political partner in peace and security. The support and cooperation with Fayyad as PA prime minister exemplified this.[148] He strove to improve PA functioning, dropping many people on the payroll for political reasons, and to eliminate armed militias outside of the PA. He used his credibility with the United States and with Israel to maximize assistance and minimize economic restrictions.

Another policy that contributed to the social and political life of Palestinians in the occupied territories was U.S. security assistance to the PA. In 2005, the office of the United States Security Coordinator for Israel and the Palestinian territories was established, through which the U.S. State Department provided direct financial and personnel assistance to Palestinian security organizations. In 2007, it began training and equipping PA Security Forces. Lt. Gen. Keith Dayton of the U. S. Army served as the coordinator from 2005 to 2010. The more professionalized Security Forces helped free economic life in the West Bank from interference by self-aggrandizing gangs. Its members could feel they were helping create the infrastructure for a Palestinian state, if they were not viewed as agents of Israeli occupation.[149]

Many American nongovernmental organizations continued to be active in seeking to influence the U.S. government, the public, and even the contending parties in the Middle East. Most prominent among these was the American Israel Public Affairs Committee (AIPAC), a lobbying group that advocates for policies generally consistent with positions of the Israeli government. Since the 1970s, it built the resources to be one of the most powerful lobbying groups in Washington.[150] Offering a different perspective, J Street was founded in April 2008 as a nonprofit advocacy group promoting American leadership to resolve the Arab-Israeli and Israel-Palestinian conflicts peacefully and diplomatically. It supports nonmilitary solutions, multilateral approaches, and dialogue over confrontation. It seeks to provide political and financial support to candidates for federal offices who believe in supporting the establishment of a Palestinian state side by side with Israel, which will advance U.S. interests in the Middle East and promote lasting peace and security for Israel and the region.

Many American-based NGOs engaged in Track Two activities between Israeli Jews and Palestinians.[151] These activities included workshops at which particular contentious issues were examined and discussed in order to increase mutual understanding and develop solutions that could be incorporated in official diplomatic meetings.

During the 1990s, NGOs acting in solidarity with Palestinians increased in the United States and many other countries. Solidarity organizations may contribute to constructive ways to advance equitable agreements by reducing asymmetries that result in one-sided domination. Non-Palestinian allies may help create space where Palestinians can express their views and have them heard or seek to directly pressure Israel. They may belong to NGOs such as Jewish Voice for Peace, Christians United for Justice in Israel-Palestine, and Students for Justice in Palestine. The allies may base their work on their understanding of religious values, of universal human rights, or other shared concerns. However, they can sometimes strengthen resistance insofar as they engage in actions that seem to threaten the existence of the state of Israel.

In concluding this section, I suggest that despite many constraining circumstances it is conceivable that during Bush's second term a more constructive conflict approach would have produced better results. Following Arafat's death, more might have been done to bolster the PA's standing among Palestinians. The United States might have encouraged the Israeli government to work more cooperatively with the PA and at least modify its unilateral disengagement strategy. The United States might have done even more to support NGOs, providing training and advice to moderate Palestinian parties about running political campaigns, and certainly to warn about the dangers of running competing candidates for the same legislative seats. A more active U.S. engagement in the Olmert-Abbas negotiations after the Annapolis conference might have aided reaching a conclusion or established the understandings reached as a basis for future negotiations.[152]

At various times, a more explorative approach with Hamas during its efforts to cooperate and even unify with Fatah in governance might have opened new constructive possibilities. There were indications in many statements by Hamas leaders that a two-state solution, with assistance of the international community, could be acceptable.[153] The experience with other insurgent groups committing terrifying acts of violence that later abandoned those tactics to make an accommodation indicates that the tactics are not necessarily the essence of those groups.

Constructive Conflict Approach Applications, 2001–2008

The developments in the constructive conflict approach, discussed in the previous chapter, continued in the first decade of the second millennium. This was particularly evident for constructive conflict escalation, especially relating to intervention. The dangers of international intervention became an area of attention, as indicated at several points in this chapter. There also was more systematic assessment of smart, targeted sanctions and specification of the conditions contributing to their effectiveness.[154] International mediation was studied more intensively, with both quantitative and qualitative research methods, including examining mediation in intractable conflicts.[155]

Considerable research was done during this period on peacebuilding. One topic that continued to attract research and theorizing was reconciliation, with growing attention to comparative analyses.[156] The role of religion, not only as a basis for contention, but also a source of bridging and shared identities and values, was increasingly investigated.[157] The profound difficulties in making a transition from oppressive societies or societies rent by years of violence into more democratic and tolerant societies were increasingly examined.[158] The further difficulties in developing sustained peace and overcoming the dangers of would-be spoilers of peace also were analyzed.[159] Important research continued on the incidence of wars, attesting to global decreases in wars and deaths in combat.[160]

Finally, it is noteworthy that at the beginning of the new millennium, the realities of the new global circumstances, and the understandings of the constructive conflict approach had converged in many ways.[161] Insofar as traditional national security thinking and practice had to deal with the new realties, they also should, and to some degree did, converge with the understandings and applications of the constructive conflict approach. The world was going through many interrelated changes that called for new ways of managing large-scale conflicts. The world had become increasingly integrated, and therefore conflicts became more widely visible and more extensive in their effects. Security threats were increasingly seen in environmental challenges, refugee flows, and increased visibility of grave economic disparities. The expanding availability of large and small deadly weapons fostered vulnerability. The growing proliferation and importance of transnational governmental organizations and of norms and values provide new bases for controlling mass violence. Finally, increasing familiarity with research and experience with constructive conflict ways of thinking offered less destructive ways to handle conflicts.

Conclusions

U.S. involvement in foreign conflicts during George W. Bush's presidency was greatly shaped by the September 11, 2001 attacks. But it was the president and his associates' choices about how to respond to those attacks that made them so important. Many chose the Global War on Terror framing to view world affairs in order to enact policies guided by neoconservative thinking. The foreign policies undertaken by many, but not all, members of the Bush administration generally adhered to the neoconservative approach. This approach stressed reliance on coercion, with undue confidence in new technological warfare. It assumed American global dominance and strove to maintain it. It sometimes resulted in what others in the world viewed as presumptuous and arrogant conduct. The result was often failures and sometimes counterproductive consequences. Instead of forcing others to submit, their actions often aroused greater resistance to American policies.[162]

The neoconservative ideological approach included breaks from the traditional foreign policy establishment policies. Its applications often differed from the long-prevailing American public views, which inclined to caution and multilateral approaches. It is also noteworthy that the neoconservative approach also drew from some long-standing elements in American thought and practice. That includes the belief in the value of American ways for the world, in American exceptionalism, and in the global triumphalism of America after the fall of the Soviet Union.

Many foreign policy decisions made by the leading figures of the Bush administration were at great variance from the constructive conflict approach and those decisions had many disastrous consequences for the United States. This can be viewed as support for the utility of the constructive conflict approach. Admittedly, however, if some other approaches were applied, disastrous consequences also probably would not have happened. Thus, realist policies guided by more pragmatic and less ideological thinking and more modest and less grandiose goals would have averted a great many deaths and human dislocations, the costly burdens imposed on the American economy, and the great decline in the standing of the United States in the world. Indeed, there were dissenters from the most egregious policies pursued by the Bush administration, both within it and certainly in the country as a whole.

The framing of the response to the 9/11 attacks as a war against terrorism had other grave implications for all the engagements in foreign conflicts discussed in this chapter. Leaders in the Bush administration took the attacks seriously and wanted to take actions to minimize the chances of more such attacks. They enhanced the fears in order to mobilize American resources to counter such attacks. But the broad framing tended to conflate every foreign conflict as a manifestation of the GWOT. That obscured the particularities of the contentions with the North Korean and Iranian governments and the mediation of the Israeli-Palestinian conflict.

If Americans in various offices, institutions, and organizations had drawn more from the constructive conflict approach, the United States might have not only avoided some costly developments, but plausibly achieved significantly more positive effects. As discussed in this chapter, this is imaginable even in difficult cases such as in the struggle against al Qaeda and the Taliban, Saddam Hussein's regime in Iraq, and the governments of North Korea and Iran. Many institutional failures enabled mistaken decisions to be made, ratified, and implemented.

The constructive conflict approach draws attention to the utility of using a broad range of inducements, including soft power. It also directs attention to giving careful consideration of the perspectives, interests, and concerns of other major engaged actors, and even of enemies. Indeed, looking at a conflict from the enemy's point of view can be especially useful. Furthermore, each actor considering the multiplicity of other actors is increasingly advisable; for example, it is ever more important to regard citizens in contending countries not as puppets but as agents. Finally, as will be discussed in the last chapter, further development of the infrastructures for more constructive policies are needed if they are to be actually undertaken.

7   Attempted Course Change after 2008

WHILE EXAMINING EPISODES of American involvement in foreign conflicts after 2008, it is useful to recall the fifth reality about conflicts noted in Chapter 1; conflicts are dynamic; they wax and wane in intensity and in extension; they emerge, escalate, become transformed and often are renewed in an altered form. This chapter revisits old conflicts and examines new ones, as they were contentiously socially constructed. Many of the conflicts discussed are actively underway as these pages are written and will have changed when the pages are read. My suggested constructive ways of Americans engaging in particular conflicts may no longer be applicable or they may have become less feasible. The suggestions are made to stimulate the readers' thinking about new options, not as final answers.

Domestic Social and Political Circumstances

The U.S. presidential election of November 2008 was in part a referendum on the foreign policy of George W. Bush and his administration. But to an even larger degree it was waged and decided on domestic issues, most notably the terrible state of the failing American economy. Nevertheless, the Democratic victory in the 2008 elections would seem to presage a fundamental shift toward a more constructive American approach to foreign conflicts, after the many disastrous policies carried out in alignment with neoconservative thinking. There were public, personality, governmental, and other circumstances that would support that shift, but there were also strong counterforces. Both kinds of factors warrant attention.

AMERICAN PUBLIC OPINION

The American public had experienced the tragedies of engagement in foreign conflicts characterized by American unilateralism and over-reliance on military might. The grandiosity of George W. Bush's rhetoric and actions had been costly in lives and the economy and they had not succeeded. The 2003 war in Iraq, which was generally supported by the public at its start, by mid-2005 was regarded as a mistake by a majority of Americans.[1] Nevertheless, in a 2008 CBS poll, 50% of the public thought Bush had made the country safer and 23% said he had made it less safe.[2]

As discussed in Chapter 5, American public opinion consistently approved of the United Nations and upholding international law.[3] Resorting to military force to protect world order was thought to be correct sometimes, preferably done with UN authorization. Despite these indications of consensus, there were segments of the population which rejected that consensus. Some on the Right were suspicious of the UN and favored U.S. unilateral militancy as the appropriate form of U.S. world leadership. On the other side of the mainstream, some segments of the public were strongly opposed to the U.S. government's over-reaching goals and its excessive reliance on military force, exercised unilaterally.

The American public continued to become even more politically polarized, intensified by the election of the first black president.[4] Some white people felt threatened and angry at their decline in societal primacy, while others were pleased and proud of this manifestation of multicultural America. Obama faced fierce opposition from significant elements of the Republican Party. Before and after his election, there were rumors of the fantastic notion that he was not born in the United States and assertions that he was a Muslim.[5] The spectacular rise of the Tea Party and the Republican capture of the House of Representatives in 2010 raised major obstacles to Obama pursuing constructive policies regarding foreign conflicts. Although the Tea Party adherents hold diverse views, particularly between insisting upon retaining traditional social values and advancing libertarian views, there are shared positions on reducing the size of the federal government.[6] Populist sentiments are somehow melded with support for government policies that aided corporate interests. This was associated with the major financial contributions of wealthy people to Tea Party–related activities.[7] Regarding foreign affairs there is a strong nationalist tendency and resistance to whatever they view as limiting U.S. sovereignty. There are also contrary tendencies between libertarian views opposing military adventurism and American exceptionalism claims that promote U.S. global leadership.[8]

NONGOVERNMENTAL FOREIGN INVOLVEMENT

In actuality, American engagement in the increasingly globalized world, discussed in Chapter 5, was expanding. Despite the American economic troubles that began in 2008, foreign direct investment in the United States and direct U.S. investment abroad continued to generally rise between 1990 and 2012.[9] Although still small in numbers, more and more American college students studied abroad for a semester or more and increasing numbers of professionals were employed abroad.[10] Their families and friends thereby often also discovered new transnational ties. The rapidly spreading use of social media enabled a growing number of Americans to keep in contact with "friends" in many other countries. The popular culture was ever more internationally blended.

Along with growing international experiences through those channels, nongovernmental organizations continued to increase in number and size. Growing numbers of Americans worked in both non-profit and profit-making organizations that provided humanitarian services including improving health, assisting economic development, and training in conflict resolution in ever more countries.[11]

U.S. GOVERNMENT OFFICIALS

To set the stage for examining U.S. government involvement in foreign conflicts in 2009–2014, the major government offices pertaining to foreign relations and the persons filling them should be considered. I begin with President Barack Obama. Many personal qualities of Obama were noted by analysts around the time of his election to the presidency. They included his high intelligence, unique international experience, his pragmatic and non-ideological approach, his considerable self-discipline, and his rhetorical skills. Other qualities particularly relevant for shaping foreign policies also were noted: he seemed to view conflicts as complex and interconnected and to recognize the different perspectives among antagonists in a conflict. Furthermore, he was viewed as inclined to seek consensus among contending groups. Finally, he had significant acquaintanceship with the effectiveness of nonviolent action, derived partly from his attention to the civil rights struggle in the United States. These qualities would tend to be congruent with taking a constructive approach to foreign conflicts.

Obama's leadership style was widely recognized to be markedly different than George W. Bush's. Obama's self-confidence did not preclude giving attention to diverse views. As a leader, he seemed to be capable of multi-tasking, very persuasive, calm, ambitious, pragmatic, thoughtful about options, and self-disciplined. A comprehensive analysis of biographical reports and media sources concluded that Obama's profile suggested a confident, competitive conciliator.[12]

Systematic analyses of political leaders can help provide relevant parameters in characterizing Obama. Thus, Margaret G. Hermann's research identifies three major leadership styles: ideological, pragmatic, and strategic.[13] Obama seemed to best fit the strategic style of leadership. Strategic leaders have a set of goals, but how they try to achieve them is dependent on the particular situation. They are relatively open to information and challenge constraints directly and indirectly. They focus on process in policymaking and deal with conflicts on a case-by-case basis.

There was little consensus, however, in characterizing the content of Obama's primary values and substantive goals. This is partly attributable to his relatively brief political career and to the self-interest of those who seek to define him negatively or positively. Furthermore, his pragmatic and non-ideological approach would reduce the salience of his long-term objectives. Most pertinent for the issues addressed in this book, Obama's personal characteristics and leadership style seem quite appropriate for playing a conciliating mediator role. In foreign policy he aligned himself with the more realist-pragmatic approach of George Kennan, whose work he read, and Zbigniew Brzezinski, with whom he consulted.[14] But he had foreign policy ambitions: "to bend history's arc in the direction of justice, and a more peaceful, stable world order."[15]

Whatever Obama's personal predilections may be, as President of the United States, he has powerful resources available to him, but he also encounters many constraints and pressures. Regarding U.S. involvements in foreign conflicts, it should be recognized that Obama inherited the ever-expanding role for the president's own national security staff, led by his own national security adviser.

As president, Obama oversaw all the federal departments and agencies and appointed or nominated the highest leaders of these bodies, for confirmation by the Senate. But all the departments and agencies have long-employed staffs with their own interests and perspectives about their tasks. Most notable in determining U.S. foreign policy are the Department of State, the Department of Defense, and the intelligence agencies.

However much Obama may have wanted to break with Bush's policies, he selected a few persons for his administration who had helped construct Bush's policies in his second term, notably Robert Gates as secretary of defense. He selected persons with hawkish backgrounds, but also with pragmatic inclinations, for other important positions; they included retired Marine General Jim Jones as national security advisor and Admiral Dennis Blair as director of national intelligence. He also relied on many persons associated with Bill Clinton's presidency; most notably, he chose Hillary Clinton, his rival for the Democratic Party's candidate for the presidency, for secretary of state.[16]

Nevertheless, Obama and many of those appointed to the less visible positions were from a new generation.[17] They had not been directly impacted by the Vietnam War and concerned about overcoming its consequences. They confronted new realities, including the evident limitations and heavy costs of America's resorting to large-scale military operations, the severe domestic economic challenges, and the rise of other major international powers. The hubris and the resulting failures of George W. Bush's foreign policies were to be avoided.

On the whole, as examined in this chapter, disasters were avoided and Obama was re-elected. Some turnover in leading positions occurred, but that did not mark any fundamental change in direction. Senator John Kerry became secretary of state and former senator Charles Hagel replaced Gates as secretary of defense. The House of Representatives remained under control of the Republican Party.

The natural body to guide and execute U.S. foreign policy is the Department of State. U.S. embassies function in countries around the world, providing information back to Washington and conducting a wide range of activities for visiting Americans and the local population. Major contributions to peace-building that helps to prevent conflicts, to recover from them and to avoid their recurrence are provided by USAID.[18] The Agency was first established in 1961 and flourished for several years until budgetary cutbacks reduced its activities. During George W. Bush's administration U.S. foundations greatly expanded contributions for foreign assistance and many special presidential initiatives to provide foreign assistance were established, reducing USAID's centrality, and it was moved into the Department of State. When Obama became president and Rajiv Shah was appointed Administrator of USAID in January 2010, the budget and staffing of USAID was increased. Moreover, the programming has shifted away from awarding contracts to large corporations and to funding local organizations for specific projects.

In recent decades, the State Department has expanded its range of activities, entering needed fields of work. The U.S. government was ill-prepared to provide assistance to countries recovering from violent conflict or transforming after authoritarian oppression. For example, this was evident in Afghanistan and Iraq after U.S. military forces ousted the governments there. U.S. policy leaders recognized that the military forces experienced problems in building local governance systems. In 2004 the Office of the Coordinator for Reconstruction and Stabilization was created within the State Department to improve coordination between civilian organizations and the military. This was upgraded to become the Bureau of Conflict and Stabilization Operations, which expanded the coordinating role of its predecessor to directly intervene in conflicts in order to advance U.S. national security by breaking cycles of violent conflict and mitigating crises in countries facing high risks of mass violence.[19] Its members in the field engage in conflict prevention and in crisis response, aiming to address the underlying causes of destabilizing violence. They work with a variety of local groups and strive to be innovative and catalytic in their operations.

Finally, the Department of State and USAID have expanded support of local organizations around the world contributing to the infrastructure needed for a long-lasting democratic order. Understandably, the governments in some countries at some periods regard such support as unwanted meddling in their affairs; yet many governments welcomed participation. As an example, one regional project, the Leaders for Democracy Fellows program, brings young activists and professionals from the Middle East and North Africa to the United States for short periods to learn about nongovernmental organizations and social change.

As discussed in the previous chapter, the Department of Defense has vast capabilities and close ties to governments around the world. Those resources and connections give it influence and special interests of its own, which a president cannot ignore. Its great capacities compared to the State Department make it likely to be chosen for actions when some kind of intervention is needed. The commanding officers of the armed forces are mindful of their obligations to serve under civilian control, which has been forceful and produced great changes at times, as it did when Donald Rumsfeld was secretary of defense. Furthermore, the wars waged in Afghanistan and Iraq were not the kind of wars military forces had prepared to fight. New doctrines and strategies had to be developed in waging counter-insurgency struggles, and that entailed working more closely with local civilians, as well as armed forces.

The intelligence community is another major provider of information and counsel about developments around the world. The scope of intelligence operations greatly expanded after the September 11, 2001 attacks. The CIA also expanded its covert special operations, particularly in countering terror attacks. The move toward massive databases to be searched by computer algorithms for intelligence became a new source of resentment in many foreign countries and concern in the United States.

Finally, although the executive branch of government has considerable latitude in shaping foreign policy, the legislative branch has significant powers in affecting U.S. policies abroad, including confirmation of nominations to major offices, the ratification of treaties, and the funding for and the oversight over a wide array of possible operations. The members of Congress have narrower constituencies than does the president and therefore some are closely associated with particular lobbying influences. For example, this helps account for the recurrent resolutions to move the U.S. embassy from Tel Aviv to Jerusalem and other resolutions in support of the Israeli government.[20] It also helps to account for the decades of embargos against Cuba.

What was particularly remarkable from the outset of Obama's presidency was the animus of many political figures in the Republican Party. Many sought his failure and consistently opposed whatever he favored.[21] This was most apparent on domestic issues, but it also affected Republican judgments on foreign policy. When Democrats controlled both houses of Congress this was of less consequence, but it mattered greatly after the Republicans won control of the House of Representatives in 2010. The intensity of Republican antagonism was raised even higher by the eruption of the Tea Party movement and the increased leverage that highly wealthy persons came to have in spending large sums of money to support candidates and policies that they favored.

American Engagements against Adversaries

In January 2009, when Barack Obama was sworn in as president, he faced several international adversarial relations, including active engagement in two wars. The Bush administration had promoted a conflict framing that linked the global war against terrorism (GWOT) with fighting against the Taliban in Afghanistan and waging a war to overthrow Saddam Hussein to produce a friendly, democratic Iraq. Obama sought to narrow the scope of the war on terrorism to focus on a winnable fight against al Qaeda and associated organizations. The combat in Iraq, not originally related to al Qaeda, was to be ended as soon as possible. In Afghanistan the fight against the Taliban might be ended by their defeat or negotiation, minimizing the dangers of al Qaeda havens there. These three related conflict fronts are now discussed.

COUNTERTERRORISM

In the view of the American public, the primacy of the fight against terrorism had subsided considerably in the context of the domestic and international changes since September 11, 2001. By 2007, a Pew survey found that the percentage of the public that believed that terrorism posed a very big problem for the United States had fallen to 44%.[22] Obama entered the presidency intending to reframe an endless global war on terrorism into a more focused struggle against al Qaeda and similar organizations attacking the United States. That struggle could be ended and won. It was waged in many ways, including making a case for it domestically.[23]

In practice, however, Obama maintained the rules and regulations related to the operations of the Department of Homeland Security. Some intelligence gathering and counterterrorism operations were expanded and intensified, but large-scale military operations were to be concluded as soon as was feasible. Some steps to narrow the focus of countering terrorism were attempted. For example, Obama sought to close the Guantanamo Bay detention center in Cuba to end widely condemned U.S. conduct there and to signal a shift away from war to more judicial proceedings. On January 22, 2009, President Obama signed the order to shut down the center by the end of the year.[24] This did not happen because of congressional opposition to moving prisoners into facilities within the United States for detention or trial. Congressional resistance to Obama's policies was to mark his administrations.

At the outset of his presidency, Obama and secretary of state Clinton sought to improve American relations with the governments of allied countries and of other countries around the world, relations which had been damaged by the previous administration's approach to foreign affairs. This would enable more cooperative and effective operations to be taken to prevent future terror attacks. In particular Obama reached out to people in the Islamic world. In June 2009, Obama spoke at Cairo University, expressing his intention "to seek a new beginning between the United States and Muslims around the world, one based on mutual interest and mutual respect, and one based upon the truth that America and Islam are not exclusive and need not be in competition." He went on to defend U.S. policies, but in the context of noting his close, personal associations with and respect for Muslims. These and other actions noted in this chapter could be expected to help isolate al Qaeda and similar militant Islamic organizations by reducing their supporters and improving cooperation in combatting them.

As promised in his campaign for the presidency, Obama increased deadly U.S. attacks on members of al Qaeda and related organizations. He insisted upon intensive efforts to locate Osama bin Laden, and in August 2010 bin Laden's compound was located in Abbottabad, Pakistan, close by a Pakistan military academy.[25] After months of watching for more evidence that bin Laden was living in the compound, many discussions ensued about alternate policies to be followed: watch and wait, or conduct an air strike, or a drone attack, or a commando raid. Late on April 28, 2011, the National Security Council met and differed about which option to choose, after which Obama left to reflect and decide on the course of action. The next morning he told his senior White House national security team his decision was to undertake the raid. It was conducted successfully on May 1, despite a helicopter mishap. Bin Laden was killed and all the Navy Seals involved returned safely, without Pakistani knowledge.

U.S. officials had been concerned that conducting a commando raid in Pakistan without informing officials there would disrupt relations between the two countries. As noted in the previous chapter, however, there was reason to believe that some Pakistani officials, particularly in the intelligence service, were supportive of some militant Islamic groups and therefore would not keep information about a possible raid confidential.[26] In any case, this incursion into Pakistan did worsen the often-difficult relations between the two countries.

By 2009, al Qaeda's capacities to conduct terror attacks had been greatly diminished in Afghanistan and elsewhere, but new individuals and small groups attempted deadly attacks in several localities. Affiliated al Qaeda organizations include: al-Qaeda in the Islamic Maghreb, al-Qaeda in Yemen, al-Qaeda in the Arabian Peninsula, al Qaeda in Iraq, and al Qaeda Kurdish battalions.[27] Many of these organizations may be influenced by core al Qaeda leaders in the general directions and actions they take, but they remain relatively independent in their respective regions. U.S. officials generally are able to work with the governments in these regions in combating the al Qaeda affiliates. In addition, new organizations, with some similar goals and strategies, have arisen as competitors; for example, ISIS (Islamic State in Iraq and Syria).

Overall, the U.S. fight against militant Islamic organizations, despite the killing of many of their leading figures, was not steadily advancing everywhere. Some new fighters and organizations emerged and moved from one front to another. New safe havens emerged as government controls weakened or disappeared in particular areas and as some governments assisted the militant groups they favored. In addition, local people in the United States and elsewhere sometimes discussed, attempted, or executed terror attacks on their own initiative, as was the case in the bombing at the Boston Marathon in 2013.

The approach taken by the Obama administration to defeat al Qaeda affiliates included greatly increasing raids on their compounds and deadly strikes by drone aircraft, attacks which were carried out by the CIA and the U.S. military's Joint Special Operations Command.[28] The resulting "targeted killings" were deemed legal under the Authorization for the Use of Military Force, passed by Congress in 2001 following the 9/11 attacks.[29] Accurate distant strikes required a high level of current intelligence and careful execution or innocent persons would be killed. Despite close oversight, innocent people were killed fueling anger and opposition to the practice from the affected region and from groups within the United States. It also yielded new revenge-seeking fighters.[30]

This offshore strategy in some ways was to replace the emphasis on counterinsurgency that entailed extensive fighting to hold territory. Although overemphasis on this strategy can prove counterproductive, Obama and his team could not come up with a better alternative.[31] In reality, Obama and his team had a wider approach that combined a variety of strategies, which were joined together in particular evolving ways for specific countries and antagonistic organizations. These strategies are discussed later, in analyzing American involvement in particular countries.

Domestic events also resounded abroad. In Gainesville, Florida, Terry Jones declared that he would burn 200 Korans on the anniversary of the September 11 attacks. He received widespread media attention that aroused international outrage and pleas to cancel his plans. Although Jones cancelled the plans in September 2010 and said he would never burn a Koran, many protests against him broke out in the Middle East and Asia, with at least twenty deaths. Then, on March 20, 2011, Jones held a "trial" of the Koran in his church, found it guilty, and burned it in the church. Deadly protests erupted in many places, including in Afghanistan.[32] Officials in Gainesville imposed sanctions against Jones and his church and a wide range of political leaders spoke against Jones' conduct. Even greater public condemnation of Jones' actions and protests by American religious and political leaders might have limited the damage done by Jones. If his actions had generated immediate reactions of solidarity with people of all faiths in supporting religious diversity, Jones' actions might have been cut short and shown to be unrepresentative of America. Too often, a few religious and political leaders stir fears and build resistance rather than lead their followers to adhere to American civic values. Such positive leadership would help enhance domestic and international security against terrorist attacks.[33]

COUNTER-INSURGENCY IN IRAQ

By the time Barack Obama was elected, the war in Iraq was widely recognized by Americans to have been a tragic mistake. The costs at home and abroad were immense. The monetary costs of waging the war and attempting to reconstruct Iraq afterward were amazingly high, with lasting burdens on the U.S. economy. The death toll was great and the physical and mental damage to survivors will endure for many decades. Yet there were no great benefits. No weapons of mass destruction were found in Iraq. The war did not result in a friendly democratic government, thereby providing more security for the United States.

The Iraqi government, dominated by the Shiite majority and led by Prime Minister Nuri Kamal al-Maliki, was highly oppressive, especially to the Sunni minority. Furthermore, the Iranian government strove to be influential in Iraqi affairs, with mixed results.[34] The war and its consequences harmed U.S. relations with European allies as well as with countries having largely Islamic populations. The U.S. capacity to threaten or use military force in future crises was lessened. Individuals and groups that had enhanced their skills in fighting with various deadly weapons, including bombs, went home or elsewhere to serve in al Qaeda-like organizations.[35]

Ending U.S. military engagement in Iraq was politically easy for Obama since president George W. Bush had reached a withdrawal agreement in November 2008.[36] Under its provisions, U.S. combat forces would withdraw from Iraqi cities by June 30, 2009, and all U.S. forces would be out of Iraq by the end of December 2011. Obama held to his commitment to end U.S. military engagement in Iraq and its combat role was over even earlier, on August 31, 2010.[37]

Despite efforts, the U.S. government did not, and probably could not, create a system of pluralistic governance in which people of diverse identities would work cooperatively to maximize common benefits. Sunni-Shiite strife had persisted and electoral processes were troubled.[38] For example, the March 2010 elections to the Council of Representatives of Iraq did not produce a clear victory for any party. The Iraqiya Party representing many Sunnis and headed by Ayad Allawi, a secular Shiite and former prime minister, won 91 seats; Maliki's State of Law Party won 89 seats; and the Iraqi National Alliance, a Shiite coalition party, won 70 seats. Maliki remained in power as prime minister while Iraqi political leaders struggled to form a new government. Christopher R. Hill, then the U.S. ambassador to Iraq, and vice president Joseph Biden supported forming a government in which Shiites and Sunni shared power.[39] After eight months of contentious negotiations, a deal was reached on November 10, 2010: Jalal Talabani, a Kurd, kept his position as president, Maliki remained prime minister, and Allawi's alliance would hold the position of speaker of the Council of Representatives.[40] But in December 2011, Maliki created a political crisis with accusations against rivals, and by the end of February 2012 had established his authoritarian rule.[41] This provided an opening for ISIS forces to rise in Iraq, build a base in Syria, and sweep back into Iraq in June 2014.

The U.S. government had little capacity to avert the Iraqi political descent into renewed sectarian violence. Sadly, but understandably, after many years of horrible violence, often perpetrated by and against Iraqis of different religious and other identities, and also by and against foreign Islamic fighters and U.S. military personnel, an authoritarian strong-man would have popular appeal. Obama, in any case, did not want to set nation-building goals. Achieving them would be highly demanding in time and resources, and probably unattainable by the U.S. government, particularly given the domestic economic crisis and the public's war-weariness. Facing further deterioration in Iraq related to the ISIS presence, however, some U.S. military role was renewed as well as efforts to help create a more inclusive government. Success would need cooperation from other governments, which slowly was achieved to a limited degree.

Creating a pluralistic Iraqi political system would also require a supportive civil society. No such society existed under Saddam Hussein and would be difficult to achieve while sectarian wars, insurgencies, and counter-insurgencies were being fought. Implementing a broad range of non-governmental as well as governmental policies might have contributed to the growth of a pluralistic civil society. One such policy would be greater support for non-governmental organizations in Iraq. Initially, following the overthrow of Saddam Hussein, many nongovernmental organizations were quickly established. From the outset, however, the U.S. government sometimes failed to build on local resources. This was notably the case regarding the Iraqi anti-trade union policies.

In 1987, Saddam Hussein's government had imposed laws prohibiting unions and collective bargaining in the public sector, which applied to the oil industry and more than 80% of the nation's economy.[42] These harsh anti-trade union laws were not rescinded following the 2003 invasion, while Lewis Paul "Jerry" Bremer III was in charge of the Coalition Provisional Authority in Iraq from May 2003 until June 2004. They remained in effect after Iraq had its own government and continued thereafter.

This decision was not unrelated to U.S. policymakers' fear that a resurgent Iraqi union movement would oppose their plans for privatization of state-owned enterprises and resulting foreign control of Iraq's oil resources.[43] The Iraqi governments that took over from the Provisional Authority persisted in failing to reform the anti-union laws. Nevertheless, Iraqi workers have struggled to organize unions while the authorities seized union treasuries and offices, deployed troops against strikers, and prosecuted union leaders. So far, even during Obama's presidency, the Iraqi government has not changed its anti-union policies.

American trade unions might be expected to support organizing independent trade unions in Iraq. As noted in Chapter 2, American trade unions were active during the Cold War in supporting unions, particularly in Western Europe and in Latin America, which were competing against unions with Communist Party ties. Aiding independent trade unions in Iraq could contribute to the country's civil society and democratic infrastructure. A major vehicle for such endeavors is the American Center for International Labor Solidarity, known as the Solidarity Center, a non-profit organization affiliated with the AFL-CIO labor federation, which helps channel U.S. foreign aid. The Solidarity Center's mission is to help build a global labor movement by strengthening effective, independent, and democratic unions. It supports the Iraqi labor movement's efforts to create new laws that support workers' fundamental rights to form unions and bargain collectively. Since 2011, the Solidarity Center has joined with unions in Iraq to improve conditions in workplaces that receive loans from the World Bank's International Finance Corporation. The AFL-CIO also has called on the U.S. government to protect rights of Iraqi workers.[44] Clearly much more attention and popular mobilization in the United States and Iraq are needed to bring about appropriate reforms.

Many other nongovernmental organizations in the United States and in Iraq contributed to overcoming the legacies of Saddam Hussein's brutally oppressive rule and the wars that followed. For example, the Iraqi and American Reconciliation Project

founded in 2005, links Minneapolis, Minnesota and Najaf, Iraq in a wide range of activities, including art exhibits by American and Iraqi artists, person-to-person exchanges, and working to provide clean water for Iraqi schools.[45] Also related to the
Reconciliation Project, is an Iraqi-registered NGO, Muslim Peacemaker Teams, which
responds to local controversies and humanitarian needs. Although there was a great
surge in the number of NGOs in Iraq in the first years following Saddam's ouster, the
number soon fell, and their dearth hampers progress toward sustainable Iraqi peace.[46]

Difficult as it may be, progress toward coexistence is an important ingredient at
the local as well as the national level in building a pluralistic and peacefully sustainable Iraq. Since conflicts are socially constructed, they also can be re-constructed,
re-framed, and thereby transformed. Knowing that every large collectivity engaged
in conflict is internally diverse in many ways makes it reasonable to expect that some
persons and groups on each side may move toward coexistence, while others may
oppose such movement.

Finally, mediation, one of the core realities of the constructive approach,
needs to be discussed. The multiplicity of interconnected conflicts in Iraq could
be ameliorated to some degree by mediation at many levels. Mediation, like
reconciliation, is a process shaped by cultural factors. David A. Steele, noting
that cultural anthropologists distinguish between shame-oriented and guilt-
oriented societies to contrast many tradition-based, communal societies from
Western societies, cites studies of Arab culture that suggest the pursuit of honor
and the avoidance of shame are primary motivators of conduct.[47] Honor is acknowledged by one's community; therefore, dishonor brings shame on both the
individual and the individual's group. Furthermore, in many tradition-based,
communal societies, honor is achieved from relations with one's peers and
viewed as a zero-sum game, whereby one person's acquisition of honor is at the
expense of the other.

Steele examines many ways that cultural and religious obstacles to effective mediation and reconciliation can be overcome, by reference to Islamic beliefs and by
conflict resolution processes. For example, he points out that the Prophet Mohammed condemned unconditional loyalty to family or tribe as contrary to the spirit of
Islam. Rather, "honor of virtue" is emphasized, stressing honesty, hospitality, and
conciliation. A lack of honesty injures one's own sense of self-respect, which can be
repaired by humility, resulting from honest self-assessment. Contending groups can
be helped to acknowledge their own accountability for their conflict by a process of
parallel and separate self-examination; knowing that the other group is undergoing
the same exercise and by meeting, first, in private caucus so that no group is shamed
in front of its adversaries. Such practices are congruent with traditional Arab dispute settlement procedures.[48]

The Baghdad office of the United States Institute of Peace's Center for Post-Conflict Peace and Stability Operations conducted a variety of projects utilizing such insights, starting early in the occupation. They included workshops for Iraqi national and local officials and for tribal and civil society leaders regarding relationship building, negotiation, and problem-solving processes. They also included a dialogue process led by Iraqi facilitators, which produced a peace agreement signed by thirty-two Sunni and Shiite sheiks in Mahmoudiyah in Babil Governorate.

With the exception of the Kurdish region, Iraq continues to suffer ongoing violence related to power differences along sectarian lines. This contributes to widespread economic hardships. Much more work for reconciliation and constructive conflict transformation is needed at all levels of Iraqi society. Ultimately, this is the challenge for Iraqis to meet. However, Americans having made mistakes in going to war and in the subsequent occupation of Iraq bear some responsibility for the tragic circumstances that ensued.

AL QAEDA AND THE TALIBAN IN AFGHANISTAN AND PAKISTAN

In Obama's campaign and in his mind, the war in Afghanistan was a necessary war, unlike the disastrously mistaken war in Iraq. However, he and his advisors did not want an open-ended war with grand nation-building goals, let alone unrealizable objectives of ending global terrorism.[49] Some members of the Democratic Party in and outside the administration, however, would be reluctant to allow the Taliban to exercise power that would impose restrictions on women's education, employment, and other human rights.[50] This included Hillary Clinton and Nancy Pelosi, Speaker of the House of Representatives, who were inclined to a more militant idealist perspective. The main objective for Obama and his national security advisors was to defeat al Qaeda and prevent Afghanistan and Pakistan from being havens for al Qaeda.

Meanwhile, however, the military situation in Afghanistan was deteriorating, as resources had been drawn out of Afghanistan to fight the war in Iraq. After reviews and discussions a counter-insurgency strategy was adopted. General David Petraeus is recognized as a primary formulator, advocate, and implementer of this strategy. It emphasizes protecting the local population and winning their support against insurgents. This allows for more constructive methods than does a strategy of simply trying to kill enemies. Petraeus and Richard Holbrooke, the presidential envoy for Afghanistan and Pakistan, were to oversee the implementation of the new strategy in Afghanistan.

Two major problems for a counter-insurgency strategy are that it takes much time to be effective and it requires many soldiers. The U.S. military commanders requested a large number of troops be sent to Afghanistan to carry out the new strategy and turn the deteriorating situation around. The requests were not wholly confidential and Obama felt that military leaders sought to box him in, forcing him to send the requested number of troops. Robert Gates, writing after ending his service as secretary of defense, observed that Obama may have had reason to believe that, but there was no plot to do so.[51] In any case, with the support of Gates and Clinton, Obama did decide to order a surge with an additional deployment to Afghanistan of 40,000 soldiers. At the same time, he set a deadline for beginning a U.S. military withdrawal from Afghanistan.

In addition to the size of the military force needed, another difficulty in conducting a counter-insurgency strategy is that soldiers are generally not prepared to perform the necessary tasks.[52] Two existing programs, drawing upon civilians to work with military personnel, were expected to help overcome the resulting problems. One program was the Provincial Reconstruction Teams. They consist of military personnel, diplomats, and reconstruction specialists, which began supporting reconstruction projects in Afghanistan in 2002. Another program, begun in 2007, the Human Terrain System, incorporated anthropologists and other social scientists to analyze local cultural and social patterns.[53] Providing such information was intended to ameliorate some of the immense difficulties that arise from waging armed conflicts within a civilian society. Basically, however, the fight in Afghanistan was waged militarily.

NATO forces helped train and build a national Afghan army. A stable political system was achieved, with popular elections in 2004 and 2009, when Hamid Karzai was elected, and then in July 2014 when Abdullah Abdullah and Asraf Ghani competed in a dangerously contested runoff election. Secretary of state Kerry mediated the dispute and changed a zero sum fight over who would be president into a shared victory with a unity government in which two major offices were structured, prime minister and chief executive.[54] After a recount, the one with the most votes would be president and the other (or his nominee) would be the prime minister and a new constitution would be written.

Despite many challenges, USAID carried out wide-ranging programs in agriculture, democracy and governance, health, education, economic development and infrastructure.[55] These programs contributed to increases in literacy rates, life expectancy, and the number of girls attending school, and thereby aided security.[56] The American public showed indications of interest in and sympathy for the Afghan people. For example, Khaled Hosseini, an Afghan-American, wrote *The Kite Runner,* about Afghan boys of different ethnicities, which was a best-selling novel;[57] and Gregg Mortenson's best-selling book, *Three Cups of Tea,* spurred contributions to build schools for girls in Afghanistan.[58]

The threat of al Qaeda resurgence, however, was not eliminated. The Taliban, and very significantly leaders in Pakistan, had not agreed to join in preventing any resurgence. That would require negotiating political understandings. Holbrooke, who had campaigned for Clinton during her nomination battle against Obama, was appointed to conduct such diplomatic efforts, which he was deemed to have accomplished successfully in the former Yugoslavia (discussed in Chapter 5). This did not happen in Afghanistan. He was not part of the younger team of security advisors who had close political relations with Obama and he was unable to get a hearing from Obama.[59] Furthermore, his forceful style of operations may have worked in dealing with Milošević, but it produced a rupture with President Karzai. Then, suddenly he died in December 2010, and the difficulties with Pakistan persisted. In general, more constructive U.S. strategies to counter al Qaeda in Afghanistan and Pakistan would involve relations with other countries with which those conflicts are interlocked. One issue arises from the assistance some members of the Pakistan ISI give to al Qaeda and Taliban elements, as discussed in Chapter 6. They presumably believed that this would provide Pakistan greater influence in Afghan affairs and be useful in its struggle against India and to gain control of Kashmir. The Obama administration might have enhanced its leverage in this matter by drawing closer to one or more nearby regional powers, such as India and Iran. This might improve relations with them. For example, as discussed in the previous chapter, Iranian leaders had demonstrated their common interest with the United States in countering al Qaeda, a hostile Sunni force. Their help was briefly taken, but excluded afterward. Giving continuing attention to shared interests and acknowledging Iran's regional importance could help overcome the tensions between the U.S. and Iran.

IRANIAN RELATIONS

Obama entered office with a strong commitment to preventing nuclear weapons proliferation. This also had been stressed in George W. Bush's antagonism against the governments in North Korea and Iran. Obama, however, framed that contentious issue more constructively in significant ways.[60] As a senator, Obama had spoken of the unacceptability of Iran acquiring nuclear weapons, but said nothing about nuclear enrichment. Iranians had claimed the inalienable right to enrich uranium, as provided for in the nonproliferation treaty, but the Bush administration had rejected Iranian enrichment. Immediately, as president, Obama spoke of possible direct negotiations with Iran and of the importance of mutual respect. This new approach was generally viewed favorably by European allies, except for British and French concerns that Obama might be giving way too readily in regard to uranium enrichment. Sunni Arab leaders, particularly those in Saudi Arabia and Egypt, were worried that Obama would tilt in favor of their primary regional rival, Iran. They saw Iran as meddling in Arab affairs, outflanking them by supporting Hamas and Hezbollah and being more pro-Palestinian than they were. Finally, Israeli leaders were extremely concerned at any lessening of U.S. opposition to Iranian nuclear development, since they regarded the Iranian government as posing an existential threat to Israel.

In actuality, Obama's approach toward Iran was not entirely different from Bush's. He was prepared to conduct a harsher sanctions campaign against Iran. His more multilateral approach and improved standing in the world enabled him to gain greater international cooperation in imposing economic sanctions. Moreover, Stuart Levey, who had developed effective tools to block undesired international money transfers while in Bush's administration, was asked to remain in office.[61] Levey, a neoconservative Republican, working in the Treasury Department, gathered information from U.S. intelligence agencies to track money going to individuals and groups believed to be engaged in anti-U.S. terror attacks. This information could be used to induce banks around the world to impose sanctions blocking financial transfers to Iranian banks. Such targeted or smart sanctions are more likely to be widely imposed, thereby being more effective.

The prospects for the election of Obama raised hopes among many Iranians for achieving better relations between America and Iran. This was indicated by a remarkable Track Two channel initiated before Obama's election. Opening this channel derived from the Pugwash Conference on Science and World Affairs, discussed in Chapter 2. In 2008, its then-secretary general, Professor Paolo Cotta-Ramusino, brought together current and former American officials with representatives of the ruling conservative factions of Iran.[62] American participants were led by a former secretary of defense, William Perry, then a member of the national security working group of Obama's presidential campaign. They included prominent official and nonofficial members of the Washington foreign policy community. The Iranian participants were led by Mojtaba Samareh Hashemi, a close friend and political associate of Mahmoud Ahmadinejad, and included representatives from the office of Sayyid Ali Khamenei, the Supreme Leader. Foreign policy experts from Europe and Canada also participated.

The intensive talks dealt with nuclear issues and ways mistrust between the two sides could be overcome. Some progress was made in understanding each other's positions and underlying interests. Furthermore, personal relations were forged between persons who would be officially engaged in the ensuing months.

As the Obama administration took shape and began developing relations with the Iranian government, Iranian reformers retained hopes that a transformation of relations with the U.S. government was possible. Iranian hardliners, however, mistrusted the U.S. leadership. For example, Ali Ardashir Larijani, the chairman of the

Parliament of Iran, denounced Obama's "carrots and sticks" policy as savagery.[63] He asserted that Iranian national interests would not be compromised by bribes or threats; tactical changes in policy would not suffice—rather, a thorough change in strategy was needed.

Indeed, from a constructive conflict perspective, the effects of any particular co-ercive action depend on the context of other inducements and on the objectives sought. Severe negative sanctions are likely to produce resistance, particularly if the goals sought are highly objectionable to the targeted leadership, as noted in the pre-vious chapter regarding Iraq, Iran, and North Korea. Attention to the perceived interests and concerns of the other side tend to make for more effective policies. In this case, the reasons for Iranian mistrust of the U.S. leadership are evident. Iranian cooperation with the United States in the aftermath of the 9/11 attacks did not pro-duce continuing reciprocating cooperation. Furthermore, the U.S. long-term goal of overturning the Iranian system of government persisted in the judgment of many Iranian leaders. Therein lay the grounds for the Iranian call for the United States to choose a new strategic policy. Obama did present a respectful approach. Within that context, the U.S. policy regarding Iranian nuclear developments seemed more flexible than it was in the Bush administration, and the sanctions regime was tougher.

Meanwhile, important political changes within Iran were underway.[64] In 2011 relations between Iran's supreme leader and its president were deteriorating, a man-ifestation of growing divisions and rivalries within the conservative establishment. After Ahmadinejad's 2005 presidential election, two conservative factions became politically dominant in Iran: the pragmatic conservatives and the ultranationalists. The pragmatists were the Islamic Republic's traditional "Old Guard," which gener-ally supported continuing clerical rule and expanding Iran's international influence, but they also recognized the importance of reforming Iran's economic and political systems. The pragmatists tended to have close ties to the Iranian Revolutionary Guard Corps and to the elite clerical and merchant families. The ultranationalists challenged the Old Guard's grip on power. They too favored a more assertive foreign policy, but they sought to curb the influence of Iran's clerics relative to a techno-cratic-military class drawn from their own membership. Unlike the pragmatists, the ultranationalists come from a younger generation and from lower socio-economic classes. Ahmadinejad was one of the prominent members of this faction.

In the presidential elections in 2005, Khamenei had supported Ahmadinejad, seeing him as a hardliner who would support an aggressive foreign policy and move domestic policy in a more conservative direction, after the presidencies of Ayatollah Akbar Hashemi Rafsanjani and Seyyed Mohammad Khatami. However, Ahma-dinejad and his supporters tried to alter Iran's power structures, arousing strong resistance from the Old Guard. For that purpose they stressed the messianic belief in the imminent arrival of the Mahdi (prophesied redeemer of Islam). They stressed furthermore that Shiite Muslims have a personal connection to the Mahdi, implying that Iranians do not need the clerical class to govern in the Mahdi's absence. Such challenges produced a direct rivalry between Ahmadinejad and Khamenei.

The election of June 14, 2013, had results that could become a turning point in U.S.-Iranian relations.[65] The clerical establishment wanted to avoid an outcome that would provoke popular protest, as had happened in 2009. Therefore candidates were to have some popular appeal, yet exclude persons deemed too radical and objectionable for Khamenei and the clerical establishment. As a result a space was created for a reformist establishment figure to win. In the election, Iranians jammed polling stations to elect Hassan Rouhani, a Shiite cleric who campaigned on a pledge of "reconciliation and peace." His victory touched off spontaneous street celebrations. White House press secretary Jay Carney stated: "We respect the vote of the Iranian people and congratulate them for their participation in the political process, and their courage in making their voices heard."

About 72% of Iran's electorate voted in the election in which Rouhani had overcome a divided conservative field of candidates and won a majority of the votes by a small margin but enough to avoid a runoff. Rouhani had led Iran's nuclear negotiating efforts from 2003 to 2005. He had resigned the post after Ahmadinejad became president, and then became a harsh critic of Ahmadinejad's economic and foreign policy.

Soon after the election, international negotiations began regarding Iran's nuclear development programs. In the United States, the election results and the Iranian agreement to begin such negotiations are largely attributed to the coercive sanctions. The Obama administration stressed this in order to assert its toughness and effectiveness. However, that complicates the negotiations from the Iranian point of view, since concessions by the Iranian government would more likely be viewed as signs of weakness by its electorate. Furthermore, in reality U.S. and allied sanctions are only part of the changes. The election results were largely due to internal politics, with overreaching by Ahmadinejad and public restiveness under the state's heavy hand. The latter factor was partly enhanced by American soft power, the attractiveness of its lifestyle. Finally, the changes were assisted by a sense of hopefulness about American readiness to transform relations, after Obama's re-election as president.

In February 2014, serious negotiations were begun in Geneva. Iran and six world powers set a timetable and framework for negotiating a comprehensive agreement to end the confrontation over Iran's nuclear program.[66] In July, with some progress made, the negotiators agreed to extend the timetable four more months.

RUSSIA AND UKRAINIAN CRISIS

Upon beginning his presidency, Obama attempted to reverse the deterioration that had occurred in relations with Russia during the Bush administration. Indeed, considerable progress was made working with Dmitry Medvedev when he was president of Russia. Members of the Obama administration chose to treat Medvedev as an independent actor, but they recognized that Vladimir Putin retained ultimate authority in Russia.[67] Putin had been elected president of Russia in 2000 and was re-elected in 2004. Constitutionally mandated term limits made Putin ineligible to run for a third consecutive presidential term in 2008. Dmitry Medvedev won the 2008 presidential election and appointed Putin as prime minister. Medvedev was relatively young and his professional career began in a post–Cold War world.

Early in Obama's first term, several actions demonstrated the possibilities of cooperation between the United States and Russia. For example, this occurred in regard to the Russian provision of fuel for the U.S. airbase in Kyrgyzstan, which helped supply American troops in Afghanistan.[68] In another example, the Obama administration decided not to implement the Bush administration's plan to build a missile defense system in Poland and the Czech Republic. Instead it would be deployed on ships near Iran, which had posed the ostensible threat that the system was to be the defense against. In other actions, Russia joined the United States in UN Security Council resolutions imposing sanctions on Iran and North Korea, and the United States supported Russia's entry into the World Trade Organization.

Nevertheless, there were also issues of contention between Russia and the United States, particularly associated with troubles between Russia and the former Soviet republics that had become independent as the USSR dissolved. The troubles were exacerbated and became sources of contention with the United States due to NATO enlargement. This was the case during Bush's administration when the moves for Georgia's membership in NATO contributed to the outbreak of war between Georgia and Russia. In Obama's administration, three developments contributed to the eruption of a major crisis in American-Russian relations related to Ukraine: political changes in Russia, domestic developments in Ukraine, and possible NATO enlargement.

In Russia, after a law extended the presidential term from four years to six, Putin announced that he would seek a third, nonconsecutive term as president and he won the election in March 2012; he then choose Medvedev as prime minister. The prearranged switch with Medvedev upset many Russians and Putin instituted repressive measures against the resulting protests.[69] He had participated in the Cold War as a KGB officer and readily rallied support by voicing the sense of humiliation and the anger felt by many Russians at the loss of respect from the United States and the West. Acting assertively abroad, Putin could win support domestically, at least in the short term.

The recent history of Ukraine also contributed to the crisis that engulfed Russia, Europe, and the United States. Ukraine had long been part of Tsarist Russia and of the Soviet Union. In 1954, Nikita Khrushchev enlarged Ukraine's borders to incorporate the Crimea, a peninsula in the Black Sea with a large Soviet naval base and a largely Russian population. The breakup of the Soviet Union and consequent independence of Ukraine then required a detailed agreement for Russia to maintain its control of its naval base now in Ukraine.

Members of the governments in Ukraine failed to guide economic development and engaged in corrupt deals with foreign oligarchs. Those failings and authoritarian methods of ruling prompted popular dissent. Political contentions also arose based on differences about having closer ties with Russia or with Western Europe. Thus, in the 2004 presidential election, Viktor Yanukovych favored closer ties with Russia while the main opposition candidate, Viktor Yushchenko, favored turning to the West. In a runoff election, Yanukovych officially won by a narrow margin, but Yushchenko and his supporters alleged massive fraud, especially in eastern Ukraine. Nonviolent protests, constituting the Orange Revolution, spread throughout the country from November 2004 to January 2005. The Supreme Court declared a second runoff was necessary, which was won by Yushchenko. The presidential election of 2010 was another three-way race, which Yanukovych then won.

NATO enlargement also contributed to the eruption of the Ukrainian crisis. Its expansion to include countries bordering Russia could readily be regarded as a threat by Russian leaders. [70] Ukrainian partnering with or joining NATO was varyingly pursued since 1994. In 2008, Ukraine applied to take steps leading to NATO membership and NATO decided it would prepare an Annual National Program to assist Ukraine in implementing reforms needed to join the alliance. However, plans for Ukrainian membership to NATO were dropped by Ukraine following the 2010 election of Yanukovych, who opted to keep Ukraine a non-aligned state. This was confirmed by a vote of the Ukrainian Parliament. Nevertheless, co-operation with NATO was not excluded. Indeed, in 2011 a cooperation plan with NATO was agreed upon. [71] In a May 2009 Gallup survey, however, 40% of the Ukrainian public viewed NATO as a threat and only 17% viewed it as a protection; one in three said it was neither. It would seem Yanukovych was trying to please the U.S. and Russia at the same time, which was proving difficult.

Taking into serious consideration how Putin and many Russians would view the circumstances, the U.S. government might have taken a more constructive approach by making it easier for Ukraine to have good relations with both Russia and the United States. NATO membership for Ukraine could have been taken off the table. Important Ukrainian reforms could have been pursued through the EU, which might be more acceptable for Russia when NATO membership was ruled out. Admittedly, this would have been difficult. Russian leaders wanted Ukraine to join its own free trade system consisting of Russia, Belarus and Kazakhstan. Nevertheless, discussions might have generated new ideas of special provisions for Ukraine or a broader European customs union over time.

The Ukrainian crisis began on November 21, 2013, with nonviolent demonstrations on Kiev's Independence Square (Maidan).[72] The demonstrators were protesting President Yanukovych's decision, made under Russian pressure, not to sign an association agreement with the EU. On November 30, a grave escalation occurred when riot police violently attempted to disperse the crowd. Intimidation failed and the crowds grew, as did their demands, which now included the government's resignation. Massive crowds remained at the Maidan as seizures of government offices spread.

Finally, on February 21, 2014, an agreement to overcome the crisis was signed by opposition leaders and President Yanukovych.[73] It foresaw early elections and reduced presidential powers. The agreement was reached through negotiations mediated by the foreign ministers of France, Germany, and Poland and the EU foreign affairs high representative. Russia participated in the negotiations, but then did not sign the agreement. The agreement was rejected by the Maidan protesters opposing compromises with Yanukovych, who then fled the capital and went to Russia.

At that point, U.S. intervention would have had limited remediable possibilities. The crowds in the streets opposing Yanukovych, the militancy of pro-Russian separatists, and Putin's readiness to use covert and overt coercion produced great volatility and were not subject to much U.S. influence in the short run. From most any perspective, acting ineffectively is generally worse than not acting at all; and resorting to large-scale force ineffectively is much worse.

Meanwhile, a graver development emerged in the Crimea, as Putin seized what seemed a great opportunity. Separatist pro-Russian militants, including elements sent from Russia, began to take over Ukrainian offices there. On March 1, the Russian legislature approved using armed force in Ukraine to protect ethnic Russians. On March 6, the Crimean parliament voted to join Russia and scheduled a referendum, which was claimed to result in 97% of the voters favoring union with Russia. On March 18, Putin reclaimed Crimea as an integral part of Russia and denounced the dominating American behavior after the dissolution of the Soviet Union.[74] In late March, a heavy Russian military buildup on the Ukrainian border appeared, although Putin said he had no intention to further divide Ukraine.

The U.S. government imposed travel and economic sanctions against several individuals closely associated with Putin, and Obama tried to organize major Western countries to impose sanctions.[75] The sanctions were to inflict costs and to deter further Russian actions to separate eastern Ukraine from the country as a whole. At the same time, the Obama administration continued to cooperate with Russia, trying to limit the dangers of an expanding Ukraine crisis.[76]

The crisis escalated on July 17, when a Malaysia Airlines passenger plane was struck by a sophisticated missile and crashed in territory controlled by Ukrainian rebels, killing 298 persons on board. The evidence that the missile (probably supplied by Russia) was dispatched by the rebels was strong and the delays in retrieving all the victims and in allowing experts to examine the site aroused widespread anger at Putin and Russia and an expansion of sanctions by the United States and the major countries of Europe. Putin intensified his celebration of Russia, its independence and civilization.

In retrospect, as each party in the Ukrainian crisis escalated the fight, each tended to see their struggle against others as a zero-sum fight. From a constructive conflict perspective, the United States should have avoided pushing Ukrainians to choose sides between Russia and America. In addition, the U.S. government should have recognized Russian concerns in regard to relations with Ukraine and tried to find mutually beneficial options years earlier, before Putin was first elected president or in the years of Medvedev's presidency. Even the difficulties associated with the status of Crimea might have been recognized and new options generated to take into more account its Russian population and being the site of a major Russian naval base. Obviously, too, Ukrainian or Russian leaders could have pursued much more constructive policies and likely gained benefits at less cost.

Finally, the many other conflicts with which the U.S.-Russian contention in the Ukraine is interlocked should be considered. They give leverage to Russia in some places and to the United States in other places, which makes trade-offs and grand bargains conceivable. They also create dilemmas about what course of action is most constructive. Thus, the constructive course of American-Iranian negotiations discussed earlier was aided by Russian support of UN sanctions imposed on Iran. On the other hand, as discussed later in this chapter, the disastrous civil wars in Syria are perpetuated in part by the failure of Russia to join in UN-authorized sanctions against the Syrian government. To what extent such linkages should affect policies regarding Ukraine raises moral and empirical questions of great complexity. Sometimes isolating one crisis, and maintaining some cooperative relations, makes the crisis more amenable to solution.[77]

Interventions in Arab Uprisings

In 2010, most Arab countries had long been ruled by authoritarian governments and many had stagnated economically. American soft power, its manifestation of personal freedom and high standard of living, contributed to popular resentment at these conditions. In some ways it also contributed to fostering constructive ways to change those conditions.

AMERICAN NONPROFIT ORGANIZATIONS

American nongovernmental organizations have long been active in the Arab world. They include for-profit business corporations and various non-profit organizations providing humanitarian relief, education, development assistance, human rights advocacy, and other services and goods. I first discuss the often-overlooked nonprofit organizations whose actions have relevance for the Arab uprisings that began in 2011. Afterward, the U.S. government interventions in the Middle East and North Africa (MENA) region pertinent to the uprisings are examined.

Many national and international NGOs provide training and experience in a variety of conflict resolution methods in numerous parts of the Arab region. The Israeli-Palestinian conflict absorbs much of conflict resolution programs' attention, but not all of it. For example, Search for Common Ground, based in Washington, has programs designed to foster constructive conflict resolution at all societal levels in many countries in the MENA region. Illustratively, it has projects to promote civic engagement through the media and to help diffuse mediation in Morocco, making it routine in many institutions.

Significantly too, former president Jimmy Carter and the staff of the Carter Center conducted conflict resolution work at the grassroots level, and also at the level of leading decision-makers in the MENA region. Thus, President Carter sometimes facilitated communication between governments and groups which have severe handicaps in communicating with each other, for example when they have involved Hamas, leaders since Hamas is designated a terrorist organization by the U.S. and many other governments.

One of the most dramatic non-governmental new developments in the MENA region is the establishment of numerous international branch campuses (IBCs) of universities, most notably in the United Arab Emirates (UAE), Saudi Arabia, Qatar, and Bahrain.[78] For example, in 2012, there were thirty-seven IBCs in the UAE. An IBC is a "higher education institution that is located in another country from the institution which either originated it or operates it, with some physical presence in the host country, and which awards at least one degree in the host country that is accredited in the country of the originating institution."[79] The IBCs may serve as safety valves, providing youth the opportunity to advance personal professional careers, keeping many youth busy, and allowing for a gradual and guided assimilation of modernity. On the other hand, they also can serve as a locus for youth mobilization when grievances markedly rise.

American individuals and groups also engaged in citizen diplomacy with people in Arab countries. An instance of this is the work that Rabbi Marc Gopin, a professor with the School for Conflict Analysis and Resolution at George Mason University, has done in Syria for several years.[80] He worked particularly with the Grand Mufti of Syria, Sheikh Ahmed Hassoun, and a Christian Arab, Hind Kabawat, in discussing a vision of a peaceful civil society in the Middle East. In the midst of the civil war in Syria, he raised funds for Syrian refugees and provided training and experience that contributes to women's empowerment and the development of civil society organizations.

To understand the course of the Arab uprisings beginning in 2010 the reliance on nonviolent action must be accorded great attention. Of course, the effectiveness of mass adoption of nonviolent struggle was widely recognized in the fight for Indian independence led by Mohandas Gandhi and the fight for civil rights in the United States led by Martin Luther King Jr. But these cases seemed unique and distant events for many people. Beginning in the 1970s, research and theorizing about the reasons for the effectiveness of nonviolent action began to develop. The work of an academic sociologist, Gene Sharp, was highly influential in this development.[81] He based his analysis on the idea that power is held only if people obey the supposed powerful officials. Therefore, when people refuse to obey particular office-holders, those officials lose their authority and cease to have power.

Peace and conflict scholars and peacemaking organizations such as the Fellowship of Reconciliation developed the ideas and trained people in nonviolence. Then, in the 1980s and more widely in the 1990s, nonviolent revolutionary struggles were waged against authoritarians, and nonviolent independence movements spread across Eastern Europe and the former Soviet Union. Sharp wrote short pamphlets about specific methods to be used for particular problems; notably, ending authoritarian rule.[82] Videos were produced about the force of nonviolence and its successful applications, which were widely viewed.[83] Young people in Tunisia and Egypt read and discussed Sharp's work and viewed the video about the Otpor uprising in Serbia that defeated Slobodan Milošević.[84] The people in Tunisia and Egypt who undertook the nonviolent demonstrations were forethoughtful, disciplined, and creative in conducting their struggle to change their authoritarian governments.

U.S. PROGRAMS IN MENA

The U.S. government has had close relations to most Arab governments and has counseled them to introduce democratic reforms. The Obama administration changed and expanded some of the programs supportive of democratic governance and economic development that the Bush administration had undertaken in the MENA region following the attacks of September 11, 2001. President Obama tried to improve America's role in the Arab world.

Several specific long-term programs to foster political reforms in Arab countries were undertaken within the Department of State, including the Middle East Partnership Initiative MEPI. Early in the Obama administration, the prior reliance on bilateral government arrangements was shifted to more local arrangements. Thus, MEPI provides significant direct funding to individuals and organizations for local activities. An example of this approach is the Leaders for Democracy Fellowship (LDF) program. MEPI contracted with Syracuse University's Maxwell School of Citizenship and Public Affairs to design and implement the LDF program beginning in 2007. Each year, Syracuse University hosts twenty to twenty-five young democratic reformers, activists, journalists, and human rights workers from as many as fifteen Arab countries.[85] The men and women in the program participate in a five-week academic program with courses on democracy, leadership, communication and conflict resolution. They then spend seven weeks in Washington, DC, completing professional assignments at American NGOs or government agencies.

The LDF participants have come from nearly every Arab country, but the numbers vary from country to country and from year to year. Territories that have had the largest number of participants have been Lebanon, Palestine, Egypt, Yemen, and Tunisia. Alumni of the program gather each year in a MENA country to exchange information about their activities, helping to sustain a network of mutual support for change. In the summer of 2011 an additional workshop was inaugurated, conducted in Arabic and based at the American University of Beirut. The former LDF participants engage in a variety of civic undertakings upon their return to their home countries, including building new non-governmental organizations. In addition, they form a regional network to exchange information about what works well and what does not. Such initiatives may be aided by a U.S. fund, which makes awards on a competitive basis.[86]

The much-larger National Endowment for Democracy (NED), established in 1983 to foster democratic reform and roll back Soviet global influence, also deserves attention. It consists of four institutes: the National Democratic Institute for International Affairs (NDI), the International Republican Institute (IRI), the American

Center for International Labor Solidarity, and the Center for Private Enterprises. The NDI and IRI have emphasized building the infrastructure for electoral politics and were channels for supporting local movements and organizations. The goal of promoting democracy was blended with spreading a belief in the value of a free market and friendship with the United States. The early work in Latin America included efforts to oust Fidel Castro's government in Cuba and the IRI's support of the opposition to Jean-Bertrand Aristide in Haiti. After the September 11, 2001 al Qaeda attacks, the Bush administration wished to encourage democratic reform in the Middle East, which resulted in more attention to the Middle East by NED. The work was generally focused on enhancing civil society organizations within the Arab countries, and winning support for U.S. policies.

In addition, Freedom House, based in Washington is a nonprofit organization receiving its funding mainly from the State Department. Freedom House's programs support advocates of human rights and democracy in their efforts to promote open government, defend human rights, strengthen civil society and facilitate the free flow of information and ideas. Freedom House primarily offers assistance through trainings, international exchange programs, grant giving, and networking activities. In addition, Freedom House offers support through advocacy and visible demonstrations of solidarity on behalf of counterparts abroad. Freedom House conducts programs in over two dozen countries in all regions of the world. Primary funding for Freedom House's programs comes in grants from USAID and the State Department, as well as grants from other governments and from private foundations, including the John D. and Catherine T. MacArthur Foundation, the Open Society Foundations, and NED.[87]

Although these governmental actions did not transform the Arab societies nor their public's unfavorable views of the United States, the proportion viewing America favorably did increase, at least in the first year of the Arab Spring. In 2010, only 10% of the Arabs surveyed had favorable views about the United States but in 2011 this had risen to 26%.[88] Asked in 2011 what two steps by the United States would improve their views of the United States, the most respondents, 55%, said reaching an Israeli-Palestinian peace agreement, and 42% said stopping aid to Israel.

ARAB UPRISINGS AND U.S. RESPONSES

The Arab uprisings that began in late 2010 drew great public attention in the United States and initially there was immense enthusiasm for the protestors, which was reflected in referring to these events as the Arab Spring, or later, as the Arab Awakening. U.S. government policies and actions have contributed in varying ways to the course of the many uprisings.[89] Of course, those contributions usually have quite small influences compared to the powerful effects of domestic conditions and actors. Regional factors and actors also often help shape what happens within each society. However, over the long-term or at a particular pivotal moment, American actions may significantly affect an uprising's course. The U.S. government's interventions in countries in the MENA region are often explained and justified as fostering democracy, preserving secure oil supplies, countering terrorism, demonstrating U.S. power, upholding international law, and helping our allies. The relative importance of various purposes varies with the intervention, but their multiplicity often means they are served in contradictory ways so that serving one purpose undermines another.

This section discusses various uprisings and American policies relating to them, with particular attention to Egypt, Libya, and Syria. The uprisings began with non-violent demonstrations that erupted in Tunisia in December 2010.[90] The Tunisian events were soon followed by mass demonstrations in Tahrir Square in Cairo, Egypt. The Tunisian and Egyptian eruptions, however, had been preceded by two years of collaborative discussions between and among many civil groups in those countries.[91] The relatively swift success of massive non-violent protests that removed Zine al-Abidine Ben Ali and Hosni Mubarak from office in Tunisia and Egypt, respectively, raised expectations of dissatisfied people in many neighboring countries and beyond. Concerns about economic stagnation, corruption and political repression had long been widespread. Protest is likely when people come to believe change can be made to happen if fear is put aside. The relatively quick and successful overthrow of the government leaders in Tunisia and Egypt gave hope and spurred action elsewhere.[92]

The course of changes in Tunisia was relatively successful in initiating a pluralistic, democratic governance system. The level of civil society organizations and institutions was comparatively high; these local independent associations included community groups; labor unions; charities; and political, professional, and faith-based associations, and this propelled change.[93] Furthermore, and significantly, the largest and most influential Islamist movement in Tunisia is the Ennahda, the most moderate Islamist movement in the Arab world.[94] There was relatively limited direct American engagement in preparing the ground for the Tunisian transition to democratic governance.[95]

U.S. engagement in Egypt has been much greater and its strategic value more important. The United States has had very close ties with the Egyptian military forces and has provided large amounts of financial aid to Egypt since the signing of the Egyptian-Israeli peace treaty in 1979. Egyptian foreign policy was allied with America's policies in the struggle against attacks by militant Islamists and in mediation efforts in Israeli-Palestinian relations. For many years, Mubarak had been advised to introduce some democratic reforms, but his authoritarian control remained. As the anti-government protests grew and he resorted to violent suppression, however, U.S. officials encouraged him to resign; the military establishment agreed that was necessary and he did.

In the first months after Mubarak's fall, the coalition of students, workers, women, and liberal-leaning Islamist youth organizations that had led the uprising in Tahrir Square did act to continue the Egyptian revolution.[96] They helped force out Mubarak's allies controlling television and newspapers, closed the State Security and police ministries, seized police files on dissidents, and established new political parties. However, the Muslim Brotherhood survived Mubarak's constraints and emerged as a broadly supported national organization. It seemed to become allied with the military leadership, but that proved short-lived. In June 2012, as Mohamed Morsi, the Brotherhood candidate, was about to win the presidential election, the military leadership closed the Brotherhood-controlled Parliament. In August, Morsi dismissed the leading generals, who he believed opposed him, and chose Abdul Fattah el-Sisi to head the military forces. In June 2013, demonstrations erupted against the government and the military staged a coup that was immediately followed by a ruthless suppression of the Muslim Brotherhood. In May 2014 el-Sisi won election as president with an overwhelming majority, but with a low turnout of voters.

U.S. influence on these tumultuous events was limited. As the Muslim Brotherhood gained political power its leadership reassured the U.S. government it would respect Egypt's treaty obligations with Israel.[97] Once Morsi was president, the U.S. government sought to be highly engaged with his government.[98] But the Morsi government did not govern in an inclusive, pluralistic manner, nor was it effective in directing economic growth. The el-Sisi government hardly promises an open democratic political system and widely shared economic progress. The long-standing U.S. policy of emphasizing support for the Egyptian military forces does not appear to have been effective in advancing many important U.S. goals in relations with Egypt. Expanding programs of support for local civil society organizations, for non-military political and judiciary officials, and for economic development projects benefiting rural areas and the urban poor could have been more constructive.

In Yemen, the initial demonstrations in January 2011 were against poor economic conditions and widespread corruption as well as opposition to government proposals to change the Yemini constitution. Demands quickly escalated to calls for the resignation of the long-ruling President, Ali Abdullah Saleh. Mass defections from his government and the military forces swiftly followed. Saleh accepted but then rejected an agreement for a transition of power mediated by the Gulf Cooperation Council. After more fighting in which Saleh was injured, he left the country for treatment and effectively lost power.

In Morocco, after demonstrations in February 2011 calling for government reforms, King Mohammed VI promised comprehensive constitutional reforms, and
he proposed specific changes. They were ratified in September and in accord with
them, a parliamentary election was held in November 2011. Moderate Islamists
from the Justice and Development Party won the most seats for the House of Representatives, and its leader, Abdelilah Benkirane, formed a coalition government.
Although he lost some power, the king retains ultimate authority and controls the
military, police, and intelligence services. The U.S. and Moroccan governments
have mutually supportive foreign policies.[99]

Bahrain also experienced protests in February 2011. Initially, protesters sought
increased political freedom and equality for the Shia majority.[100] The application of
violent government force to suppress the protests produced expanded demands,
including an end to King Hamad bin Isa Al Khalifa's rule. The king offered minor
concessions that were deemed inadequate by the demonstrators. In March, the
Gulf Cooperation Council, upon the king's request, sent troops and police to help
suppress the protests. Unrest and repression mixed with slight concessions have
continued. The United States has a large military base in Bahrain and close ties
with the king, which may be viewed critically as reasons for acquiescing in very
limited concessions. Conversely, the United States might have used its large
military-to-military aid to enhance its leverage in opposing repressive actions by
the King's government.[101]

In Libya the quest for change quickly took the form of a civil war to end Muammar Gaddafi's rule. He had dominated Libya for forty-two years as a ruthless, erratic
dictator and lacked any major international allies. The spark igniting the civil war
occurred in February 2011 when security forces violently suppressed protests against
the arrest of a human rights campaigner. These events in the eastern city of Benghazi rapidly escalated into warfare between rebels and government forces. In
March, the UN Security Council authorized a no-fly zone over Libya and air strikes
to protect civilians. The Obama administration facilitated NATO operations that
served to defend the rebels.[102] This low-profile U.S. engagement and use of NATO
forces was dubbed "leading from behind," and ridiculed by Republican leaders, but
was militarily effective.[103]

In July 2011, the international Contact Group on Libya recognized the main opposition group, the National Transitional Council, as the legitimate government of
Libya. After see-saw fighting, the pro-Gaddafi forces were defeated and on October
20, Gaddafi was seized and killed by rebel forces. Assassinations and violent battles
among various militia groups, however, persisted even after the elections in July 2012
of the General National Congress and other steps were taken to establish formal
government structures.

In the context of ongoing disorder, in September 2012, armed men stormed the U.S. consulate in Benghazi, killing the U.S. ambassador and three other Americans. The Republican Party leadership focused on this event and talking points about it for Sunday talk shows. They did not discuss the conditions in Libya nor larger matters pertaining to the Obama administration's policies in relation to the civil war in Libya. Indeed, there was barely any discussion within the United States about alternative strategies.

An important alternative approach actually was attempted. The African Union (AU) undertook a peace initiative for Libya during 2011, based on recognizing the grave dangers of civil war in Libya and the limitations of forcing a change of regime.[104] Combining NATO or UN pressure and AU diplomacy might have avoided some of the severe costs during and after the civil war in Libya. The United States, France, and Britain, however, dismissed the AU efforts and demonstrated their reliance on NATO. This drove UN policy and interfered with AU actions. Thus, the AU tried to send its ad-hoc high-level committee to Libya in order to facilitate dialogue leading to political reforms that would yield a peaceful and sustainable solution. Mauritania provided a plane to fly a panel from the ad hoc committee to Tripoli on March 20, but that was the day when the no-fly zone entered into effect. The United States and the UN curtly informed the panel members that if they proceed with their mission, their security could not be guaranteed. No serious consideration was given to relying on regional governments and the UN Security council as a whole. Rather, NATO was relied upon, seriously angering the Russians.[105]

Finally, the Syrian civil war must be discussed as another illustration of the possible tragic consequences when implications of interconnected conflicts are not well-recognized. In March 2011, protest demonstrations erupted against the authoritarian government, led by President Bashar al-Assad. He had become president in 2000, after the death of his father, Ḥafiz al-Assad, who had ruthlessly ruled Syria since 1971. The Assads were Alawites, a small religious community in Syria, following a branch of Shia Islam. Their political party, the secular Arab Socialist Ba'th Party, dominated political life.

The Syrian government responded to the protests with deadly violence. It also tried to win support by claiming that the protests resulted from foreign conspiracies and sectarian tensions. In April, it also made a few concessions aimed at Syria's conservative Muslims and the Kurdish minority.[106] At the same time, Assad declared the lifting of Syria's emergency law, although the Syrian opposition regarded that as a ruse. Opposition militias began to form and large-scale fighting grew and government security forces escalated their use of violence against protesters. Very soon, outside governments picked sides in the fight, largely in terms of their own interests and rivalries with each other, and thereby set the stage for engaging in proxy wars. For example, the Iranian support for the Assad government and the Saudi support for the Sunni Islamist opponents also reflected rival regional power aspirations. Russian support for the Assad government was in part based on past shared foreign policies and Russian military sales to Syria. The Turkish government lent support to rebel groups to counter Shia'a Islamists opposing the Syrian government. The U.S. and European governments favored the rebels, who were regarded as moderate or secular in religious matters and seeking pluralistic democratic governance. This complexity would greatly hamper cooperation among the opponents of the Assad government. It also would hamper effective international intervention, as noted next.

In February 2012, after a year of terrible violence, an international "Friends of Syria" conference was organized by the United Nations and the Arab League. Seventy countries attended the conference, which Russia and China did not attend, given their usual reluctance to support UN intervention in a country's domestic affairs. The conference chose Kofi Annan as their envoy to Syria, and in March he presented a six-point peace plan to the UN Security Council. The plan asked the Syrian regime "to address the legitimate aspirations and concerns of the Syrian people," stop fighting, and pull back military concentrations from towns, and simultaneously the envoy would seek similar commitments from the Syrian opposition and other elements.[107]

Initially it appeared that the Syrian regime would comply with the peace plan. Syrian compliance, however, was viewed skeptically by the United Kingdom's foreign secretary, William Hague, and by the U.S. ambassador to Syria, Robert S. Ford.[108] Within the Department of State and then openly after he resigned in February 2014, Ford argued consistently that more U.S. military support be provided the Free Syrian Army (FSA). In any case, heavy regime violence in May 2012 and the FSA's resumption of its operations made evident that the peace initiative was not progressing. In June, Annan convened a meeting in Geneva to revive his peace plan; Iran, Assad's strongest ally, and Saudi Arabia, supporter of Assad's enemies, were not included. In July Annan convened another meeting of world powers, but Russia and China blocked the others from calling for Assad's ouster, agreeing on a plan for a political transition that would have little chance of implementation.

As the fighting went on, the prospects of Assad's remaining in power fluctuated, which affected every power's calculation of its best policy course. For example, in July 2012, when there were signs of fracturing in Assad's regime, secretary of state Clinton said that President Bashar al-Assad's "days are numbered."[109] Annan was unable to win UN Security Council agreement to threaten the Syrian government and the rebels with consequences for failure to comply with his peace plan.

In August 2012, Kofi Annan resigned as Envoy due to the intransigence of the Syrian government, increasing militancy of the Syrian rebels and the failure of the UN Security Council to agree to forcefully support the implementation of his peace plan.

From a constructive conflict perspective, perhaps closer U.S. cooperation with Russia and China in the UN Security Council and with the external intervening governments of Saudi Arabia, Iran, and Turkey might have influenced the calculations of the Assad regime and of the rebels against it to find a path to a transforming Syrian transition. The surprising U.S.-Russian agreement in September 2013 regarding the removal of chemical weapons from Syria was largely successful. The leaders on both sides recognized they had mutual interests in the deal and seized it. Perhaps other agreements might have been, or might yet be, reached to reduce the horrible tragedies of the Syrian wars. As it came to be, countless lives have been lost, huge refugee movements have occurred, foreign fighters from Hezbollah and al Qaeda have joined the fighting, and neighboring countries have suffered destabilizing challenges.

In concluding this section, it is clear that the hopes aroused in America by the Arab uprisings were largely unfulfilled. Moreover, the interventions by the U.S. government were often checked by foreign policy goals of higher priority than fostering democratic change. This opened up the United States to charges of hypocrisy. The Obama administration's recognition of the limitations of externally imposing democratic governance, if articulated more forthrightly, might help blunt such charges. The administration's caution in military interventions is in line with that recognition. More long-term programs of respectful assistance in moving in the peaceful directions that local people wish to move can be broadly beneficial. More public awareness of such programs, provided by USAID and other organizations, would help expand and strengthen them.

Mediation of Israeli-Palestinian Conflict

When Barack Obama became president, he had important reasons to act quickly to help resolve the Israeli-Palestinian conflict.[110] Its persistence and the widespread Muslim view that the United States unfairly supported Israel in its occupation of Palestinian territories hampered the defeat of al Qaeda and similar organizations and generally harmed American interests in the Middle East. Resolving the conflict would be difficult and would take time, so it was advisable to start early.

Any mediation effort would have to take into account the concerns of a wide array of domestic constituencies relevant to U.S. Middle East policies. For many Americans, Israel was considered an asset in fighting terrorism. Many Jewish-American organizations mobilized support for elected officials and U.S. policies that were congruent with Israeli government policies, even as they change. Also, many Christian groups strongly support the state of Israel as consistent with the fulfillment of biblical prophecy. In addition, some Americans hold negative stereotypes of Arabs and especially of Palestinians in part due to bombings and other attacks against civilians by militant Palestinian groups.

On the other hand, many Americans objected to Israeli policy toward Palestinians. Some believed that Israeli policies aroused anti-American sentiments among Arabs and Muslims. Others sympathized with the plight of Palestinians and held Israel responsible for their difficult circumstances. Still others regarded Israeli policies in occupying Palestinian territories as violating UN resolutions and international law.

Whatever Obama's preferences may have been, he also had to work with the realities of the Israeli-Palestinian circumstances. The Israeli elections on February 10, 2009, enabled Benjamin Netanyahu, leader of the Likud Party, to form a nationalist, right-wing coalition government. The Israeli peace camp was still devastated by the failure of the Oslo process and the second Intifada.[111]

Arab Palestinian political factionalism had reached new heights after Arafat died in November 2004. As discussed in the previous chapter, Mahmound Abbas was elected president of the Palestinian Legislative Council in January 2005, but Fatah was stunningly defeated by Hamas in the January 2006 elections.[112] A unity government was formed but functioned poorly and was dissolved in June 2007 when Hamas seized control of Gaza. Hamas escalated hostilities with Israel, and in December 2008 Israel conducted a massive military operation in Gaza. It was concluded shortly before Obama took office in January 2009. In the West Bank, Prime Minister Salam Fayyad, with assistance from Western states, made progress to develop the Palestinian economy, provide basic social welfare, and build up the physical and social infrastructure.[113]

In dealing with Israeli-Palestinian relations, Obama exhibited notable continuities with those of President Bill Clinton.[114] He selected Hillary Clinton as secretary of state and she chose Dennis Ross, the primary official for Israeli-Palestinian negotiations during Clinton's presidency, to be her senior aide with responsibilities for Southwest Asia, particularly Iran. However, in June 2009, Ross was appointed special assistant to the president and senior director of the Central Region at the National Security Council.[115] George J. Mitchell, who had been appointed by President Clinton to head the commission investigating the second Intifada, was appointed special envoy for Israeli-Palestinian relations.[116]

Obama continued the program, begun four years before he became president, to train Palestinian security forces for deployment in the West Bank.[117] The program was led by Lt. Gen. Keith Dayton and was intended to thwart criminal groups and Hamas actions in the West Bank. Recruits were vetted by U.S. and Israeli security forces. They improved everyday security in Nablus and other places, and thereby helped improve local economic conditions. They won considerable support among Palestinians in the West Bank, but it was said that if they did not soon become part of the security force of a Palestinian state, they would be widely seen as collaborators.[118]

The Obama administration might have been expected to use a much more multilateral approach in its peacemaking effort in the Middle East than had President Bush. However, there was not great reliance on international organizations and other governments to develop and implement coordinated policies. There were consultations, but the United States was the lead actor in setting goals and deciding on policies to attain them.

Obama's overall Middle East policies did break from Bush's in important ways. Notably, Obama promptly initiated active engagement in the Israeli-Palestinian case and he asserted that he would not accord the Israeli government uncritical support of its policies. Consistent with a constructive conflict perspective, he also demonstrated his recognition of the numerous linkages of the Israeli-Palestinian conflict.

In July 2009, Obama met with leaders from fourteen major Jewish-American organizations and discussed his policies relating to Israel, and particularly to Jewish settlements in the West Bank and Jerusalem.[119] He won acquiescence and some support for his efforts to halt further expansion of Jewish settlements there. The American Israel Public Affairs Committee (AIPAC), with a history of supporting hardline Israeli policies, did not oppose the new stance and the new stance was supported by the new Jewish-American organization, J-Street.[120]

In relating to the Israeli government, Obama tried to use the interconnections among Middle East conflicts to attain the trade-offs he desired. He linked Israeli concerns about the threat from Iran with reaching an accommodation with the Palestinians. He noted that while Iran posed an existential threat to Israel, halting settlement construction did not, and he assured the Israeli government that the U.S. would handle the Iranian nuclear development problem.[121] In another kind of linkage, the Obama administration adjusted arms sales to sustain Israel's military edge relative to its Arab neighbors.[122]

The primary initial mediation effort was undertaken by George Mitchell who made frequent visits to the region and met with officials in the PA and in the Israeli government.[123] The focus of the mediation was to restart direct negotiations between the PA and the new Israeli government. The primary issue in accomplishing this was a halt to building Jewish settlements while negotiations were underway. Secretary of State Clinton and President Obama became intensely engaged in achieving Israeli agreement to this provision, but won only a ten-month partial freeze, which Netanyahu announced on November 25, 2009. The U.S. then convinced the Palestinians to undertake negotiations on that basis, and direct bilateral negotiations finally began. Despite some progress in the negotiations, however, the Israeli government would not extend the freeze, which expired on September 26, 2010, whereupon the negotiations became dormant. The initial U.S. insistence that the Israeli government stop further construction of settlements in the West Bank and Jerusalem failed to be effective.[124] Expectations were raised at times that Mitchell would present a basic proposal to which each side could react, but this did not happen.

After the failure of bilateral negotiations and U.S. mediation efforts, the Palestinian leadership turned to international options.[125] In October 2011, despite strong opposition from the United States, Israel, and several European states, the Palestinian Authority gained approval on its bid for full membership in the United Nations Educational, Scientific and Cultural Organization (UNESCO) despite great skepticism.[126] This demonstrated a form of nonviolent leverage that reduced the asymmetry of relations with Israel. However, it was not presented in a context to allay Israeli concerns, presumably out of consideration of looking tough in the eyes of its constituents.

Shortly after John Kerry took over as secretary of state on February 1, 2013, he and President Obama tried to revive the Israeli-Palestinian peace negotiations. In the context of the turmoil of the Arab Awakening, Kerry drew upon actions of other major stakeholders to foster effective negotiations. He brought Arab leaders together to reinvigorate the Arab Peace Initiative of 2002, adding more flexibility on borders.[127] He supported a World Economic Forum initiative to invest $4 billion in Palestinian economic development and supported an Israeli-Palestinian joint business initiative. He succeeded in winning concessions from Israeli and Palestinian leaders that enabled direct negotiations to begin in July 2013. The Palestinian Authority agreed to hold off applying for recognition from international organizations, and the Israeli government agreed to release 104 Palestinian prisoners who had been incarcerated since before the 1993 Oslo Accord.

April 29, 2014, was set as the deadline to reach a broad outline of an agreement ending the Israeli-Palestinian conflict. Martin Indyk, former U.S. ambassador to Israel during the Clinton administration, was appointed to oversee the negotiations. In addition, Kerry met frequently with Abbas and even more frequently with Netanyahu. The two sides' negotiation teams met in various locations and the content of the discussions was held in confidence, which was widely deemed positive. However, Abbas and Netanyahu each made public statements asserting his side's positions that were known to be unacceptable to the other side.

By January 2014, the negotiations were clearly in trouble. Jewish settlement expansions continued, as did disagreements about recognizing Israel as a Jewish state. Disagreements about monitoring the border between Jordan and a future Palestinian state and the overall borders also persisted. Kerry tried to get an agreement based on trade-offs among these various issues, but the negotiations broke down before that could be agreed upon.[128] On March 28, 2014, Israel held up the release of the last group of Palestinian prisoners. Abbas thereupon took steps to sign fifteen international conventions regarding human and social rights. Israel then approved the expansion of settlements in greater Jerusalem, across the 1967 Green Line. On April 23, 2014, Fatah and Hamas agreed to form a unity government. The peace negotiations were officially ended, with mutual recriminations that the other side was responsible for the failure.

The Israeli insistence on its terms for an agreement was stiffened by hardliners in the Israeli coalition government.[129] A change in the political composition of the coalition would have been necessary to achieve an agreement and that change could be brought about if Netanyahu chose to form it or defections from the coalition could bring it down.[130] At least 60% of the members of the Knesset are estimated to accept the peace deal that Kerry was developing in the negotiations.

Abbas certainly knew that many Palestinians were opposed to accepting the peace deal that might emerge with the compromises Kerry might develop. Nevertheless, he could expect that a referendum among Palestinians in the West Bank and Gaza Strip probably would accept it. However, the existence of a militant independent force, Hamas, was a grave challenge. The improvement of political, security, and economic conditions in the West Bank probably contributed to the recent rise in the standing of Fatah relative to Hamas.[131] Furthermore, support for Hamas was seriously reduced with the changes in Egypt and with its support for opposition groups in Syria, contrary to Iran's position. Abbas and Fatah could expect that they could secure good terms in reaching agreements with Hamas.

In any case, a Palestinian government including Hamas need not have been a barrier to negotiating an enduring peace. It could mean that if an agreement were reached, it would have greater likelihood of being sustained. Significantly, a June 2009 survey found that 50% of Israelis support talks with Hamas "if needed to reach a compromise agreement with the Palestinians," and 62% favor talks with a Palestinian government composed jointly of Fatah and Hamas.[132] The U.S. government announced on June 2, 2014, that it planned to work with the new Palestinian unity government and would continue to disburse aid to the PA while monitoring that it upholds certain principles, including recognizing Israel, rejecting terror, and honoring prior agreements. This was an important decision, demonstrating to the Israeli government that the United States. would not defer to it on all such matters.

This might have had constructive benefits, but that was not appreciated by the Hamas leadership. Instead, celebrating the kidnapping and killing of three teenage Jewish hitchhikers in June 2014 undercut that initiative. Hamas-Israeli hostility quickly escalated into a fierce war in Gaza.

The terrible costs of the weeks of violence again demonstrated the importance of reaching a negotiated solution between Israeli Jews and Palestinians. Mutual recourse to violence is mutually self-defeating. Negotiation must be done primarily by representatives of both sides, but other stakeholders can help or hinder that process. The Obama administration made two valiant efforts to help, but they were not sufficient to overcome the obstacles inherent in the nature of the conflict.

There are ways Americans can be more helpful, derived from the constructive conflict approach. First, it should be recognized that the general outlines of what an acceptable solution would look like are known. The precise terms of a two-state solution were almost fully agreed upon between Abbas and Olmert, the former Israeli prime minister, as discussed in the previous chapter. For many years, the people on both sides have supported a two-state solution, but did not believe the other side wanted it so it would not happen.[133] The stronger position of Israel relative to the Palestinians enables hardliner segments of the Israeli society to insist on terms that are unacceptable to most Palestinians. Failing to reach a mutually acceptable accommodation, however, is costly to both sides. Although Israeli society is prosperous in many ways, its democratic character is undermined by the ongoing conflict. The Palestinians experience limitations and humiliations. Both groups fear suffering violence. The 2014 war in Gaza demonstrated the reality of the fears.

The suggested possible actions that American officials and nongovernmental actors may pursue to enhance effective peacemaking derive from the conflict transformation and constructive conflict schools of thought and practice. I first consider actions that focus on the negotiation process and subjective ways of reframing the conflict, and then discuss actions that take a longer time perspective and involve structural factors that reduce the conflict's great asymmetry.

Recent developments in Israel and in the occupied territories could be used to achieve greater negotiating progress. Consider the striking economic growth in Israel and the emerging improvements in the West Bank economy. The flourishing Israeli economy might be construed as an asset that is a source of security and that also could help bear some of the costs of making peace.[134] For the Palestinians, the economic gains made even under the present difficult circumstances could help make credible a vision of future viability and much greater progress once a peace settlement is reached.

U.S. intermediaries might do more to help generate a vision of a future Israeli-Palestinian relationship that would yield mutual benefits. There is evidence that future-oriented peace accords tend to be more enduring than backward-looking agreements.[135] This future could include economic gains from accessing oil deposits off the coast of Gaza and water supplies from Turkey. A mutually acceptable accommodation would certainly enhance the global standing of Palestinians and Israelis and open new markets for both. Peace should not be viewed as requiring only painful compromises, but as offering major joint benefits.

Interestingly in this regard, the RAND Corporation has conducted analyses of the requirements for a successful Palestinian state.[136] It has issued reports about various approaches to constructing a backbone of infrastructure for that state. The reports provide a detailed vision of a transportation system linking urban centers and neighborhoods. Attention should be given to that vision and to the initial steps that can be taken to actualize it.

More attention also should be given to the socioemotional elements in the conflict.[137] Palestinians often speak of their feelings of humiliation from the way the Israeli Jews treat them and many are bitter and angry for the losses resulting from the establishment of the state of Israel. Conversely, Israeli Jews are angry about terror attacks upon Jews and fear an existential threat from a hostile Arab world. Many people on each side hold derogatory stereotypes of each other and are aware of the negative way they are viewed by people in the other community. Intermediary efforts should include encouraging members of each side to be respectful of the other, which in the long run will better serve their own interests. American attention should be given when such gestures are made as Abbas did in calling the Holocaust a heinous crime.[138]

There is evidence that in regard to sacred matters, being offered tangible benefits to yield in those matters is seen as bribery and it therefore would be dishonorable to make concessions.[139] Intangible expressions of respect and the acknowledgment of the importance of what is sacred to the other side are more likely to win concessions than humiliating coercion.[140] Intermediaries and Track Two channels can help formulate and orchestrate statements by representatives of one side recognizing the sites holy to the other.

Members of each side can demonstrate their respect for each other in many ways, which do not place themselves in great danger. Intermediaries can help communicate how that can be done effectively and help coordinate the actions so that they are conducted reciprocally. One way is for members of each side to emphasize what is positive in the actions that the members of the other side have taken. For example, the economic progress that members in each nation are making might be commended by people in the other nation.

In this case, at this time, the acknowledgement of pain and loss that members of one side have suffered, sometimes at the hands of the other, is very difficult.

Apologies are probably too difficult and dangerous to be made. But each side can acknowledge the pain the other side has endured and is suffering arising from the conflict.[141] Israeli leaders can acknowledge the pain of Palestinians who lost the homes and land their families had. Palestinian leaders can acknowledge the Israeli fear and anguish from prior bombings and attacks against Jewish civilians. More positively, open recognition by each of what the other people hold sacred in Jerusalem and the Holy Land should be encouraged.

More can be done to encourage respectful conduct that enables egalitarian interaction. At present, the checkpoints within the Palestinian territories interfere with economic and social activities and these should be eliminated, or at least greatly reduced and monitored in ways that allow for speedy and respectful passage. To complement the training being given to Palestinian security forces, the United States might support nonofficial as well as official efforts in the West Bank to protect Palestinians from harassment by Jewish settlers. Such actions would increase the credibility that a peaceful accommodation will be achieved.

Another area for improvement is the respectful depiction of each people in the textbooks used by the students of the other nation. Efforts to compose histories by Palestinians and Jewish authors working together should be sponsored and encouraged by foreign donors and organizations.

In order to build an enduring peace, members at many levels on each side must support a peace agreement, or at least not try to disrupt it. Intermediaries should help engage people at the grassroots and sub-elite levels and provide information to the public on each side about constructive actions that members of the other side have taken. More peacemaking work should be encouraged, recognized, and supported through diverse NGOs, which may be based on religion, profession, or business. Of course some of this was done during and after the Oslo process, but too often the participants were already committed to coexistence. Joint undertakings not directly fostering mutual understanding need to be expanded and promoted, for example relating to the arts, sports, business, and the environment.

Finally, rather than rely on essentially bilateral direct negotiations between Israeli and Palestinian leaders, Americans might develop agreements based on extensive negotiations with each side together with other interested parties. The agreements would need to be supported by a wide spectrum of stakeholders committed to their realization and maintenance. The chances of attempting this action and it succeeding will be enhanced if some of the ideas discussed below were also implemented.

The constructive conflict approach is broader than mediation and negotiation understood only in terms of cognitive and emotional factors. Structural factors have been integral to the approach, since peace studies was one of its sources of development.[142] The use of terms like conflict transformation by workers in the field indicates that the goal of adversaries and intermediaries need not be to end a conflict but to change it so that the adversaries struggle in ways they deem legitimate and acknowledge each other's interests and concerns. Even small achievements in transforming the conflict should be given more attention. In this matter, intermediaries should not expect to be neutral and rely only on persuasive inducements, but use appropriate negative and positive sanctions.

This broader perspective is particularly relevant for reducing the forms of conflict asymmetry that hamper reaching equitable, mutually acceptable agreements.[143] Many partisans and analysts stress the asymmetries in the Israeli-Palestinian conflict that obstruct reaching such an agreement. One kind of conventional response is to call for the United States to pressure Israel. This is often urged from many sides but rarely has been employed.[144] U.S. officials have been reluctant to follow this path, and not only out of American domestic considerations. They point out that such efforts are not likely to be effective and rather emphasize the need to reassure Israelis that U.S. protection will reduce the inherent risks in making peace with the Palestinians and the Arab world supporting them.

One way the United States might reinforce the Palestinian claim that the capital of the Palestinian state will be in Palestinian-inhabited portions of Jerusalem is that some U.S. official and non-official transactions with PA officials would be held in the U.S. consulate office in East Jerusalem or in offices of Palestinian organizations there. This would make the Palestinian presence in East Jerusalem more visible and legitimate to Israeli Jews.

Another way to reduce asymmetries in this conflict is to increase Palestinian capacities to resist Israeli actions that hamper Palestinian economic and political activities. To do this in a way that is not highly threatening and yet not easily ignored is challenging. This was achieved in some measure in the first Intifada, but not in the second, which incorporated armed violence.[145] Presently, there are increasing instances of nonviolent demonstrations in West Bank villages. Palestinians have been joined by Israeli Jews and people from other countries in many of these demonstrations.[146]

Peace Now, a major Israel peace movement organization, has been gathering information about the titles of the land that has been used for building settlements for Jews.[147] Peace Now discovered many violations of Israeli laws in transferring land and building housing. It has won court orders to stop construction; however, the orders are generally not implemented. Increasing official and non-official American attention to these local campaigns will bolster their effects and raise the costs of expanding the settlements for the Israeli government.

A fundamental way to redress the asymmetries that hamper movement towards an equitable Israeli-Palestinian accommodation is to strengthen the bargaining position of the Palestinians. This can be done in nonprovocative ways, buttressing the Palestinians' economic conditions and normative claims. One way to do that is to further increase economic aid for Palestinian economic development, and monitor its use. Significantly, such aid is going directly to the Palestinian Authority. This may be a path to reconstruction efforts in Gaza.

It is crucial that the United States act in ways that are manifestly new. As part of a new approach, it is important to actually start doing new things that help improve Palestinian-Israeli relations, creating new facts on the ground quickly, not merely making promises about the future. For example, action could begin in the near term to create an international fund for the compensation and resettlement of Palestinian refugees.[148] The international fund, with money from Arab countries, Israel, European countries, and the United States, would provide assistance in the resettlement of Palestinian refugees and their families in the occupied Palestinian territories, in neighboring Arab countries, and elsewhere where many Palestinians now live.[149]

Joint economic programs should be discussed and where feasible actually begin to be implemented. These may include projects to expand and improve water supplies and to undertake exploration and drilling for oil off the Gaza shore. It also could include jointly produced and marketed products and services entering expanding markets. USAID has supported small-scale projects of this kind. For example, with USAID funds, the Near East Foundation has been helping in the modernization and development of the Palestinian olive oil industry and is developing ways to foster related joint Palestinian-Israeli activities.[150]

The United States should work more closely with international governmental organizations and with other states and NGOs. For example, the Palestinian economic efforts in the West Bank would benefit from PA preliminary membership in the World Trade Organization.[151] The U.S. government should support this, and the WTO rules would be safeguards for Israel and other countries. To be effective, multilateral efforts are needed, but they should be coordinated so they do not interfere with each other. Russia, Turkey, the European Union, and many other entities can help greatly in peacemaking.

Another international project should be given more active attention. Israeli abandonment of its policy of ambiguity regarding its possession of nuclear weapons, in the context of establishing a Middle East zone free of weapons of mass destruction (WMD), could have security benefits not only for Israel but for all countries in the region.[152] It would help protect the countries from the threats of nuclear, chemical and biological weapons.

The adoption of many such policy prescriptions could help provide the context within which the methods of negotiation and mediation of the narrower conflict resolution approach could be effective. In that context, negotiations for an Israeli-Palestine peace accord may yet be successful in reaching mutually acceptable agreements. This discussion has presumed that a two-state solution was the goal of the mediation effort. There is increasing skepticism, however, that Palestinian and Jewish states existing side by side in peace and security is feasible. Actually, a variety of state characteristics can be imagined, with more or less integration between the states and more or less porous borders. Various forms of association between them and with other states may be developed over time. These might include shared authorities for particular places or functions.

Improving living conditions in the Palestinian territories may be perceived by some Palestinians as a way of keeping them quiet and acquiescent about the Israeli occupation of their lands. The improvements should be understood by them and others as part of self-directed nation-building by Palestinians. Even when projects are undertaken jointly with Israeli organizations, they should be clearly contributing to the viability and independence of a Palestinian state.

In addition to direct attempts to influence the policies of the adversaries, intermediaries can help change linked conflicts and other structural factors so as to influence the adversaries indirectly. Such changes in the context can help to reframe the conflict so that opportunities for better security, social welfare, and political institutions will seem likely to Israelis and Palestinians as their relations move toward a more constructive transformation.

The Obama administration has pursued peace in the Middle East in ways that are somewhat more congruent with the constructive conflict approach than its predecessors did, but it has not been applied comprehensively and with audacity. It may be that the president cannot overcome domestic constraints to implement a more creatively constructive approach. And it may be that the adversaries are too far apart in what they each believe is required for a peaceful accommodation for any kind of U.S. intervention to be effective. It may be that one or both sides must change what they deem is required for a settlement, and such changes will follow only after still more pain and anguish.

Nevertheless, the present analysis suggests that a fresh, more comprehensive constructive approach could help transform the Israeli-Palestinian conflict. It is important for external intermediaries to work with local developments in any conflict they seek to moderate. Intermediary efforts that help transform intractable conflicts need to be applied to reshape the conflict context. The efforts can draw upon a wide array of inducements, including both coercive and noncoercive inducements; but the coercion must be constrained and exercised within a broadly constructive context.

Nongovernmental actions within the United States also can have important effects in influencing the U.S. government or impacting on the relationship between Israeli Jews and Palestinians. Thus, the growth of J-Street and the shift within the Jewish-American community away from automatic support for the positions of the hardline Israeli government has produced more open congressional support for a negotiated peace between Israel and the Palestinians.

In addition, some nongovernmental organizations with Jewish and non-Jewish memberships have acted in solidarity with Palestinians. This can contribute to reducing the asymmetry of the conflict by imposing moral and economic sanctions against Israel. Thus, in recent years, some nongovernmental organizations in the United States have taken actions associated with an international campaign of boycotts, divestment, and sanctions (BDS) against Israel. This was prompted by the 2005 Palestinian Civil Society call for sanctions against Israel until it complied with international law and Palestinian rights. Several churches and other nongovernmental organizations in the United States and other countries began to mobilize selected sanction actions. These coercive acts of solidarity were intended to help influence the Israeli government to negotiate in a more conciliatory manner, but some activist BDS campaigners sought a one-state solution. More often, the groups waging sanction campaigns targeted products and corporations associated directly with the Israeli occupation of the West Bank. Such targeting could be presented as not challenging the existence of the state of Israel, thereby lessening the possible counterproductive effects of such campaigns. For example, in 2012, the General Assembly of the Presbyterian Church (USA) called for a boycott of Israeli products made in the Palestinian territories; and in June 2014, the General Assembly voted (very narrowly) to sell stock in Caterpillar, Hewlett-Packard, and Motorola due to their activities against Palestinians in the West Bank.[153]

Finally, the constructive conflict approach recognizes the reality that large-scale conflicts such as the Israeli-Palestinian conflict do not end. There will not be a postconflict stage of unchanging harmonious peace. The Israeli-Palestinian conflict will continue, but in time not as destructively as it has often been waged in the past. Over time it will become transformed and ultimately waged in mutually acceptable ways. Indeed, the larger Arab-Israeli conflict already has been significantly transformed. It is important to recognize the ways transformation has already occurred in the Israeli-Palestinian conflict and take more transformative actions self-consciously now. Taking transformative actions now holds out the credible promise of further actions that will hasten and deepen the process of transformation. The challenge is to make the transformation substantially equitable, and thereby more stable.

Current Issues in the Constructive Conflict Approach

Three sets of challenges generated by the growth of the constructive conflict approach raise issues that deserve attention. The challenges relate to specialization, standards to assess constructiveness, and the diffusion and unwitting applications of the approach's ideas.

SPECIALIZATION

The field of conflict resolution broadly understood has grown and matured greatly in the last decade. The number of graduate programs offering degrees and certificates in the conflict resolution field and other related fields has continued to grow, and these degrees are now widely available in the United States and in many other countries. New doctoral programs have also been established in the United States. In addition, training in conflict resolution and experience with it has diffused in all school levels and in many governmental and nongovernmental organizations. The ideas are so prevalent that persons who have had no formal learning in the field unwittingly use some of its concepts and practices.

As the field has grown and expanded, it has become ever-more specialized and differentiated. Workers in the fields of peace studies and conflict resolution, broadly understood, cultivate different conflict arenas, including family settings, intra- and interorganizational systems, and national and international societal relations. They focus on different conflict stages including underlying structural conditions, escalating contention, negotiation and mediation, and recovery from oppression and mass violence. They concentrate on different kinds of actors, including officials in the UN system and other international governmental organizations, nongovernmental conflict resolvers, and members of various other nongovernmental organizations, political leaders, official military forces and militias, and mass social movements. Finally they emphasize different kinds of practices including negotiation and mediation, dialogue workshops, transitional justice mechanisms, Track Two diplomacy, reconciliation processes, electoral procedures, legal tribunals, and nonviolent actions.

Problems arise from too much specialization. They can result from applying a particular specialty's methods to aspects of conflicts for which other specialties also have great or greater relevance. The growing differentiation and specialization calls for research comparing the effects of different choices of applications for similar conflict circumstances. It also calls for efforts by all workers in the fields of conflict resolution and peace studies to keep informed about developments in many other specialties. That task is eased by the recent publication of the four-volume *Oxford International Encyclopedia of Peace* and numerous handbooks with entries relating to the abundance of topics within the many specializations.[154]

The constructive conflict approach is one way to draw from many specialized sub-fields and synthesize them into a comprehensive way to deal with a particular range of conflicts. These are large-scale conflicts, persisting over long time periods, in which the actuality or threat of violence is present. This approach is empirically grounded and encompasses the multiple levels and extensions such large-scale conflicts entail.

STANDARDS TO ASSESS CONSTRUCTIVENESS

As noted in earlier chapters, the number of assessments of conflict resolution projects and operations have been increasing and are now widely done. Much of this research focuses on the degree to which particular projects achieved their intended goals.[155] This is essential and valuable work, providing guides to "best practices" for other practitioners. Thinking about evaluation prods people undertaking conflict resolution applications to reflect on their practice. For example, one framework in evaluation research emphasizes the theory of change that practitioners use to conduct their conflict resolution project.[156] Making that explicit is undoubtedly useful.

Such research, however, tends to consider short-term gains, giving relatively little attention to undesired effects, interactions, and complementary effects with other efforts and long-term and indirect effects.[157] Furthermore, there is relatively little attention to the underlying standards by which desired effects are differentiated from undesired ones. That, of course, is central to determining various degrees of constructiveness and was discussed in Chapter 1. As evident in my analyses of different policies and judgments about their constructiveness, universal norms are not precise enough to guide attributing definitive degrees of constructiveness.

In this book, I have examined many conflict engagements and passed judgments on them as well as offering alternatives I deem to be more constructive. In doing so, I have relied on several criteria to judge a policy as having been more or less constructive. For example, I have often given weight to long-term consequences, rather than immediate feelings and judgments about actions taken. I have also given weight to the costs as well as the benefits of particular policy courses. By focusing on American foreign conflict engagements, I have tended to stress constructiveness for Americans. However, the effects upon all stakeholders in any conflict are important for the concept of constructiveness and I tried to keep that in mind. Finally, I did give weight in assessing destructiveness to the numbers of lives lost in pursuing various courses of action.

Developing standards of constructiveness needs much more attention. It is probably useful to distinguish various dimensions of constructiveness and indicators of degrees of destructiveness and constructiveness along each dimension. As discussed in the first chapter, factual evidence about the effects of different policies as well as clarity about values are both relevant.[158]

DIFFUSION AND UNWITTING APPLICATIONS

The constructive conflict approach has emerged by synthesizing ideas and practices from the fields of conflict resolution and peace studies and other related fields and by applying them to all stages of large-scale conflicts. Consequently, their concepts, insights, propositions and practices have diffused into many spheres of American life and in countries around the world. Academics doing research and theorizing about the constructive conflict approach and related fields as well as the self-identified practitioners in these arenas want that diffusion. They feel gratified when government officials, business leaders, social activists, and philanthropists use some of their ideas or adopt some of their techniques. Of course, some of the best ideas and practices in the field have been drawn from the activities of persons who did not think of themselves as workers in the field of conflict resolution. Instances of this kind of interaction appear throughout this book.

Acting on elements taken from the field, however, may be poorly done. Techniques may be misapplied and concepts misunderstood when taken out of the context of the broad constructive conflict approach. Methods reduced to tricks fail to work constructively. Research is needed about the essential context for effective adoption of particular methods from the constructive conflict approach. Familiarity with the basic realities stressed in the approach may be very useful in this regard.

There are a few kinds of relationships that persons engaging directly in large-scale conflicts could establish with analysts working in the field of conflict resolution and in developing the constructive conflict approach that would increase the chances that American engagements in foreign conflicts would be increasingly constructive. Too often, analysts and practitioners in the conflict resolution field join activists in peace movement organizations in opposing U.S. major military escalations without proposing alternate ways to deal with a foreign conflict. Sometimes just saying "no" is not enough.

It would be helpful to develop specific plans for responding to an emerging crisis in a timely fashion. Of course that is not easy. Groups must have substantial knowledge of the relevant areas in which a crisis is arising and the time-space to reflect and discuss constructive paths. Few such bases exist for such efforts, but interpersonal networks might sometimes help generate plausible alternatives. Groups might be formed with ongoing relations between analysts/researchers and policymakers/

activists. For example, some such collaboration exists in relationship to the application of nonviolent action as a method to challenge and transform an oppressive relationship. Another arena for collaborative work lies in developing the infrastructure that would be supportive of constructive ways to engage in foreign conflicts. Important ways American society might be changed to create such an infrastructure are discussed in Chapter 8.

Conclusion

At many points in earlier chapters of this book, I suggested alternative policies that might have been better than the ones taken. They were not intended to be blueprints to be followed in the future, but as catalysts to stimulate fresh thinking. This is especially true for the suggestions made in this chapter about conflicts that were intensely ongoing as I wrote about them. My suggestions were written with the limited information that I had at the time and about conflicts at a particular moment in time, which is already past when these pages are read. I presented them to prompt creative constructive ideas in the reader's mind for new circumstances in the future.

This chapter dealt with a particular challenge. President Obama seemed to have understandings and preferences that would be conducive to adopting and utilizing a constructive conflict approach before undertaking U.S. involvement in foreign conflicts. Furthermore, the American public, U.S. officials, and attentive leading figures had seen the unfortunate consequences of many governmental and nongovernmental actions in the preceding eight years that had been so contrary to that approach. Indeed, many official and non-official efforts pursued after 2008 had significant constructive conflict qualities. This was true to some degree in adversarial relations with Iran, interventions related to the Arab uprisings, and mediation attempts in the Israeli-Palestinian conflict.

The results, however, have been mixed in their positive consequences. The United States did militarily extricate itself from Iraq and Afghanistan, leaving each country at least initially stabilized. Al Qaeda itself posed less of a threat to America than it did in 2008. In other cases, somewhat better relations were achieved, as with Iran. In some cases, possibly worse consequences had been avoided, as in relations with Libya and Russia.

Of course, some critics of Obama's foreign policy, whether neocons or liberal interventionists, argue that the policy was erroneous. They argue that a more muscular U.S. interventionist approach would have produced better results.[159] I believe that the evidence presented in this book demonstrates that such a course would have yielded more destructive consequences for Americans than the approach taken.

The failure to achieve more successful results, I believe, is attributable to five broad reasons. First, the very intractability of many conflicts and of the adverse domestic and regional conditions affecting people in other countries can be affected only marginally by any American actions, particularly in the short term. In many cases, no actions by a president of the United States or of a nongovernmental organization could prevent an adversary from harming some American interest. No governmental or nongovernmental American actor can intervene abroad to resolve a profound conflict within or among other countries.

Second, the great resistance and obstructiveness of domestic opponents of the Obama administration were often harmful distractions, sometimes obstacles that could not be overcome, and sometimes enticements to inappropriate compromises by members of the Obama administration. Furthermore, sometimes such opponents influenced people abroad so as to undermine the administration's policies. This was the case at times in relations with Israel and with predominantly Muslim countries.

Third, the skills and talents of Obama and his many advisors had their own human limitations, and naturally they sometimes erred in their judgments about what was the right course and what was politically possible. They always operated with limited information and sometimes under terrific time pressures and lacking needed capabilities for implementing worthwhile ideas. Nevertheless, they have expanded the realm of thinking about how Americans can and should engage in foreign conflicts.

Fourth, the inertias and internal concerns of government departments and agencies and of various interest groups and lobbies hampered better foreign policy decision-making and effective implementation of policies. Such inertias and concerns can reduce creativity and give undue weight to narrow, self-serving, and short-term goals.

Finally, traditional ways of thinking about recourse to military options, vested interests, and simplistic notions of realism versus idealism fostered adapting old policies for new circumstances. I argue that a more comprehensive constructive approach offers better options in the presently evolving world. Some of the engagements in foreign conflicts discussed in this chapter had elements in accord with the constructive conflict approach, but in quite limited ways. They were often accompanied by other elements that were contrary to such an approach, which undermined the constructive elements.

Much needs to be changed in American society to improve chances that constructive conflict applications are undertaken more often and applied more effectively. In Chapter 8, needed changes in American society are discussed that would help realize the potentialities of a more constructive way of waging conflicts.

8   Building the Conditions for Constructive Strategies

THE PRECEDING CHAPTERS have demonstrated that constructive ways of contending and of intervening in foreign conflicts often have been urged and sometimes have been used by Americans, in and outside of political offices. For several reasons this is an opportune time for increasing applications of the constructive conflict approach. As discussed in Chapter 5, the approach is in harmony with many of the technological, social, and economic developments and trends in the increasingly integrated world. This is evident in the increasing speed of global communications, the growing worldwide engagement of nongovernmental actors, and the deepening global interdependence. As discussed in Chapter 6, acting in ways that are contrary to a constructive conflict approach has been deleterious to the United States and its friends and allies. Furthermore, Chapter 7 discussed the American public's wariness of the burdens of overreliance on military force. This is particularly worrisome as the capabilities of China and other emerging powers grow. The United States cannot and should not try to disengage from the world. Many Americans would be attracted to a realistic way for America to continue to be engaged in the world in a leading way, but to reduce the costs and risks of doing so contentiously.

Implementing more ideas and practices of a constructive conflict approach, however, must overcome many obstacles. In this chapter, I discuss how the conditions that obstruct taking constructive actions can be diminished and can be changed so as to make beneficial involvement in foreign conflicts increasingly likely.

In seeking changes in American conditions so that they would minimize destructive American foreign policies, we should keep in mind that no policy implemented in a large-scale conflict will be purely destructive or purely constructive. There are numerous effects of every policy and they differ in degree among the various groups directly involved in the conflict or more distantly affected by it. Furthermore, the effects often differ between the time of their implementation and in their consequences years or decades later. Overall assessments of the constructiveness or destructiveness of particular American strategies should be compared to other alternatives.

Changes might be made in four broad arenas so that Americans can and do conduct themselves more constructively when they engage in foreign conflicts. First, changes are needed in the prevailing ways of thinking among government officials and the population at large about foreign policies. Second, the functioning of American civic life could be improved in a variety of ways so the public can directly and indirectly act in ways that minimize destructive foreign policy actions. Third, certain governmental arrangements that have contributed to undue reliance on methods that fostered relatively damaging forms of engagement and hampered reliance on more constructive methods could be altered. Fourth, greater participation with the United Nations system could enable greater use and effectiveness of the constructive conflict approach.

Ways of Thinking

What Americans think about foreign conflicts is important in determining the course of American involvement in them. This is true for the general public as well as for the attentive elites and the governing officials. American political leaders certainly influence their constituents and have considerable independence in their actions abroad, but they generally feel some need to take into account what they believe are the views of the diverse American public. Certainly the thinking of the political, military, economic, and other elites of the United States have particular relevance for the conduct of American foreign policy. This was evident in the earlier discussions of neoconservatism, the Washington rules, the militarization of foreign policy, American exceptionalism, and other belief patterns.[1]

If Americans knew more about alternative ways to engage in foreign conflicts constructively, they would probably be more likely to endorse them. This knowledge would likely result in foreign engagements that are more constructive. In this book's first chapter, I identified seven realities providing the base for the constructive conflict approach. The possible future value of attending to those realities can now be discussed in the context of the previous chapters' analyses of American involvement in foreign conflicts, which were varyingly constructive and often quite destructive.[2] Obviously, the policies that turned out to be counterproductive were chosen in the belief that they would be successful. Good intentions, however, do not ensure good results.

Furthermore, too often people act in the mistaken belief that there are no alternatives to the bad choices they feel compelled to make. Too often they accept that social conflicts are inevitable in social life and fail to recognize that they might be conducted with little destructiveness. The overarching belief of the constructive conflict approach is that social conflicts can be broadly beneficial for the adversaries, albeit in varying degrees. Indeed, we have seen many instances of American engagement in foreign conflicts that had significantly beneficial consequences for substantial periods. That truth needs to be recognized so involvement is not avoided, with unfortunate consequences. On the other hand, many American foreign conflict engagements have had profoundly somber results for many parties within and beyond the United States. The United States cannot and should not try to withdraw from international engagements. When done well the engagements can be widely beneficial.

It is important to recognize that at times official and non-official American engagements have been significantly constructive. This has been the case when Americans have been one of the primary adversaries in a conflict. For example, this happened in important ways in the course of the gradual transformation of the Cold War. Significant constructiveness also was apparent when president Jimmy Carter's administration negotiated treaties with the Panamanian government to transform the conflict between the United States and Panama about the disposition of the Panama Canal. There were also relatively constructive de-escalations in U.S.-Iranian and U.S.-North Korean contentions, for short periods.

Very often, however, Americans have waged conflicts at great costs and with widespread destructive consequences. This was most tragically the case in the war in Vietnam during the 1960s and the war begun in Iraq in 2003. It was the case for covert operations that overthrew democratically elected governments in Guatemala in 1954 and in Iran in 1953. It was true for militarized responses when diplomatic activities might have contributed to constructive conflict transformations that avoided decades of antagonism. It even was sometimes the case when humanitarian interventions, too coercively pursued, contributed to deadly escalations. On the other hand, foreign engagement at times was avoided because only a violent intervention was considered and that was recognized as perhaps contributing to even greater destructiveness.

Many people tend to think that conflicts are bad and should be avoided or think of them as good for the winners and bad for the losers. What is crucial in the approach stressed here is that conflicts can have broad benefits if the conflict is done well, and if it is concluded constructively. Recognizing the possibilities of the seven realities stressed in the constructive conflict approach provides guides to better conduct.

SOCIAL CONFLICTS ARE CONDUCTED WITH VARYING METHODS

Conflicts are widely viewed as necessarily entailing coercion, imposing or threatening to impose pain on the opponent. That often is the case; however, other forms of power also are generally used as inducements by each side to get what it wants from the other. In reality, people waging a fight often incorporate some promises of benefits in the future and they usually attempt to persuade their adversary of the virtue of what they seek and even that it would be of benefit to the other side. Members of an adversary entity may be convinced by offers of future benefits or arguments convincing them that their interests and values will be served by agreeing to the changes being sought.

Such blandishments by leaders of one side may simply serve to rally their own supporters, who thereby feel better about what they seek. In actuality, it has been an important tool for Americans in their engagement in many foreign fights. Persuasive inducements were highly influential in transforming and ending the Cold War. That is attributable to the attractiveness of certain human rights values; for example, the effects of the human rights provisions of the Conference on Security and Cooperation in Europe. Also many aspects of the expansive consumerism in the United States and its popular culture had great allure to the people, especially the youth, of the Soviet Union.

The delivery and the promise of material economic benefits that might flow from cooperation with the United States was and is attractive to many people at every economic level in countries around the world. This is particularly the case for government officials and local business people in developing countries. The American power deriving from such benefits binds many people to the United States as allies. The benefits also can be converted to coercive threats or deeds, so that reducing or severing those benefits can yield compliance.

The United States has great power to fend off attacks and advance its own goals. It has unequaled soft power. America is widely admired and people from all over the world want to come to the United States to visit, to study, and even to live. All this contributes to knowledge about the United States and receptivity to the interests and concerns of Americans.

Nevertheless, when all this noncoercive power is exerted to advance short-term and narrowly defined American interests, and without due respect to those others, some pushback is likely. When accompanied by barely veiled possible coercive power, the pushback can become quite strong. This helps account for the success of populist leaders in many developing countries, challenging what they regard as American hegemony. The brashness and unilateralism of Ronald Reagan and George W. Bush's foreign policies tended to exacerbate these problems.

Certainly, the large role of coercion in foreign conflicts must be recognized. Coercion is manifested in a wide variety of violent and nonviolent strategies. In conflicts when adversaries rely greatly on large-scale direct violence, however, all sides are likely to suffer some undesirable impacts. Violence turns out to be a very blunt weapon. Yet Americans, like many people elsewhere, revel in the possession of large and powerful instruments of destruction, such as long-range missiles, drones, and smart bombs. An added attraction of some of these weapons is that their use does not expose the executioner of the deeds to direct counterattacks.

In recent decades recognition of the power of nonviolent actions in waging conflicts has greatly expanded along with growing appreciation of their greater effectiveness compared to violent strategies. Evidence of the effectiveness of nonviolent action accumulated in quantitative research, case studies, and actual uprisings. For example, Chenoweth and Stephan analyzed 323 violent and nonviolent resistance campaigns between 1900 and 2006. They found that the "nonviolent resistance campaigns were nearly twice as likely to achieve full or partial success as their violent counterparts."[3] American officials and non-officials play important roles in spreading information and providing training about nonviolent challenges to authoritarian rule.

EACH SOCIAL CONFLICT IS SOCIALLY CONSTRUCTED

Members of each side in a conflict tend to develop a shared view of who they are and who is their opponent and what issues are in contention. However, no one of them can unilaterally define the conflict of the other. Members of each adversarial side in a conflict strive to construct their own identity and the identity of the enemy; disagreements about that tend to be contentious. Members of each adversarial party conceive what issues are at stake and how the antagonists are endangering or hampering the realization of their hopes.

Characterization of the other affects each side's self-conception. During the Cold War, being anti-Communist was central for many Americans in characterizing what being American meant. If the other side is characterized by religious, ethnic, ideological, or other kinds of qualities, one's own side tends to be defined in terms of the same qualities, but a different kind of religion, ethnicity, or ideology. Ways of fighting, however, may be mimicked and the other side's cruelty and brutality can be used to justify such conduct against them.

The socially constructed character of social conflicts makes them amenable to constructive reframing. With the end of the Cold War, fights framed in terms of ideological differences could be overcome as erstwhile antagonists focus on common interests against poor economic conditions or authoritarian domination. Of course, sometimes the reframing takes on new destructive forms, fighting for power and status along ethnic or religious lines, as happened in some African countries. Which direction reframing goes depends on shifts in the broader context of the conflict and changes within one or more of the antagonists.

EACH PARTY IN A LARGE-SCALE CONFLICT IS HETEROGENEOUS

Among the many possible differences among members of each adversary party, the most relevant for affecting the course of a conflict are the different interests and concerns that are held by leaders and among all the other people in a contending country or adversarial entity. Indeed, it is a common theme in conflicts for leaders on each side to assert that they have no quarrel with the people in the opposing camp, but only with their bad leaders. Leaders themselves are not uniform and unitary; there are different interests among rivals and even allied groups.

Domestic conflicts are intermingled with foreign conflicts. For the United States, political party contests and intra-party rivalries are constantly impacting official decision-making about engaging and how to engage in foreign conflicts. When this is done constructively it can help produce better decisions. However, sometimes one political party or faction undermines or contravenes a rival's undertaking in order to make it fail, damaging long-range improved relations for all. For example, the Republican Party's acts to oppose President Clinton's moves toward greater mutual accommodation with North Korea and Iran damaged U.S. credibility with each country.

The heterogeneity within America's opponents in a conflict opens up opportunities for constructive conduct. For example, in the struggle against al Qaeda, initially its leadership was a very small circle of visionary true believers. Its fighters were a larger circle of devout young adventurers. Major funders, with their own diversity of origins and beliefs, were another important kind of associated supporters. Still-wider circles of admirers and enthusiastic supporters could and did play various roles in enabling the al Qaeda leaders to execute well-planned and orchestrated attacks. Each of the various categories making up the al Qaeda camp were varyingly committed to the cause and vulnerable to a distinctive set of coercive and noncoercive strategies to induce them to leave the al Qaeda camp. This was understood and acted upon to some degree by U.S. officials and other Americans fighting al Qaeda. However, not making that reality more explicit sometimes confounded carrying out a complex set of strategies effectively.

CONFLICTS ARE INTERLOCKED

As demonstrated time after time in the previous chapters, conflicts are often significantly linked over time, each waxing and waning in scale and intensity. Others are embedded in social space, small ones being nested simultaneously in a series of ever-larger conflicts. Furthermore, each adversary is involved contemporaneously in conflicts with another set of adversaries, some of which may be overlapping. Finally, each side in a major conflict encompasses some internal ones. Shifts in the salience of one or another conflict affect the significance of other interconnected conflicts.

This reality is significant for American intermediary interventions as well as conflicts in which America is confronting an antagonist. The United States may intervene or otherwise engage in a conflict in the belief that the engagement is in the primary conflict, but later discovers that some of the adversaries are giving higher priority to quite other conflicts, perhaps relating to religion or control over resources. Too little attention to such possibilities can contribute to misguided and ineffective efforts.

Consideration of the multiplicity of interlocking conflicts can help in identifying possible allies in the pursuit of the goals in the engagement. Furthermore, the policies are more likely to be helpful if done in concert with other countries, particularly ones in the same region.

CONFLICTS ARE DYNAMIC

Conflicts tend to move through stages and can be transformed to be more constructively waged at various conflict stages. They emerge, escalate, begin to de-escalate, then move toward an ending (imposed or agreed-upon), and the resulting outcome becomes the ground for renewed contention or a stable new relationship. There are no clearly demarcated stages with all members of the antagonistic sides moving together, in an unvarying sequence.

Conflicts are never totally static. Even when seemingly stuck in stalemates or intractability, the context of the conflict is shifting and internal elements of each side are slowly altering. Such changes can result in abrupt and unforeseen breakthroughs into conflict escalations or transformative de-escalations, as occurred in the move to negotiations between the U.S. and Iranian governments discussed in the previous chapter.

A particular tactic's effectiveness depends upon the timing of its implementation. The possible opportunity for positive change needs to be seized for the opportunity to be realized.

Thinking ahead about different possible paths forward can stimulate reflection on more constructive pathways. Unfortunately, too often reactions to the current situation are made based on short-term calculations. This may have contributed to U.S. overreaching when the United States was advancing in triumph. This was evident to some degree in the decision to march north in Korea towards the Chinese border after fighting back to the former boundary between North and South Korea. The apparent quick victory in overthrowing the Taliban in Afghanistan may have contributed to the decision by George W. Bush and his advisors to move speedily to invade Iraq, and not to plan for what would likely follow.

Considering the future course of a low-grade conflict can prompt early entry, before self-perpetuating destructive interactions become entrenched. There have been a multitude of times when the U.S. government intervened to help save lives of people dying from hunger, illness, or gun-fighting during a destructively escalated civil war in another country. Such interventions are often tardy and of limited benefit. U.S. officials and other Americans are more likely to undertake policies that have constructive effects if well considered actions are taken at early stages of a conflict.

MEDIATION CONTRIBUTES TO CONSTRUCTIVE TRANSFORMATION

Adversaries locked into conflicts that persist with varying degrees of destructiveness may benefit from the intervention of well provided mediation. Americans often do provide mediating services that help the parties in contention and also the Americans providing the service. In addition, more frequent U.S. use of mediation would be beneficial for America when it is involved as an adversary in a foreign conflict. There are times when intermediaries can help de-escalate or settle a dispute that the United States is waging. This was the case with the Algerian government's assistance in managing the 1981 release of the U.S. embassy personnel held for 444 days by the Iranian hostage-takers. Sometimes, it is allied governments that provide informal mediation services between the U.S. government and governments with whom disagreements cannot be overcome. This sometimes occurred during the Cold War and U.S.-Soviet arms control negotiations.

More attention should be given to the possible use of mediation services provided by the UN Secretary General's office or other governmental international organizations. Public awareness of the past and present contributions of non-official diplomacy should be expanded, thereby improving the likelihood of increased usage of such channels. In Chapter 2, the important roles of the Dartmouth and Pugwash conferences were discussed. Currently, unofficial Track Two meetings are particularly important when official meetings are very limited, as in U.S. talks with North Korea.

CONSIDERING THE OTHER SIDE'S INTERESTS AND CONCERNS

Shared benefits tend to follow when each side takes the interests and concerns of the other side into account. Such considerations, even if made unilaterally at first, can guide contentious conduct toward stable, mutually acceptable accommodations among adversaries. Establishing enduring legitimate relations among adversaries is more likely when they take a long-term perspective and take into account each other's concerns and interests. It is not the interests and concerns of oppressive autocratic leaders that must be considered so much as those of the great majority of people within each side in the conflict.

Seriously considering the opponent's interests may lead to altering the goals of American involvements in foreign conflicts. It can mean renouncing seeking total victory and the enemy's total defeat, at least of the broadly conceived enemy. Thus, the transformation of the Cold War was furthered with the negotiations about European security that incorporated the Western powers' agreement that they would not try to forcefully change the borders in Eastern Europe established after World War II. This was part of the Helsinki Accords concluded after years of negotiations, when the Final Act of the CSCE was signed in 1975.[4]

In short, recognizing that conflicts can be waged more constructively should give people hope that they can act to advance peace, justice, freedom, and many other important values and avoid severe destructive consequences. This holds true even in the face of seemingly intractable conflicts such as the one between Israelis and Palestinians. Conflicts are a major way people seek to challenge and rectify injustices, to win autonomy and more control of their own lives. This holds for actions taken by the U.S. government abroad, as well as for the many parties involved in conflicts everywhere in the world.

Changes in American Society and Its Institutions

Two of the major ongoing societal changes in America are conducive to adopting aspects of the constructive conflict approach to involvement in foreign conflicts. The growing multicultural character of the American population raises the likelihood of understanding and appreciating the concerns of other people elsewhere in the world, a central idea of the approach. With the changing population comes a growing appreciation of cultural differences and a strengthening of norms of tolerance and of opposition to discrimination. This helps reduce American ethnocentrism. Furthermore, this enhances regard for America by other people and America's increased credibility as a model for interreligious and interethnic coexistence among many people in other countries.

In two primary ways, the women's movement and the diffusion of feminist thinking also contribute to the adoption of the constructive conflict approach.[5] First, women are gradually increasing their participation in higher ranks of political, intellectual, economic, and other spheres of public life. There is evidence, discussed in Chapter 5, that countries with greater participation by women in public affairs are less likely to be engaged in violent wars. In general, women are less likely than men to support military action in international conflicts.[6] Second, the rigid masculine and feminine gender roles of the past have become much looser. Men and women have become increasingly liberated to act in less stereotyped ways. Therefore, men are less likely to feel and believe they must act coercively when in contention with others, while women become freer to express anger and bellicosity.

Many of the changes in American society that would foster using the constructive conflict approach are consistent with those two major social changes. Admittedly, however, some people are troubled by these changes and push against them, but with declining effect. This discussion focuses on specific new societal developments that could bolster utilizing the constructive conflict approach.

SOCIALIZATION AND EDUCATION

The discussion begins with changes that would have quite long term, indirect benefits. Children growing up with little loving support and suffering material and emotional deprivations do tend to act more aggressively as they mature. Programs and policies that reduce childhood poverty and maltreatment will decrease the interpersonal violence and participation in violence-prone organizations. Certainly, with the high and increasing income inequality in the United States, good and affordable preschool programs should be greatly expanded. This is also true for making good education available at all levels of formal education for families at low as well as high income levels.

National legislation can help overcome the disturbingly high rates of poverty and poor childrearing experience of American children, which ill-prepares them for formal education and socially productive lives.[7] Legislation should include provisions for paid parental leaves and provision of high-quality child-care facilities. Such expenditures would greatly improve the well-being of the American people and thus their human security.

More directly relevant to the issues discussed here, learning skills and having experiences that help young people deal with conflicts nonviolently can have enduring benefits. Indeed, exposure to conflict resolution negotiation and mediation is widely increasing in elementary and secondary schools; for example, by experience with youth courts.

A growing number of colleges and universities have undergraduate and graduate programs in conflict resolution and in peace studies, which include studying about and practicing conflict resolution skills.[8] These programs include undergraduate majors or minors and graduate degrees or certificates. Students interested in future careers in international relations study basic conflict resolution ideas and skills in such programs, sometimes in conjunction with other degrees. Knowledge about constructive conflict ideas and practices should be included in the basic courses relating to international relations.

Government officials and others working directly in American foreign affairs should have greater familiarity with the constructive conflict approach generally, and with possible constructive strategic alternatives specifically. The Department of State has its Foreign Service Institute and the Department of Defense has four Senior Service Colleges, the National Defense University, the Army War College, the Naval War College, and the U.S. Air Force Academy. These are excellent institutions, providing opportunities to reflect on past military experiences and consider future developments that help guide responses to current military challenges. Inevitably, however, they function within the cultures and structures of their respective organizations.

Some academic institutions, policy centers, and professional associations in the fields of conflict resolution, peacebuilding, and conflict transformation do help in many ways to connect practitioners (in and out of government service) with analysts of foreign policies. For example, in July 1992, the United States Institute of Peace organized a large conference that delivered what its name promised: "Dialogues on Conflict Resolution: Bridging Theory and Practice." In later years, more narrowly focused projects were undertaken with cooperating practitioners and scholars; for example, it awarded funds for a workshop on timing in the de-escalation of intractable international conflicts.[9] The USIP itself convened a series of meetings that resulted in a book examining the possible transforming effects of mediation in large-scale intractable conflicts.[10]

A further kind of bridging development is needed to enhance the application of the constructive conflict approach by American officials and non-officials involved in foreign conflicts. This is the establishment of venues for ongoing interactions between practitioners and analysts who do their work based on the ideas of this approach with practitioners and analysts whose work is based on more traditional ways of thinking. This is happening, particularly in the Washington, DC area. For example, the Alliance for Peacebuilding was founded in 2003 to develop and disseminate innovative approaches to peacebuilding and link related fields including development, relief, human rights, democracy, and security sector reform.[11] It convenes annual conferences and works collaboratively on issues that are too large for any one organization to carry out by itself.

NONGOVERNMENTAL ORGANIZATIONS

Voluntary associations have always been an outstanding feature of American society. Many of them play highly important and effective roles in American involvement in foreign conflicts. This is true for many religious and interreligious organizations, ethnic and interethnic organizations, and fraternal service organizations. Thus, many local religious and interreligious organizations provide important services in resettling refugees from countries beset by wars and oppression. This not only represents humanitarian assistance for the refugees, but it reduces the burdens in the regions and countries they leave that otherwise may fuel more wars and oppression. It also increases the understanding among Americans of people in other lands, and enhances the regard for America among people around the world.

Many interreligious and multiethnic organizations have long existed; for example, among Catholics, Protestants, and Jews, and more recently they have expanded to include Muslims and an even wider variety of religious faiths. Often these groups constitute networks among the clergy and leaders of these faiths. They may visit and share congregational events. This not only contributes to substantial tolerance but provides channels of communication to avert escalating misunderstandings. They provide models for peoples in other countries about how to build effective multicultural societies.[12]

Some of these organizations take the form of dialogue groups, with diaspora members from communities that are in contention with each other in their homelands. The dialogue topics may range from exchange and sharing of elements of their cultures to focusing on intense conflicts in their places of origin. In the latter case, they may try to find common ground and seek support for their shared policy ideas from other members of their respective communities and from U.S. political figures. There are many such groups relating to the Israeli-Palestinian conflict, some of which advocate for various U.S. foreign policies in the Middle East.[13]

The attacks of September 11, 2001, spurred interest in learning about Islam and the Middle East. However, only isolated organizations focusing on Muslim and non-Muslim relations in the United States or elsewhere were formed. Muslim representatives may have joined the preexisting interreligious organizations but the special issues relating to Muslims in the United States were not widely addressed. Given concerns about homegrown terrorism and the dangers arising from prejudice against Muslims, much more effort at focusing on building good relations between Muslims and others would be worthwhile. At the national level, the American-Arab Anti-Discrimination Committee, founded in 1980, works to protect Arab civil rights, promote mutual understanding with non-Arabs, and preserve the Arab American cultural heritage.[14]

Some American voluntary service organizations devote major programs to providing humanitarian services abroad and to foster international bonds and understanding. For example, Rotary International was established in Chicago in 1905 as one of the world's first service organizations, and within sixteen years it had clubs on six continents. It functions internationally and with several partners on major projects, particularly related to health. In addition, Rotary Youth Exchange offers the opportunity for American youths, fifteen to nineteen years old, to live abroad, and for youths from abroad to be hosted by families in the United States.

Finally, it is worth noting that Americans belong to various kinds of associations related to their work: professional associations, business associations, and trade unions. Most of these kinds of organizations operate at the local, national, and also at the international levels. Many individuals and members from national organizations participate in regularly held conferences advancing their individual and collective interests. These and other kinds of international nongovernmental organizations are increasing in number and level of work.[15]

The constructive conflict approach draws attention to the reality that large-scale conflicts are waged at several levels, not only between leaders of the opposing sides. Positive conflict transformation also occurs at many social levels. This is particularly important in conflicts involving one or more nongovernmental adversary. This should be obvious in the struggle between the United States and al Qaeda. The competition and rivalry among various Muslim and non-Muslim transnational organizations is a major arena in which the American struggle to counter al Qaeda is necessarily waged.

MILITARY-INDUSTRIAL COMPLEX

In the 1950s and 1960s, there was intensive research and discussion about the effective interdependence of the weapons industry, the military establishment, and the members of Congress, which collectively make up the military-industrial complex.[16] In his 1961 farewell speech, President Dwight D. Eisenhower famously warned, "In the councils of government we must guard against the acquisition of unwarranted influence, whether sought or unsought by the military-industrial complex."[17]

Currently, however, there is relatively little public attention paid to the concept. There are, nevertheless, many analyses of particular elements of the complex. Clearly, the strong ties between weapons manufacturing corporations, the military establishment, members of Congress, think tanks, and other major American institutions drive up military defense costs while thwarting the adoption of more constructive foreign policies. Several processes sustain these linkages.

The jobs provided in the weapons production industries throughout the United States are extremely attractive and people in various cities and states compete with each other for arms production contracts. Members of Congress too often vote to fund particular weapons systems that yield jobs in their districts, even if they are not the Pentagon's preferred use of funds.[18] In addition, the corporations that produce various weapons systems lobby members of Congress and discretely make large campaign contributions.[19] These corporations also produce weapons for sale around the world, making the United States the world's largest arms dealer. The Department of Defense plays a key role in fostering such arms sales, often in circumstances that exacerbate conflicts. The arms sales contribute to the militarization of many countries' foreign and domestic policies, increasing the likelihood of destructive foreign conflicts.[20]

The recent concerns about the federal deficit and federal spending have spurred attention to waste in Pentagon operations and funding for unnecessary weapons; for example, by the Project on Government Oversight and Taxpayers for Common Sense.[21] Targets for cutbacks in weapons spending include the M1 tank and the V-22 Osprey. Other proposed reductions in military defense spending include downblending highly enriched uranium and selling it as low-enriched uranium and withdrawing a number of U.S. troops from Europe.[22] Furthermore, the increased threat from nonstate actors and the absence of states with large-scale weapons systems comparable to those possessed by the United States leaves room for slower enhancements of U.S. military capacities. Robert M. Gates was proud to report that as Secretary of Defense he cut out 36 unnecessary weapons systems.[23]

Of course, corporations in the weapons production industry promote their products in many ways, including lobbying members of Congress. They also provide high-level positions to some officials in the military and civilian services after they retire from their government employment. Additionally, they try to influence the attentive public by advertising and by making contributions to relevant think tanks.[24] Revelations about these relations are important to countering dysfunctional effects, as discussed later.

NEWS COVERAGE AND POPULAR CULTURE

Two recent developments combine to reduce the breadth of information about current foreign conflicts that the general public receives. The developments are the decline in newspapers and in journalists reporting news they gather firsthand, and also the political polarization of many mass media political sources. Americans' attention to foreign affairs has generally been relatively low. Those new developments make it more difficult for people to have well-informed grounds for choosing whether or how to participate in foreign conflicts.

Fortunately, there are other developments that open new channels for getting more information about events abroad. The increased integration of the world means that people have more international involvements. There is greater travel experience for more adults and young people. There is rapidly expanding transnational work experience among the younger generations. The Internet and social media expose more Americans to foreign events and perspectives. All these sources tend to be somewhat independent of governmental or corporate control and management, compared to the reliance on traditional one-directional mass media.

In addition, non-U.S.-based news sources have become more available in the broad range of cable television channels. This is evident in the expansion of Al Jazeera, based in Qatar, into the United States. It is also evident in a few television programs that give extended periods of time to very different points of view, as in CSPAN's Book Channel, Charlie Rose's interviews on Public Broadcasting System channels, and Fareed Rafiq Zakaria's weekly wide-ranging news program on CNN.

How news about international conflicts is interpreted and understood is critical in formulating better responses to the conflicts. Undoubtedly, the coverage generally focuses on violent conflicts, and the public seems more attracted to knowing about those conflicts than about slower-moving peaceful transformations of bloody conflicts or oppressive conditions. In this regard, the popular culture also is important. On the whole, films, television programs, electronic and video games, and other areas of popular culture give relatively little attention to cooperative conflict transformations. Destructive engagements in foreign conflicts are treated as inevitable. Monuments, museums, and holidays generally celebrate and honor warriors and their leaders from past wars. Without denigrating their valor and sacrifice, celebrations of persons and events that exhibited alternative ways of defending and advancing American values and interests should be created.

There are some manifestations of honoring leaders of nonviolent struggles for equal justice and freedom. Notably, Martin Luther King Jr. is widely celebrated and the power of nonviolent action in the struggle for civil rights for African Americans has been analyzed and reported. His opposition to U.S. engagement in the Vietnam War, however, is not so widely recognized, examined, and discussed.

Americans who are recognized for their contributions to international peacemaking are rarer. Ralph Bunche is one of the few widely recognized exemplars of constructive peacemaking. He received the 1950 Nobel Peace Prize for his mediating work between Israel and its Arab neighbors in 1949. He served as Under-Secretary-General of the UN and as UN mediator in several major conflicts. He is publically celebrated by several monuments in the United States.

In addition, in many American localities, there are monuments celebrating peace, the concept itself or some aspect of it, such as friendship, hope, or reconciliation.[25] They may take the form of a great bell (at Oak Ridge, Tennessee), a sculpture (on Raoul Wallenberg Walk in New York, New York), a fountain (at the University of Arkansas, in Fayetteville, Arkansas), or a wall mural (in Philadelphia, Pennsylvania).

Centers and museums hosting exhibits and providing educational experiences related to peace, diplomacy, and nonviolent conflict resolution are small in number and scope. However, there are some. For example, the United States Institute of Peace (USIP) moved into its new headquarters on the National Mall in 2011. It conducts a wide range of activities that help to teach, train, and inform policymakers, practitioners, students, and the public at large about the challenges of conflict prevention, management, and resolution and how to respond to those challenges.

Finally, individuals and organizations produce a wide range of books and other educational material about the reality and the possibilities of constructive ways to conduct and to resolve foreign conflicts. These are intended for policymakers, students and teachers, children, and the general public.[26] Many focus on the roles of individual heroic peacemakers, as in biographical films about Mohandas Gandhi and Nelson Mandela. Other works document accounts of historic changes and large-scale social movements.[27] Still others offer analyses and explanations of why some ways of trying to advance peace fail and others succeed.[28] On the whole, however, news coverage and popular culture do not convey the evidence that wars and mass violence have been decreasing in the world for decades, and probably longer. The idea that conflicts can be conducted relatively constructively is not conventional wisdom.

PEACE MOVEMENTS AND ORGANIZATIONS

Within the United States, peace movement activity has sharply risen in opposition to particular wars, or sometimes against particular military policies that were deemed to be dangerous. In the intervals between such bursts of energy, peace movement conduct has been expressed at a low level, to some extent sustained by local and national peace organizations maintained by persons committed to opposing particular kinds of weapons (nuclear weapons, landmines, or drones) or any direct deadly violence, or what they regard as imperialistic interventions.[29] Many religious communities advocate for peace actions as a regular part of their services and activities and some are associated with organizations dedicated to supporting peacemaking policies; for example, Pax Christi USA for Catholics, American Jewish World Service for Jews, and the American Friends Service Committee for Quakers.

At this time, a substantial number of advocacy organizations oppose foreign policies that emphasize reliance upon particular militarized foreign engagements. Such peace movement organizations also support institutional and policy developments that produce better conflict strategies. Sometimes it seems that peace movement organizations and demonstrations are aroused only to say "No!" They seem to be saying no to various aggressive U.S. government actions without offering alternative ways of dealing with the problems that the government policies are purporting to solve. With the development of the constructive conflict approach, opposition is more often now complemented with support for alternative options. For example, in 1987, two anti-war and disarmament organizations, SANE and the Nuclear Weapons Freeze Campaign, merged to form SANE/FREEZE, which in 1993 was renamed Peace Action. Peace Action is the largest grassroots peace organization in the United States, affirming its commitment to resolving international conflicts peacefully and upholding international cooperation and human rights.[30]

This is evident in varying degrees in the work of the previously mentioned Alliance for Peacebuilding. It is also evident to varying degrees in the work of long-standing and new peace movement organizations, such as Win Without War, a coalition of about forty nongovernmental organizations formed in 2002. It opposes the "overmilitarization of our foreign policy and its effects at home and abroad . . . [believing] that international cooperation and international law provide the greatest security for the United States and the world."[31] Another national coalition network is United for Peace and Justice; it was founded in October 2002 during the buildup to the U.S. invasion of Iraq in 2003. It is opposed to what it regards as the U.S. government's policy of permanent warfare and empire-building.[32]

Many peace movement organizations focus on trying to influence the members of Congress and the president to alter their policy regarding particular foreign conflicts. This used to typically take the form of letter-writing and telephone campaigns, and now often are mobilizations manifested by electronically submitted petitions. In addition, letters to newspapers or statements on social media platforms are organized. Face-to-face lobbying of senators and representatives also is conducted. On some issues, organizations or coalitions are able to mount street demonstrations that may garner local newspaper reports.

Acts of civil disobedience are also sometimes undertaken by members of local and of national organizations. Persons undertaking such actions may incur fines or even jail sentences, but do so to witness or simply announce their opposition to what they regard as immoral conduct. Thus, two Catholic priests, the brothers Daniel and Philip Berrigan, carried out many campaigns of civil disobedience to oppose the nuclear arms race and the Vietnam War. For example, in May 1968 they joined with seven other Catholics to seize draft-board files in Catonsville, Maryland, which they destroyed with chicken blood.[33]

Sometimes activists undertake more narrowly focused campaigns seeking to bring about limited changes in U.S. government foreign policies. They create newsworthy events, including acts of civil disobedience, as illustrated by the School of the Americas Watch. It was spurred by the March 1980 assassination of Archbishop Óscar Romero in El Salvador.[34] He had preached against the oppressive El Salvadoran government, supported by the U.S. government. Roy Bourgeois, an ordained priest in the Roman Catholic Church's Maryknoll Society, learned that officers from El Salvador's army and other Latin American armies had been trained at the School of the Americas at Fort Benning in Georgia. They undertook a campaign of public education, congressional lobbying, demonstrations, and nonviolent actions. After the murders of six Jesuit priests in El Salvador in 1989, they began holding annual demonstrations at Fort Benning. These events grew and in 2000, Congress renamed the school the Western Hemisphere Institute for Security Cooperation. Curriculum changes also were made, including at least eight hours of classes on human rights and civilian control of the military. The annual demonstrations continue calling for the closure of the Institute.

Peace movement organizations in periods of mass mobilization have influenced U.S. policies regarding participation in the Gulf and Iraq wars, the Vietnam War, and in countering U.S. involvement in civil wars in Central America. Peace movement organizations during periods lacking mass mobilizations have mitigated particular U.S. policies that had destructive implications, as noted in regard to the School of the Americas.

American peace movement organizations also persist in efforts to gain U.S. adherence to international agreements banning or limiting particularly egregious military policies. They did so in association with international nongovernmental campaigns that successfully resulted in two international treaties. First, the International Campaign to Ban Landmines succeeded in bringing about the 1997 Mine Ban Treaty, for which it was awarded the Nobel Peace Prize. Second, Child Soldiers International, formerly the Coalition to Stop the Use of Child Soldiers, was formed to prevent the recruitment and exploitation of children in warfare, which helped bring about the UN General Assembly adoption, in 2000, of the Optional Protocol on the involvement of children in armed conflict to the Convention on the Rights of the Child. The Protocol requires that ratifying governments ensure that while their armed forces can accept volunteers below the age of 18, they cannot be conscripted and "shall take all feasible measures to ensure that members of their armed forces who have not attained the age of 18 years do not take a direct part in hostilities."[35] In 2008, the United States passed legislation supporting that policy.

ALTERNATIVE THINK TANKS

A possible basis for creative fresh thinking about applying the constructive conflict approach to American participation in foreign conflicts is the establishment of more numerous and influential think tanks that develop constructive alternative foreign policies. As discussed in Chapter 5, American think tanks tend to be mainstream or right wing in their orientation, yet persons associated with those think tanks often are consulted by policymakers and appear on television and radio talk shows.

Individual academic scholars, policy analysts, and bloggers may formulate better conflict options regarding a specific foreign conflict. However, they are not likely to have access to the resources of an organization with members possessing wide-ranging knowledge and experience about many parts of the world and possessing familiarity with a comprehensive constructive approach to participating in foreign conflicts. They are also not likely to have a platform that would help get their ideas about options heard.

Large think tanks that blend regional expertise with familiarity with conflict resolution are needed to provide creative alternative ways of responding to specific looming conflicts. There are several centers, organizations, and networks that partially fulfill the functions of such alternative think tanks. I briefly point out a few of them.

The *Carnegie Endowment for International Peace*, founded in 1910, is the oldest international affairs think tank in the United States, yet it provides fresh independent analysis and policy options.[36] In 2006 it began to transform itself and has become a global think tank, establishing centers beyond Washington in Beijing, Beirut, Brussels, and Moscow. The centers employ local experts who report on national, regional, and global issues, collaborating with colleagues around the world. The result provides governments and civil institutions with well-grounded analyses and new ideas about policy problems. Carnegie does not take institutional positions and does not engage in lobbying. Its scholars have diverse political views, but it is viewed as a centrist institution within the American political spectrum.

The *World Policy Institute* seeks to identify critical emerging global issues in this increasingly interdependent world and provides new global perspectives to offer innovative policy solutions. It originated in the post–World War II movement of moderate internationalists, being founded in New York City in 1961 as the Fund for

Education Concerning World Peace through World Law. In 1982, the World Policy Institute adopted its current name to reflect a shift from a primarily educational focus to incorporating a strong policy character.[37] It founded the *World Policy Journal* as a forum for accessible policy analysis and public debate.

The *International Center on Nonviolent Conflict* provides information about nonviolent conflict and collaborates with educational institutions and nongovernmental organizations in several projects. It uses television broadcasting, the Internet, and other media to disseminate video programming and books, as well as learning materials for schools and universities. It holds workshops, meetings, and briefings, cosponsors conferences, and distributes articles, books, and films to encourage international institutions and decision-makers to facilitate the activity of civilian-based nonviolent movements. The Center does not assist activists in planning, organizing, or conducting any actions; it does support research and other educational projects by other nongovernmental organizations and individuals. It accepts no grants, contracts, or funding of any kind from any government or government-related organization, or from any foundation, corporation, or institution, being funded entirely by the founding chair, Peter Ackerman.

In summary, many aspects of American society are quite congruent with the basic ideas of the constructive conflict approach. Some of the ongoing developments in American society together with realizing some of the proposed new developments discussed here could bolster the awareness of this congruence and foster a more widespread adoption and utilization of those ideas. Furthermore, enhanced public understanding and application of the core ideas would help overcome the obstacles to their governmental implementation that exist in the American political system.

Changes in the American Political System

Many interrelated changes are needed in the American political system to foster constructive foreign policies and to overcome the factors that contribute to destructive policies. Often, the government-based obstacles to acting constructively reinforce each other, but necessarily they are discussed separately. I begin with aspects of the American presidency and the executive branch of the U.S. government, and give particular attention to the military establishment.

The American goals being sought are obviously related to the choice of approach toward engagement in foreign conflicts. It is striking that U.S. international goals are only vaguely discussed and not widely debated in any specificity. The most authoritative statements of U.S. goals and means are presidential decision directives (PDD).

These are executive orders issued by the U.S. President with the advice and consent of the National Security Council. The directives generally focus on narrowly delimited national security policy and military strategies, and many PDDs are classified. They change over time with different presidents.

Overall, international U.S. goals are indicated in speeches and inferred from conduct. But what is said and what is done often are at variance, making for ambiguity in the eyes of many people in the United States and worldwide. Generally, the words and deeds tend to suggest claims for American primacy and leadership in the world, which rely on the overwhelming U.S. military capabilities. Other framings of what the U.S. role in the world is and ought to be are articulated to varying degrees by different presidents and other American leaders.

The constructive conflicts approach, as presented in this book, has implications about what American goals in the world should be. It recognizes many of the changing world realities that set parameters for American choices. These include demographic and climatic changes, increasing global integration and also differentiation, and increasingly shared information and unequal access to resources. Within those contexts, the United States has been well favored in natural resources and in synthesizing human cultures from around the world. The American way of life is widely attractive. Its economic and military capabilities allow it to play a predominant role in world affairs. On those bases, the ideas of the constructive conflict approach suggest that Americans can be reasonably influential in the world. However, the approach would also suggest that it would be a mistake to presume and insist upon one-way American influence unconstrained by consideration of others. Over-reliance on coercion would naturally produce resistance and push-backs. The recourse to coercion is best done selectively and with attention to the concerns and interests of others, as well as to the unintended consequences of such actions in the longer term.[38]

THE WHITE HOUSE AND THE CIVILIAN DEPARTMENTS

In recent decades, decision-making in foreign policy has been increasingly concentrated in the executive branch of government and in the president's office. Despite the constitutional mandates for congressional power, Congress has exercised decreasing authority in regard to engagement in foreign conflicts. Several trends converge to raise the likelihood that foreign policy decisions are made within the executive branch departments and agencies, and particularly within the presidential office. The increasing technological capacities for rapid communication enable persons in Washington to oversee and direct actions by their subordinates wherever they may be, thus reducing their autonomy. In addition, the increasing integration of the world and the interdependence of various spheres of activity mean that any particular foreign policy issue is highly connected with a multitude of other issues. Therefore, a decision on any single matter has broad implications in many other realms, which argues for a person with broad areas of knowledge and responsibilities making decisions about many specific issues. The president would reasonably be considered at the pinnacle of possessing the most and best information, but that does not mean that any one person can possibly have good information about all relevant matters. The high value placed on secret information further privileges the president and his associates' capabilities to make foreign policy decisions. These tendencies are further enhanced by the militarization of foreign policy and the president's role as Commander in Chief.

Given the complexity of every significant foreign conflict, and the diversity of the federal entities that may bear on it, consultation and coordination are vital. The National Security Council (NSC) was created in 1947 because President Harry Truman and his associates believed that the diplomacy of the State Department was no longer adequate to wage the Cold War. The NSC was to ensure coordination among the Navy, Marine Corps, Army, Air Force, and other instruments of national security policy such as the CIA. The composition of the NSC expanded over the years, particularly as concerns about homeland security rose after September 11, 2001. The Global War on Terrorism resulted in vast increases in domestic institutions and policies to prevent, to mitigate, and to recover from terror attacks. The Department of Homeland Security was created by bringing together elements from relevant departments and agencies into one new department. Forms of surveillance of communication and control of movement across the country's borders were greatly expanded. Some of these actions were effective, but some of them were overblown and counterproductive.[39] A discussion of more narrowly focused domestic policies and their possible benefits goes beyond the parameters of this book.

The concentration of foreign policy decision-making sometimes is drawn very tightly into a small circle of advisers and the president. This was the case notably in George W. Bush's administration. For various reasons, the consequences are likely to be unfortunate. Generally, U.S. presidential elections are won and lost on domestic, not international, issues. Many American presidents have not entered office with extensive knowledge and experience with foreign affairs. They sometimes select persons to be secretary of state for reasons other than their great experience in foreign affairs. The risks of this conduct are greater as presidents have developed national security teams associated with their office, reducing their reliance on the established departments and agencies with long-experienced personnel.

In general, the centralized concentration of foreign policy decision-making forgoes the knowledge and perspective that broader participation would provide.

It also results in a lack of public understanding and support that greater public engagement would likely generate. Congressional debates and hearings at some periods in the not-too-distant past did provide broader counsel and stimulate public discussion. Unfortunately, the standing and influence of the Senate Committee on Foreign Relations and the House Committee of Foreign Affairs have greatly declined since the early years of the Cold War.[40]

The Department of State is the natural body to help provide the infrastructure for improved U.S. policies regarding foreign conflicts. In recent years, the department has expanded its range of activities, entering new fields of work. For example, as discussed in the previous chapter, the Bureau of Conflict and Stabilization Operations was established within the Department of State to advance U.S. national security by breaking cycles of violent conflict and mitigating crises.[41] Working in countries facing high risks of mass violence, its teams are involved in conflict prevention and in crisis response and stabilization, striving to overcome the causes of destabilizing violence. They work closely with a wide range of local groups and seek to be innovative, catalytic, and agile in their operations. Nation-building projects are not best met under military direction, and various ways of expanding Department of State capacities to undertake such missions are possible and deserve consideration.[42]

Greater visibility and more public awareness of such activities could help the Department of State gain much needed additional resources. The greater resources would enable it to do more and it would likely be called on more often for its judgment and services. Congressional hearings about more innovative undertakings and potential new undertakings could help in these regards.

THE MILITARY ESTABLISHMENT

Since the end of the Cold War, there are no real challengers to U.S. global military primacy. After a short-time decline in U.S. military expenditures, they rose sharply after the September 11, 2001 attacks.[43] With the winding down of U.S. military engagement in Iraq and in Afghanistan, a reduction in the number of military personnel has occurred. Nevertheless, U.S. military expenditures throughout the post–Cold War years have been very high, almost equal to the rest of the world's expenditures combined. Since 9/11, the United States seems to have entered into a permanent war in some regards.[44] This seems more domestically driven than by any massive external military threat. As documented earlier, international wars and violent deaths have declined in recent decades and are less often the way international and civil conflicts are conducted and concluded.

The Department of Defense 2005 Base Structure Report stated that U.S. military forces maintained more than 700 bases overseas in 120 countries.[45] It failed, however, to include bases at that time in Afghanistan and Iraq, as well as in Kosovo, Israel, Kyrgyzstan, Qatar, and Uzbekistan. A complete count would probably be over 1,000 U.S. military bases overseas. With the end of the Cold War, some shifting of bases was begun, closing some in Germany and elsewhere in Europe while opening new bases in many other parts of the world. As Secretary of Defense William S. Cohen explained in 1998:

> We have to be forward deployed in Europe and Asia in order to shape people's opinions about us in ways that are favorable to us. To shape events that will affect our livelihood and our security. And we can do that when people see us, they see our power, they see our professionalism, they see our patriotism, and they say that's a country that we want to be with.[46]

That is hardly a universal response. The investment in overseas military bases is immense and certainly could be pruned without increasing American security risks; indeed, as discussed later, such reductions can enhance American security and influence.

The U.S. global military dominion is also indicated by the division of the world into regional commands.[47] At present the world is divided into five regions, each led by a Combatant Commander. The regions are: Europe, Asia-Pacific, the Western Hemisphere, Africa, and Near-East-South Asia.[48] The commanders, four-star generals or admirals, control great resources, which enable them to carry out a wide range of activities including drawing together a variety of officials, including U.S. ambassadors, for regional meetings. In addition, the U.S. military forces provide professional training of military officers from many countries around the world. In some cases, such as for Egypt and Saudi Arabia, close interpersonal ties develop that provide channels for mutual exchanges of information and influence.

The hyper-militarization of American foreign policy often hampers conducting better international policies.[49] The heavy global footprint of the U.S. government is likely to be viewed by people in other countries as overbearing and is often experienced as interfering in their domestic affairs. Consequently, other governments and peoples resist and find ways to pushback against the United States. That is one of the ways that over-reliance on military power can be counterproductive.

Overall, the great U.S. military resources and capability too often mean that when U.S. leaders see a challenge or problem somewhere in the world, their choice in response is to apply military force or do nothing. In the absence of strong alternatives, the U.S. military forces are too often tasked to undertake missions for which they are not well-suited, such as peacebuilding, nation building, or counterinsurgency. United States Secretary of Defense Robert M. Gates said:

> What is dubbed the war on terror is, in grim reality, a prolonged, world-wide irregular campaign—a struggle between the forces of violent extremism and moderation. In the long-term effort against terrorist networks and other extremists, we know that direct military force will continue to have a role. But we also understand that over the long term, we cannot kill or capture our way to victory. Where possible, kinetic operations should be subordinate to measures to promote better governance, economic programs to spur development, and efforts to address the grievances among the discontented from which the terrorists recruit. It will take the patient accumulation of quiet successes over a long time to discredit and defeat extremist movements and their ideology.[50]

Savings from the Department of Defense could be used to strengthen agency work suited to counter-insurgency and constructive recoveries from wars or oppression. They could increase the capabilities exercising persuasive inducements and offering attractive benefits in the future.

One way to approach overcoming the problems of the overly militarized U.S. foreign policy is to reduce the size of the defense budget. The over-militarization means that some activities are counterproductive to advancing American values, security, and interests. Savings from cuts could increase utilization of soft power and enable greater and more effective use of noncoercive inducements. More money could then be spent on countering erroneous anti-American views and on improving welfare abroad. Existing effective programs could be expanded and creative new programs could be developed in collaboration with recipient countries. Such programs should include educational and cultural exchanges, humanitarian assistance, and Peace Corps-type international service activities. They should be guided by working with people abroad to move in directions they desire, not to necessarily act in precisely American ways. Those kinds of programs would have immediate and direct benefits to Americans, enhancing their knowledge and skills.

Robert M. Gates, when he was Secretary of Defense, frequently pointed out that Congress funds Defense Department personnel far more easily than it funds State Department employees. He often told the story that there are about 6,000 Foreign Service officers, adding that former Secretary of State "Condi Rice used to say, 'We have more people in military bands than they have in the Foreign Service'. She was not far wrong."[51]

There are a few areas of Department of Defense operations that if reduced or transferred to other departments would not only reduce defense expenditures, but would contribute to more helpful American involvement in foreign conflicts. The Defense Department is heavily engaged in cooperative military activities in and with many countries. These include maintaining overseas bases, training of military personnel and even police from other countries, and engaging in joint military maneuvers.

To begin, there are benefits in reducing the number of military bases beyond U.S. territories. Establishing and maintaining foreign bases are sometimes counterproductive, producing ill-will toward America, particularly by the people living near the bases.[52] The image and reality of U.S. power sets America up as responsible for being blamed when bad things happen. Fundamentally, money spent on establishing and maintaining these bases should not be calculated by comparison to past years or percentage of GDP. It should be weighed against expenditures for the many other ways to promote American values, security, and interests. It is expensive to close down and dismantle bases. More might be done to turn over certain bases to the host country. Another option worth consideration is to transfer some to the UN to maintain for humanitarian disasters and other needs.

As discussed previously, the Department of State has begun to take on some stabilization operations that military forces might otherwise try to fulfill. Increased resources for such activities could replace U.S. military forces from such tasks. Other kinds of transfers would also be desirable. Presently, the United States trains at least 100,000 foreign soldiers and police from more than 150 countries each year.[53] Most are trained in their home countries, but many of them study in the United States at approximately 275 military schools and installations. This training is purported to instill respect for human rights, civilian rule, and democratic institutions. However, the training programs generally do not include such material, and the forces trained have poor human rights records. Unless the training actually fosters conduct supportive of human rights and democratic governance, the programs should not be continued. Instead the training should be transferred to civilian institutions. Even more usefully, the Department of Justice could be tasked to provide training of police, lawyers, and judges.

The training functions for helping build the infrastructure for stable democratic systems could be more effective if they were done by international organizations. Suspicions of U.S. interference and control would be lessened and more cultural sensibility would be added if UN or regional organizations cooperated in the training. That would also reduce U.S. defense expenditures.

Finally, instead of depending upon military ties to build relations with other countries, nonmilitary operations could be undertaken. For example, joint training exercises should be undertaken to respond to increasingly devastating natural disasters. This could be done or facilitated through regional organizations or through

UN auspices. Such exercises and plans for them could bring knowledgeable people together among friendly and not-so-friendly neighboring countries. These ties could very well contribute to preventing the outbreak of violent conflicts.

THE CONGRESS

Congress has important powers accorded it by the constitution pertaining to foreign affairs, including the power to declare war. The U.S. Senate must approve a treaty by a two-thirds vote to ratify it. Congress must pass a budget authorizing all government expenditures and can pass legislation regarding specific areas of foreign policy conduct. In addition, each house has committees that provide oversight of the executive branch's actions and help frame public debate. The influence of Congress over foreign policy varies with different issues. It is low in matters of crisis, moderate in strategic policy matters, and more substantial in structural policy issues.[54]

The activism and the influence of Congress have varied greatly with different administrations and with differences in political control of the two houses of Congress.[55] During much of the early years of the Cold War, Congress was actively engaged in foreign policy. There was considerable consensus between members of Congress and the presidents regarding a militarized anti-Communist approach. Criticism from Congress was more likely to come from the Right, warning of softness toward Communism, than from those urging a less-aggressive approach. During the war in Vietnam, initial acquiescence as seen in support for the Tonkin Gulf resolution was followed by congressional dissent, particularly in the Senate.[56] This encouraged and was encouraged by large-scale popular protests. One result was the effort to reassert Congressional engagement in foreign and defense policymaking. Thus, as noted in Chapter 6, the War Powers Resolution of 1973 was intended to deter presidents from sending troops into combat without consulting with Congress beforehand.[57] It requires the president to send a report to Congress within forty-eight hours of introducing troops equipped for combat into hostile situations. The 1973 resolution also provides that Congress can compel the president to withdraw troops at any time by passing a concurrent resolution to that effect. Congress, however, has not acted to implement the resolution.

Congressional dissent and influential actions were again high in the early 1980s, in opposition to Reagan's anti-Soviet activism in Central America and elsewhere. The September 11, 2001 attacks produced another era of considerable congressional and presidential consensus, as Congress yielded to extraordinary presidential determination of foreign policy. Republicans in Congress, however, have opposed many of president Obama's efforts to change his predecessor's policies relating to waging the war against terrorism and to other involvements in foreign conflicts.

Members of Congress also try to influence U.S. policy in regard to specific foreign conflicts. This may be responsive to particular constituency concerns related, for example, to ethnicity and ancestral ties. Since America has attracted immigrants and refugees from countries around the world, it is quite natural that many Americans tend to be sympathetic to one side or another in foreign conflicts. Since certain localities in the United States tend to have high concentrations of such communities, members of Congress from those districts tend to be solicitous of their sentiments. Historically, this has been noted for Irish Catholics, Germans, Cubans, Jews, and many others. In this book, this has been noted particularly in relationship to the American mediation of the Israeli-Palestinian conflict. Members of Congress are also subject to lobbying efforts by foreign governments, as was the case by the Kuwaiti government after Iraq invaded Kuwait.

Such sources of influence provide information and insight and can be constructive when there is competition among them. What is crucial is the context within which they are received by the members of Congress. The desirable context incorporates members of Congress who are generally knowledgeable about the relevant areas of foreign policy and the wide gamut of American interests, values, and concerns.

Finally, one area frequently cited as an example of congressional actions that harm national security policy relates to treating some components of defense spending as jobs programs and subject to pork-barrel politics. For many years, it was difficult to close military bases in the United States even when the military commanders deemed some closures and relocations as desirable and cost-efficient.[58] Often, members of Congress objected to closing bases in the district or state they represented. This problem was overcome by creating a system that took the selection of base closings out of the regular legislative process. Initiated in 1988, the system was enacted into law as the Defense Base Realignment and Closure Act of 1990. The process consists of a nine-member commission, appointed by the president, evaluating recommendations made by the Secretary of Defense. The Commission investigates the proposed recommendations and sends them on, possibly amended, to the president, who then sends them to Congress to be approved or disapproved as a whole. Several commission reports and related base closures have ensued.

Congressional problems continue to be related to the development and production of major weapons systems.[59] As discussed earlier, too often congressional support for new weapon systems is driven more by the jobs associated with large corporations and by corporate lobbying and campaign contributions than by the judgments of U.S. military leaders. Provisions to significantly help localities adjust to large, abrupt cuts in defense contracts could ease the difficulties in making the most rational choices regarding defense expenditures.

Members of Congress should and could play more useful roles in making U.S. participation in foreign conflicts more constructive. They could help provide real debates about alternative strategies, which would be enlightening to the public.[60] They could participate more fully in shaping U.S. strategies that are more effective in foreign conflict engagements. To fulfill these roles, institutional changes would be helpful. To bring about such changes the voting public would probably have to support them and the candidates who would advance them. The damaging extreme partisanship in Congress and in the country needs to be confronted and overcome. The media could help by not simply providing platforms for the most extreme exemplars of unremitted partisanship buttressed by deception. They should provide more factual information and investigative reporting that counters or places in context distortions and fabrications.

Within Congress, the status of the Senate Foreign Relations Committee, the House Foreign Affairs Committee, and the other committees dealing with defense and foreign policy matters needs to be restored. The diminishing of those committees is partly a result of the party leaders in the Senate and the House of Representatives amassing great power to represent their parties. Members of these committees, particularly their chairs, develop knowledge and sensibility over time that should be recognized. Their senior members should receive more recognition from the media and the executive branch of government. Those developments could help moderate the destructive level of partisanship impacting U.S. foreign policy.

Of course, many structural and policy changes in the political system are needed to reduce the extreme partisanship and obstructionism that hampers developing and implementing sound constructive policies regarding engagement in foreign conflicts. They pertain to the gerrymandering of House of Representative districts, to the vast increase in funds needed for electoral campaigns, to the huge increase in corporate electoral spending, and the poor level of information and interest the public has about foreign affairs. Those matters, however, extend beyond this book's limits.

Participation in the United Nations System

The UN has significantly contributed to the notable peaceful progress that occurred since the Cold War ended. Its peacekeeping and peacebuilding operations have helped prevent and shorten civil wars and have helped prevent their recurrence. There is clear evidence that cease-fires in civil wars are more likely to hold so that wars do not recur when there are external interventions.[61] However, the UN often has failed to act or has been unsuccessful when peacekeeping operations were undertaken because the mandates for the operations were too limited and slow, and the operations were inadequately resourced. The U.S. government and public has not maximized what the UN could do that would be to American and global benefit. In this final section, I discuss changes in the UN that could produce more positive outcomes for American involvements in foreign conflicts. Signs of some of these changes can be discerned and deserve further thought and support by the American government and people.

IMPROVING UN CAPABILITIES AND PRACTICES

Major UN reforms are possible and considerable progress has been made, despite the mistrust regarding the UN fomented by some leading Republicans.[62] These reforms include the UN Millennium Development Goals and the Responsibility to Protect project. The UN Millennium Development Goals program has focused attention and helped coordinate activities to achieve eight goals by 2015 starting from 1990.[63] One goal was eradicating extreme poverty, and indeed by 2008 extreme poverty was greatly reduced in every developing region. Another goal was to significantly improve child survival rates, and indeed the under-five deaths have declined worldwide. These improvements are consistent with and serve American interests and concerns. U.S. aid programs, undertaken in the context of the UN Millennium Development project, are amplified by what other countries contribute.

Nevertheless, the gap between countries with the highest and lowest well-being of its citizens greatly increased in the 1990s.[64] The UN's human development reports assess progress, combining income, life expectancy, and literacy measures. The results reveal that human development actually fell in twenty-one countries in the 1990s, but had fallen in only four countries in the 1980s.[65] This is shaped by unequal benefits in investment and trade patterns.

Global economic inequalities are also manifested in the way some countries lag far behind the highly developed countries of North America, Western Europe, and Japan. For example, consider the economic and social circumstances of the Arab countries. Despite the great petroleum reserves in several Arab countries, economic growth in the region has been extremely weak. During the 1990s, per capita gross domestic product increased only 0.7% there, compared to 2.9% in the developing world as a whole and 5.5% in East Asia.[66] Foreign direct investment in Arab countries is very low compared to other regions of the world. Most significantly, domestic actors have not pursued policies that would generate broad economic development.

The other major conflict-relevant UN development is the Responsibility to Protect project. It was a response to the failure of international actors to intervene in large-scale violent conflicts when that seemed to be needed and the inadequacies of interventions when they were undertaken.[67] Several of these failures and inadequacies were examined in the previous chapters and there was no consensus about what was to be done. For example, during the wars breaking up Yugoslavia, debates erupted around the world about whether or not and how to intervene when mass atrocities were underway. Addressing the General Assembly in 1999 and in 2000, Secretary-General Kofi Annan called for international consensus about not allowing gross violations of human rights and yet not assaulting state sovereignty. In September 2000 the government of Canada joined by major foundations announced the establishment of the International Commission on Intervention and State Sovereignty.

A year later, the Commission released its report, Responsibility to Protect (R2P). It presented two basic principles.[68] They are: (1) State sovereignty implies responsibility and the primary responsibility for the protection of its people lies with the state itself; (2) Where a population is suffering serious harm, as a result of internal war, insurgency, repression or state failure, and the state in question is unwilling or unable to halt or avert it, the principle of non-intervention yields to the international responsibility to protect. These basic principles are founded on the UN charter, international and national laws, developing state practices, and obligations inherent in the idea of sovereignty.

R2P has three components: (1) the responsibility to *prevent* harms by addressing the causes of those harms; (2) the responsibility to *respond* appropriately to the situations of great need, and resort to military force only in extreme circumstances; and (3) the responsibility to *rebuild*. Furthermore, the responsibility to *prevent* should have the highest priority. Security Council authorization should be sought in all cases, but if the Security Council does not authorize action, the General Assembly may be asked to consider the response.

Acceptance of the idea that the international community has a responsibility to protect, as prescribed in the report, has speedily grown.[69] This acceptance was recognized at the September 2005 United Nations' World Summit by the world's heads of state and governments. In 2007 Secretary-General Ban Ki-moon took steps to institutionalize the Responsibility to Protect. An international coalition of NGOs is engaged in strengthening the normative and institutional character of R2P (http://responsibilitytoprotect.org). It is also noteworthy that on March 28, 2011, President Obama used some of the language of R2P in explaining and justifying the U.S. intervention in Libya.

Finally, the expanding work of the UN peacekeeping forces should be recognized. Since 1948, there have been sixty-eight UN peacekeeping operations and in 2013, there were fifteen ongoing operations.[70] Those fifteen operations were staffed by 98,014 uniformed personnel, with 83,343 troops, 12,807 police, and 1,864 military observers, and also 16,822 civilian personnel. The number of operations has risen greatly since the end of the Cold War, and in 1992, the Department of Peacekeeping Operations was established.

In 2000, the Brahimi Report set out an agenda of needed reforms, many of which were subsequently instituted. This included a larger headquarters staff funded by the regular UN budget and not peacekeeping assessments. UN peacekeeping operations should be undertaken in a more timely fashion, which would increase their effectiveness. Establishing a standing UN peacekeeping force would make this feasible. The idea of maintaining UN forces ready for deployment is strongly supported by the public in the United States and other nations.[71] The standing force could include small contingents of soldiers from the five permanent members of the UN Security Council, greatly enhancing its capabilities. The five permanent members, having veto power on undertaking any operation, should be willing to so serve.

In 2005, the UN created a Peacebuilding Commission.[72] This is designed to help countries make the difficult transitions from war to peace. The projects it supports include ones related to the formerly fighting forces, referred to as disarmament, demobilization, and reintegration processes. They also include projects dealing with civil security and with truth and reconciliation efforts.

The UN represents an increasingly salient perspective, that the world is one and humankind faces shared threats and opportunities. Global warming and environmental pressures impact all humans and require global responses to reduce the growing threats, defend against them, and to recover from the disastrous consequences. U.S. interests and concerns would be advanced as it joins other countries to make progress in these and other global issues.

AMERICANS WORK WITH THE UN

The preeminent global position of the United States means that its role within the UN is crucial and UN actions tend to complement U.S. conduct. Furthermore, as documented in Chapter 6, the American public generally approves of the UN and favors U.S. multilateralism. However, a significant segment of the American political leadership has strong ideological convictions exalting American exceptionalism and unilateralism. Reducing the influence of this segment would enhance the abilities of the UN to function effectively to the benefit of peoples around the world, including the American people.

Organized nongovernmental approval for the UN does exist in the United States, and could provide the bases for mobilizing greater support for the UN. Important nongovernmental supporting organizations include the United Nations Association of the United States of America and the Business Council for the United Nations, which contribute to understanding the UN and draw attention to innovative business opportunities between member companies and the UN. The Model United Nations is a very widespread phenomenon in the United States whose high school and college participants role-play as diplomats representing a country or an NGO in a simulated session of the United Nations, such as the Security Council or the General Assembly.

Much greater efforts should be undertaken in the United States to increase public awareness of the achievements and potentialities of the UN and of the U.S. role in the UN. Respected public figures and especially political leaders should vouch for the benefits of the UN activities, as well as discuss its limitations and reasons for them. Unrealistic fears about the changing nature of sovereignty in an increasingly integrated world then would be countered by serious, well-grounded discussions.

The UN provides vehicles for Americans to promote their own service goals, which often have indirect pertinence to preventing foreign conflicts. This has been the case in some degree with the conferences on women, the environment, sustainable development, and other matters.[73] It also has occurred for specific projects in cooperation with the UN; for example, with former president Bill Clinton as special envoy on tsunami recovery and later for Haiti. Cooperation also has taken the form of grants for UN projects from the Bill and Melinda Gates Foundation. In 1998, Ted Turner created The United Nations Foundation with a $1 billion gift to support UN activities. The Foundation fosters public-private partnerships to address major world problems, and also works to strengthen public support for the UN.

In short, there are many ways in which Americans can enhance their participation in waging, averting, and recovering from conflicts in other countries by doing so in conjunction with the UN. Greater American collaboration with the UN can help bring about needed reforms of the UN and it will help make American efforts in foreign conflicts be more effective and less costly in money and in lives.

Concluding Words

No one of these suggested actions or developments will by itself assure that Americans will conduct foreign conflict engagements more constructively. However, several of them, taken by many people, will tend to make American involvement more widely beneficial. Everyone can do some things that will combine with what other people do to produce more constructive American involvements in foreign conflicts.[74] Those things include raising their children with loving support and attention, acquiring training in the knowledge and skills of conducting conflicts constructively, learning more about the reasons foreign adversaries view

U.S. actions as antagonistic, communicating to persons engaged in American foreign policy what they believe would be better options, and joining organizations that are advancing relatively constructive strategies.

Certainly, in numerous circumstances, choosing a more constructive strategy may appear risky. An adversary may try to take advantage of a relatively conciliatory gesture or policy, but the evidence in this book demonstrates that risking a harsher, punishing approach often fails and proves counterproductive. The overall lesson to draw from the analyses in this work is that relatively constructive options should be imagined and weighed before automatically moving to highly coercive strategies. The episodes analyzed here indicate that better strategies can be applied before harmful escalations occur, while they are occurring, or even after they have largely ended. The analyses also suggest what mixtures of tactics can be particularly beneficial in specific circumstances.

If the ideas of this book become more accepted in the United States, fewer destructive foreign involvements will occur. As the ideas continue to be adopted in other countries, their use by Americans will be more likely to be effective. The evidence presented in this book indicates that these ideas are realistic. They are becoming part of the way that peace is realized. In good measure this is because the ideas are congruent with many social, cultural, and economic trends and emerging global institutions.

I do not expect any readers of this book to agree with everything I wrote here. In a year or two I myself will probably disagree with some of the assertions I have made. I do wish that every reader will be prompted to think freshly about how Americans have been involved in large-scale foreign conflicts and how those involvements might have been conducted better. I wish even more fervently that readers will consider current and impending involvements and how they might be done relatively well, doing them the best way they could be done for all people in the long run.

Notes

CHAPTER 1

1. Elizabeth N. Saunders, *Leaders at War: How Presidents Shape Military Interventions* (Ithaca, NY: Cornell University Press, 2011).

2. Andrew J. Bacevich, *The New American Militarism: How Americans Are Seduced by War* (New York: Oxford University Press, 2005).

3. Steven Pinker, *The Better Angels of Our Nature: Why Violence Has Declined* (New York: Viking, 2011).

4. Nils Petter Gleditsch, "The Liberal Moment Fifteen Years On," *International Studies Quarterly* 52 (4):681–712 (2008); Joshua S. Goldstein, *Winning the War on War: The Decline of Armed Conflict Worldwide* (New York: Penguin, 2011); Andrew Mack, ed. *Human Security Report 2013: The Decline in Global Violence: Evidence, Explanation, and Contestation*, Human Security Report Project (Vancouver: Simon Fraser University, 2014).

5. Richard K. Betts, *American Force: Dangers, Delusions, and Dilemmas in National Security* (New York: Columbia University Press, 2012). pp. 5–6.

6. The approach is presented fully in Louis Kriesberg and Bruce W. Dayton, *Constructive Conflicts: From Escalation to Resolution*, 4th ed. (Lanham, MD: Rowman & Littlefield, 2012).

7. The word *approach* or *perspective* is used rather than *theory* because the concept of theory usually refers to a precise set of inter-related concepts and propositions that explain a specified range of phenomena. There is no comprehensive theory of all aspects of social conflicts. There are numerous small-scale, middle-range, or mini theories about particular aspects of social phenomena relevant to conflicts. Some such partial theories are incorporated in the constructive conflict approach.

8. West Europeans, in particular, have contributed significantly to the constructive conflict approach, usually in the field they refer to as peace research. Other names for highly related fields are peace science, conflictology, and polemology.

9. Robert Jervis, *Perception and Misperception in International Politics* (Princeton, NJ: Princeton University Press, 1976).

10. Johan Galtung, "Violence, Peace, and Peace Research," *Journal of Peace Research* 3 (3):167–191 (1969). Goldstein, *Winning the War on War: The Decline of Armed Conflict Worldwide*.

11. Many works document the evolution of the conflict analysis and resolution field and its current characteristics. Oliver Ramsbotham, Tom Woodhouse, and Hugh Miall, *Contemporary Conflict Resolution*, 3rd ed. (Cambridge, UK: Polity, 2011); Dennis J. D. Sandole, Sean Byrne, Ingrid Sandole-Staroste, and Jessica Senehi, *Handbook of Conflict Analysis and Resolution* (Abingdon, UK: Routledge, 2009); Jacob Bercovitch, Viktor Kremenyuk, and I. William Zartman, ed. *Sage Handbook of Conflict Resolution* (London: Sage, 2009); Kriesberg and Dayton, *Constructive Conflicts: From Escalation to Resolution*.

12. Illustratively, see: Ole R. Holsti, Richard A. Brody, and Robert C. North, "Measuring Affect and Action in International Reaction Models: Empirical Materials from the 1962 Cuban Crisis," *Journal of Peace Research* 3–4:170–189 (1964); Jeffrey Z. Rubin, ed. *Dynamics of Third Party Intervention: Kissinger in the Middle East* (New York: Praeger, 1981); Eileen F. Babbitt, "Jimmy Carter: The Power of Moral Suasion in International Mediation," in *When Talk Works: Profiles of Mediator*, ed. Deborah M. Kolb (San Francisco, CA: Jossey-Bass, 1994). C.H. Mike Yarrow, *Quaker Experiences in International Conciliation* (New Haven, CT: Yale University Press, 1978); I. William Zartman, *The 50% Solution: How to Bargain Successfully with Hijackers, Strikers, Bosses, Oil Magnates, Arabs, Russians, and Other Worthy Opponents in This Modern World* (Garden City, NY: Anchor Press, 1976); John Paul Lederach, *Building Peace: Sustainable Reconciliation in Divided Societies* (Washington, DC: United States Institute of Peace Press, 1997).

13. Lewis F. Richardson, *Statistics of Deadly Quarrels* (Pittsburgh, PA: The Boxwood Press, 1960). Jacob Bercovitch, "International Mediation: A Study of the Incidence, Strategies and Conditions of Successful Outcomes," *Cooperation and Conflict* 21:155–168 (1986); J. David Singer and Melvin Small, *The Wages of War, 1816–1965: A Statistical Handbook* (New York: John Wiley, 1972); John R. Oneal and Bruce Russett, "The Classical Liberals Were Right: Democracy, Interdependence, and Conflict, 1950–1985," *International Studies Quarterly* 41:267–294 (June 1997); Russell J. Leng and Hugh Wheeler, "Influence Strategies, Success and War," *Journal of Conflict Resolution* 23:655–684 (December 1979); Bruce Russett and John R. Oneal, *Triangulating Peace: Democracy, Interdependence, and International Organization* (Princeton, NJ: Princeton University Press, 2001); John Vasquez, *The War Puzzle* (Cambridge, UK: Cambridge University Press, 1993); Karl W. Deutsch et al., *Political Community and the North Atlantic Area* (Princeton, NJ: Princeton University Press, 1957).

14. Morton Deutsch, *The Resolution of Conflict: Constructive and Destructive Processes* (New Haven, CT: Yale University Press, 1973); Howard Raiffa, *The Art and Science of Negotiation* (Cambridge and London: Harvard University Press, 1982); Muzafer Sherif, *In Common Predicament* (Boston: Houghton Mifflin, 1966).

15. John W. Burton, *Conflict and Communication: The Use of Controlled Communication in International Relations* (New York: Free Press, 1969); Herbert C. Kelman, "Contributions of an Unofficial Conflict Resolution Effort to the Israeli-Palestinian Breakthrough," *Negotiation*

Journal 11:19–27 (January 1995). Ronald Fisher, *Interactive Conflict Resolution* (Syracuse, NY: Syracuse University Press, 1997).

16. Louis Kriesberg, "Conflict Resolution and Applications to Peace Studies," *Peace and Change* 16 (Fall):400–417 (1991); Elizabeth S. Dahl, "Oil and Water? The Philosophical Commitments of International Peace Studies and Conflict Resolution," *International Studies Review* 14 (2):240–272 (2012).

17. There is a large body of literature on positive and negative sanctions as means to influence conduct. David A. Baldwin, "The Power of Positive Sanctions," *World Politics* 24:19–38 (October 1971). Persuasion is often added as a third form of influence. See, for example, William A. Gamson, *Power and Discontent* (Homewood, IL: Dorsey Press, 1968). Deutsch, *The Resolution of Conflict*.

18. Joseph S. Nye, Jr., *Soft Power: The Means to Success in World Politics* (New York: Public Affairs, 2004).

19. Richard L. Armitage and Joseph S. Nye, Jr., "A Smarter, More Secure America," (Washington, DC: Center for Strategic and International Studies, 2007).

20. Peter L. Berger and Thomas Luckman, *The Social Construction of Reality* (New York: Doubleday, 1966); Franke Wilmer, *The Social Construction of Man, the State, and War: Identity, Conflict, and Violence in the Former Yugoslavia* (New York and London: Routledge, 2002).

21. Jacob Bercovitch, ed. *Studies in International Mediation: Essays in Honor of Jeffrey Z. Rubin* (London and New York: Palgrave/Macmillan, 2002); Bercovitch, *Sage Handbook of Conflict Resolution*; Peter Wallensteen and Isak Svensson, "Talking Peace: International Mediation in Armed Conflicts," *Journal of Peace Research* 51 (2):315–327 (2014).

22. Kriesberg and Dayton, *Constructive Conflicts: From Escalation to Resolution*, 4th ed., p. 2.

23. Louis Kriesberg, "The Conflict Transformation Field's Current State of the Art," in *Berghof Handbook for Conflict Transformation*, ed. Martina Fischer, Joachim Giessmann, and Beatrix Schmelzle (Farmington Hills, MI: Barbara Budrich Publishers, 2011).

24. Roger Fisher and William Ury, *Getting to Yes* (Boston: Houghton Miflin Company, 1981).

25. Louis Kriesberg, "Changing Conflict Asymmetries Constructively," *Dynamics of Asymmetric Conflict* 2 (1):4–22 (March 2009). Christopher R. Mitchell, "Asymmetry and Strategies of Regional Conflict Reduction," in *Cooperative Security: Reducing Third World Wars*, ed. I; William Zartman and Victor A. Kremenyuk (Syracuse, NY: Syracuse University Press, 1995).

26. Pinker, *The Better Angels of Our Nature*. Goldstein, *Winning the War on War*.

27. Peter Ackerman and Christopher Kruegler, *Strategic Nonviolent Conflict* (Westport, CT/London: Praeger, 1994); Gene Sharp, *Waging Nonviolent Struggle: 20th Century Practice and 21st Century Potential* (Boston: Porter Sargent, 2005); Erica Chenoweth and Maria J. Stephan, *Why Civil Resistance Works: The Strategic Logic of Nonviolent Conflict* (New York: Columbia University Press, 2011).

28. Herbert C. Kelman, "Informal Mediation by the Scholar Practitioner," in *Mediation in International Relations*, ed. Jacob Bercovitch and Jeffrey Z. Rubin (New York: St. Martin's Press, 1992).

29. Roger Fisher, Elizabeth Kopelman, and Andrea Kupfer Schneider, *Beyond Machiavelli* (New York: Penguin, 1996). Fisher and Ury, *Getting to Yes*; ibid.

30. Babbitt, "Jimmy Carter: The Power of Moral Suasion in International Mediation." Jimmy Carter, *Keeping Faith* (New York: Bantam Books, 1982).

31. Elements of the conflict resolution field are introduced in many graduate programs in international relations and public administration and in law schools. In addition, M.A. programs in conflict resolution are widespread and prepare graduates for international work with governmental and nongovernmental organizations.

32. This is stressed in the constructivist approach, which emphasizes that people together socially construct their reality and act in terms of the reality as they define it. Alexander Wendt, "Anarchy Is What States Make of It: The Social Construction of Power Politics," *International Organization* 46 (2) (1992, Spring). Berger and Luckman, *The Social Construction of Reality*.

33. Paul R. Viotti and Mark V. Kaupp, *International Relations Theory: Realism, Pluralism, Globalism, and Beyond* (Boston: Allyn and Bacon, 1999).

34. John J. Mearsheimer, *The Tragedy of Great Power Politics* (New York: W.W. Norton, 2014). Kenneth N. Waltz, *Theory of International Politics* (Reading, MA: Addison-Wesley, 1979).

35. Andrew Moravcsik, "Taking Preferences Seriously: A Liberal Theory of International Politics," *International Organization* 51 (4):513–553 (1997).

36. Anne-Marie Slaughter, "International Relations, Principal Theories," in *Max Planck Encyclopedia of Public International Law*, ed. R. Wolfram (New York: Oxford University Press, 2011).

37. Wendt, "Anarchy Is What States Make of It: The Social Construction of Power Politics."

38. Cynthia Enloe, *Bananas, Beaches and Bases* (Berkeley and Los Angeles: University of California Press, 1989); Betty A. Reardon, *Sexism and the War System* (Syracuse, NY: Syracuse University Press, 1996); J. Ann Tickner, *Gender in International Relations: Feminist Perspectives on Achieving Global Security* (New York: Columbia University Press, 1992); Carolyn M. Stephenson, "Gender Equality and a Culture of Peace," in *Handbook on Building Cultures of Peace*, ed. Joseph de Rivera (New York: Springer Science + Business Media, 2009).

39. G. John Ikenberry, "The Liberal International Order and Its Discontents," in *After Liberalism? The Future of Liberalism in International Relations*, ed. Rebekka Friedman, Kevork Oskania, and Ramon Pacheco Pasrdo (New York: Palgrave MacMillan, 2013).

40. Sanjay Seth, ed. *Postcolonial Theory and International Relations* (New York: Routledge, 2013).

41. Eric Laferrière and Peter J. Stoett, *International Relations Theory and Ecological Thought: Towards a Synthesis* (New York: Routledge, 2002).

42. James Mann, *Rise of the Vulcans* (New York: Viking, 2004). Also see Bill Keller, "The I Can't Believe I'm a Hawk Club," *New York Times*, February 8, 2003.

43. John J. Mearsheimer and Stephen M. Walt, "An Unnecessary War," *Foreign Policy* 134:51–59 (Jan/Feb 2003).

44. Louis Kriesberg, "Convergences between International Security Studies and Peace Studies," in *Millennial Reflections on International Studies*, ed. Michael Breher and Frank Harvey (Ann Arbor: University of Michigan Press, 2002).

45. Philip S. Gorski, "Beyond the Fact/Value Distinction: Ethical Naturalism and the Social Sciences," *Social Science and Modern Society* 50 (6):543–553 (2013).

46. Louis Kriesberg, "Moral Judgments, Human Needs and Conflict Resolution: Alternative Approaches to Ethical Standards," in *Beyond Basic Needs: Linking Theory and Practice*, ed. Christopher R. Mitchell and Kevin Avruch (Oxford, UK: Routledge, 2013).

47. Ernest Fahr and Simon Gächter, "Altruistic Punishment in Humans," *Nature* 415 (10):137–140 (January 2002); Hillard Kaplan and Kim Hill, "Food Sharing among Ache

Foragers: Tests of Explanatory Hypotheses," *Current Anthropology* 26 (2):223–239 (1985); Elliott Sober and David Sloan Wilson, *Unto Others: The Evolution and Psychology of Unselfish Behavior* (Cambridge, MA: Harvard University Press, 1998).

48. John Mueller, *The Retreat from Doomsday: The Obsolescence of Major Wars* (New York: Basic, 1989); Pinker, *The Better Angels of Our Nature*; Stephen D. Krasner, *International Regimes* (Ithaca, NY: Cornell University Press, 1983).

CHAPTER 2

1. Other interpretations include the role of the harsh terms of the Versailles Treaty after the First World War in contributing to the rise of Nazism in Germany. They also include the weakness of the League of Nations which was attributable in part to the absence of the United States from its membership and U.S. non-engagement in efforts at collective security in Europe. Another interpretation relates to the strength of anti-Soviet views that precluded anti-Fascist cooperation.

2. Historians disagree about the likelihood that the war might have been ended earlier if clearer guarantees about the Emperor remaining on his throne had been made, without nuclear bombing of Hiroshima and Nagasaki. Douglas Lackey, "Why Hiroshima Was Immoral: A Response to Landesman," *Philosophical Forum* 34 (1):29–42 (2003); Barton J. Bernstein, "Understanding the Atomic Bomb and the Japanese Surrender: Missed Opportunities, Little-Known near Disasters, and Modern Memory," *Diplomatic History* 19 (2):227–273 (1995).

3. Bruce Cumings, *The Origins of the Korean War: Liberation and the Emergence of Separate Regimes 1945–1947* (Princeton, NJ: Princeton University Press, 1981), p. 28.

4. Ibid., pp. 116–118. In 1953, I published an article suggesting that a neutralized Formosa might resolve the crisis about Formosa and that a neutralized Korea might resolve the Korean war, Louis Kriesberg, "An Independent Formosa," *Christian Century* 70 (27) (July 8, 1953).

5. For possible reasoning by Stalin, see William Stueck, *Rethinking the Korean War: A New Diplomatic and Strategic History* (Princeton and Oxford: Princeton University Press, 2002), pp. 22–24.

6. Allan R. Millett, *The War for Korea, 1945–1950* (Lawrence, KS: University Press of Kansas, 2005), pp. 43–71; Chae-Jin Lee, *A Troubled Peace: U.S. Policy and the Two Koreas* (Baltimore, MD: Johns Hopkins University Press, 2006).

7. Stueck, *Rethinking the Korean War: A New Diplomatic and Strategic History*, pp. 32–33. Also see Bruce Cumings, *The Origins of the Korean War: The Roaring of the Cataract, 1947–1950*, vol. II (Princeton, NJ: Princeton University Press, 1990), pp. 306 ff.

8. Stueck, *Rethinking the Korean War: A New Diplomatic and Strategic History*, p. 69.

9. Ibid., pp. 35–38.

10. Cumings, *The Origins of the Korean War: The Roaring of the Cataract, 1947–1950*, vol. II, pp. 268–290, 396.

11. On January 12, 1950, Secretary of State Dean Acheson delivered a speech at the Press Club in Washington, DC, about the Asia policy. His intentions and the effects of the speech in the onset of the Korean War have been heatedly debated. Following the North Korean invasion, Republicans charged (and some analysts concluded) that Acheson had failed to clearly assert U.S. intentions to defend South Korea from attack and thereby undercut effective deterrence. See Alexander L. George and Richard Smoke, *Deterrence in American Foreign Policy: Theory*

and Practice (New York: Columbia University Press, 1974). This was, and for some has remained, the conventional interpretation. Later analyses questioned this view. The speech was not delivered casually, but carefully crafted by Acheson. The immediate response from the Soviet Union and North Korea did not see any U.S. departure from their understanding of past U.S. policy. See Cumings, *The Origins of the Korean War: The Roaring of the Cataract, 1947–1950*, vol. II, pp. 408–438.I believe the North Korean invasion was not prompted or invited by Acheson's speech. For the United States to have prevented the attack would have required a much grander strategy about the future of Korea and of the relations among the major powers engaged in Northeast Asia that were more accommodating of their interests and ambitions. Deterrence is more likely to be effective if it is not accompanied by threats to vital interests of the target. However, the goals of Acheson and other leaders were too oppositional to the Soviet Union at that time for such a strategy.

12. The United States won UN support because the Soviet Union was absent, having withdrawn earlier from participation in the Security Council affairs in protest. Glenn Paige, *The Korean Decision* (New York: Free Press, 1968).

13. Initially, U.S. military deaths in the Korean War were reported to be over 54,000, but that included non-theater deaths. In-theater deaths officially are reported to have been 36,574, of which 33,739 were hostile deaths. See Anne Leland and Mari-Jana "M-J" Oboroceanu, "American War and Military Operations Casualties: Lists and Statistics." Congressional Research Service. 7-5700 RL32492 Washington, DC, 2010.

14. One might also consider the weight to be given to Koreans in the North and South who might not favor the imposition of the South Korean system by U.S. military forces.

15. William A. Gamson and Andre Modigliani, *Untangling the Cold War* (Boston: Little, Brown, 1971).

16. In February 1946, George Kennan sent a "Long Telegram," while stationed in the American Embassy in Moscow, which set forth the containment strategy. It was later published anonymously in *Foreign Affairs* as, X, "The Sources of Soviet Conduct," *Foreign Affairs* 15 (2):566–582 (July 1947).

17. Quotation is from the conclusion to Kennan's "Long Telegram." http://www.gwu.edu/~nsarchiv/coldwar/documents/episode-1/kennan.htm

18. Lawrence S. Wittner, *Rebels against War: The American Peace Movement, 1941–1960* (New York and London: Columbia University Press, 1969).

19. Three important world government organizations were established after the Second World War ended: Americans United for World Government, Student Federalists, and World Federalists, USA. Ibid., pp. 170–171. In 1945, Robert M. Hutchins and many others formed a committee at the University of Chicago to draft a world constitution, To Frame a World Constitution Committee, *Preliminary Draft of a World Constitution* (Chicago: University of Chicago Press, 1948).

20. Wittner, *Rebels against War: The American Peace Movement, 1941–1960*, p. 196.

21. Louis Kriesberg, *International Conflict Resolution: The U.S.-USSR and Middle East Cases* (New Haven, CT: Yale University Press, 1992).

22. Melvyn P. Leffler, *For the Soul of Mankind: The United States, the Soviet Union, and the Cold War* (New York: Hill and Wang, 2007); Adam B. Ulam, *Expansion and Coexistence: Soviet Foreign Policy, 1917–73*, 2nd ed. (New York: Praeger, 1974).

23. Leffler, *For the Soul of Mankind*, pp. 106–108.

24. Quotations from Foreign Relations of the United States, 1952–54, 595, cited in Leffler, 2007, 133–134.

25. Sven Allard, *Russia and the Austrian State Treaty* (University Park, PA: University of Pennsylvania Press, 1970); Louis Kriesberg, "Noncoercive Inducements in U.S.-Soviet Conflicts: Ending the Occupation of Austria and Nuclear Weapons Tests." *Journal of Political and Military Sociology* 9:1–16 (1981).

26. Vladislav M. Zubok, *A Failed Empire: The Soviet Union in the Cold War from Stalin to Gorbachev* (Chapel Hill, NC: University of North Carolina Press, 2007).

27. Alva Myrdal, *The Game of Disarmament: How the United States and Russia Run the Arms Race* (New York: Pantheon, 1982); David Tal, *American Nuclear Disarmament Dilemma: 1945–1963* (Syracuse, NY: Syracuse University Press, 2008).

28. David Tal, "The Secretary of State versus the Secretary of Peace: The Dulles-Stassen Controversy and US Disarmament Policy, 1955–58." *Journal of Contemporary History* 41 (4):721–740 (2006).

29. David Tal, *American Nuclear Disarmament Dilemma: 1945–1963*.

30. Zubock, pp. 112–113.

31. Vladislav M. Zubok, *A Failed Empire: The Soviet Union in the Cold War from Stalin to Gorbachev* (Chapel Hill, NC: University of North Carolina Press, 2007), p. 180.

32. Yale Richmond, *U.S.-Soviet Cultural Exchanges, 1958–1986* (Boulder, CO: Westview, 1987).

33. Louis Kriesberg, "U.S. and U.S.S.R. Participation in International Non-Governmental Organizations," in *Social Processes in International Relations*, ed. Louis Kriesberg (New York: John Wiley & Sons, 1968).

34. Matthew Evangelista, *Unarmed Forces: The Transnational Movement to End the Cold War* (Ithaca, NY and London: Cornell University Press, 1999), p. 375.

35. David Cortright, *Peace Works: The Citizen's Role in Ending the Cold War* (Boulder, CO: Westview Press, 1993); Evangelista, *Unarmed Forces*.

36. Norman Cousins, *The Impossible Triumvirate* (New York: Norton, 1972). James Voorhees, *Dialogue Sustained: The Multilevel Peace Process and the Dartmouth Conference* (Washington, DC: U.S. Institute of Peace Press, 2002).

37. Louis Kriesberg, "Contemporary Conflict Resolution Applications," pp. 873–894 in *Leashing the Dogs of War: Conflict Management in a Divided World*, edited by C. A. Crocker, Fen Osler Hampson, and Pamela Aall (Washington, DC: United States Institute of Peace Press, 2007).

38. For example, see Kenneth Boulding, *Conflict and Defense* (New York: Harper & Row, 1962); Theodore F. Lentz, *Towards a Science of Peace* (New York: Bookman Associates, 1961); Thomas C. Schelling, *The Strategy of Conflict* (Cambridge, MA: Harvard University Press, 1960).

39. Mary Caprioli and Mark A. Boyer, "Gender, Violence, and International Crisis," *The Journal of Conflict Resolution* 45 (4):503–518 (2001).

40. Johan Galtung, "Violence, Peace, and Peace Research," *Journal of Peace Research* 3 (3):167–191 (1969).

41. Joshua S. Goldstein, *Winning the War on War: The Decline of Armed Conflict Worldwide* (New York: Penguin, 2011), pp. 204–209.

42. Johan Galtung, *Peace by Peaceful Means: Peace and Conflict, Development and Civilization* (London: Sage Publishers, 1996).

43. Kurt Lewin, *Resolving Social Conflicts* (New York: Harper and Brothers, 1948); Lewis A. Coser, *Continuities in the Study of Social Conflict* (New York: Free Press, 1967); Kenneth E. Boulding, *Conflict and Defense; a General Theory* (New York: Harper, 1962); Ralf Dahrendorf, *Class and Class Conflict in Industrial Society* (Palo Alto, CA: Stanford University Press, 1959).

44. William A. Gamson, "Rancorous Conflict in Community Politics," *American Sociological Review* 31:71–81 (February 1966).

45. The report, which I prepared when teaching at Columbia University, was the basis for a small but influential book: James S. Coleman, *Community Conflict* (New York: Free Press, 1957).

46. Mary Parker Follet, *Dynamic Administration* (New York: Harper and Brothers, 1942).

47. Robert R. Blake, Herbert A. Shephard, and Jane S. Mouton, *Managing Intergroup Conflict in Industry* (Houston, TX: Gulf Publishing, 1964).

48. Wilfred Bion, *Experience in Groups* (London: Tavistock Institute, 1961).

49. Morton Deutsch, "Trust and Suspicion," *The Journal of Conflict Resolution* 2 (4):265–279 (1958). Morton Deutsch, *The Resolution of Conflict: Constructive and Destructive Processes* (New Haven, CT: Yale University Press, 1973).

50. C. Wright Mills, *The Power Elite* (New York: Oxford University Press, 1956).

51. Morton Grodzins, *The Loyal and the Disloyal* (Chicago: University of Chicago Press, 1956).

52. Crane Brinton, *The Anatomy of Revolution* (New York: Vintage, 1955); Daniel Lerner and Lucille W. Pevsner, *The Passing of Traditional Society: Modernizing the Middle East* (Glencoe, IL: The Free Press, 1958).

53. Singer, J. David, and Melvin Small, *The Wages of War, 1816–1965: A Statistical Handbook* (New York: John Wiley, 1972).

54. Robert C. North, Ole R. Holsti, M. George Zaninovich, and Dina Zinnes, *Content Analysis* (Evanston, IL: Northwestern University Press, 1963); Snyder, Richard C., H. W. Bruck, and Burton Sapin, *Foreign Policy Decision Making* (New York: The Free Press, 1962).

55. Game theory evolved from the work of mathematicians; see: J. von Neumann and O. Morgenstern, *Theory of Games and Economic Behavior* (Princeton, NJ: Princeton University Press, 1944).

56. Anatol Rapoport and Albert M. Chammah, *The Prisoner's Dilemma: A Study in Conflict and Cooperation* (Ann Arbor: University of Michigan Press, 1965).The prisoner's dilemma supposes that two men carried out a robbery and were later arrested by police and placed in separate cells for interrogation. The police seek confessions from each, implicating the other. If each would confess to save himself from a harsher sentence (twelve years) if he did not confess and his confederate did. The individually rational choice is to confess, with the result being both serve nine years. If they trusted each other to hold out they would do better, serving only one year (assuming police had evidence for only a lesser crime).

57. Robert Axelrod, *The Evolution of Cooperation* (New York: Basic Books, 1984).

58. Muzafer Sherif, *In Common Predicament* (Boston: Houghton Mifflin, 1966).

59. Charles E. Osgood, *An Alternative to War or Surrender* (Urbana: University of Illinois Press, 1962).

60. Karl W. Deutsch, Sidney A. Burrell, Robert A. Kann, Maurice Lee Jr., Martin Lichterman, Raymond Lindgren, Francis L. Loewenheim, and Richard W. Van Wagenen, *Political Community and the North Atlantic Area* (Princeton, NJ: Princeton University Press, 1957); Ernst B. Haas, *The Uniting of Europe* (Palo Alto, CA: Stanford University Press, 1958); David Mitrany, *A Working Peace System* (Oxford, UK: Oxford University Press, 1944).

61. My research built on the work of Mitrany and Haas, cited in the previous note. Louis Kriesberg, "German Businessman and Union Leaders and the Schuman Plan," *Social Sciences* 35:114–121 (April 1960).

62. For example, see Robert Cooley Angell, *Peace on the March: Transnational Participation* (New York: Van Nostrand Reinhold, 1969), pp. 59–67.

63. Louis Kriesberg, "Peace Movements and Government Peace Efforts," pp. 57–75 in *Research in Social Movements Conflicts and Change*, vol. 10, edited by Louis Kriesberg, Bronislaw Misztal, and Mucha, Janusz (Greenwich, CT and London: JAI Press, 1988); John Lofland, *Polite Protestors: The American Peace Movement of the 1980's* (Syracuse, NY: Syracuse University Press, 1993).

64. Christopher Mitchell, "From Controlled Communication to Problem Solving: The Origins of Facilitated Conflict Resolution," *The International Journal of Peace Studies* 6 (1) (2001); Ronald Fisher, *Interactive Conflict Resolution* (Syracuse, NY: Syracuse University Press, 1997).

65. John W. Burton, *Conflict and Communication: The Use of Controlled Communication in International Relations* (New York: Free Press, 1969).

66. Zubock, pp. 114–115.

67. Zubock, pp. 115–117.

68. In addition to the many other conflicts associated with the Cold War and the Arab-Israeli conflict, a major conflict existed between the United Kingdom and Egypt. In accordance with the 1936 Anglo-Egyptian Treaty, the British maintained a large military base at the Suez Canal. In 1951, the Egyptian government unilaterally abrogated the treaty, which the British rejected, resulting in demonstrations that escalated in the deaths of Egyptians and British citizens. This helped precipitate the Egyptian military coup that overthrew the monarchy in 1952. The British government undertook to improve relations with the new Egyptian government, and among other actions, an agreement for the phased withdrawal of British troops from Suez was reached in October 1954, which was to be completed within 20 months.

69. The Baghdad Pact was encouraged and aided by the U.S. government. It was formed initially with Iraq, Turkey, Iran, Pakistan, and the United Kingdom as members. Iraq withdrew in March 1959, when it became a republic.

70. Elmore Jackson, *Middle East Mission: The Story of a Major Bid for Peace in the Time of Nasser and Ben-Gurion* (New York: W. W. Norton & Company, 1983). Nancy Gallagher, *Quakers in the Israeli-Palestinian Conflict* (Cairo and New York: American University in Cairo Press, 2007), pp. 145–163.

71. Jackson, *Middle East Mission: The Story of a Major Bid for Peace in the Time of Nasser and Ben-Gurion*, pp. 83–85.

72. Barry Rubin, "America and the Egyptian Revolution, 1950–1957," *Political Science Quarterly* 97 (1):73–90 (1982).

73. Jon D. Glassman, *Arms for the Arabs: The Soviet Union and War in the Middle East* (Baltimore and London: The John Hopkins University Press, 1975), pp. 8–21. Also see Mohamed Heikal, *The Sphinx and the Commissar: The Rise and Fall of Soviet Influence in the Middle East* (New York: Harper & Row, 1978).

74. U.S. military assistance to Egypt was urged by Assistant Secretary of State Henry Byroade and John Foster Dulles's brother, the director of the Central Intelligence Agency, Allen Dulles. But John Foster Dulles opposed this until it was too late to stop the Soviet-Egyptian agreement; Rubin, "America and the Egyptian Revolution, 1950–1957."

75. Glassman, *Arms for the Arabs: The Soviet Union and War in the Middle East.*

76. The Suez Canal was operated by the Suez Canal Company, with France and Great Britain being the major shareholders. Nasser announced that the stockholders would be paid for their shares at the day's closing price.

77. I was in London in August 1956 and saw Prime Minister Anthony Eden on television insisting that Nasser was like Adolph Hitler and his aggression had to be stopped. Such

characterizations may be used to mobilize support, but they obviously confound clear thinking about the unique conflict that is being confronted.

78. Chalmers Johnson, *Blowback: The Costs and Consequences of American Empire* (New York: Henry Holt, 2000).

79. Elizabeth N. Saunders, *Leaders at War: How Presidents Shape Military Interventions* (Ithaca, NY: Cornell University Press, 2011).

80. Hugh Wilford, *The Mighty Wurlitzer: How the CIA Played America* (Cambridge, MA: Harvard University Press, 2008).

81. See Harold H. Saunders, *A Public Peace Process: Sustained Dialogue to Transform Racial and Ethnic Conflicts* (New York: St. Martin's Press, 1999). Also see http://copy_bilderberg. tripod.com/ccf.htm.

82. Based on personal interviews I conducted in 1955 with persons associated with those efforts, including then-current and former officials of the AFL and CIO, including Jay Lovestone (August 25), Victor Reuther (August 31), Arnold Beichman (August 3 and October 3), William Gomberg (October 24), Jacob Potofsky (September 27), and several others. See John P. Windmuller, *American Labor and the International Labor Movement, 1940–1953* (Ithaca, NY: The Institute of International Industrial and Labor Relations, Cornell University, 1954).

83. Stephen Kinzer, "Revisiting Cold War Coups and Finding Them Costly," *New York Times*, November 30, 2003, p. 3; Tim Weiner, *Legacy of Ashes: The History of the CIA* (New York: Doubleday, 2007).

84. Jorge I. Dominguez, "Pipsqueak Power: The Centrality and Anomaly of Cuba," pp. 57–58 in *The Suffering Grass: Superpowers and Regional Conflict in Southern Africa and the Caribbean*, edited by T. G. Weiss and J. G. Blight (Boulder, CO: Lynne Rienner, 1992).

85. Herbert S. Dinerstein, *The Making of a Missile Crisis: October 1962* (Baltimore and London: The Johns Hopkins University Press, 1962); Tim Weiner, *Legacy of Ashes: The History of the CIA* (New York: Doubleday, 2007).

86. Tim Weiner, *Legacy of Ashes: The History of the CIA*.

87. Graham Allison, *The Essence of Decision* (Boston: Little, Brown, 1971); Robert F. Kennedy, *Thirteen Days: A Memoir of the Cuban Missile Crisis* (New York: W. W. Norton, 1971).

88. Some analysts regard the exchanges as a demonstration of the effectiveness of a tit-for-tat strategy; Ole R. Holsti, Richard A. Brody, and Robert C. North, "Measuring Affect and Action in International Reaction Models: Empirical Materials from the 1962 Cuban Crisis," *Journal of Peace Research* 3–4:175–189 (1964); Rapoport and Chammah, *The Prisoner's Dilemma: A Study in Conflict and Cooperation*. However, in the conflict resolution literature, tit-for-tat entails a series of reciprocations of positive and negative acts. See: Axelrod, *The Evolution of Cooperation*.

89. Kennedy actually had ordered that to be done shortly after taking office, but the orders were not implemented. The fact that the Soviets were willing to allow the United States' concession to remain secret also indicates Khrushchev's recognition of the importance of face-saving. Despite the success of the negotiations in averting an immense disaster, the Soviet military afterwards launched a major buildup of long-range missiles, so as not to be overwhelmed by U.S. nuclear capability again.

90. Louis Kriesberg, "Contemporary Conflict Resolution Applications," in *Leashing the Dogs of War: Conflict Management in a Divided World*, ed. Chester A. Crocker, Fen Osler Hampson, and Pamela Aall (Washington, DC: United States Institute of Peace Press, 2007), p. 231.

91. Amitai Etzioni, "The Kennedy Experiment." *The Western Political Quarterly* 20:361–380 (1967). Etzioni argued that the GRIT strategy was consciously followed, since an article by Osgood describing the strategy had been passed on to the White House before the American University speech (personal conversation). However, the congruence with the GRIT strategy was probably unwitting. Theodore Sorenson, who had drafted the speech, said in a personal interview (March 20, 1979) that he did not recall any such strategy and simply was trying to include some material that he knew the Soviets wanted to hear. Moreover, discussions about what steps would be taken associated with the speech were conducted prior to the speech. (Personal interview with Arthur Schlesinger Jr., October 9, 1978.) See: Norman Cousins, *The Impossible Triumvirate* (New York: Norton, 1972). Such official or nonofficial conversations are valuable in making a GRIT strategy effective. See: Louis Kriesberg, "Noncoercive Inducements in U.S.-Soviet Conflicts: Ending the Occupation of Austria and Nuclear Weapons Tests." *Journal of Political and Military Sociology* 9:1–16 (1981).

92. William L. Ury, *Beyond the Hotline: How We Can Prevent the Crisis that Might Bring On a Nuclear War* (Boston: Houghton Mifflin, 1985).

93. Lawrence S. Wittner, *One World or None: A History of the World Nuclear Disarmament Movement through 1953*, 3 vols., vol. 1, "The Struggle against the Bomb" (Palo Alto, CA: Stanford University Press, 1993).

94. Nuclear weapons tests in Nevada sent radioactive materials into the atmosphere that fell to earth and were absorbed into plants that cows ate. The result was radioactivity in the milk that humans drank, which increased the risk of thyroid cancer and leukemia. Steven L. Simon, André Bouville, and Charles E. Land, "Fallout from Nuclear Weapons Tests and Cancer Risks," *American Scientist* 94 (1):48–58 (2006).

95. Wittner (1969), p. 241.

96. Charles DeBenedetti and Charles Chatfield, *An American Ordeal: The Antiwar Movement of the Vietnam Era* (Syracuse, NY: Syracuse University Press, 1990); Sam Marullo and John Lofland, eds., *Peace Action in the Eighties* (New Brunswick and London: Rutgers University Press, 1990); Robert Kleidman, *Organizing for Peace: Neutrality, the Test Ban, and the Freeze* (Syracuse, NY: Syracuse University Press, 1993).

97. Jeffrey W. Knopf, *Domestic Society and International Cooperation: The Impact of Protest on Us Arms Control Policy* (Cambridge, UK: Cambridge University Press, 1998).

98. Louis Kriesberg, *International Conflict Resolution: The U.S.-USSR and Middle East Cases* (New Haven, CT: Yale University Press, 1992).

99. Melvyn P. Leffler, *For the Soul of Mankind: The United States, the Soviet Union, and the Cold War* (New York: Hill and Wang, 2007), pp. 198–201.

100. Arthur M. Schlesinger Jr., *A Thousand Days* (Boston: Houghton Miflin, 1965), pp. 340–342.

101. Seemingly small operations often required large numbers of support personnel. For example, each hour a military helicopter flew it needed 24 hours of maintenance, which required many people, and they required a supply unit with more personnel. David T. Ratcliffe, *Understanding Special Operations: 1989 Interview with L. Fletcher Prouty* (Roslindale, MA: rat haus reality press, 1999).

102. David Halberstam, *The Best and the Brightest* (New York: Fawcet, 1973).

103. For example, on February 3, 1964, Johnson said in a taped telephone conversation with John S. Knight, chairman of the board, *Miami Herald*, "Almighty, what they said about leaving China would just be warming up with what they'd say now." Michael R. Beschloss, ed. *Taking Charge: The Johnson White House Tapes, 1963–1964* (New York: Simon & Schuster, 1997), p. 213.

104. Indeed in February 1979, a brief war was fought when Chinese forces invaded Vietnam.

105. Robert S. McNamara, *In Retrospect: The Tragedy and Lessons of Vietnam* (New York: Random House, 1995), pp. 129–136.

106. Later, some of those who voted for the resolution, such as Senator William Fulbright, claimed that Johnson misled them to get the resolution passed.

107. www.lbjlib.utexas.edu/johnson/archives.hom/speeches.hom/650407.asp

108. Bombing as a policy tool in "Vietnam: Effectiveness," A staff study based on the Pentagon Papers, study no. 5. Robert E. Biles (Washington: U.S. Govt. Print. Office, 1972). http://congressional.proquest.com/congressional/docview/t21.d22.cmp-1972-for-0022?accountid=14,214

109. Michael R. Beschloss, *Reaching for Glory: Lyndon Johnson's Secret White House Tapes, 1964–1965* (New York: Simon & Schuster, 2001).

110. Data are from: http://www.rjsmith.com/kia_tbl.html. In addition to those killed in action, military personnel die in noncombat circumstances as well. I cite only those killed in action so the numbers are comparable for non-U.S. casualties, for which noncombat deaths are not available.

111. William Bundy, *A Tangled Web: The Making of Foreign Policy in the Nixon Presidency* (New York: Hill and Wang, 1998), pp. 35–48.

112. William B. Quandt, *Peace Process: American Diplomacy and the Arab-Israeli Conflict since 1967* (Washington, DC: The Brookings Institution; Berkeley and Los Angeles: University of California Press, 1993).

113. O. Edmund Clubb, *China & Russia: The "Great Game"* (New York and London: Columbia University Press, 1971).

114. J. William Fulbright, ed., *The Vietnam Hearings* (New York: Vintage Books, 1966), p. 112.

115. This should have been evident in 1962 when U.S. government leaders participated in planning a coup to overthrow the South Vietnamese government led by President Ngo Dinh Diem. John F. Kennedy was shocked to learn on November 2 that Diem had been assassinated by the coup leaders. McNamara, *In Retrospect: The Tragedy and Lessons of Vietnam*, pp. 48–85.

116. Michael R. Beschloss, ed. *Reaching for Glory: Lyndon Johnson's Secret White House Tapes, 1964–1965* (New York: Simon & Schuster, 2001), p. 137. It is not likely that would be kept secret.

117. Scott Atran, Robert Axelrod, and Richard Davis, "Sacred Barriers to Conflict Resolution," *Science* 317:1039–1040 (August 24) (2007).

118. Roger Fisher, Elizabeth Kopelman, and Andrea Kupfer Schneider, *Beyond Machiavelli: Tools for Coping with Conflict* (New York: Penguin, 1994), pp. 46–47.

119. Christopher Mitchell, *Gestures of Conciliation: Factors Contributing to Successful Olive Branches* (New York: St. Martin's Press, 2000); Louis Kriesberg and Bruce W. Dayton, *Constructive Conflicts: From Escalation to Resolution*, 4th ed. (Lanham, MD: Rowman & Littlefield, 2012), pp. 204–222.

120. McNamara, *In Retrospect: The Tragedy and Lessons of Vietnam*, p. 322.

121. Roger Fisher, William Ury, and Bruce patton, *Getting to Yes: Negotiating Agreement without Giving in*, 2nd ed. (New York: Penguin, 1991); Rachel Fleishman, Catherine Gerard, and Rosemary O'Leary, ed. *Pushing the Boundaries: New Frontiers in Conflict Resolution and Collaboration* (Bingley, UK: Emerald, 2008).

122. Irving L. Janis, *Victims of Groupthink* (Boston: Houghton Mifflin, 1972).

123. Joel Brockner and Jeffrey Z. Rubin, *Entrapment in Escalating Conflicts: A Social Psychological Analysis* (New York: Springer Verlag, 1985).

CHAPTER 3

1. Henry Kissinger, *Nuclear Weapons and Foreign Policy* (New York: Harper & Row, 1957); Jussi Hanhimäki, *The Flawed Architect: Henry Kissinger and American Foreign Policy* (Oxford and New York: Oxford University Press, 2004).

2. William Bundy, *A Tangled Web: The Making of Foreign Policy in the Nixon Presidency* (New York: Hill and Wang, 1998); Henry Kissinger, *White House Years* (Boston: Little, Brown, 1979); Tad Szulc, *The Illusion of Peace: Foreign Policy in the Nixon Years* (New York: The Viking Press, 1978).

3. Nixon liked the idea of appearing to be capable of irrational actions, of being a "madman"; Bundy, *A Tangled Web: The Making of Foreign Policy in the Nixon Presidency*, p. 73.

4. Ibid., p. 153.

5. Charles DeBenedetti and Charles Chatfield, *An American Ordeal: The Antiwar Movement of the Vietnam Era* (Syracuse, NY: Syracuse University Press, 1990), pp. 279–280.

6. The program, under the leadership of Neil Katz, became an undergraduate minor and later shifted to focus on conflict resolution. It played an important role in the establishment of the Program on the Analysis and Resolution of Conflicts (PARC) at Syracuse University in 1986.

7. Bundy, *A Tangled Web: The Making of Foreign Policy in the Nixon Presidency*; Kissinger, *White House Years*.

8. David A. and Robert D. Benford Snow, "Ideology, Frame Resonance, and Participant Mobilization," in *International Social Movement Research*, ed. Hanspeter Kriesi, Bert Klandermans, and Sidney Tarrow (Greenwich, CT: JAI Press, 1988).

9. According to a Gallup poll of January 26, 1973, 58% of the respondents thought the terms of the agreement constituted "peace with honor," and 26% did not. But only 34% thought the peace agreement would last and 41% thought it would not, cited in Bundy, *A Tangled Web: The Making of Foreign Policy in the Nixon Presidency*, p. 370.

10. The attacks, largely by B-52s, dropped nearly 20,000 tons of bombs, which killed slightly more than 2,000 people according to North Vietnamese authorities. The attacks were widely criticized by members of Congress and the American public. Ibid., pp. 361–362.

11. Szulc, *The Illusion of Peace: Foreign Policy in the Nixon Years*.

12. Arnold R. Isaacs, *Without Honor: Defeat in Vietnam and Cambodia* (Baltimore: Johns Hopkins University Press, 1983), pp. 62–63; cited in agreement in Bundy, *A Tangled Web: The Making of Foreign Policy in the Nixon Presidency*, p. 364.

13. Bundy, *A Tangled Web: The Making of Foreign Policy in the Nixon Presidency*, pp. 372–373.

14. David Rudenstine, *The Day the Presses Stopped: A History of the Pentagon Papers Case* (Berkeley: University of California Press, 1996).

15. Bundy, *A Tangled Web: The Making of Foreign Policy in the Nixon Presidency*, pp. 110–123.

16. Christopher Davis and Murray Feshback, "Rising Infant Mortality in the Ussr in the 1970s," (Washington, DC: U.S. Department of Commerce, Bureau of the Census, 1980); John Dutton Jr., "Changes in Soviet Mortality Patterns, 1959–77," *Population and Development Review* 5:267–291 (June 1979).

17. Kissinger, *White House Years*. But such back-channel procedures could leave major agencies of the government, and their expert knowledge, locked out of deals that were reached. Gerald Smith, *Double Talk: The Story of the First Strategic Arms Limitation Talks* (New York: Doubleday, 1960). Also see: John Newhouse, *Cold Dawn: The Story of SALT* (New York: Holt, Rinehart and Winston, 1973).

18. Anthony Wanis-St. John, *Back Channel Negotiation: Secrecy in the Middle East Peace Process* (Syracuse, NY: Syracuse University Press, 2011).

19. Jeffrey W. Knopf, *Domestic Society and International Cooperation: The Impact of Protest on US Arms Control Policy* (Cambridge, UK: Cambridge University Press, 1998), pp. 196–197.

20. Janie Leatherman, *From Cold War to Democratic Peace* (Syracuse, NY: Syracuse University Press, 2003). Vladislav M. Zubok, *A Failed Empire: The Soviet Union in the Cold War from Stalin to Gorbachev* (Chapel Hill, NC: The University of North Carolina Press, 2007).

21. Weigle Marcia and Jim Butterfield, "Civil Society in Reforming Communist Regimes: The Logic of Emergence," *Comparative Politics* 25 (1):1–23 (1992). Daniel C. Thomas, *The Helsinki Effect: International Norms, Human Rights, and the Demise of Communism* (Princeton and Oxford: Princeton University Press, 2001).

22. Thomas, *The Helsinki Effect: International Norms, Human Rights, and the Demise of Communism*.

23. Hanhimäki, *The Flawed Architect: Henry Kissinger and American Foreign Policy*.

24. Tim Weiner, *Legacy of Ashes: The History of the CIA* (New York: Doubleday, 2007), pp. 306–317.

25. Hanhimäki, *The Flawed Architect: Henry Kissinger and American Foreign Policy*, p. 23.

26. William B. Quandt, *Peace Process: American Diplomacy and the Arab-Israeli Conflict since 1967* (Washington, DC: The Brookings Institution and Berkeley and Los Angeles: University of California Press, 1993), pp. 76–85.

27. Ibid., pp. 80, 94–98.

28. Bundy, *A Tangled Web: The Making of Foreign Policy in the Nixon Presidency*, pp. 128–129; Hanhimäki, *The Flawed Architect: Henry Kissinger and American Foreign Policy*, pp. 94–98.

29. Mohamed Heikal, *The Sphinx and the Commissar: The Rise and Fall of Soviet Influence in the Middle East* (New York: Harper & Row, 1978). Bundy, *A Tangled Web: The Making of Foreign Policy in the Nixon Presidency*, pp. 337–338.

30. Anwar el-Sadat, *In Search of Identity: An Autobiography* (New York: Harper & Row, 1978). Also see Quandt, *Peace Process: American Diplomacy and the Arab-Israeli Conflict since 1967*, pp. 122–129.

31. Matti Golan, *The Secret Conversations of Henry Kissinger: Step-by-Step Diplomacy in the Middle East*, trans. R. G. Stern and S. Stern (New York: Bantam, 1976).

32. The participants in this assessment were: Jeffrey Z. Rubin, Edward R. F. Sheehan, Roger Fisher, Thomas A. Kochan, Dean G. Pruitt, I William Zartman, Davis B. Bobrow, P. Terrence Hopmann, Daniel Druckman, Kenneth Kressel, and Donald B. Straus. See: Jeffrey Z. Rubin, ed. *Dynamics of Third Party Intervention: Kissinger in the Middle East* (New York: Praeger, 1981).

33. Ibid., p. 280.

34. Louis Kriesberg and Stuart J. Thorson, eds., *Timing the De-Escalation of International Conflicts* (Syracuse, NY: Syracuse University Press, 1991).

35. Harty Martha and John Modell "The First Conflict Resolution Movement, 1956–1971: An Attempt to Institutionalize Applied Interdisciplinary Social Science," *Journal of Conflict Resolution* 35 (4):720–758 (1991).

36. Louis Kriesberg, "The Evolution of Conflict Resolution," in *Sage Handbook of Conflict Resolution*, ed. Jacob Bercovitch, Victor Kremenyuk, and I. William Zartman (London: Sage, 2009).

37. Peter S. Adler, "Is ADR a Social Movement?," *Negotiation Journal* 3 (1):59–66 (1987).

38. Larry Ray, "The Alternative Dispute Resolution Movement," *Peace & Change* 8:117–128 (Summer 1982).

39. John Lofland, *Polite Protesters: The American Peace Movement of the 1980's* (Syracuse, NY: Syracuse University Press, 1993); Ibid.

40. See the personal account of this in Herb Kelman's profile at: http://www.beyond intractability.org/audio/10637/. Also see: Ronald Fisher, *Interactive Conflict Resolution* (Syracuse, NY: Syracuse University Press, 1997).

41. C. H. Mike Yarrow, *Quaker Experiences in International Conciliation* (New Haven, CT: Yale University Press, 1978); Maureen R. Berman and Joseph E. Johnson, eds., *Unofficial Diplomats* (New York: Columbia University Press, 1977).

42. Thomas C. Schelling, *The Strategy of Conflict* (Cambridge, MA: Harvard University Press, 1960); I. William Zartman, ed. *The Negotiation Process* (Beverly Hills and London: Sage, 1978, 1977); Morton Deutsch, *The Resolution of Conflict: Constructive and Destructive Processes* (New Haven, CT: Yale University Press, 1973); I. William Zartman, ed. *The Fifty Percent Solution* (Garden City, NY: Doubleday, 1976); Jeffrey Z. Rubin and Bert R. Brown, *The Social Psychology of Bargaining and Negotiation* (New York: Academic Press, 1975).

43. Glenn H. Snyder and Paul Diesing, *Conflict among Nations: Bargaining, Decision Making, and System Structure in International Crises* (Princeton, NJ: Princeton University Press, 1977).

44. Gene Sharp, *The Politics of Nonviolent Action* (Boston: Porter Sargent, 1973).

45. Snyder and Diesing, *Conflict among Nations: Bargaining, Decision Making, and System Structure in International Crises*; Graham Allison, *The Essence of Decision* (Boston: Little, Brown, 1971); Glenn Paige, *The Korean Decision* (New York: Free Press, 1968).

46. Adam Curle, *Making Peace* (London: Tavistock, 1971). Deutsch, *The Resolution of Conflict: Constructive and Destructive Processes*. Louis Kriesberg, *The Sociology of Social Conflicts* (Englewood Cliffs, NJ: Prentice-Hall, 1973); Paul Wehr, *Conflict Regulation* (Boulder, CO: Westview, 1979).

47. In 1973, Adam Curle was appointed to the first chair in peace studies at Bradford University in Britain.

48. Ronald Pagnucco and John D. McCarthy, "Advocating Nonviolent Direct Action in Latin America: The Antecedents and Emergence of Serpaj," in *Religion and Politics in Comparative Perspective*, ed. Bronislaw Misztal and Anson Shupe (Westport, CT: Praeger, 1992).

49. Louis Kriesberg, *International Conflict Resolution: The U.S.-USSR and Middle East Cases* (New Haven, CT: Yale University Press, 1992).

50. Melvyn P. Leffler, *For the Soul of Mankind: The United States, the Soviet Union, and the Cold War* (New York: Hill and Wang, 2007).

51. Ivo H. Daalder and James M. Lindsay, *America Unbound: The Bush Revolution in Foreign Policy* (Washington, DC: Brookings Institution Press, 2003); James Mann, *Rise of the Vulcans* (New York: Viking, 2004). Also see Jerry W. Sanders, *Peddlers of Crisis* (Boston: South End Press, 1983).

52. Zubok, *A Failed Empire: The Soviet Union in the Cold War from Stalin to Gorbachev*.

53. Strobe Talbott, *Endgame: The Inside Story of SALT II* (New York: Harper & Row, 1979).

54. Carter, *Keeping Faith*; Leffler, *For the Soul of Mankind: The United States, the Soviet Union, and the Cold War*.

55. Talbott, *Endgame: The Inside Story of SALT II*.

56. Mann, *Rise of the Vulcans*.

57. Strobe Talbott, *Deadly Gambits* (New York: Knopf, 1984).

58. Carter, *Keeping Faith*, pp. 454–457.

59. Many Iranians also failed to grasp the nature of the revolution's course. I recall conversing with several Iranian university students and expressed my support for change in Iran, but also my concern about the Ayatollah Khomeini and the establishment of a theocracy. They all assured me that he would be controlled by the secular reformers.

60. Leffler, *For the Soul of Mankind: The United States, the Soviet Union, and the Cold War*, pp. 329 ff.

61. Steve Coll, *Ghost Wars: The Secret History of the CIA, Afghanistan, and Bin Laden, from the Soviet Invasion to September 10, 2001* (New York: The Penguin Press, 2004), p. 46.

62. Leffler, *For the Soul of Mankind: The United States, the Soviet Union, and the Cold War*, cited on p. 328.

63. Coll, *Ghost Wars: The Secret History of the CIA, Afghanistan, and Bin Laden, from the Soviet Invasion to September 10, 2001*, cited on p. 49.

64. The Iranian revolution also meant the loss of U.S. installations in Iran that were used to monitor Soviet missile tests, an essential element in arms control agreements.

65. Jimmy Carter, *Keeping Faith* (New York: Bantam Books, 1982); J. Michael Hogan, *The Panama Canal in American Politics: Domestic Advocacy and the Evolution of Policy* (Carbondale, IL: Southern Illinois Press, 1986).

66. Carter, *Keeping Faith*, pp. 163–164.

67. Ibid., pp. 273–429.

68. Quandt, *Peace Process: American Diplomacy and the Arab-Israeli Conflict since 1967*.

69. Ibid., pp. 262–263.

70. For the text of the speech and other documents, see: Walter Laqueur and Barry Rubin, eds., *The Israel-Arab Reader*, 4th ed. (New York: Penguin Books, 1984).

71. Christopher Mitchell, *Gestures of Conciliation: Factors Contributing to Successful Olive Branches* (New York: St. Martin's Press, 2000).

72. Louis Kriesberg, "Varieties of Mediating Activities and of Mediators," in *Resolving International Conflicts*, ed. Jacob Bercovitch (Boulder, CO: Lynne Rienner, 1995).

73. Quandt, *Peace Process: American Diplomacy and the Arab-Israeli Conflict since 1967*.

74. Harold H. Saunders, *The Other Walls: The Politics of the Arab-Israeli Peace Process* (Washington, DC: American Enterprise Institute for Public Policy Research, 1985).

75. Christian Smith, *Resisting Reagan: The U.S. Central America Peace Movement* (Chicago and London: University of Chicago Press, 1996).

76. Sharon Erickson Nepsted, "Creating Transnational Solidarity: The Use of Narrative in the U.S.-Central America Peace Movement," in *Globalization and Resistance*, ed. Jackie Smith and Hank Johnston (Lanham, MD: Rowman & Littlefield, 2002).

77. The Iran-Contra operation was a misguided and illegal attempt to free the captives in Lebanon. In 1985 and 1986, transactions were undertaken whereby U.S. arms were sold to Iran, through Israel and then private intermediaries, to induce the Iranian government to influence Lebanese Shi'a groups to free the hostages they held. The profits from the sales were diverted to provide arms to the Contras. When this scheme was exposed, it was quickly halted. Congressional investigations were held, followed by criminal indictments of National Security Advisor John Poindexter and his aide, Colonel Oliver North.

78. Pam Solo, *From Protest to Policy* (Cambridge, MA: Ballinger, 1988), p. 55.

79. For an analysis of congressional support and a discussion of building the coalition, see David S. Meyer, *A Winter of Discontent* (New York: Praeger, 1990), pp. 183–188.

80. This had particularly important consequences for religious developments in the Ukraine. See: Catherine Wanner, "Missionaries of Faith and Culture: Evangelical Encounters in Ukraine," *Slavic Review* 63 (4):732–755 (2004).

81. http://www.fas.org/irp/offdocs/nsdd/23-2222t.gif. Also see Đorđević, "Hesitant to Engage: US Intervention in the Balkans from Yugoslav Dissolution to the Kosovo Campaign." Chossudovsky, *The Globalization of Poverty, Impacts of IMF and World Bank Reforms.*

82. Gibbs, *First Do No Harm: Humanitarian Intervention and the Destruction of Yugoslavia,* pp. 175–178.

83. Louis Kriesberg, Bronislaw Misztal, and Janusz Mucha, eds., *Social Movements as a Factor of Change in the Contemporary World,* vol. 10, *Research in Social Movements, Conflict and Change* (Greenwich, CT: JAI Press, 1988).

84. Louis Kriesberg, "Assessing Past Strategies for Countering Terrorism, in Lebanon and by Libya," *Peace and Conflict Studies* 23 (2):1–20 (2006).

85. https://www.cia.gov/news-information/cia-the-war-on-terrorism/terrorism-faqs.h

86. Ronald Reagan, *An American Life* (New York: Simon and Schuster, 1990). p. 291.

87. Bob Woodward, *Veil: Secret Wars of the CIA 1981–1987* (New York: Simon and Schuster, 1987), pp. 93–97.

88. Ronald Bruce St. John, *Libya and the United States: Two Centuries of Strife* (Philadelphia: University of Pennsylvania Press, 2002).

89. Zeev Schiff, "The Green Light," *Foreign Policy,* Spring 1983.

90. Quandt, *Peace Process: American Diplomacy and the Arab-Israeli Conflict since 1967.*

91. Sami G. Hajjar, "Hizballah: Terrorism, National Liberation, or Menace?" (Carlisle, PA: U.S. Army War College, Strategic Studies Institute, 2002).

92. Tom and Jean Sutherland, *At Your Own Risk* (Golden, CO: Fulcrum Publishing, 1996).

93. Robin Wright, *Sacred Rage: The Wrath of Militant Islam* (New York: Simon & Schuster, 1986).

94. David C. Wills, *The First War on Terrorism: Counter-Terrorism Policy During the Reagan Administration* (Lanham, MD: Rowman & Littlefield, 2003), p 213.

95. See the National Security Archive Electronic Briefing Book No. 82, *Shaking Hands with Saddam Hussein: The U.S. Tilts toward Iraq, 1980–1984,* edited by Joyce Battle, February 25, 2003.

96. Robert Pear, "U.S. Agrees to Talks with P.L.O., Saying Arafat Accepts Israel and Renounces All Terrorism," *New York Times,* December 15, 1988.

97. The nonviolence included greater reliance on Palestinian goods and services and demonstrations. Deadly weapons were not to be used. Stone-throwing, however, was widely used by young protesters who were then pursued and sometimes beaten by Israeli soldiers. This won widespread sympathy for the Palestinian cause, even among Jewish Israelis.

98. Raymond L. Garthoff, *The Great Transition: American-Soviet Relations and the End of the Cold War* (Washington, DC: The Brookings Institution, 1994). Jermi Suri, "Explaining the End of the Cold War: A New Historical Consensus?" *Journal of Cold War Studies* 4 (4):60–92 (Fall 2002); Don Oberdorfer, *From the Cold War to a New Era: The United States and the Soviet Union, 1983–1991* (Baltimore and London: The Johns Hopkins University Press, 1998).

99. Robert M. Gates, *From the Shadows: The Ultimate Insider's Story of Five Presidents and How They Won the Cold War* (New York: Simon and Schuster, 1996), pp. 131–134, 143–149; and Suri, "Explaining the End of the Cold War: A New Historical Consensus?"

100. Ronald Reagan, *An American Life* (New York: Simon and Schuster, 1990), p. 589.

101. Oberdorfer, *From the Cold War to a New Era: The United States and the Soviet Union, 1983–1991*, pp. 142–143, 261; Garthoff, *The Great Transition: American-Soviet Relations and the End of the Cold War*, p. 145.

102. James Mann, *The Rebellion of Ronald Reagan: A History of the End of the Cold War* (New York: Viking, 2009).

103. Yale Richmond, *U.S.-Soviet Cultural Exchanges, 1958–1986* (Boulder, CO: Westview, 1987), p. 107. Also see Lofland, *Polite Protesters: The American Peace Movement of the 1980's*.

104. Matthew Evangelista, *Unarmed Forces: The Transnational Movement to End the Cold War* (Ithaca and London: Cornell University Press, 1999), p. 255.

105. Evangelista, *Unarmed Forces: The Transnational Movement to End the Cold War*, pp. 187–189; Jorgen Dragsdahl, "How Peace Research Has Reshaped the European Arms Dialogue," in *Annual Review of Peace Activism, 1989* (Boston: Winston Foundation for World Peace, 1989).

106. Chester Pach, "The Reagan Doctrine: Principle, Pragmatism, and Policy," *Presidential Studies Quarterly* 36 (1):75–88 (2006); Robert C. Rowland and John M. Jones, "Reagan at the Brandenburg Gate: Moral Clarity Tempered by Pragmatism," *Rhetoric & Public Affairs* 9 (1):21–50 (2006).

107. Mikhail Gorbachev address to the 43rd U.N. General Assembly Session, December 7, 1988.

108. The Soviet Peace Committee and an informal U.S. group, led by Rabbi Sheldon W. Moss from California, organized the meeting that was coordinated by the Center for Soviet-American Dialogue based in New York.

109. For example, Denise Williams, a graduate of the Program on Conflict Analysis and Resolution at Syracuse University, in the summer of 1989, joined the International Association of Ecopolis of Peace where conflict resolution and nonviolence training was being provided. Indeed, Educators for Social Responsibility had been conducting workshops in Leningrad and Novosibirsk for the preceding two years. Denise Williams, "Ecopolis of Peace Staraya Ladoga, U.S.S.R.," *PARC Newsletter*, October 1989.

110. Leffler, *For the Soul of Mankind: The United States, the Soviet Union, and the Cold War*, pp. 403–404.

111. Coll, *Ghost Wars: The Secret History of the CIA, Afghanistan, and Bin Laden, from the Soviet Invasion to September 10, 2001*, p. 59.

112. Garthoff, *The Great Transition: American-Soviet Relations and the End of the Cold War*, p. 600 ff.

113. Steve Coll, *The Bin Ladens: An Arabian Family in the American Century* (New York: Penguin, 2008).

114. Lawrence Wright, *The Looming Tower: Al-Qaeda and the Road to 9/11*, 1st ed. (New York: Knopf, 2006), p. 131.

115. Louis Kriesberg, "Peace Movements and Government Peace Efforts," in *Research in Social Movements Conflicts and Change*, ed. Louis Kriesberg, Bronislaw Misztal, and Janusz Mucha (Greenwich, CT and London: JAI Press, 1988); DeBenedetti and Chatfield, *An American Ordeal: The Antiwar Movement of the Vietnam Era*; David S. Meyer, *A Winter of Discontent: The Nuclear Freeze and American Politics* (New York: Praeger, 1990).

116. Lofland, *Polite Protesters: The American Peace Movement of the 1980's*.

117. Yeshua and Thomas Weber Moser-Puangsuwan, ed. *Nonviolent Intervention across Borders* (Honolulu: Spark M. Matsunaga Institute of Peace, University of Hawaii, 2000).

118. Patrick G. Coy, "Cooperative Accompaniment and Peace Brigades International in Sri Lanka," in *Transnational Social Movements and Global Politics: Solidarity Beyond the State*, ed. Jackie Smith, Charles Chatfield, and Ron Pagnucco (Syracuse, NY: Syracuse University Press, 1997); Liam Mahony and Luis Enrique Eguren, *Unarmed Bodyguards: International Accompaniment for the Protection of Human Rights* (West Hartford, CT: Kumarian, 1997). These actions were inspired by Gandhi's Shanti Sena peace brigades. See: Thomas Weber, *Gandhi's Peace Army: The Shanti Sena and Unarmed Peacekeeping* (Syracuse, NY: Syracuse University Press, 1995).

119. Roger Fisher and William Ury, *Getting to YES* (Boston: Houghton Miflin Company, 1981).

120. Howard Raiffa, *The Art and Science of Negotiation* (Cambridge and London: Harvard University Press, 1982).

121. Deborah M. Kolb, *The Mediators* (Cambridge, MA: MIT Press, 1983).

122. Kenneth Kressel and Dean G. Pruitt, *Mediation Research* (San Francisco/London: Jossey-Bass, 1989).

123. Carolyn M. Stephenson, ed. *Alternative Methods for International Security* (Washington, DC: University Press of America, 1982).

124. James H. Laue, Sharon Burde, William Potapchuk, and Miranda Salkoff, "Getting to the Table: Three Paths," *Mediation Quarterly* no. 20 (1988); Janice Gross Stein, ed. *Getting to the Table: The Process of International Prenegotiation* (Baltimore and London: John Hopkins University Press, 1989).

125. Lawrence Susskind, *Breaking the Impasse: Consensual Approaches to Resolving Public Disputes* (New York: Basic, 1987).

126. Gail Bingham, *Resolving Environmental Disputes* (Washington, DC: The Conservation Foundation, 1990); Rosemary O'Leary and Lisa Bingham, eds., *The Promise and Performance of Environmental Conflict Resolution* (Washington, DC: Resources for the Future Press, 2003).

127. Among such former diplomats and political leaders who have followed distinctive careers in advancing the practice and theory of contemporary conflict resolution, five are discussed in this book: John W. Burton, Jimmy Carter, John MacDonald, Joseph V. Montville, and Harold Saunders.

128. Joseph V. Montville and William D. Davidson, "Foreign Policy According to Freud," *Foreign Policy* 45 (Winter 1981–82).

129. John W. McDonald and Diane B. Bendahmane, eds., *Conflict Resolution: Track Two Diplomacy* (Washington, DC: Foreign Service Institute, U.S. Department of State, 1987).

130. John W. McDonald, "Further Explorations in Track Two Diplomacy," in *Timing the De-Escalation of International Conflicts*, ed. Louis Kriesberg and Stuart J. Thorson (Syracuse, NY: Syracuse University Press, 1991).

131. Subcommittee of the Committee on Labor and Public Welfare Education, "Hearing, George Washington Peace Academy Act, 1976," ed. U.S. Senate (Washington, DC: U.S. Government Printing Office, 1976).

132. The other members were representatives John M. Ashbrook and Dan Glickman, Arthur H. Barnes, John R. Dellenback, and John P. Dunfey. The fact that so many members were experienced in domestic matters reflected the early idea that the Peace Academy would have a broad area of work and this would give it a larger constituency and wider support.

133. David Kovick, "The Hewlett Foundation's Conflict Resolution Program: Twenty Years of Field-Building, 1984–2004," (Menlo Park, CA: Hewlett Foundation, 2005).

CHAPTER 4

1. Paul N. Stockton, "Congress and Defense Policy-Making for the Post-Cold War Era," in *Congress Resurgent*, ed. Randall B Ripley and James M. Lindsay. (Ann Arbor, MI: The University of Michigasn Press, 1993), cited on p. 240.

2. James A. Baker III with Thomas M. DeFrank, *The Politics of Diplomacy: Revolution, War and Peace, 1989–1992* (New York: G. P. Putnam's Sons, 1995).

3. Mary Elise Sarotte, *1989: The Struggle to Create Post-Cold War Europe*, Princeton Studies in International History and Politics (Princeton, NJ: Princeton University Press, 2009), pp. 22–25.

4. James A. Baker with Thomas M. DeFrank, *The Politics of Diplomacy: Revolution, War and Peace* (New York: G. P. Putnam, 1995), p. 42.

5. In December 1988, I witnessed a large rally in Gorky Park at which speakers asserted that the Soviet Union lost 30 million people in the war resisting the Nazi invasion. But the speakers went on to point out that Stalin killed even more people and they called for criminal trials of the persons responsible for those deaths, which did not happen.

6. Rey Koslowski and Friedrich V. Kratochwil, "Understanding Change in International Politics: The Soviet Empire's Demise and the International system," *International Organization* 48 (2) (1994). Louis Kriesberg and David R. Segal, ed. *The Transformation of European Communist Societies*, vol. 14, Research in Social Movements Conflicts and Change (Greenwich, CT: JAI Press, 1992).

7. Louis Kriesberg, *International Conflict Resolution: The U.S.-USSR and Middle East Cases* (New Haven, CT: Yale University Press, 1992).

8. Timothy Garton Ash, *The Magic Lantern: The Revolution of '89 Witnessed in Warsaw, Budapest, Berlin and Prague* (New York: Random House, 1990).

9. Angela Stent, *Russia and Germany Reborn: Unification, the Soviet Collapse, and the New Europe* (Princeton, NJ: Princeton University Press, 1999), pp. 83–84; Charles Gati and Center for Strategic and International Studies (Washington, DC), *The Bloc That Failed: Soviet-East European Relations in Transition* (Bloomington: Indiana University Press, 1990), pp. 167–178.

10. Melvyn P. Leffler, *For the Soul of Mankind: The United States, the Soviet Union, and the Cold War* (New York: Hill and Wang, 2007), pp. 432–436.

11. Such an action would violate the treaty between Hungary and East Germany, which required that East Germans in Hungary seeking to enter West Germany be expatriated back to East Germany. Stent, *Russia and Germany Reborn: Unification, the Soviet Collapse, and the New Europe.* pp. 86 ff.

12. Ibid., pp. 88 ff.

13. Ibid., pp. 92 ff.

14. Ibid.; Micahel R. Beschloss and Strobe Talbott, *At the Highest Levels: The Inside Story of the End of the Cold War* (Boston: Little, Brown & Co., 1993); Mary Elise Sarotte, *The Collapse: The Accidental Opening of the Berlin Wall* (New York: Basic Books, 2009).

15. Beschloss and Talbott, *At the Highest Levels: The Inside Story of the End of the Cold War*, p. 137.

16. Stent, *Russia and Germany Reborn: Unification, the Soviet Collapse, and the New Europe*, p. 99.

17. Ibid., pp. 105–106.

18. Perhaps Gorbachev saw some value of continued U.S. engagement in Europe, via NATO, as a way to control a powerful Germany; Ibid., p. 114.

19. Baker, *The Politics of Diplomacy: Revolution, War and Peace*, pp. 198–205.

20. Stent, *Russia and Germany Reborn: Unification, the Soviet Collapse, and the New Europe*, p. 140.

21. Sarotte, *1989: The Struggle to Create Post-Cold War Europe*.

22. Stent, *Russia and Germany Reborn: Unification, the Soviet Collapse, and the New Europe*, p.106.

23. Raymond L. Garthoff, *The Great Transition: American-Soviet Relations and the End of the Cold War* (Washington, DC: The Brookings Institution, 1994), pp. 398–399; and Kriesberg, *The Transformation of European Communist Societies*.

24. Beschloss and Talbott, *At the Highest Levels: The Inside Story of the End of the Cold War*, p. 191.

25. Ibid., pp. 234–237; William M. Evan, *Knowledge and Power in a Global Society* (Beverly Hills: Sage Publications, 1981).

26. As of 2010, there were twenty-eight member-states, including Albania, Estonia, Poland, and Slovenia. There were twenty-two partner states, including Armenia, Azerbaijan, Belarus, Kazakhstan, Russia, and Ukraine.

27. Actually, some changes were made to the Conference on Security and Cooperation in Europe (CSCE), and it was renamed the Organization on Security and Cooperation in Europe Conflict Prevention Centre of OSCE, OSCE Guide on Non-Military Confidence-Building Measures (CBMS), (Vienna, Austria: Organization for Security and Co-Operation in Europe), http://www.osce.org/cpc91082.

28. Beschloss and Talbott, *At the Highest Levels: The inside Story of the End of the Cold War*, p. 233.

29. Jermi Suri, "Explaining the End of the Cold War: A New Historical Consensus?" *Journal of Cold War Studies* 4 (4):60–92 (Fall 2002); Kriesberg, *International Conflict Resolution: The U.S.-USSR and Middle East Cases*; Kriesberg, *The Transformation of European Communist Societies*.

30. Derisively called Star Wars, the SDI was to use ground and space-based systems to protect the United States from attack by strategic nuclear ballistic missiles. It was widely criticized as being unrealistic and as threatening a first strike once a protective shield was in place.

31. James Mann, *Rise of the Vulcans* (New York: Viking, 2004).

32. See Randall Collins and David Waller, "What Theories Predicted the State Breakdowns and Revolutions of the Soviet Bloc?" in *Research in Social Movements, Conflicts and Change*, ed. Louis Kriesberg and David R. Segal (Greenwich, CT: JAI, 1992).

33. John Lewis Gaddis, *The Long Peace: Inquiries into the History of the Cold War* (New York: Oxford University Press, 1987). *The Cold War: A New History* (New York: Penguin Books, 2005).

34. John Vasquez, *The War Puzzle* (Cambridge, UK: Cambridge University Press, 1993); Vladislav M. Zubok, *A Failed Empire: The Soviet Union in the Cold War from Stalin to Gorbachev* (Chapel Hill, NC: University of North Carolina Press, 2007).

35. Matthew Evangelista, *Unarmed Forces: The Transnational Movement to End the Cold War* (Ithaca, NY and London: Cornell University Press, 1999); David Cortright, *Peace Works: The Citizen's Role in Ending the Cold War* (Boulder, CO: Westview Press, 1993).

36. Zubok, *A Failed Empire: The Soviet Union in the Cold War from Stalin to Gorbachev*; Richard Ned Lebow and Janice Gross Stein, "Reagan and the Russians," *The Atlantic Monthly*, February 2004, pp. 35–37.

37. See Philip Zelikow and Condoleezza Rice, *Germany Unified and Europe Transformed: A Study in Statecraft*, 1st Harvard University Press pbk. ed. (Cambridge, MA: Harvard University Press, 1997).

38. Richard Ned Lebow and Janice Gross Stein, *We All Lost the Cold War* (Princeton, NJ: Princeton University Press, 1994).

39. Joshua S Goldstein and John R. Freeman, *Three-Way Street: Strategic Reciprocity in World Politics* (Chicago: The University of Chicago Press, 1990).

40. Stephen Sestanovich, "Gorbachev's Foreign Policy: A Diplomacy of Decline," *Problems of Communism* (January–February 1988), pp. 1–15.

41. Kriesberg, *International Conflict Resolution: The U.S.-USSR and Middle East Cases.*

42. The Maastrict Treaty or the Treaty on European Union was signed in February 1992 by twelve member-states of the European Community. It evolved from the European Coal and Steel Community.

43. David Remnick, *Lenin's Tomb: The Last Days of the Soviet Empire* (New York: Random House, 1993), pp. 216–233.

44. Ibid., p. 223.

45. Frank Möller, *Thinking Peaceful Change: Baltic Security Policies and Security Community Building* (Syracuse, NY: Syracuse University Press, 2006).

46. The incorporation of the Baltic countries in 1940 was in accord with the Molotov-Ribbentrop Pact, the non-aggression treaty between Hitler's Nazi Germany and Stalin's Soviet Union. The agreement produced the German and Soviet invasions and division of Poland and the initiation of World War II.

47. In January 1991, Soviet authorities used force in attempting to suppress the elected government; fourteen unarmed civilians were killed and seven hundred were injured. Moscow, however, took no further action and the Lithuanian government continued to function autonomously.

48. Remnick, *Lenin's Tomb: The Last Days of the Soviet Empire*, pp. 372–373.

49. Michael R. Beschloss and Strobe Talbott, *At the Highest Levels: The Inside Story of the End of the Cold War*, 1st ed. (Boston: Little, Brown, 1993), p. 47.

50. They included the chairman of the KGB, Vladimir Kryuchkov; the USSR defense minister, Dmitriy Yazov; the internal affairs minister, Boris Pugo; the prime minister, Valentin Pavlov; the vice president, Gennady Yanayev; and the CPSU central committee secretary, Oleg Shenin.

51. Jeffrey D. Sachs, "What I Did in Russia," Jeffsachs.org (2012), http://jeffsachs.org/2012/03/what-i-did-in-russia/

52. Stephen Cohen, *Failed Crusade: Ameria and the Tragedy of Post Communist Russia* (New York: W. W. Norton, 2000).

53. Beschloss and Talbott, *At the Highest Levels: The Inside Story of the End of the Cold War*, pp. 59–61. The quotation of Shevarnadze was made after a meeting with Ambassador Jack Matlock in May 1989.

54. Geoffrey Wiseman, *Concepts of Non-Provocative Defence: Ideas and Practices in International Security*, St. Antony's Series (New York: Palgrave in association with St. Antony's College, Oxford, 2002), p. 183.

55. Ibid., pp. 183–184.

56. Roland Paris, *At War's End: Building Peace after Civil Conflict* (Cambridge, UK: Cambridge University Press, 2004). Nevertheless, new civil wars did not erupt. See discussion in Joshua S. Goldstein, *Winning the War on War: The Decline of Armed Conflict Worldwide* (New York: Penguin, 2011), pp. 106–107.

57. Steve Coll, *Ghost Wars: The Secret History of the CIA, Afghanistan, and Bin Laden, from the Soviet Invasion to September 10, 2001* (New York: The Penguin Press, 2004), p. 59.

58. Ibid., pp. 176–177.

59. Beschloss and Talbott, *At the Highest Levels: The inside Story of the End of the Cold War*, p. 62.

60. Najibullah warned of this consequence. Coll, *Ghost Wars: The Secret History of the CIA, Afghanistan, and Bin Laden, from the Soviet Invasion to September 10, 2001*, p. 234.

61. Tim Weiner, *Legacy of Ashes: The History of the CIA* (New York: Doubleday, 2007), pp. 384–385.

62. Bob Woodward, *The Commanders* (New York: Simon & Schuster, 1991).

63. Paul A Gigot, "A Great American Screw-Up: The U.S. And Iraq," *Wall Street Journal* 1990, December 18.

64. The Iraqi government released a version of the meeting of U.S. Ambassador April Glaspie with President Saddam Hussein and the Iraqi Deputy Prime Minister Tariq Aziz on July 25, 1990, which is available in the *International New York Times*, September 23, 1990.

65. Kriesberg, *International Conflict Resolution: The U.S.-USSR and Middle East Cases*.

66. Baker, *The Politics of Diplomacy: Revolution, War and Peace*.

67. John R. MacArthur, *Second Front: Censorship and Propaganda in the Gulf War* (Berkeley, CA: University of California Press, 1992). John Stauber and Sheldon Rampton, *Toxic Sludge Is Good for You: Lies, Damn Lies and the Public Relations Industry* (Monroe, ME: Common Courage Press, 1995). Martin A. Lee, *Unreliable Sources: A Guide to Detecting Bias in News Media* (New York: Lyle Stuart, 1991).

68. Lawrence Wright, *The Looming Tower: Al-Qaeda and the Road to 9/11*, 1st ed. (New York: Knopf, 2006), pp. 156–157.

69. The actions of bin Laden were not known to U.S. officials at that time. See Richard A. Clarke, *Against All Enemies: Inside America's War on Terror* (New York: Free Press, 2004), p.59.

70. Thomas L. Friedman, "Mideast Tensions; U.S. Jobs at Stake in Gulf, Baker Says," *New York Times*, November 14, 1990.

71. Roger Fisher, "Winning without War," *Boston Globe*, November 4, 1990; Howard Raiffa, Jeffrey Z. Rubin, and Jeswald W. Salacuse, "Mideast Peace Can Be Negotiated," *Newsday*, December 14, 1990; Louis Kriesberg, "Forcing Iraq's Withdrawal," *The Post-Standard*, October 10, 1990.

72. Roger Fisher, Andrea Kupfer, and Douglas Stone, "How Do You End a War?" *Boston Globe*, February 8, 1991.

73. This is fully discussed in a later book: Roger Fisher, Elizabeth Kopelman, and Andrea Kupfer Schneider, *Beyond Machiavelli: Tools for Coping with Conflict* (New York: Penguin, 1994).

74. Roger Fisher, William Ury, and Bruce Patton, *Getting to YES: Negotiating Agreement without Giving in*, 2nd ed. (New York: Penguin, 1991), p. 54.

75. Woodward, *The Commanders*, pp. 299–302.

76. Secretary of State Baker reports that such an effort would make even Bush's critics unable to say that he had not gone "the extra mile for peace." Baker, *The Politics of Diplomacy: Revolution, War and Peace*, p. 350.

77. Michael Massing, "The Way to War," *New York Review of Books* (March 28, 1991), pp. 17–22.

78. Scott Ritter, *Frontier Justice: Weapons of Mass Destruction and the Bushwhacking of America* (New York: Context Books, 2003), pp. 59–64.

79. Dana Priest and Walter Pincus, "U.S. 'Almost All Wrong' on Weapons," *Washington Post*, October 7, 2004, p. A01.

80. Glenn Kessler, "Hussein Pointed to Iranian Threat," *Washington Post*, July 2, 2009, http://articles.washingtonpost.com/2009-07-02/news/36847839_1_interviews-saddam-hussein-weapons-of-mass-destruction. Piro spoke about his interrogation of Hussein, on CNN on January 27, 2008, and at Syracuse University on January 17, 2013.

81. Michael Barkun, *A Culture of Conspiracy: Apocalyptic Visions in Contemporary America* (Berkeley: University of California Press, 2003).

82. Daniele Conversi, "German-Bashing and the Breakup of Yugoslavia," in *The Donald W. Treadgold Papers 16* (Seattle: The Henry M. Jackson School of International Studies, p. 88; The University of Washington, 1998); Misha Glenny, *The Fall of Yugoslavia* (New York: Penguin, 1992).

83. Howard Clark, *Civil Resistance in Kosovo* (London: Pluto Press, 2000).

84. Jon Western, "Sources of Humanitarian Intervention: Beliefs, and Advocacy in the U.S. Decisions on Somalia and Bosnia," *International Security* 26 (4):112–142 (2002). A best-selling account of the long history of ethnic hatred in the Balkans contributed to aversion to intervention, see Robert D. Kaplan, *Balkan Ghosts: A Journey through History* (New York: St. Martin's Press, 1993).

85. Baker, *The Politics of Diplomacy: Revolution, War and Peace, 1989–1992*, pp. 478–483. William Hyland, *Clinton's World: Remaking American Foreign Policy* (Westport, CT: Praeger, 1999), p. 30.

86. See the discussion in the previous chapter. Also see David N. Gibbs, *First Do No Harm: Humanitarian Intervention and the Destruction of Yugoslavia* (Nashville, TN: Vanderbilt University Press, 2009); Richard C. Holbrooke, *To End a War* (New York: Random House, 1998).

87. Jeffrey D. Sachs, *The End of Poverty: Economic Possibilities for Our Time* (New York: Penguin, 2005), p. 127. Warren Zimmerman, *Origins of a Catastrophe: Yugoslavia and Its Destroyers* (1999).

88. Gibbs, *First Do No Harm: Humanitarian Intervention and the Destruction of Yugoslavia*, pp. 64–65.

89. Jon Western, "Sources of Humanitarian Intervention: Beliefs, Information, and Advocacy in U.S. Decisions on Somalia and Bosnia," in *The Domestic Sources of American Foreign Policy*, ed. Eugene R. Wittkopf and James M. McCormick (Lanham, MD: Rowman & Littlefield, 2008).

90. John R. Bolton, "Wrong Turn in Somalia," *Foreign Affairs* 73 (1):56–66 (1994).

91. C. H. Mike Yarrow, *Quaker Experiences in International Conciliation* (New Haven, CT: Yale University Press, 1978). Nancy Gallagher, *Quakers in the Israeli-Palestinian Conflict* (Cairo & New York: The American University in Cairo Press, 2007).

92. American Friends Service Committee, *Search for Peace in the Middle East* (Philadelphia, American Friends Service Committee, 1970). Everett Mendelsohn and American Friends Service Committee, *A Compassionate Peace: A Future for the Middle East: A Report Prepared for the American Friends Service Committee* (New York: Hill and Wang, 1982).

93. Hussein Agha, Shai Feldman, Ahmad Khalidi, and Zeev Schiff, *Track-II Diplomacy: Lessons from the Middle East* (Cambridge, MA; London: MIT Press, 2003). John Davies and Edward (Edy) Kaufman, ed. *Second Track/Citizens' Diplomacy: Concepts and Techniques for Conflict Transformation* (Lanham, MD: Rowman & Littlefield, 2002).

94. Esra Çuhadar and Bruce W. Dayton, "Oslo and Its Aftermath: Lessons Learned from Track Two Diplomacy," *Negotiation Journal* 28 (2):155–179 (2012).

95. Herbert C. Kelman, "Contributions of an Unofficial Conflict Resolution Effort to the Israeli-Palestinian Breakthrough" (January 1995). Also see Agha, *Track-II Diplomacy: Lessons from the Middle East*. pp. 25–27.

96. Çuhadar and Dayton, "Oslo and Its Aftermath: Lessons Learned from Track Two Diplomacy."

97. Louis Kriesberg, "Mediation and the Transformation of the Israeli-Palestinian Conflict," *Journal of Peace Research* 38 (3):373–392 (2001). William B. Quandt, *Peace Process: American Diplomacy and the Arab-Israeli Conflict since 1967*, 3rd ed. (Washington, DC, and Berkeley, CA: Brookings Institution Press and University of California Press, 2005).

98. Baker, *The Politics of Diplomacy: Revolution, War and Peace, 1989–1992*, pp. 510–513.

99. David Makovsky, *Making Peace with the PLO: The Rabin Government's Road to the Oslo Accord* (Boulder, CO: Westview, 1996); Nabil Shaath, "Interview with Nabil Shaath," *Journal of Palestine Studies* 23 (89):5–13 (Autumn 1993).

100. The unacceptability of the PLO to the U.S. officials mediating the conflict was accurate. See Rashid Khalidi, *Brokers of Deceit: How the US Has Undermined Peace in the Middle East* (Boston: Beacon Press, 2013), pp. 55–56.

101. http://www.un.org/en/peacekeeping/. Also see Goldstein, *Winning the War on War: The Decline of Armed Conflict Worldwide*, pp. 73—108.

102. The new agenda was set forth by Secretary-General Boutros Boutros-Ghali, "An Agenda for Peace," United Nations (New York: United Nations, 1992).

103. Robert A. Rubinstein, *Peacekeeping under Fire: Culture and Intervention* (Boulder, CO: Paradigm, 2008).

104. Louis Kriesberg and Bruce W. Dayton, *Constructive Conflicts: From Escalation to Resolution, 4th Ed.*, 4th ed. (Lanham, MD: Rowman & Littlefield, 2012), p. 255; Human Security Project Report, "The Shrinking Costs of War," in *Human Security Report*, ed. Andrew Mack (Vancouver, Canada: Simon Fraser University, 2009); Lotta Harbom and Peter Wallensteen, "Armed Conflicts, 1946-2009," *Journal of Peace Research* 47 (4):501–509 (July 2010).

105. Edward Azar and Nadia Farah, "The Structure of Inequalities and Protracted Social Conflict: A Theoretical Framework," *International Interactions* 4:317–335 (1981). Edward E. Azar, "The Analysis and Management of Protracted Conflicts," in *The Psychodynamics of International Relationships, Vol. II*, ed. Vamik D. Volkan, Joseph V. Montville, and Demetrios A. Julius (Lexington, MA: Lexington, 1991).

106. Terrell A. Northrup, "The Dynamic of Identity in Personal and Social Conflict," in *Intractable Conflicts and Their Transformation*, ed. Louis Kriesberg, Terrell A. Northrup, and Stuart J. Thorson (Syracuse, NY: Syracuse University Press, 1989).

107. Richard H. Thompson, *Theories of Ethnicity: A Critical Appraisal* (New York: Greenwood Press, 1989). For constructionist approaches, see Benedict Anderson, *Imagined Communities: Reflections on the Origin and Spread of Nationalism*, revised ed. (London: Verson, 1991); and Paul R. Brass, *Ethnicity and Nationalism: Theory and Comparison* (New Delhi/Newbury Park/London: Sage, 1991). A hybrid approach that views ethnic consciousness as a potentiality that is realized only under certain conditions is articulated by John L. Comaroff, "Humanity, Ethnicity, Nationality: Conceptual and Comparative Perspectives on the USSR," *Theory and Society* 20:661–687 (1991); and Daniele Conversi, ed. *Ethnonationalism in the Contemporary World* (London: Routledge, 2002).

108. For a discussion of the distinction between these three forms of identity formation, see: Neal G. Jessee and Kristen P. Williams, *Ethnic Conflict: A Systematic Approach to Cases of Conflict* (Washington, DC: CQ Press, 2011).

109. Daniel Druckman, "Social Psychological Aspects of Nationalism," in *Perspectives on Nationalism and War*, ed. John L. Comaroff and Paul C. Stern (Luxembourg: Gordon and Breach, 1995).

110. Timothy D. Sisk, "Democratization and Peacebuilding: Perils and Promises," in *Turbulent Peace: The Challenges of Managing International Conflict*, ed. Chester A. Crocker, Fen Osler Hampson, and Pamela Aall (Washington, DC: United States Institute of Peace Press, 2001).

111. Chester A. Crocker, *High Noon in Southern Africa: Making Peace in a Rough Neighborhood* (New York: W. W. Norton, 1992).

112. Bruce Russett, *Grasping the Democratic Peace: Principles for a Post-Cold War World* (Princeton, NJ: Princeton University Press, 1993).

113. Boutros-Ghali, "An Agenda for Peace."

114. Louis Kriesberg, Terrell A. Northrup, and Stuart J. Thorson, eds., *Intractable Conflicts and Their Transformation* (Syracuse, NY: Syracuse University Press, 1989).

115. P. H. Gulliver, *Disputes and Negotiations: A Cross-Cultural Perspective* (New York: Academic Press, 1979). John Paul Lederach, *Preparing for Peace: Conflict Transformation across Cultures* (Syracuse, NY: Syracuse University Press, 1995); Paul Wehr and John Paul Lederach, "Mediating Conflict in Central America," *Journal of Peace Research* 28 (1):85–98 (1991). E. Victoria Shook and Leonard Ke'ala Kwan, "Ho'oponopono: Straightening Family Relationships in Hawaii," in *Conflict Resolution: Cross-Cultural Perspectives*, ed. K. Avruch, P. Black, and J. Scimecca (New York: Greenwood Press, 1991).

116. Lederach, *Preparing for Peace: Conflict Transformation across Cultures*.

117. Hendrik van der Merwe, *Pursuing Justice and Peace in South Africa* (London and New York: Routledge, 1989).

118. Susan Allen Nan, "The Roles of Conflict Resolution Scholars in Georgian–Abkhaz and Georgian–South-Ossetian Conflict and Conflict Resolution," *Cambridge Review of International Affairs* 23 (2):237–258 (2010).

CHAPTER 5

1. John Agnew, *Globalization and Sovereignty* (Lanham, MD: Rowman & Littlfield, 2009).

2. Ray Kurzweil, "The Law of Accelerating Returns," http://www.kurzweilai.net/articles/art0134.html?printable=1.

3. Galen B. Crow and Balakrishnan Mthuswamt, "International Outsourcing in the Information Technology Industry: Trends and Implications," *Communications of the International Information Association*, 3 (1), pp. 25–34, 27.

4. See Jackie Smith, Charles Chatfield and Ron Pagnucco, eds., *Transnational Social Movements and Global Politics: Solidarity Beyond the State* (Syracuse, NY: Syracuse University Press, 1997).

5. Edward A. L. Turner, "Why Has the Number of International Non-Governmental Organizations Exploded since 1960?" *Cliodynamics: The Journal of Theoretical and Mathematical History* 1:81–91 (2010); Smith, *Transnational Social Movements and Global Politics: Solidarity Beyond the State*.

6. For a detailed and nuanced analysis of this, see Paul De Graue and Filip Camerman, "How Big Are the Big Multinational Companies?" January 2002, http://www.rrojasdatabank.info/tncshowbig.pdf.

7. Gerhard E. Lenski, *Power and Privilege* (New York: McGraw-Hill, 1966).

8. Thomas Piketty *Capital in the Twenty-First Century*, translated by Arthur Goldhammer (Cambridge, MA: The Belknap Press, 2014).

9. Kevin Phillips, *Arrogant Capital: Washington, Wall Street, and the Frustration of American Politics* (Boston: Little, Brown and Co, 1994).

10. Jeff Faux and Larry Mishel, "Inequality and the Global Economy," in *Global Capitalism*, ed. Will and Anthony Giddens Hutton (New York: The New Press, 2000).

11. "The richest 1% of the world's population (around 60 million) now receives as much income as the poorest 57%, while the income of the richest 25 million Americans is the equivalent of that of almost 2 billion of the world's poorest people. In 1820, Western Europe's per capita income was three times that of Africa's; by the 1990s it was more than 13 times as high." Larry Elliott, "The Lost Decade," *Guardian*, July 9, 2003. http://www.globalpolicy.org/socecon/un/2003/0709lost.htm.

12. Nicholas Blanford, "Bleak Arab Progress Report," *Christian Science Monitor*, October 21, 2003, http://www.csmonitor.com/2003/1021/p01s04-wogi.html

13. Monty G. Marshall and Donna Ramsey, "Gender Empowerment and the Willingness of States to Use Force" (paper presented at the International Studies Association, Washington, DC, 1999); Mary Caprioli and Mark A. Boyer, "Gender, Violence, and International Crisis," *The Journal of Conflict Resolution* 45 (4):503–518 (2001).

14. Neil J. Kritz, ed. *Transitional Justice*, 3 vols. (Washington, DC: United States Institute of Peace Press, 1995).

15. Leslie Vinjamuri and Jack Snyder, "Advocacy and Scholarship in the Study of International War Crime Tribunals and Transitional Justice," pp. 345–362 in *Annual Review of Political Science* (American Political Science Association, 2004).

16. Steven Pinker, *The Better Angels of Our Nature: Why Violence Has Declined* (New York: Viking, 2011), pp. 255–268.

17. For example, see Michael N. Dobkowski and Isidor Wallimann, *The Coming Age of Scarcity: Preventing Mass Death and Genocide in the Twenty-first Century* (Syracuse, NY: Syracuse University Press, 1998).

18. William Hyland, *Clinton's World: Remaking American Foreign Policy* (Westport, CT: Praeger, 1999), pp. 54–55.

19. Donette Murray, *US Foreign Policy and Iran: American-Iranian Relations since the Islamic Revolution* (London and New York: Routledge, 2010), pp. 91–93.

20. Peter D. Feaver and Christopher Gelpi, *Choosing Your Battles: American Civil-Military Relations and the Use of Force* (Princeton and Oxford: Princeton University Press, 2004), pp. 21–63.

21. Colin Powell with Joseph E. Perisco, *My American Journey* (New York: Ballantine, 1995), pp. 576–577.

22. Also see the report of the Guatemalan Historical Clarification Commission. See John M. Broder, "Clinton Apologizes—for U.S. Support of Guatemalan Rightists," *New York Times*, March 11, 1999, p. A12. Also see Elaine Sciolino, "Vance-Owen Bosnia Move Is Surprise for Washington," *New York Times*, January 31, 1993.

23. Andrew J. Bacevich, *The New American Militarism: How Americans Are Seduced by War* (New York: Oxford University Press, 2005), pp. 117–121.

24. The data are from the Stockholm International Peace Research Institute. http://www.sipri.org/yearbook/2013/03.

25. Andrew Kohut, "Public Opinion of the UN: Strong Support, Strong Criticism," (Washington, DC: Times Mirror Center for The People & The Press, 1995).

26. John E. Rielly, "American Public Opinion," (Chicago: The Chicago Council on Foreign Relations, 1995).

27. James Mann, *Rise of the Vulcans* (New York: Viking, 2004).

28. Bill Keller, "The Sunshine Warrior," *New York Times Magazine*, September 22, 2002, pp. 48–55, 84, 88, 96–97.

29. Daalder and Lindsay, pp. 46–47.

30. Nicholas Lemann, "The Next World Order," *New Yorker* (April 1, 2002) pp. 36–44.

31. See Patrick E. Tyler, "Pentagon Drops Goal of Blocking New Superpowers," *New York Times*, May 23, 1992. Available at: http://www.disinfopedia.org/wiki.phtml?title=Defense_Policy_Guidance_1992–1994.

32. See Rebuilding America's Defenses: Strategy, Forces and Resources For a New Century A Report of The Project for the New American Century, September 2000. http://www.newamericancentury.org/RebuildingAmericasDefenses.pdf.

33. Eric Alterman, *What Liberal Media?* (New York: Basic Books, 2003), p. 82

34. See: http:www.ppionline.org/ and http://www.ndol.org/ndol.

35. Hyland, *Clinton's World: Remaking American Foreign Policy.*

36. John R. Bolton, "Wrong Turn in Somalia," *Foreign Affairs* 73 (1):56–66 (1994); Hyland, *Clinton's World: Remaking American Foreign Policy*, p. 56.

37. *Clinton's World: Remaking American Foreign Policy.* pp. 56–57.

38. Unknown to U.S. officials at that time, al Qaeda had provided advisors to Aidid and assistance in planning to shoot down the U.S. helicopters. Richard A. Clarke, *Against All Enemies: Inside America's War on Terror* (New York: Free Press, 2004), pp. 87–88.

39. This was done with leadership by President Ali Hassan Mwinyi of Tanzania. Linda Melvern, *A People Betrayed: The Role of the West in Rwanda's Genocide.* (London; New York: Zed Books, 2000).

40. Russell Smith, "The Impact of Hate Media in Rwanda," *BBC News* (December 3, 2003).

41. Responsibility for the attack was disputed, with most observers and reports proposing that government-aligned Hutu extremists opposed to negotiations with the RPF planned and carried out the assassination. Less credibly, some observers blamed the RFP.

42. For an account of the failure of the United Nations to intervene even after genocide began, see Michael Barnett, *Eyewitness to a Genocide: The United Nations and Rwanda* (Ithaca, NY and London: Cornell University Press, 2002).

43. The Belgian ambassador and several aid organizations sought international help to stop the broadcasts. But the U.S. ambassador, David Rawson, said the United States believed in free speech. Melvern, *A People Betrayed: The Role of the West in Rwanda's Genocide.*

44. James Morrell, "The Governors Island Accord on Haiti," *International Policy Report*, September 1993. http://www.haitipolicy.org/archives/Publications&Commentary/governors.htm

45. Robert J. Tata, "Haiti," *Microsoft Encarta Online Encyclopedia* (2001); Eileen F. Babbitt, "Jimmy Carter: The Power of Moral Suasion in International Mediation," in *When Talk Works: Profiles of Mediator*, ed. Deborah M. Kolb (San Francisco: Jossey-Bass, 1994); Jimmy Carter, *Keeping Faith* (New York: Bantam Books, 1982).

46. David N. Gibbs, *First Do No Harm: Humanitarian Intervention and the Destruction of Yugoslavia* (Nashville, TN: Vanderbilt University Press, 2009); Lawrence Freedman, "Why the West Failed," *Foreign Policy* 97:53–69 (Winter 1994–1995).

47. Gibbs, *First Do No Harm: Humanitarian Intervention and the Destruction of Yugoslavia.*

48. Richard C. Holbrooke, *To End a War* (New York: Random House, 1998), p .52.

49. Hyland, *Clinton's World: Remaking American Foreign Policy*, p. 34. Also see Madeleine Albright, *Madam Secretary: A Memoir* (New York: Miramax, 2003), pp. 180–186.

50. Gibbs, *First Do No Harm: Humanitarian Intervention and the Destruction of Yugoslavia*, pp. 154–160.

51. Ibid., pp. 27–32.

52. Holbrooke, *To End a War*.

53. Such percentages were matters of great moment in the negotiations. See Ibid., pp. 294–309.

54. Howard Clark, *Civil Resistance in Kosovo* (London: Pluto Press, 2000), pp. 70–94.

55. Gibbs, *First Do No Harm: Humanitarian Intervention and the Destruction of Yugoslavia*, pp. 184–191.

56. This included training and advice; Ibid., p. 186.

57. Oskar Lafontaine, *The Heart Beats on the Left* (Malden, MA: Blackwell, 2000), p. 162.

58. Andrew J. Bacevich and Eliot A. Cohen., eds., *War over Kosovo: Politics and Strategy in a Global Age* (New York: Columbia University Press, 2001).

59. Gibbs, *First Do No Harm,* pp. 200–201.

60. Suggested in conversation by colleague, Andrijana Vojnovic, a Serb high school activist at the time of the bombing, February 5, 2013, in Syracuse, NY.

61. Thomas Carothers, "Ousting Foreign Strongmen: Lessons from Serbia (2001)," in *Critical Mission: Essays on Democracy Promotion*, ed. Thomas Carothers (Washington, DC: Carnegie Endowment for International Peace, 2004). Also see Steve York, "Bringing Down a Dictator," ed. Peter Ackerman (Washington, DC, 2001).

62. Florian Bieber, "The Serbian Opposition and Civil Society: Roots of the Delayed Transition in Serbia," *International Journal of Politics, Culture and Society* 17 (1) (2003).

63. Anika Locke Binnendjik and Ivan Marovic, "Power and Persuasion: Nonviolent Strategies to Influence State Security Forces in Serbia (2000) and Ukraine (2004)," *Communist and Post-Communist Studies* 39 (3):411–429 (2006).

64. Janine di Giovanni, "Blueprint for a Revolution," *Financial Times*, March 18, 2011.

65. Thomas Carothers, "Ousting Foreign Strongmen: Lessons from Serbia," *Carnegie Endowment for International Peace Policy Outlook* (May 17, 2001) pp. 53–61.

66. The National Endowment for Democracy (NED) is a private, nonprofit foundation, funded by the U.S. Congress. NED helps strengthen democratic institutions; each year it supports more than one thousand projects of nongovernmental groups abroad who work for democratic goals in more than ninety countries.

67. Albright, *Madam Secretary: A Memoir*.

68. Lyn Boyd-Judson, "Strategic Moral Diplomacy: Mandela, Qadaffi and the Lockerbie Negotiations," *Foreign Policy Analysis* 1 (1):73–97 (March 2005).

69. National Commission on Terrorist Attacks upon the United States., Thomas H. Kean, and Lee Hamilton, *The 9/11 Commission Report: Final Report of the National Commission on Terrorist Attacks Upon the United States*, official government ed. (Washington, DC: National Commission on Terrorist Attacks upon the United States: Supt. of Docs. U.S. G.P.O., 2004), pp. 71–73. John V. Parachini, "The World Trade Center Bombings (1993)," pp. 185–206 in *Toxic Terror: Assessing Terrorist Use of Chemical and Biological Weapons*, ed. Jonathan B. Tucker (Cambridge, MA: MIT Press, 2000).

70. Clarke, *Against All Enemies: Inside America's War on Terror*, pp. 78–79.

71. Ibid., pp. 92–94.

72. Ibid., pp. 78–79. This includes Ramzi Yousef and El Sayyid Nossair.

73. Lawrence Wright, *The Looming Tower: Al-Qaeda and the Road to 9/11*, 1st ed. (New York: Knopf, 2006), pp. 205–206.

74. Clarke, *Against All Enemies: Inside America's War on Terror*, pp. 97–99. Some Republicans in the Senate and the House, in their antagonism toward the White House, opposed some of the counterterrorism measures that were sought.

75. Wright, *The Looming Tower: Al-Qaeda and the Road to 9/11*, p. 163.

76. Whether or not the Sudanese government offered to turn bin Laden over to U.S. authorities is disputed. It is claimed in Wright, pp. 220–221, and strongly denied in Clarke, *Against All Enemies: Inside America's War on Terror*, pp. 142–143.

77. See http://en.wikisource.org/wiki/Osama_bin_Laden%27s_Declaration_of_War

78. Clarke, *Against All Enemies: Inside America's War on Terror*, pp. 181 ff.

79. Wright, *The Looming Tower: Al-Qaeda and the Road to 9/11*, p. 272.

80. Ibid., p. 282.

81. By some accounts, bin Laden sold unexploded missiles to China for more than $10 million, and Pakistan perhaps used those that landed on its territory in designing its own cruise missiles. Ibid., p. 185.

82. Clarke, *Against All Enemies: Inside America's War on Terror*, pp. 205 ff.

83. National Commission on Terrorist Attacks upon the United States, Kean, and Hamilton, *The 9/11 Commission Report: Final Report of the National Commission on Terrorist Attacks Upon the United States*.

84. Murray, *US Foreign Policy and Iran: American-Iranian Relations since the Islamic Revolution*, p. 96.

85. Bruce O. Riedel, "The Clinton Administration," in *The Iran Primer*, ed. Robin Wright. http://Iranprimer.Usip.Org/Resource/Clinton-Administration (Washington, DC: United States Institue of Peace Press, 2010).

86. Murray, *US Foreign Policy and Iran: American-Iranian Relations since the Islamic Revolution*, p. 97.

87. David Crist, *The Twilight War: The Secret History of America's Thirty-Year Conflict with Iran* (New York: The Penguin Press, 2012), pp. 398–409.

88. Speech made to Foreign Policy Association, in New York, cited in Murray, *US Foreign Policy and Iran: American-Iranian Relations since the Islamic Revolution*, p.102.

89. Clarke, *Against All Enemies: Inside America's War on Terror*, pp.119–121; Riedel, "The Clinton Administration."

90. In 2001, the Justice Department charged that several members of the group were involved. The indictment noted the support of Iran's Revolutionary Guards and Lebanon's Hezbollah in the attack. Riedel, "The Clinton Administration."

91. Albright, *Madam Secretary: A Memoir*, p. 319.

92. Puneet Talwar, "Iran in the Balance," *Foreign Affairs* 80 (4):58–71 (2001). Also see R. K. Ramazani, "The Shifting Premise of Iran's Foreign Policy: Towards a Democratic Peace?" *The Middle East Journal* 52 (2):177–187 (1998).

93. Zbigniew Brzezinski, *Differentiated Containment: U.S. Policy toward Iran and Iraq, Report of an Independent Task Force Sponsored by the Council on Foreign Relations/Zbigniew Brzezinski and Brent Scowcroft, Co-Chairs, Richard W. Murphy, Project Director Also Includes*

Statement and Recommendations of Independent Study Group on Gulf Stability and Security. (Washington, DC: Brookings Institution 1997).

94. Crist, *The Twilight War: The Secret History of America's Thirty-Year Conflict with Iran,* pp. 409–411.

95. The statement is widely regarded as an apology. See Sasan Fayazmanesh, "In Memory of August 19, 1953," http://www.payk.net/mailingLists/iran-news/html/current/msg00974.html.

96. Riedel, "The Clinton Administration."

97. Clarke, *Against All Enemies: Inside America's War on Terror,* p. 118.

98. Scott Ritter, *Frontier Justice: Weapons of Mass Destruction and the Bushwhacking of America* (New York: Context Books, 2003), pp. 62–65.

99. Clarke, *Against All Enemies: Inside America's War on Terror,* pp. 79–84.

100. Brzezinski, *Differentiated Containment: U.S. Policy toward Iran and Iraq, Report of an Independent Task Force,* Sponsored by the Council on Foreign Relations/Zbigniew Brzezinski and Brent Scowcroft, Co-Chairs, Richard W. Murphy, Project Director Also includes *Statement and Recommendations of Independent Study Group on Gulf Stability and Security,* p. 7.

101. Hyland, *Clinton's World: Remaking American Foreign Policy,* pp. 172–175.

102. Ibid., pp. 77–78.

103. Leon V. Sigal, "Look Who's Talking: Nuclear Diplomacy with North Korea," *Items (Social Science Research Council)* 51 (June–September 1997). Also see *Disarming Strangers: Nuclear Diplomacy with North Korea* (Princeton, NJ: Princeton University Press, 1998).

104. Don Oberdorfer and Robert Carlin, *The Two Koreas,* 3rd ed. (New York: Basic Books, 2014), pp. 274–288.

105. Robert Carlin and John W. Lewis, "Negotiating with North Korea, 1992–2007," (Stanford University Center for International Security and Cooperation, 2008), p. 5.

106. Albright, *Madam Secretary: A Memoir,* pp. 459–470; and Bruce Cumings, Ervand Abrahamian, and Moshe Maóz, *Inventing the Axis of Evil: The Truth About North Korea, Iran and Syria* (New York and London: The New Press, 2004), pp. 52–54.

107. Janine R. Wedel, "The Harvard Boys Do Russia," *The Nation* (1998, May 14).

108. Albright, *Madam Secretary: A Memoir,* p. 167.

109. Ibid.

110. Anatol Lieven, "Russian Opposition to Nato Expansion," *The World Today* 51(10): 196–199 (1995).

111. Gerald B. Solomon, *The Nato Enlargement Debate, 1990–2007:Blessings of Liberty* (Westport, CT and London: Praeger, 1998), p. 130.

112. Ted Galen Carpenter and Barbara Conry, eds., *NATO Enlargement: Illusions and Reality* (Washington, DC: Cato Institute, 1998).

113. The United States also actively mediated between the Syrian and Israeli governments, but no agreement was reached. The U.S. mediation between the Jordanian and Israeli governments was helpful and the parties signed a peace treaty on October 26, 1994. William B. Quandt, *Peace Process: American Diplomacy and the Arab-Israeli Conflict since 1967,* 3rd ed. (Washington, DC and Berkeley, CA: Brookings Institution Press and University of California Press, 2005).

114. For example, see: Louis Kriesberg, "Transforming Conflicts in the Middle East and Central Europe," in *Intractable Conflicts and Their Transformation,* ed. L. Kriesberg, T. A. Northrup, and S. J. Thorson (Syracuse, NY: Syracuse University Press, 1989). *International Conflict Resolution: The U.S.-USSR and Middle East Cases* (New Haven, CT: Yale University Press, 1992);

"Negotiating the Partition of Palestine and Evolving Israeli-Palestinian Relations," *The Brown Journal of World Affairs* 7 (Winter/Spring 2000) pp. 63–80; "Mediation and the Transformation of the Israeli-Palestinian Conflict," *Journal of Peace Research* 38 (3):373–392 (2001).

115. There are numerous accounts of the negotiations. See for example, Mahmoud Abbas, *Through Secret Channels. The Road to Oslo: Senior PLO Leader Abu Mazen's Revealing Story of the Negotiations with Israel* (Reading: Garnet Publishing, 1995); Yossi Beilin, *Touching Peace: From the Oslo Accord to a Final Agreement* (London: Weidenfeld & Nicolson, 1999); Michael Watkins and Kirsten Lundberg, "Getting to the Table in Oslo: Driving Forces and Channel Factors," *Negotiation Journal* 14 (2):115–135 (April 1998).

116. Sidney Blumenthal, "The Handshake," *The New Yorker* 69 (32):74–76 (1993).

117. Hyland, *Clinton's World: Remaking American Foreign Policy*, pp. 155–162.

118. Nimrod Goren and Miriam Fendius Elman, eds., *Spoilers of Peace and the Dilemmas of Conflict Resolution* (Ramat Gan, Israel and Syracuse, NY: The Israeli Institue for Regional Foreign Policies [MITVIM] and the Program for the Advancement of Research for Conflict and Collaboration [PARCC], 2012).

119. The primary intellectual architects for policy in this area were Dennis Ross and Martin Indyk, former director of the Washington Institute for Near East Policy and newly appointed to the National Security Council, handling Middle East affairs. Quandt, *Peace Process: American Diplomacy and the Arab-Israeli Conflict since 1967*, 3rd ed., p. 323.

120. Aaron David Miller, *The Much Too Promised Land: America's Elusive Search for Arab-Israeli Peace* (New York: Bantam Books, 2008), pp. 204–205; Rashid Khalidi, *Brokers of Deceit: How the US Has Undermined Peace in the Middle East* (Boston: Beacon Press, 2013), pp. 55–57.

121. Anthony Wanis-St.John, *Back Channel Negotiations: Secrecy in the Middle East Peace Process* (Syracuse, NY: Syracuse University Press, 2010), pp. 152–156.

122. At the time, Yossi Beilin was a minister in the Labor Party government and advisor to Mr. Peres. Mahmud Abbas (Abu-Mazin) was secretary of the Executive Committee and a member of the Central Committee of the Fatah Movement.

123. Rabin had been subjected to a terrible campaign of defamation and demonization by political leaders of the Likud and ultra-religious parties. I visited Jerusalem in March 1995 and saw many walls covered with large posters bearing images of Rabin wearing a Palestinian keffiyeh, a Nazi SS uniform, or being the target in the cross-hairs of a rifle. I lunched with a leader of the Peace Now movement and asked why there was no evidence of pushing back against such extreme actions. She explained that "they" had so much more money than we had but we were working on the great peace rally that was to be held in Tel Aviv.

124. Dennis Ross, *The Missing Peace: The Inside Story of the Fight for Middle East Peace* (New York: Farrar, Straus and Giroux, 2004), pp. 209–215.

125. Quandt, *Peace Process: American Diplomacy and the Arab-Israeli Conflict since 1967*, 3rd ed., p. 339. Also see Hyland, *Clinton's World: Remaking American Foreign Policy*, p. 159.

126. Hebron is a major Palestinian city with a site of religious importance to Jews and Muslims. A small number of highly religious Jews were allowed by Israeli authorities to settle there. The city was divided into Jewish and Arab sectors governed by different security arrangements. An agreement signed in January 1997 was negotiated by Israeli-and Palestinian leaders regarding the disposition of Israeli security forces, aided by intensive U.S. mediation by Dennis Ross and Aaron Miller (personal interview with Aaron Miller, in Washington, DC, April 23, 1998).

127. Wanis-St.John, *Back Channel Negotiations: Secrecy in the Middle East Peace Process*.

128. Hyland, *Clinton's World: Remaking American Foreign Policy*, pp. 166–167.

129. This was articulated, for example, by Henry Kissinger ("The Mideast Deal," *Washington Post*, November 7, 1996).

130. Gilead Sher, *The Israeli-Palestinian Peace Negotiations, 1999–2001* (London and New York: Routledge, 2006), pp. 2–4.

131. Ibid.

132. Albright, *Madam Secretary: A Memoir*, p. 484.

133. Quandt, *Peace Process: American Diplomacy and the Arab-Israeli Conflict since 1967*, 3rd ed., pp. 358–373.

134. Daniel Kurtzer et al., *The Peace Puzzle* (Washington, DC: USIP Press, 2013), pp. 142–147.

135. Sher, *The Israeli-Palestinian Peace Negotiations, 1999–2001*, pp. 119–132.

136. Ibid., pp. 150–151; Quandt, *Peace Process: American Diplomacy and the Arab-Israeli Conflict since 1967*, 3rd ed., p. 373.

137. Various motives have been proposed for Sharon's actions. Sher, *The Israeli-Palestinian Peace Negotiations, 1999–2001*, p. 157. The site is sacred for both Jewish and Islamic believers. In biblical times, Jews built a temple on a platform sustained by extensive walls. When the Romans destroyed the temple and platform, some of the walls remained, and one part of the western wall became the holiest shrine for Jewish believers. When Muslims controlled Jerusalem, they constructed the Al Aksa mosque on the platform buttressed by the wall. That platform is known as the Haram al-Sharif in Arabic, or the Temple Mount.

138. Akram Hanieh, "The Camp David Papers," *Journal of Palestine Studies* 30 (2):75–97 (2001); Ron Pundak, "From Oslo to Taba: What Went Wrong," *Survival* 43 (3):31–45 (2001); Jeremy Pressman, "Visions in Collision: What Happened at Camp David and Taba?" *International Security* 28 (2):5–43 (2003); Louis Kriesberg, "The Relevance of Reconciliation Actions in the Breakdown of Israeli-Palestinian Negotiations, 2000," *Peace & Change* 27 (4):546–573 (2002).

139. Some of this was recognized by one of the architects of the Oslo peace process, Yossi Beilin. Beilin, *Touching Peace: From the Oslo Accord to a Final Agreement*. Also see Sher, *The Israeli-Palestinian Peace Negotiations, 1999–2001*, p. 15.

140. Miller, *The Much Too Promised Land: America's Elusive Search for Arab-Israeli Peace*, pp. 204–205.

141. Sher, *The Israeli-Palestinian Peace Negotiations, 1999–2001*.

142. David Aaron Miller, who admired much of the way Clinton mediated, also faults him for not being tough enough to walk away. Miller, *The Much Too Promised Land: America's Elusive Search for Arab-Israeli Peace*, pp. 309–311.

143. Sher, *The Israeli-Palestinian Peace Negotiations, 1999–2001*, pp. 157–172.

144. Similar rises in the usage of other key words occurred. Thus, publications with the words "conflict" and "stakeholders" increased greatly, rising from 32 to 220 and then to 3,900 over that period. Finally the words "win-win" in conjunction with conflict rose from 25 to 151 and then up to 1,810 in the same years.

145. Erica Chenoweth and Maria J. Stephan, *Why Civil Resistance Works: The Strategic Logic of Nonviolent Conflict* (New York: Columbia University Press, 2011), pp. 234–235.

146. Peter Ackerman and Christopher Kruegler, *Strategic Nonviolent Conflict* (Westport, CT/London: Praeger, 1994).

147. The companion book was published at the same time, Peter Ackerman and Jack Duvall, *A Force More Powerful: A Century of Nonviolent Conflict* (New York: Palgrave, 2000).

148. David Cortright and George Lopez, with Richard W. Conroy, Jaleh Dashti-Gibson, & Julia Wagler, *The Sanctions Decade: Assessing UN Strategies in the 1990s* (Boulder, CO and London: Lynne Rienner, 2000). David Cortright and George A. Lopez, *Sanctions and the Search for Security* (Boulder, CO: Lynne Rienner, 2002).

149. Commission on Preventing Deadly Conflict Carnegie, "Final Report of the Carnegie Commission on Preventing Deadly Conflict" (New York: Carnegie Corporation, 1997); Michael S. Lund, *Preventing Violent Conflicts* (Washington, DC: United States Institute of Peace Press, 1996); Louis Kriesberg, "Preventing and Resolving Communal Conflicts," in *Wars in the Midst of Peace*, ed. David Carment and Patrick James (Pittsburgh, PA: University of Pittsburgh Press, 1997); Max van der Stoel, "The Role of the OSCE High Commissioner in Conflict Prevention," in *Herding Cats: Multiparty Mediation in a Complex World*, ed. Chester A. Crocker, Fen Osler Hampson, and Pamela Aall (Washington, DC: United States Institute of Peace Press, 1999).

150. Eugene Weiner, ed., *The Handbook of Interethnic Coexistence* (New York: Continuum, 1998); Louis Kriesberg, "Paths to Varieties of Inter-Communal Reconciliation, 105-129," in *Conflict Resolution: Dynamics, Process and Structure*, ed. Ho-Won Jeong (Fitchburg, MD: Dartmouth, 1999); John Paul Lederach, *Building Peace: Sustainable Reconciliation in Divided Societies* (Washington, DC: United States Institute of Peace Press, 1997).

151. Terrence Lyons, *Demilitarizing Politics: Elections on the Uncertain Road to Peace* (Boulder, CO and London: Lynne Rienner, 2005).

152. Roland Paris, *At War's End: Building Peace after Civil Conflict* (Cambridge, UK: Cambridge University Press, 2004); Roy Licklider, "Obstacles to Peace Settlements," in *Turbulent Peace*, ed. Fen. O. Hampson Chester H. Crocker, and Pamela Aall (Washington, D.C.: United States Institute of Peace Press, 2001); Witold J. Henisz, Bennet A. Zelner, and Mauro F. Guillén, "The Worldwide Diffusion of Market-Oriented Infrastructure Reform, 1977– 1999," *American Sociological Review* 70 (6):871–897 (2005); and Lyons, *Demilitarizing Politics: Elections on the Uncertain Road to Peace.*

153. George Downs and Stephen John Stedman, "Evaluation Issues in Peace Implementation," in *Ending Civil Wars*, ed. Donald Rothchild, Stephen John Stedman, and Elizabeth M. Cousens (Boulder, CO and London: Lynne Rienner, 2002).

154. Beatrix Schmelzle and Martina Fisher, ed. *Peacebuilding at a Crossroads? Dilemmas and Paths for Another Generation*, vol. 7, Berghof Handbook Dialogue Series (Berlin: Berghof Research Center for Constructive Conflict Management, 2009). Paris, *At War's End: Building Peace after Civil Conflict.*

CHAPTER 6

1. Louis Kriesberg, "Long Peace or Long War: A Conflict Resolution Perspective," *Negotiation Journal* 23 (2):97–116 (2007).

2. John J. Mearsheimer and Stephen Walt, "An Unnecessary War," *Foreign Policy* (Jan/Feb 2003) pp. 51–59.

3. Nolan McCarty, Keith T. Poole, and Howard Rosenthal, *Polarized America: The Dance of Ideology and Unequal Riches* (Boston, MA: MIT Press, 2006).

4. In national surveys conducted in 2003, respondents were asked, "Where do you tend to get most of your news?" Print media were identified by 19% of the respondents and TV and radio by 80%. Asked which network, if any, was their primary source, 30% said two or more networks and individual networks were chosen by the following proportion of respondents: Fox, 18%; CNN, 16%; NBC, 14%; ABC, 11%; CBS, 9%; and PBS-NPR, 3%. Steven Kull, "Misperceptions, the Media and the Iraq War," (College Park, MD: University of Maryland, 2003); p. 12.

5. From debate in Winston-Salem, North Carolina, October 11, 2000; see transcript in *New York Times*, October 12, 2000.

6. Nicholas Lemann, "The Next World Order," *The New Yorker* (April 1, 2002) pp. 16–44.

7. See: http://www.newamericancentury.org/RebuildingAmericasDefenses.pdf,

8. George Packer, *The Assassin's Gate: America in Iraq* (New York: Farrar, Strraus and Giroux, 2005), pp. 37–38.

9. The emphasis was on cutting taxes, and Bush did not support the increase in military spending sought by Rumsfeld, to the consternation of some members of the neocon networkl James Mann, *Rise of the Vulcans* (New York: Viking, 2004), p. 290.

10. Leon V. Sigal, "Look Who's Talking: Nuclear Diplomacy with North Korea," *Items (Social Science Research Council)* 51 (June–September 1997) pp. 31–36. Chae-Jin Lee, *A Trroubled Peace: U.S. Policy and the Two Koreas* (Baltimore, MD: Johns Hopkins University Press, 2006).

11. National Commission on Terrorist Attacks upon the United States, Thomas H. Kean, and Lee Hamilton, *The 9/11 Commission Report: Final Report of the National Commission on Terrorist Attacks Upon the United States*, official government ed. (Washington, DC: National Commission on Terrorist Attacks upon the United States: For sale by the Supt. of Docs. U.S. G.P.O., 2004), p. 255.

12. Richard A. Clarke, *Against All Enemies: Inside America's War on Terror* (New York: Free Press, 2004), pp. 227–228, 232.

13. Peter Beinart, *The Icarus Syndrome: A History of American Hubris* (New York: Harper, 2010), p. 327. Bob Woodward, *Bush at War* (New York: Simon & Schuster, 2003), pp. 32, 62, 282.

14. Interestingly, the criticism by political leaders was muted, believing that uniting behind the president when America was so brutally attacked was not only expedient but the right thing to do. Academics and independent analysts could look at the issues in a broader and longer perspective.

15. Beinart, *The Icarus Syndrome: A History of American Hubris*. pp. 322–326.

16. Ibid., pp. 327–329.

17. Defense Science Board Task Force on Strategic Communication, "Report of the Defense Science Board Task Force on Strategic Communication" (Washington, DC: Office of the Under Secretary of Defense for Acquisition, Technology, and Logistics, 2004). Also, United States Advisory Commission on Public Diplomacy, "2004 Report of the United States Advisory Commission on Public Diplomacy" (Washington, DC: U.S. Department of State, 2004).

18. Mathieu Deflem, "Social Control and the Policies of Terrorism: Foundations for a Sociology of Counterterrorism," *The American Sociologist* 35(2): 75–92 (2004).

19. Beinart, *The Icarus Syndrome: A History of American Hubris*, p. 334.

20. The Iranian representative convinced the Northern Alliance representatives who had been insisting on heading 18 out of the 24 ministries to accept two fewer. Trita Parsi, *A Single Roll of the Dice: Obama's Diplomacy with Iran* (New Haven, CT and London: Yale University Press, 2012), pp. 39–40.

21. During the years 2003, 2004, and 2005, my colleague John Murray and I provided a simulation related to the U.S. engagement in Afghanistan to military colonels and to civilians of an equivalent standing. This was part of the National Security Studies program in the Maxwell School at Syracuse University, under a contract with the Department of Defense to provide leadership training. F. William Smullen III was then and continues as director of the NSS program; see: http://www.maxwell. syr.edu/exed/Sites/nss/. Our simulation remains available online. It is entitled "Managing Transition in a Post War Country," case number: CS 0903–34. The simulation entailed dividing the class into four teams, each simulating a deputies meeting dealing with hypothesized challenging circumstances in Afghanistan. The deputies in the simulation, as in reality, represented the principals, secretaries, and others dealing with national security affairs. I also sat in on various lectures and discussions during the course, and also the shorter course for one- and two-star generals and admirals.

22. Some members of the government found moral clarity useful and did not think it got in the way of being "realistic" in foreign affairs. Interview with Richard N. Haass, Director of Policy Planning Staff of the Department of State, May 16, 2002.

23. Chicago Council on Foreign Relations, Worldviews 2002, *American Public Opinion & Foreign Policy*, Figure 2-2 (http://www.worldviews.org/index.html).

24. Pew Research Center for the People & the Press, "America's New Internationalist Point of View" released October 24, 2001. https://www.google.com/search?q=Pew+Research+Center+ for+the+People+%26+the+Press%2C+%E2%80%9CAmerica%E2%80%99s+New+Internatio nalist+pPoint+of+View%E2%80%9D+released+October+24%2C+2001&ie=utf-8&oe=utf-8 &aq=t&rls=org.mozilla:en-US:official&client=firefox-a&channel=fflb#rls=org.mozilla:en-US :official&channel=fflb&q=Pew+Research+Center+for+the+People+%26+the+Press%2C+%E 2%80%9CAmerica%E2%80%99s+New+Internationalist+point+of+View%E2%80%9D+releas ed+October+24%2C+2001&spell=1 (http://people-press.org/reports/print.php3?PageID=22)

25. Chicago Council on Foreign Relations, Worldviews 2002, *American Public Opinion & Foreign Policy*, see: Figure 3-9 (http://www.worldviews.org/index.html.)

26. Gallup data reported in Pew Research Center for the People & the Press, "America's New Internationalist Point of View" released December 12, 2002 https://www.google.com/search?q =Pew+Research+Center+for+the+People+%26+the+Press%2C+%E2%80%9CAmerica%E2 %80%99s+New+Internationalist+pPoint+of+View%E2%80%9D+released+October+24%2C +2001&ie=utf-8&oe=utf-8&aq=t&rls=org.mozilla:en-US:official&client=firefox- a&channel=fflb#rls=org.mozilla:en-US:official&channel=fflb&q=Pew+Research+Center+ for+the+People+%26+the+Press%2C+%E2%80%9CAmerica%E2%80%99s+New+Internatio nalist+point+of+View%E2%80%9D+released+December+12%2C+2002&spell=1(http://people- press.org/reports/display.php3?PageID=166).

27. Chicago Council on Foreign Relations, Worldviews 2002, *American Public Opinion & Foreign Policy*, Figure 3.3.

28. People will rally around the flag and support the president in foreign undertakings, for peace initiatives as well as warlike initiatives. Susan Borker, Louis Kriesberg, and Abdu Abdul-Quader, "Conciliation, Confrontation, and Approval of the President," *Peace and Change* 11:31–48 (Spring 1985).

29. Alexander Todorov and Anesu N. Mandisodza, "Public Opnion on Foreign Policy: The Multilateral Public that Perceives Itself as Unilateral," Policy Briefs, Woodrow Wilson School of Public and International Affairs, 2003. http://www.princeton.edu/~policybriefs/todorov_opinion.pdf

30. Only 23% responded that the U.S. needs to act on its own to fight terrorism rather than to work with other countries, but estimated that 49% of other Americans supported that view.

31. Bob Woodward, *Plan of Attack* (New York: Simon & Schuster, 2004), pp. 1 ff; Peter Baker, *Days of Fire: Bush and Cheney in the White House* (New York: Anchor, 2014).

32. Richard N. Haass, *War of Necessity, War of Choice: A Memoir of Two Iraq Wars* (New York: Simon & Schuster, 2009); Beinart, *The Icarus Syndrome: A History of American Hubris*; Thomas E. Ricks, *Fiasco: The American Military Adventure in Iraq* (New York: Penguin Books, 2007).

33. Haass, then heading the State Department Policy Planning Board, believed that the national security advisor should ensure such conversations, but concedes Condoleezza Rice was giving Bush the process he preferred. Haass, *War of Necessity, War of Choice: A Memoir of Two Iraq Wars*, pp. 184–185.

34. Louis Fisher, "Deciding on War against Iraq: Institutional Failures," *Political Science Quarterly* 118 (3) (2003), pp. 393–394.

35. Woodward, *Plan of Attack*, pp. 19–20, 432–433.

36. Gilles Kepel, *The War for Muslim Minds: Islam and the West* (Cambridge, MA and London: Harvard University Press, 2004), p. 198.

37. Fisher, "Deciding on War against Iraq: Institutional Failures."

38. Woodward, *Plan of Attack*, pp. 283–284.

39. Larry Diamond, *Squandered Victory* (New York: Henry Holt, 2005); Ricks, *Fiasco: The American Military Adventure in Iraq*.

40. Woodward, *Bush at War*, p. 272.

41. By January 19, 2003, *TIME Magazine* reported that "as many as 1 in 3 senior officers questioned the wisdom of a preemptive war with Iraq."

42. Ricks, *Fiasco: The American Military Adventure in Iraq*, pp. 96–97.

43. In June 2004, Shinseki resigned, observing in his farewell address, "Mistrust and arrogance are antithetical to inspired and inspiring leadership." Ibid., p. 156.

44. Eric Boehlert, "I'm Not Sure What Planet They Live On," *Salon*, October 17, 2002; http://www.salon.com/2002/10/17/zinni/

45. The Center for American Progress had been newly established under John Podesta's leadership as a think tank to counter the conservative and right-wing think tanks. See James Mann, *The Obamians: The Strugle Inside the White House to Redefine American Power* (New York: Viking, 2012), pp. 49–54.

46. Of course, I was asking that they take what they could regard as undue heroic action, placing their future careers at risk. As a retired academic, I could speak out on television and write letters opposing the war without any risk. It did not involve any heroism on my part.

47. Ken Auletta, "Fortress Bush: How the White House Keeps the Press under Control," *The New Yorker*, January 19:53–65 (2004).

48. For example, Richard Clarke resigned from the government in 2001, after serving since 1997 as national counterterrorism coordinator of the National Security Council. He published a book, appeared on "60 Minutes," and in March 2004, testified before the National Commission on Terrorist Attacks upon the United States, the 9/11 Commission. He and his critical remarks about handling the war against al Qaeda were strongly attacked by some leading figures of the Bush administration (not including Secretary of State Colin Powell) and by commentators in the conservative media. For example, he was denounced in an editorial in *The Washington Times* (April 6, 2004) as a "very disgruntled former employee."

49. Michael Massing, "Now They Tell Us," *The New York Review of Books* (2004, February 26) pp. 43–49. Also see Jacques Steinberg, "Washington Post Rethinks Its Coverage of War Debate," *New York Times*, August 13, 2004, p. A14.

50. They attribute the mistakes in large measure to relying on information from a circle of Iraqi informants and exiles whose accounts "were often eagerly confirmed by United States officials convinced of the need to intervene in Iraq." See: "From The Editors: The Times and Iraq," *New York Times*, May 23, 2004, p. 16.

51. Kull, "Misperceptions, the Media and the Iraq War."; Ibid.

52. For example, the talk show programs of Mario Cuomo and Gary Hart were short-lived, and even Jim Hightower's was terminated; Alterman, p. 71.

53. Personal email communication with John Marks, president of Search for Common Ground, September 22, 2004.

54. James William Gibson, *Warrior Dreams: Violence and Manhood in Post-Vietnam America* (New York: Hill and Wang, 1995).

55. http://www.nytimes.com/packages/html/politics/20030214POLL/20030214poll_results.html

56. Danny Hayes and Matt Guardino, "The Influence of Foreign Voices on U.S. Public Opinion," *American Journal of Political Science* 55 (4):830–850 (2011).

57. Richard Benedetto, "Poll: Most Back War, but Want U.N. Support," *USA Today* (March 17, 2003). www.google.com/url?sa=t&rct=j&q=&esrc=s&source=web&cd=1&ved=0CCAQFjAA&url=http%3A%2F%2Fusatoday30.usatoday.com%2Fnews%2Fworld%2Firaq%2F2003-03-16-poll-Iraq_x.htm&ei=YxNaVPwIiJXJBMesgaAL&usg=AFQjCNEjpRpoweclcp6zNUwZ5FGBcTywgg&bvm=bv.78677474,d.aWw

58. Packer, *The Assassin's Gate: America in Iraq*, p. 45.

59. Woodward, *Plan of Attack*, p. 172. The Bumiller article was published on September 7, 2002, under the headline: "Traces of Terror: The Strategy; Bush Aides Set Strategy to Sell Policy on Iraq." Also see: Scott McClellan, *What Happened* (New York: Public Affairs, 2008).

60. Douglas C. Foyle, "Leading the Public to War? The Influence of American Public Opinion on the Bush Administration's Decision to Go to War in Iraq," *International Journal of Public Opinion Research* 16 (3):269–294 (2004).

61. Beinart, *The Icarus Syndrome: A History of American Hubris*, pp. 347–350. Lacking an alternative strategy, many Democrats sought to get the vote done and behind them before the mid-term elections. Fisher, "Deciding on War against Iraq: Institutional Failures."

62. Nick Anderson, "Liberal Gephardt Sides with Bush on Iraq War Resolution," *Los Angeles Times* 2002, October 3; Woodward, *Plan of Attack*, pp. 185–191.

63. Beinart, *The Icarus Syndrome: A History of American Hubris*, p. 347. Obama was in the Illinois legislature and in October 2002 spoke against going to war.

64. Security Council UN, "Security Council Holds Iraq in 'Material Breach' of Disarmament Obligations," Press Release SC/7564 (New York: United Nations, 2002, November 8). http://www.un.org/News/Press/docs/2002/SC7564.doc.htm

65. Woodward, *Plan of Attack*, pp. 341–345.

66. Scott Ritter, *Frontier Justice: Weapons of Mass Destruction and the Bushwhacking of America* (New York: Context Books, 2003).

67. Woodward, *Plan of Attack*.

68. UNMOVIC had been created through the adoption of United Nations Security Council Resolution 1284 of December 17, 1999.

69. http://www.un.org/Depts/unmovic/SC7asdelivered.htm

70. http://www.cnn.com/2003/US/03/07/sprj.irq.un.transcript.elbaradei/

71. Some of the refutations were immediate and others more gradually emerged. Ritter, *Frontier Justice: Weapons of Mass Destruction and the Bushwhacking of America*, pp. 143–157.

72. However, Powell did try at least to point out to Bush the likely terrible consequences of invading Iraq and trying to establish a democratic government there, at a dinner at the White House with Bush and Rice, on August 5, 2002. Woodward, *Plan of Attack*, p. 346.

73. Stephen C. Pelletiere, *Losing Iraq: Insurgency and Politics* (Westport, CT and London: Praeger Security International, 2007). pp. 78–79.

74. Fisher, "Deciding on War against Iraq: Institutional Failures."

75. Ritter, *Frontier Justice: Weapons of Mass Destruction and the Bushwhacking of America*, pp. 159–184.

76. Diamond, *Squandered Victory*.

77. The coordinated bombings in four locations killed 191 persons and injured 1,800. Perpetrated three days before the general election, they were intended to damage Jose Maria Aznar's governing Partido Popular's vote, because it was allied with the United States in Iraq.

78. Patrick G. Coy and Lynne M. Woehrle, "Constructing Identity and Oppositional Knowledge: The Framing Practices of Peace Movement Organizations During the Persian Gulf War," *Sociological Spectrum* 16: 287–327 (1996).

79. Hyunseo Hwang et al., "Media Dissociation, Internet Use, and Antiwar Political Participation: A Case Study of Political Dissent and Action against the War in Iraq," *Mass Communication and Society* 9 (4):461–483 (2006).

80. http://www.democracynow.org/2004/5/12/ex_national_security_agency_head_calls

81. Carl Boggs, "Bush, Kerry and the Politics of Empire," *Logos* 2, no. 3 (2004), http://www.logosjournal.com/boggs_election.htm

82. Dana Milbank and Jim VandeHei, "No Political Fallout for Bush on Weapons," *Washington Post*, May 17, 2003. p. A-1.

83. Jim VandeHei, "Kerry Reaffirms His Vote on Iraq / He Faults Bush for 'Rush to War'on Bad Information," *Washington Post*, August 10, 2004. p. A-1.

84. Woodward, *Plan of Attack*, pp. 431–432.

85. http://www.pollingreport.com/Iraq.htm. Scroll down through years of polls.

86. Emma Sky, "Iraq, from Surge to Sovereignity" *Foreign Affairs* (March, April 2011), http://www.foreignaffairs.com/67459. http://www.foreignaffairs.com/67459 The number of troops added to the U.S. forces in Iraq peaked at 28,000 in July and began to decline in November 2007.

87. http://www.nbcnews.com/id/8420885/ns/world_news-mideast_n_africa/t/most-suicide-bombers-iraq-are-foreigners/

88. Charles Levinson, "Sunni Tribes Turn against Jihadis," *The Christian Science Monitor*, February 6, 2006, p. 1.

89. The origins of the phrase do not indicate serious foreign policy deliberations. Bush asked Michael Gerson to draft the address. Gerson asked David Frum to write a sentence or two linking Saddam Hussein and the 9/11 attacks. Frum thought of the nexus between Iraq and the non-state terrorist organizations, and called it an Axis of Hatred, which Gerson changed to Axis

of Evil. But Condoleezza Rice and Stephen J. Hadley thought that singling out Iraq as the only state would seem very close to declaring war, so North Korea and Iran were added, although they were quite different cases. Woodward, *Plan of Attack*, pp. 85–89. For intended meaning see: Baker, *Days of Fire: Bush and Cheney in the White House*, pp. 186–187.

90. Sigal, "Look Who's Talking: Nuclear Diplomacy with North Korea"; Lee, *A Troubled Peace: U.S. Policy and the Two Koreas.*

91. Mann, *Rise of the Vulcans*, pp. 277–278. Don Oberdorfer and Robert Carlin, *The Two Koreas*, 3rd ed. (New York: Basic Books, 2014), p. 352.

92. *The Two Koreas*, p. 351.

93. Robert Carlin and John W. Lewis, "Negotiating with North Korea, 1992–2007," (Palo Alto, CA: Stanford Center for International Security and Coopertion, 2008), p. 3.

94. Oberdorfer and Carlin, *The Two Koreas*, 3rd ed., pp. 351, 354.

95. Ibid., p. 356.

96. Ibid., pp. 366–374.

97. David E. Sanger, "North Korea Says It Has a Program on Nuclear Weapons," *New York Times*, October 17, 2002; Lee, *A Trroubled Peace: U.S. Policy and the Two Koreas*, p. 223.

98. Oberdorfer and Carlin, *The Two Koreas*, 3rd ed., pp. 376–377.

99. Ibid., p. 377.

100. Mann, *Rise of the Vulcans*, pp. 344–347.

101. Lee, *A Troubled Peace: U.S. Policy and the Two Koreas*, p. 238.

102. Siegfried S. Hecker, "Lessons Learned from the North Korean Nuclear Crises," *Daedalus* (Winter 2010) pp. 44–56.

103. Mike Chinoy, "Bush on North Korea: Wrong Again," *38 North: Informed Analysis of North Korea*, http://38North.org/2010/11/Bush-on-North-Korea-wrong-again/print/ (2010, November).

104. Elisabeth Bumiller, *Condoleezza Rice: An American Life* (New York: Random House, 2007), pp. 306–308.

105. President Bush attributes this progress to his hardline toughness and imposition of sanctions. See George W. Bush, *Decision Points* (New York: Crown, 2010), p. 425.

106. George S. Bain, "One Korea," Syracuse University *Maxwell Perspective* 2009. https://www.maxwell.syr.edu/news.aspx?id=36507226702

107. See: http://dailynightly.nbcnews.com/_news/2007/10/05/4373464-tae-kwon-do-diplomacy? Vitale made a presentation on these activities at Syracuse University on April 26, 2013.

108. Daniel J. Wakin, "North Koreans Welcome Symphonic Diplomacy," *New York Times*, February 27, 2008.

109. Bruce Cumings, Ervand Abrahamian, and Moshe Maóz, *Inventing the Axis of Evil: The Truth About North Korea, Iran and Syria* (New York and London: The New Press, 2004), pp. 95–97.

110. Ibid. Also see Parsi, *A Single Roll of the Dice: Obama's Diplomacy with Iran.*

111. Woodward, *Plan of Attack*, pp. 87–88; Bumiller, *Condoleezza Rice: An American Life*, p. 174.

112. Parsi, *A Single Roll of the Dice: Obama's Diplomacy with Iran*, pp. 40–41.

113. Cumings, Abrahamian, and Maóz, *Inventing the Axis of Evil: The Truth About North Korea, Iran and Syria*, pp. 97–108.

114. Parsi, *A Single Roll of the Dice: Obama's Diplomacy with Iran*, pp. 1–5

115. Kenneth Katzman, "Iran-Iraq Relations," Washington, DC: Congressional Research Service, (August 13, 2010).

116. Stephen J. Hadley, "The George W. Bush Administration," in *Iran Primer*, ed. Robin Wright, Washington, DC: The United States Institute of Peace, 2010, p. 1; http://iranporimer.usip.org/resource/george-w-bush-adminisration?print:.

117. Ibid.

118. Kenneth M. Pollack, "A Common Approach to Iran," in *Crescent of Crisis: U.S.-European Strategy for the Greater Middle East*, ed. Ivo H. Daalder, Nicole Gnesotto, and Phillip H. Gordon (Washington and Paris: Brookings Institution Press and European Union Institute for Security Studies, 2006).

119. Scott Atran, Robert Axelrod, and Richard Davis, "Sacred Barriers to Conflict Resolution," *Science* 317:1039–1040 (August 24, 2007).

120. Ivo H. Daalder, Nicole Gnesotto, and Philip Gordon, "A Common U.S.-European Strategy on the Crescent of Crisis," in *Crescent of Crisis: U.S.-European Strategy for the Greater Middle East*, ed. Ivo H. Daalder, Nicole Gnesotto, and Philip Gordon (Washington and Paris: Brookings Institution Press and European Union Institute for Security Studies, 2006).

121. Louis Kriesberg, "Assessing Past Strategies for Countering Terrorism, in Lebanon and by Libya," *Peace and Conflict Studies* 23 (2):1–20 (2006).

122. Flynt Leverett, senior director for Middle Eastern affairs at the National Security Council from 2002 to 2003, wrote that this quid pro quo demonstrates that "to persuade a rogue regime to get out of the terrorism business and give up its weapons of mass destruction, we must not only apply pressure but also make clear the potential benefits of cooperation." Flynt Leverett, "Why Libya Gave up on the Bomb," *New York Times*, January 23, 2004. Patrick E. and James Risen Tyler, "Secret Diplomacy Won Libyan Pledge on Arms," *New York Times*, December 21, 2003, pp. A-1, 30.

123. Bruce W. Jentleson and Christopher.A. Whytock, "Who 'Won' Libya?" *International Security* 30 (3) (Winter 2005/06). The British played a major role in this process.

124. Aaron David Miller, *The Much Too Promised Land: America's Elusive Search for Arab-Israeli Peace* (New York: Bantam Books, 2008), pp. 323–324.

125. Rashid Khalidi, *Brokers of Deceit: How the US Has Undermined Peace in the Middle East* (Boston: Beacon Press, 2013), pp. 89–93; Daniel C. Kurtzer and Scott B. Lasensky, *Negotiating Arab-Israeli Peace: American Leadership in the Middle East* (Washington, DC: United States Institute of Peace Press, 2008).

126. William B. Quandt, *Peace Process: American Diplomacy and the Arab-Israeli Conflict since 1967*, 3rd ed. (Washington DC and Berkeley, CA: Brookings Institution Press and University of California Press, 2005), pp. 390–391.

127. Abrams dismissed the report for taking a "stance of total moral relativism." Elliott Abrams, *Tested by Zion: The Bush Administration and the Israeli-Palestinian Conflict* (Cambridge: Cambridge University Press, 2013), p. 7. Abrams was a senior member of the National Security Council during George W. Bush's administration, including serving as director for Near East and North Africa Affairs, December 2, 2002 to February 1, 2005.

128. Galia Golan, "Factors for De-Escalation: Israel and a Shift to Constructive Conflict," in *Waging Conflicts Constructively*, ed. Bruce W. Dayton and Louis Kriesberg (Lanham, MD: Rowman & Littlefield, Forthcoming).

129. Quandt, *Peace Process: American Diplomacy and the Arab-Israeli Conflict since 1967*, 3rd ed., pp. 396–397.

130. Miller, *The Much Too Promised Land: America's Elusive Search for Arab-Israeli Peace*, pp. 345–353.

131. Quandt, *Peace Process: American Diplomacy and the Arab-Israeli Conflict since 1967*, 3rd ed., p. 198. Daniel Kurtzer et al., *The Peace Puzzle* (Washington, DC: USIP Press, 2013).

132. Quandt, *Peace Process: American Diplomacy and the Arab-Israeli Conflict since 1967*, 3rd ed., pp. 401–405.

133. Mahmoud Abbas, *Through Secret Channels. The Road to Oslo: Senior PLO Leader Abu Mazen's Revealing Story of the Negotiations with Israel* (Reading: Garnet Publishing, 1995).

134. Quandt, *Peace Process: American Diplomacy and the Arab-Israeli Conflict since 1967*, 3rd ed., pp. 404–405.

135. Abrams, *Tested by Zion: The Bush Administration and the Israeli-Palestinian Conflict*, pp. 121–122.

136. Thanassis Cambanis, "Greenhouse Project Endangered in Gaza," *Boston Globe*, October 31, 2005.

137. Abrams, *Tested by Zion: The Bush Administration and the Israeli-Palestinian Conflict*, pp. 152–153.

138. Quotation available in Ibid., p. 166.

139. Tim Butcher, "Hamas Offers Deal If Israel Pulls Out," *Daily Telegraph* 2006, February 9; Beverley Milton-Edwards and Alastair Crooke, "Elusive Ingredient: Hamas and the Peace Process," *Journal of Palestine Studies* 33 (4):442–459 (2004).

140. Kadima was established in November 2005 by moderates from the Likud Party largely to support Ariel Sharon's unilateral disengagement plan. It also attracted some political figures from the Labor Party. It became the largest party in the Knesset after the 2006 elections.

141. Hassan M. Fattah, "Accord Is Signed by Palestinians to Stop Feuding," *New York Times*, February 9, 2007.

142. Steven Erlanger, "Palestinian Split Poses a Policy Quandary for U.S.," *New York Times*, June 17, 2007.

143. Abrams, *Tested by Zion: The Bush Administration and the Israeli-Palestinian Conflict*.

144. Ibid., pp. 180–191.

145. Bumiller, *Condoleezza Rice: An American Life*, pp. 204–206.

146. Kurtzer et al., *The Peace Puzzle*, pp. 228–229.

147. With agreement on the concept of land swaps, the precise borders still needed fine tuning. Ibid., pp. 231–233.

148. Fayyad received his Ph.D. in economics at the University of Texas and spent most of his professional career at the International Monetary Fund. Steven Erlanger, "An Economist's Task: Building a Model for His People," *New York Times*, August 25, 2007.

149. Presentation by Lt. Gen. Keith Dayton, May 5, 2009, to Middle Eastern Studies Program at Syracuse University.

150. Stephen Walt and John Mearsheimer, *The Israel Lobby and U.S. Foreign Policy* (New York: Farrar, Straus and Giroux, 2007). Stephen Zunes, "The Israel Lobby: How Powerful Is It Really," *Foreign Policy in Focus* http://www.fppif.org/fpiftxt/32702006 May 16.

151. Esra Çuhadar and Bruce W. Dayton, "Oslo and Its Aftermath: Lessons Learned from Track Two Diplomacy," *Negotiation Journal* 28 (2):155–179 (2012).

152. Kurtzer et al., *The Peace Puzzle*, p. 226.

153. Milton-Edwards and Crooke, "Elusive Ingredient: Hamas and the Peace Process"; Menachem Klein, "Hamas in Power," *Middle East Journal* 61 (3):442–459 (2007).

154. For example, see David Cortright and George A. Lopez, *Sanctions and the Search for Security* (Boulder, CO: Lynne Rienner, 2002).

155. Chester A. Crocker, Fen Osler Hampson, and Pamela R. Aall, *Taming Intractable Conflicts: Mediation in the Hardest Cases* (Washington, DC: United States Institute of Peace Press, 2004); Chester A. Crocker, Fen Osler Hampson, and Pamela Aall, ed. *Grasping the Nettle: Analyzing Cases of Intractable Conflicts* (Washington, DC: United States Institute of Peace Press, 2005); Jacob Bercovitch, ed. *Studies in International Mediation: Essays in Honor of Jeffrey Z. Rubin* (London and New York: Palgrave/Macmillan, 2002).

156. Mohammed Abu-Nimer, ed. *Reconciliation, Justice, and Coexistence* (Lanham, MD: Lexington Books, 2001); Yaacov Bar-Siman-Tov, ed. *From Conflict Resolution to Reconciliation* (Oxford: Oxford University Press, 2003); Louis Kriesberg, "Reconciliaion: Aspects, Growth, and Sequences," *International Journal of Peace Studies* 12 (1):1–21 (2007).

157. Marc Gopin, *Holy War, Holy Peace: How Religion Can Bring Peace to the Middle East* (New York: Oxford University Press, 2002). David R. Smock, ed. *Interfaith Dialogue and Peacebuilding* (Washington, DC: United States Institute of Peace Press, 2002).

158. Thomas Carothers and Marina Ottaway, eds., *Uncharted Journey: Promoting Democracy in the Middle East* (Washington, DC: Carnegie Endowment for International Peace, 2005).

159. Tristan Anne Borer, John Darby, and Siobhán McEvoy-Levy, *Peacebuilding after Peace Accords: The Challenge of Violence, Truth, and Youth* (Notre Dame, IN: University of Notre Dame Press, 2006). Kelly M. Greenhill and Solomon Major, "The Perils of Profiling: Civil War Spoilers and the Collapse of Intrastate Peace Accords," *International Security* 31 (3):7–40 (2006/07).

160. Centre Human Security, *Human Security Report 2005* (New York: Oxford University Press, 2005); Monty G. Marshall and Ted Robert Gurr, "Peace and Conflict 2003," (University Park, MD: Center for International Development and Conflict Management, University of Maryland, 2003).

161. Louis Kriesberg, "Convergences between International Security Studies and Peace Studies," in *Millenial Reflections on International Studies*, ed. Michael Brecher and Frank Harvey (Ann Arbor: University of Michigan Press, 2002).

162. Stephen M. Walt, *Taming American Power: The Global Response to U.S. Primacy* (New York: Norton, 2005).

CHAPTER 7

1. "Big Mistake," *The Economist Online* (August 31, 2010). http://www.economist.com/node/16930683/print Also see:Whitney Cox, "Timeline of Iraq War: Public Opinion Over the Past Decade," Media and Public Opinion Post Jun 7th, 2013 | http://www.mpopost.com/timeline-of-iraq-war-public-opinion-over-the-past-decade-1325.

2. Karlyn Bowman and Andrew Rugg, "Attitudes toward the War on Terror and the War in Afghanistan: A Ten-Year Review," American Enterprise Institute, 2011, see http://www.aei.org/papers/politics-and-public-opinion/polls/attitudes-towards-the-war-on-terror-and-the-war-in-afghanistan-a-ten-year-review/.

3. Council on Foreign Relations, Public Opinion on Global Issues (New York: Council on Foreign Relations, 2009).

4. Jonathan Alter, *The Center Holds: Obama and His Enemies* (New York: Simon & Schuster, 2013), pp. 41–43.

5. Ibid.

6. Walter Russell Mead, "The Tea Party and American Foreign Policy," *Foreign Affairs* 90 (2) (March/April 2011) pp. 28–44.

7. Jane Mayer, "Covert Operations: The Billionaire Brothers Who Are Waging a War against Obama," *The New Yorker*, August 30, 2010; pp. 44–55; Janie Lorber and Eric Lipton, "G.O.P. Insider Fuels Tea Party and Suspicion," *New York Times*, September 19, 2010pp. A1, 24; Will Bunch, *The Backlash: Right-Wing Radicals, High-Def Hucksters, and Paranoid Politics in the Age of Obama* (New York: Harper Collins, 2010).

8. Rand Paul is a leading spokesperson for the libertarian view that overseas military operations bolster large and powerful governments. Sarah Palin and right-wing talk show hosts often argue for unlimited American engagement in the world.

9. James K. Jackson, "U.S. Direct Investment Abroad: Trends and Current Issues," ed. Congressional Research Service, RS21118 (Washington, DC: www.crs.gov, 2013).

10. Robert A. Rhoads and Katalin Szelényi, *Global Citizenship and the University: Advancing Social Life and Relations in an Interdependent World* (Stanford, CA: Stanford University Press, 2011).

11. Kim Reimann, "A View from the Top: International Politics, Norms and the Worldwide Growth of Ngos," *International Studies Quarterly* 50 (1):45–67 (2006).

12. Aubrey Immelman, "The Political Personality of U.S. President Barack Obama," in *ISPP 33rd Annual Scientific Meeting* (San Francisco, CA, 2010).

13. Margaret G. Hermann and Catherine Gerard, "The Contributions of Leadership in the Movement from Violence to Incorporation," in *Conflict Transformation and Peacemaking: Moving from Violence to Sustainable Peace*, eds. Bruce W. Dayton and Louis Kriesberg (Oxford, UK, Routledge, 2009); Margaret G. Hermann developed a software package to analyze speeches and writings of political leaders.

14. Ryan Lizza, "The Consequentalist: How the Arab Spring Remade Obama's Foreign Policy," *The New Yorker*, May 2, 2011, pp. 44–55.

15. Martin S. Indyk, Kenneth G. Lieberthal, and Michael E. O'Hanlon, *Bending History: Barack Obama's Foreign Policy* (Washington, DC: Brookings Institution Press, 2012).

16. James Mann, *The Obamians: The Struggle inside the White House to Redefine American Power* (New York: Viking, 2012).

17. Ibid., pp. 66–75.

18. Keith Brown and Jill Tirnauer, *Trends in U.S. Foreign Assistance over the Past Decade* (Washington, DC: Management Systems International, 2009), pp. 1–51.

19. http://www.state.gov/j/cso/index.htm.

20. Regarding moving the U.S. embassy, see Akiva and Nimrod Goren Eldar, *The Jerusalem Capital Ambush: The Political Maneuvers to Relocate the American Embassy in Israel [in Hebrew]* (Jerusalem: The Jerusalem Institute for Israel Studies, 2003). Also see the book review: Itamar Rabinovitch, "The Jerusalem Hijack," *Haaretz* August 8, 2003.

21. Alter, *The Center Holds: Obama and His Enemies*, pp. 51–52.

22. Council on Foreign Relations, *Public Opinion on Global Issues*, www.cfr.or/public_opnion p. 134.

23. David Cole, "The End of the War on Terror?" *The New York Review of Books* 60 (17):59–61 (November 7, 2013).

24. Mark Mazzetti and William Glaberson, "Obama Issues Order to Shut Down Guantanamo," *New York Times* (http://www.nytimes.com/2009/01/22/us/politics/22gitmo.html, January 21, 2009); United States Department of State, "Final Report of the Guantanamo Reivew Task Force," (Washington, DC: 2011). http://www.justice.gov/ag/guantanamo-review-final-report.pdf,

25. Alter, *The Center Holds: Obama and His Enemies*, pp. 145–158.

26. Rachel Maddow, *Drift: The Unmooring of American Military Power* (New York: Crown, 2012), pp. 188–189; Carlotta Gall, "What Pakistan Knew About Bin Laden," *New York Times Magazine*, March 23, 2014, pp. 30–35, 45.

27. http://www.stanford.edu/group/mappingmilitants/cgi-bin/groups/view/21

28. Lloyd C. Gardner, *Killing Machine: The American Presidency in the Age of Drone Warfare* (New York, London: The New Press, 2013).

29. Alter, *The Center Holds: Obama and His Enemies*, pp. 144–145.

30. Stanford Law School International Human Rights and Conflict Resolution Clinic and Global Justice Clinic at NYU School of Law, "Living under Drones: Death, Injury and Trauma to Civilians from US Drone Practices in Pakistan," (http://livingunderdrones.org: Stanford Law School and NYU School of Law, 2012).

31. Gardner, *Killing Machine: The American Presidency in the Age of Drone Warfare*, pp. 245–249.

32. Kevin Sieff, "Florida Pastor Terry Jones's Koran Burning Has Far-Reaching Effect" *Washington Post* (April 2, 2011).

33. Cameron Notions, "Dust and Ash: Reflections on Terry Jones' "Trial" of the Koran," (April 5, 2011) http://www.faithlineprotestants.org/2011/04/05/dust-and-ash-reflections-on-terry-jones-trail-of-the-koran/.

34. Kenneth Katzman, "Iran-Iraq Relations," (Washington, DC: Congressional Research Service, August 13, 2010); Michael Eisenstaadt, Michael Knights, and Ahmed Ali, "Iran's Influence in Iraq Countering Tehran's Whole-of-Government Approach," (Washington, DC: The Washington Institute for Near East Policy, 2011).

35. Daniel L. Byman, "Al Qaeda's M&A Strategy," Brookings (December 7, 20100 http://www.brookings.edu/research/opinions/2010/12/07-al-qaeda-byman

36. Mann, *The Obamians: The Struggle Inside the White House to Redefine American Power*, p. 119.

37. Robert M. Gates, *Duty: Memoirs of a Secretary at War* (New York: Alfred A. Knopf, 2014), p. 472.

38. Kenneth Katzman, "Iraq: Politics, Governance, and Human Rights," (Washington, DC: Congressional Reserch Service, 2014).

39. Michael Gordon and Anthony Shadid, "U.S. Urges Iraqis to Try New Plan to Share Power," *New York Times*, September 9, 2010.

40. Martin Chulov, "Iraq's Leaders Back Fragile Power-Sharing Deal," *The Guardian*, November 11, 2010.

41. Tim Arango, "Iraq's Prime Minister Gains More Power after Political Crisis," *New York Times*, February 27, 2012.

42. Iraqi workers had begun the struggle to form trade unions soon after World War I, led by longshoremen and petroleum and railway employees. By 1959, there were an estimated 250,000 union members in Iraq. However, in 1963, a Baathist regime took over the country and largely

supressed the unions. By 1968, Iraq's organized labor had become an instrument of Baathist public relations. http://www.counterpunch.org/2010/02/19/iraq-s-labor-unions/.

43. Steve Early, "Iraqi Labor Unions Still Struggling with U.S. Occupation's Yoke," *Labor Notes* (August 21, 2012). http://www.labornotes.org/blogs/2012/08/iraqi-labor-unions-still-struggling-us-occupation%E2%80%99s-yoke#sthash.IMWYlhaq.dpuf

44. See reports of AFL-CIO efforts: http://www.aflcio.org/Blog/Global-Action/AFL-CIO-Calls-on-Iraq-and-Fiji-Governments-to-Improve-Labor-Rights; also see http://www.aflcio.org/Press-Room/Press-Releases/President-Sweeney-Joins-Iraqi-Labor-Leaders-in-Jordan/. On failures of U.S. government to aid trade union efforts, http://www.labornotes.org/2010/08/us-pulling-plug-iraqi-workers.

45. This program was initiated by an Iraqi-American, Sami Rasouli, a 25-year resident of Minneapolis, from Najaf. http://reconciliationproject.org/2012/about/

46. Matt Bradley, "With the U.S. Gone from Iraq, Non-Governmentl Organizations Are Becoming Scarce," *The Wall Street Journal* (May 26, 2013).

47. David A. Steele, "Reconciliation Strategies in Iraq," in *Special Report* (Washington, DC: United States Institute of Peace, October 2008).

48. Paul Salem, ed., *Conflict Resolution in the Arab World: Selected Essays* (Beirut: American University of Beirut, 1997); Mohammed Abu-Nimer, ed. *Reconciliation, Justice, and Coexistence* (Lanham, MD: Lexington Books, 2001).

49. Mann, *The Obamians: The Struggle Inside the White House to Redefine American Power*, pp. 120–141.

50. Lizza, "The Consequentalist: How the Arab Spring Remade Obama's Foreign Policy."

51. Gates, *Duty: Memoirs of a Secretary at War*.

52. Interestingly, military chaplains sometimes cooperate with local religious leaders. They are careful not to serve as informants, but strive to help solve local problems. See George Adams, "Chaplains as Liasons with Religious Leaders: Lessons from Iraq and Afghanistan," in *Peaceworks No. 56* (Washington, DC: United States Institute of Peace, 2006).

53. The Human Terrain System is intended to provide military commanders and staff with an understanding of the local population in the regions of their deployment. They gather information about local leaders, tribes, social groups, and political disputes. This information was used to advise military staff and commanders. This became highly controversial and many anthropologists thought such activities were professionally unethical.

54. Carlotta Gall and Maththew Rosenberg, "Anxious Moments for an Afghanistan on the Brink," *New York Times*, July 15, 2014, p. A10; Michael R. Gordon and Rod Nordland, "Afghan Rivals Back a Deal. Once More, for President," *New York Times*, August 9, 2014, p. A4.

55. USAID, "USAID in Afghanistan: Partnership, Progress, Perseverance," USAID Afghanistan Report 270312 (http://www.usaid.gov/sites/default/files/documents/1871/USAID%20Afghanistan%20Report%20270312.pdf, September 23, 2013). Tom Vanden Brook, "Aid Agency Accused of Coverup in Afghanistan," *USA TODAY* (April 2, 2014).

56. Andrew Beath, Fotini Christia, and Ruben Enikolopov, "Winning Hearts and Minds Through Development Aid: Evidence from a Field Experiment in Afghanistan," in CEFR/NES Working Paper Series (Moscow, Russia: Centre for Economic and Financial Research at New Economic School, October 2011).

57. Khaled Hosseini, *The Kite Runner* (New York: Riverhead Books, 2003).

58. Greg Mortenson and David Oliver Relin, *Three Cups of Tea: One Man's Mission to Promote Peace . . . One School at a Time* (New York: Viking, 2006).

59. Mann, *The Obamians: The Struggle Inside the White House to Redefine American Power*, pp. 229–240.

60. Trita Parsi, *A Single Roll of the Dice: Obama's Diplomacy with Iran* (New Haven, CT and London: Yale University Press, 2012), pp. 1–30.

61. Mann, *The Obamians: The Struggle inside the White House to Redefine American Power*, pp. 191–195.

62. Parsi, *A Single Roll of the Dice: Obama's Diplomacy with Iran*, pp. 31–42.

63. Ibid., pp. 38–39.

64. Artin Afkhami, "A Presidency on the Brink: Ahmadinejad & the Crisis of Iran's Conservative Elite," *Muftah* (June 28, 2011) . http://muftah.org/a-presidency-on-the-brink-ahmadinejad-the-crisis-of-irans-conservative-elite/#.U30b6ij3GKJ

65. Ali Reza Eshraghi, "How 'Ayatollah Ali Khamenei's Candidate' Lost the Election," *The Guardian* (July 4, 2013).

66. Steven Erlanger, "Iran and 6 Powers Agree on Terms for Nuclear Talks," *New York Times* (February 20, 2014). http://www.nytimes.com/2014/02/21/world/middleeast/iran.html?_r=0

67. Mann, *The Obamians: The Struggle inside the White House to Redefine American Power*, p. 185. Putin served sixteen years as an officer in the KGB, rising to the rank of lieutenant colonel before he retired to enter politics in 1991. In 1996 he joined President Boris Yeltsin's administration, where he rose quickly, becoming acting president on December 31, 1999, when Yeltsin unexpectedly resigned.

68. Mann, *The Obamians*, pp. 186–187.

69. George Soros and Gregor Peter Schmitz, "The Future of Europe, from Iran to Ukraine: An Interview," *The New York Review of Books*, April 24, 2014, pp. 67–69.

70. John J. Mearsheimer, "Getting Ukraine Wrong," *New York Times* (March 13, 2014). John J. Mearsheimer, Why the Ukraine Crisis is the West's Fault", *Foreign Affairs* 93 (5)(September/October 2014), pp. 77–89 and Mary Elise Sarotte, "A Broken Promise?" *Foreign Affairs* 93(5) September/October, 2014, pp. 90–97.

71. Worldwide News Ukraine, "Ukraine-NATO Cooperation Plan 2011 Approved," *Worldwide News Ukraine* (April 15, 2011).

72. Intrernational Crisis Group, "Ukraine: Running out of Time" (Brussels: International Crisis Group, May 2014).

73. Andrew Higgins and Andrew E. Kramer, "Ukraine Has Deal, but Both Russia and Protesters Appear Wary," *New York Times* (February 21, 2014), pp. A1, A8.

74. Steven Lee Myers and Ellen Barry, "Putin Reclaims Crimea for Russia and Bitterly Denounces the West," *New York Times*, March 19, 2014.

75. Michael D. Shear, Allison Smale, and David M. Herszenhorn, "Obama and Allies Seek Firm, United Response to Russia on Crimea," *New York Times.*, March 24, 2014, pp. A1, A8.

76. Local nonviolent demonstrations successfully dislodged armed pro-Russian separatists who had held key buildings in the eastern Ukrainian city of Mariupol and in other cities in eastern Ukraine, in latter part of May. Erica Chenoweth and Stephen Zunes, "A Nonviolent Alternative for Ukraine," *Foreign Policy* (May 28, 2014) http://www.foreignpolicy.com/articles/2014/05/28/a_nonviolent_alternative_for_ukraine.

77. The issues were exemplified in regard to U.S.-Russian cooperation in scientific matters. David E. Sanger and William J. Broad, "U.S. Nuclear Deal with Russia Fails as Tensions Rise," *New York Times*, August 3, 2014, pp. A1, A7.

78. *The Search for Peace in the Middle East—Documents and Statements, 1967–88* (Buffalo, NY: W. S. Hein, 1989).

79. William Lawton and Alex Katsomitros, "International Branch Campuses: Data and Developments" (The Observatory on Borderless Higher Education, January 2012), p. 3.

80. Marc Gopin, *To Make the Earth Whole: The Art of Citizen Diplomacy in an Age of Religious Militancy* (Lanham, MD: Rowman & Littlefield, 2009); "A Mufti, a Christian and a Rabbi," *Common Ground News Service,* March 11, 2008. See website: http://crdc.gmu.edu.

81. Gene Sharp, *The Politics of Nonviolent Action* (Boston: Porter Sargent, 1973); Peter Ackerman and Christopher Kruegler, *Strategic Nonviolent Conflict* (Westport, CT/London: Praeger, 1994).

82. These were translated into Arabic and numerous other languages and were accessible through the Internet. For example, Gene Sharp, "From Dictatorship to Democracy," at http://www.aeinstein.org (Boston: The Albert Einstein Institution, 2010).

83. The videos include, "A Force More Powerful" and "Bringing Down a Dictator." Their distribution is aided by the International Center on Nonviolent Conflict.

84. Sheryl Gay Stolberg, "Shy U.S. Intellectual Created Playbook Used in a Revolution," *New York Times*, February 17, 2011, pp. A1, A11; Sharp, "From Dictatorship to Democracy."

85. This includes Arabs from Israel, the West Bank, and Gaza.

86. Some of them organize new nongovernmental organizations. http://www.iwpr.org/blog/2011/12/15/one-on-one-with-former-iwpr-leadership-in-democracy-fellow-intisar-al-adhi/. Other alumni become engaged in the expanding opportunities for electoral politics. For example, Mater Ebrahim Matar was a 2008 Fellow from Bahrain who was elected to its parliament in October 2010; when demonstrations erupted in February 2011, he spoke out for peaceful negotiations and joined seventeen other members of Parliament in resigning their positions.In May he was abducted by masked men in civilian clothes, confined and beaten for forty-five days and, then released in August and subsequently placed on trial.

87. http://www.freedomhouse.org. Freedom House was established in 1941, with the quiet encouragement of President Franklin D. Roosevelt, to encourage popular support for American involvement in World War II at a time when isolationist sentiments were running high in the United States. From the beginning, Freedom House was notable for its bipartisan character.

88. Shibley Telhami, "2010 Arab Public Opinion Poll" (Washington, DC: Brookings Institution, 2010); Shibley Telhami, "The 2011 Arab Public Opinion Poll," (Washington, DC: Brookings Institution, 2011). In 2010, 3,976 people were interviewed, June 29–July 20, in Egypt, Saudi Arabia, Morocco, Jordan, and the United Arab Emirates. In 2011, three thousand people were interviewed in October, in the same countries, not including Saudi Arabia.

89. Many assessments of democracy-promoting American efforts since the 9/11 attacks were made before and after the 2010–2011 uprisings. Thomas Carothers and Marina Ottaway, eds., *Uncharted Journey: Promoting Democracy in the Middle East* (Washington, DC: Carnegie Endowment for International Peace, 2005); Katerina Dalacoura, "US Democracy Promotion in the Arab Middle East since 11 September 2001: A Critique," *International Affairs* 81 (2005); pp. 963–979; Louis Kriesberg, "Reverberations of the Arab Spring," *Palestine-Israel Journal of Politics,Economics and Culture* 18(1); (2012) pp. 88–92; Rick Gladstone, "Resigning as Envoy to Syria, Annan Casts Wide Blame," *The New York Times*, August 2, 2012 http://www.nytimes.

com/2012/08/03/world/middleeast/annan-resigns-as-syria-peace-envoy. html?pagewanted=all&_r=0.

90. See analyses from Kenneth M. Pollack, ed. *The Arab Awakening: America and the Transformation of the Middle East*, Saban Center at the Brookings Institution (Washington, DC: Brookings Institution, 2011); Marc Lynch, *The Arab Uprising: The Unfinished Revolutions of the New Middle East*, 1st ed. (New York: PublicAffairs, 2012).

91. David D. Kirkpatrick and David E. Sanger, "A Tunisian-Egyptian Link That Shook Arab History," *New York Times*, February 14, 2011.

92. Louis Kriesberg, "Reverberations of the Arab Spring," *Palestine-Israel Journal of Politics, Economics and Culture* 18 (1) (2012).

93. Shelley Deane, "Transforming Tunisia: The Role of Civil Society in Tunisia's Transition," (London: International Alert, 2013).

94. Marwan Muasher, *The Second Arab Awakening and the Battle for Pluralism* (New Haven, CT and London: Yale University Press, 2014), pp. 55–60.

95. Vincent Durac and Francesco Cavatorta, "Strengthening Authoritarian Rule through Democracy Promotion? Examining the Paradox of the US and EU Security Strategies: The Case of Bin Ali's Tunisia," *British Journal of Middle Eastern Studies* 36 (1):3–19 (2009).

96. Paul Amar, "Egypt after Mubarak: On Campuses, in Syndicates and Even Inside the Muslim Brotherhood—the Revolution Lives On," *The Nation*, May 23, 2011.

97. Ben Birnbaum, "Muslim Brotherhood Seeks U.S. Alliance as It Ascends in Egypt," *The Washington Times*, April 5, 2012.

98. Roger Cohen, "Working with the Muslim Brotherhood," *New York Times*, October 22, 2012.

99. Stephen Zunes and Jacob Mundy, *Western Sahara: War, Nationalism, and Conflict Resolution* (Syracuse, NY: Syracuse University Press, 2010).

100. International Crisis Group, "Popular Protests in North Africa and the Middle East (III): The Bahrain Revolt," (Brussels: International Crisis Group, 2011).

101. Joost R. Hiltermann, "Pushing for Reform in Bahrain: Washington's Leverage over the Khalifa Regime," *Foreign Affairs*, September 7, 2011. http://www.foreignaffairs.com/print/68167.

102. Mann, *The Obamians: The Struggle inside the White House to Redefine American Power*, pp. 281–301.

103. Roger Cohen, "Leading from Behind," *New York Times*, October 31, 2011. http://www.nytimes.com/2011/11/01/opinion/01iht-edcohen01.html?_r=0.

104. Alex De Waal, "The African Union and the Libya Conflict of 2011," *World Peace Foundation* (December 19, 2012http://sites.tufts.edu/reinventingpeace/2012/12/19/the-african-union-and-the-libya-conflict-of-2011/); Stephan R Weissman, "A Way Forward in Syria," *In These Times* June 2012.

105. Konstantin Garibov, "The War on Libya: NATO Uses and Abuses the United Nations. The Role of Russia," *Global Research* (August 30, 2011).

106. On April 6, the government addressed two grievances of conservative Muslims by closing Syria's only casino and reversing a 2010 law prohibiting female teachers from wearing a veil that covers the face. It also announced that Nōrūz, a New Year festival celebrated by Kurds, would be made a state holiday.

107. Kofi Annan, "Annan's Peace Plan for Syria," *Council on Foreign Relations* (March, 2012) http://www.cfr.org/syria/annans-peace-plan-syria/p28380.

108. Ian Black, "Syria's Nod to Un Peace Plan Greeted with Scepticism," *The Guardian* (March 27, 2012).

109. Thomas Erdbrink, "Annan in Tehran for Talks on Syria Peace Plan," *New York Times* (July 10, 2012).

110. Some of these matters were discussed in an earlier paper; Louis Kriesberg, "Obama, Conflict Resolution, and Mediating the Israeli-Palestinian Conflict," in *International Studies Association Conference* (New Orleans 2010).

111. Oren Barak, "The Failure of the Israeli-Palestinian Peace Process, 1993–2000," *Journal of Peace Research* 42 (6):719–736 (2005); Louis Kriesberg, "The Growth of the Conflict Resolution Field," in *Turbulent Peace*, ed. Fen Osler Hampson, Chester H. Crocker, and Pamela Aall (Washington, DC: United States Institute of Peace, 2001); Louis Kriesberg, "The Relevance of Reconciliation Actions in the Breakdown of Israeli-Palestinian Negotiations, 2000," *Peace & Change* 27 (4):546–571 (2002).

112. International Crisis Group, "Gaza's Unfinished Business," in *Middle East Briefing No. 85* (Brussels 2009); Shlomo Brom, "A Hamas Government: Isolate or Engage?" in *USIP Peace Briefing* (Washington, DC: United States Institute of Peace, March 2006).

113. Adam Robert Green, "Economic Peace in the West Bank and the Fayyad Plan: Are They Working?" in *Middle East Institute Policy Brief* (Washington, DC: Middle East Institute, January 2010).

114. Stephen Zunes, "Obama Gathering a Flock of Hawks to Oversee U.S. Foreign Policy," *AlterNet* January 30 (2010). http://www.alternet.org/story/123508/

115. Nathan Guttman, "Some See Extended Olive Branch for Israel in Ross Appointment to Nsc," *Forward.com* (2009). http://www.forward.com/articles/108792/.

116. A former U.S. senator, Mitchell served as a mediator in the civil strife in Northern Ireland conflict.

117. Robert Dreyfuss, "US General Builds a Palestinian Army," *The Nation* May 10 (2009).

118. This assessment was made by Khalil Shikaki in a personal interview in Jerusalem, January 10, 2010. It also has been articulated by Lt. General Dayton; see Ibid.

119. Ron Kampeas, "At White House, U.S. Jews Offer Little Resistance to Obama Policy on Settlements," *JTA* (July 13, 2009); http://www.peacenow.org/printview.asp?sid=2&cid=6428&rid=&p.

120. The AIPAC president was a supporter of Obama and another director contributed money to his presidential campaign. For information about J-Street, go to: http://www.jstreet.org.

121. Oren Barak, in commenting on this, observes that Obama should have said the opposite: that the continuation of the (de facto) binational state in Israel-Palestine threatens Israel's existence, while Iran is—and will continue to be—effectively deterred by the United States.

122. Barak Ravid and Aluf Benn, "U.S., Israeli Officials Claim Bush's Arms Sales Threaten IDF's Qualitative Edge," *Haaretz*, January 10, 2010; Leslie Susser, "Obama Sharpens His Focus," *The Jerusalem Report*, February 15, 2010.

123. Daniel Kurtzer et al., *The Peace Puzzle* (Washington, DC: USIP Press, 2013).

124. The observation is based upon newspaper accounts and personal conversations with many Israeli Jews in January 2010, in Tel Aviv and Jerusalem. Some Israelis called the U.S. demand for a total freeze on settlement construction a blunder. Susser, "Obama Sharpens His Focus."

125. Ethan Bronner, "Palestinians Shift Focus in Strategy for Statehood," *New York Times*, October 21, 2010.

126. Scott Sayare and Steven Erlanger, "Palestinians Win a Vote on Bid to Join UNESCO," *New York Times*, October 5, 2011. U.S. legislation mandates the cutoff of money to the United Nations or any of its agencies if they grant full membership as a state to any organization that lacks the internationally recognized attributes of statehood. When membership was accorded, the United States stopped making its contribution to the UNESCO budget.

127. The initiative was inspired by Prince Abdullah bin Abdul Aziz, crown prince of Saudi Arabia, and was adopted by the Council of Arab States.

128. Mouin Rabbani, "It's Not over until It's Over," *Journal of Palestine Studies* 43 (3) (Spring 2014).

129. Mark Landler, "Mideast Peace Effort Pauses to Let Faliure Sink In," *New YorkTtimes* 2014. Barak Ravid and Aluf Benn, "U.S. Envoy Indyk Likely to Resign Amid Talks Blowup," *Haaretz* May 4, 2014, http://www.haaretz.com/misc/article-print-page/.premium-1.588834?tra ilingPath=2.169%2C2.216%2C2.217%2C.

130. J. J. Goldberg, "Why Benjamin Netanyahu May Look at the Math – and Cut Deal on Peace Plan," January 20, 2014. http://forward.com/articles/191068/why-benjamin-netanyahu-may-look-at-the-math-and/?p=all.

131. See International Crisis Group, "Gaza's Unfinished Business." Brom, "A Hamas Government: Isolate or Engage?"

132. For the Advancement of Peace, The Harry S. Truman Institute, "Poll #28: Pessimism among Israelis and Palestinians Regarding the Prospects for a Settlement and a Palestinian State in the Next Few Years, but Majorities on Both Sides Support a Two-State Solution.," in *Israeli-Palestinian Public Opinion Polls* (Jerusalem: The Hebrew University of Jerusalem, June 2009), p. 2.

133. Shibley Telhami and Steven Kull, "Israeli and Palestinian Public Opnion on Negotiating a Final Status Peace Agreement," in *Program for Public Consultation* (Washington, DC: Brookings Institution, 2013).

134. That the economy is doing well may be a disincentive for change. To overcome that, concerns that future growth may be stunted by boycotts and other international sanctions may be usefully raised in warnings by U.S. intermediaries.

135. I. William Zartman and Victor Kremenyuk, eds., *Peace Versus Justice: Negotiating Forward- and Backward-Looking Outcomes* (Lanham, MD: Rowman & Littlefield, 2005).

136. http://www.rand.org/pubs.

137. Vamik Volkan, *The Need to Have Enemies and Allies: From Clinical Practice to International Relationships* (New York: Jason Aronson, 1988). Thomas J. Scheff, *Bloody Revenge: Emotions, Nationalism, and War* (Boulder, CO: Westview, 1994).

138. A statement that Netanyahu unfortunately branded a stunt. Gregg Carlstrom, "Abbas: Holocaust Was a 'Heinous Crime'," *Al Jazeera AmericaArabic*, April 27, 2014, http://www.aljazeera.com/news/middleeast/2014/04/abbas-holocaust-was-heinous-crime-20144271573558 2213.html.

139. Scott Atran, Robert Axelrod, and Richard Davis, "Sacred Barriers to Conflict Resolution," *Science* 317 (August 24, 2007).

140. The importance of humiliation in perpetuating conflicts is beginning to receive more recognition. See Victoria Fontan, *Voices from Post-Saddam Iraq: Living with Terrorism, Insurgency and New Forms of Tyranny* (Westport, CT: Praeger, 2008).

141. Anwar el-Sadat expressed this simply when he addressed the Israeli Knesset in November 1977. He spoke forthrightly about the past, but also said that, "Any life lost in war is the life of a

human being, entitled to live in a happy family, Arab or Israeli. The wife who becomes widowed is a human being, entitled to live in a happy family, Arab or Israeli."

142. Louis Kriesberg, "The Evolution of Conflict Resolution," in *Sage Handbook of Conflict Resolution*, ed. Jacob Bercovitch, Victor Kremenyuk, and I. William Zartman (London: Sage, 2009).

143. Louis Kriesberg, "Changing Conflict Asymmetries Constructively," *Dynamics of Asymmetric Conflict* 2 (1):4–22 (March 2009).

144. Most frequently cited, President George W.H. Bush did hold off granting loan guarantees to the Likud-led Israeli government. This contributed to the defeat of Likud in subsequent Israeli elections.

145. David Hartsough, "Active Non-Violence in Palestine and Israel," *Pulse* (2010) http://pulsemedia.org; Steven Kull, "The Potential for a Nonviolent Intifada II," Washington, DC: Program on International Policy Attitudes (PIPA) and Search for Common Ground, December 9, 2002, pp. 1–10. Don Peretz, *Intifada* (Boulder, CO: Westview, 1990).

146. Isabel Kershner, "An Eviction Stirs Old Ghosts in a Contested City," *New York Times* March 9 2010. http://www.nytimes.com/2010/03/10/world/middleeast/10jerusalem.

147. See http://www.peacenow.org.il.

148. Walter Russell Mead, "Change They Can Believe In: To Make Israel Safe, Give Palestinians Their Due," *Foreign Affairs* 88 (1) (2009), pp. 59–76 .

149. Donna E. Arzt, *Refugees into Citizens: Palestinians and the End of the Arab-Israeli Conflict* (New York: Council on Foreign Relations, 1997).

150. See http://www.neareast.org.

151. Green, "Economic Peace in the West Bank and the Fayyad Plan: Are They Working?"

152. Work on this project has been underway for several years at the Centre for International Studies and Diplomacy at the School of Oriental and African Studies in London.

153. Rebecca Shimoni Stoil, "'We Cannot Profit from the Destruction of Homes and Lives,' Presbyterians Say," *The Times of Israel*, http://www.timesofisrael.com/we-cannot-profit-from-the-destruction-of-homes-and-lives-presbyterians-say/?utm_source=The+Times+of+Israel+Daily+Edition&utm_campaign=f636ab4e10-2014_06_21&utm_medium=email&utm_term=0_adb46cec92-f636ab4e10-54549289 (June 21, 2014).

154. Nigel Young, ed. *The Oxford International Encyclopedia of Peace,* 4 vols. (New York: Oxford University Press, 2010). Dennis J. D. Sandole, Sean Byrne, Ingrid Sandole-Staroste, and Jessica Senehi, *Handbook of Conflict Analysis and Resolution* (Abingdon, UK: Routledge, 2009); Jacob Bercovitch, Viktor Kremenyuk, and I. William Zartman, ed. *Sage Handbook of Conflict Resolution* (London: Sage, 2009); Peter T. Coleman, Morton Deutsch, and Eric C. Marcus, eds., *The Handbook of Conflict Resolution: Theory and Practice*, 3rd ed. (San Francisco, CA: Jossey-Bass, 2014); Martina Fischer, Joachim Giessmann, and Beatrix Schmelzle, eds., *Berghof Handbook for Conflict Transformation* (Farmington Hills, MI: Barbara Budrich Publishers, 2011).

155. Esra Cuhadar Gürkaynak, Bruce W. Dayton, and Thania Paffenholz, "Evaluation in Conflict Resolution and Peacebuilding," in *Handbook for Conflict Analysis and Resolutio*, ed. Dennis Sandole, et al. (London: Routledge. 2008).

156. Susan Allen Nan with Mary Mulvihul, "Theories of Change and Indicator Development in Conflict Management and Mitigation. USAID June, 2010, Http://Www.Dmeforpeace.Org/Sites/Default/Files/Nan%20and%20mulvihill_Theories%20of%20change%20and%20indicator%20development.Pdf ".

157. For other concerns, see: Cheyanne Scharbatke-Church, "Peacebuilding Evaluation: Not yet all it Could Be," in *Advancing Conflict Transformation*, ed. B. Austin, M. Fischer, and H. J. Giessmann, http://www.nerghof-handbook.net/documents/publications/Scharbatke_Church_Handbook.Pdf (Opladen/Farmington Hills, MI: Barbara Budrich, 2011).

158. Louis Kriesberg, "Moral Judgments, Human Needs and Conflict Resolution: Alternative Approaches to Ethical Standards," in *Beyond Basic Needs: Linking Theory and Practice*, ed. Christopher R. Mitchell and Kevin Avruch (Oxford, UK: Routledge, 2013); *The Search for Peace in the Middle East—Documents and Statements, 1967–88*. Thomas Matyók, Jessica Senehi, and Sean Byrne, eds., *Critical Issues in Peace and Conflict Studies: Theory, Practice, and Pedagogy* (Lanham, MD: Lexington Books, 2011).

159. Jason Horowitz, "Historian's Critique of Obama Foreign Policy Is Brought Alive by Events in Iraq," *New York Times* (June 16, 2014), p. A7.

CHAPTER 8

1. Andrew J. Bacevich, *Washington Rules: America's Path to Permanent War* (New York: Metropolitan Books, 2010).

2. Louis Kriesberg and Bruce W. Dayton, *Constructive Conflicts: From Escalation to Resolution, 4th Ed.*, 4th ed. (Lanham, MD: Rowman & Littlefield, 2012).

3. Erica Chenoweth and Maria J. Stephan, *Why Civil Resistance Works: The Strategic Logic of Nonviolent Conflict* (New York: Columbia University Press, 2011), p. 7. Also see: .Gene Sharp, *Waging Nonviolent Struggle: 20th Century Practice and 21st Century Potential* (Boston: Porter Sargent, 2005); Stephen Zunes, Lester R. Kurtz, and Sarah Beth Asher, ed. *Nonviolent Social Movements: A Geographical Perspective* (Malden, MA: Blackwell, 1999).

4. Daniel C. Thomas, *The Helsinki Effect: International Norms, Human Rights, and the Demise of Communism* (Princeton and Oxford: Princeton University Press, 2001). Such reassurances are crucial; their absences in dealing with North Korea and Iran have obstructed potential transformations in the past.

5. Admittedly, the salience of the women's movement in the United States is a source of contention with some people in traditional cultures.

6. Kriesberg and Dayton, *Constructive Conflicts: From Escalation to Resolution*, 4th ed. Counter anecdotal arguments may be heard pointing to the militancy of Prime Ministers Golda Meir of Israel and Margaret Thatcher of the United Kingdom. But as women moving up a male hierarchy they had to demonstrate their toughness.

7. Madeleine. M. Kunin, *The New Feminist Agenda: Defining the Next Revolution for Women, Work, and Family* (White River Junction, VT: Chelsea Green, 2012).

8. http://www.gradschools.com/search-programs/conflict-peace-studies. http://www.wtb.org/?page_id=6.

9. Louis Kriesberg and Stuart J. Thorson, eds., *Timing the De-Escalation of International Conflicts* (Syracuse, NY: Syracuse University Press, 1991).

10. Chester A. Crocker, Fen Osler Hampson, and Pamela R. Aall, *Taming Intractable Conflicts: Mediation in the Hardest Cases* (Washington, DC: United States Institute of Peace Press, 2004).

11. http://www.allianceforpeacebuilding.org/about-us/ AfP. This is a membership association of more than seventy peacebuilding organizations and more than one thousand professionals from 153 countries.

12. In Syracuse, New York, there are several such organizations. When young activists from the Middle East and North Africa participate in the Leaders for Democracy Fellows program of the U.S. State Department at Syracuse University, they often meet with members of such organizations. Seeing local Jews, Christians, and Muslims discussing Israeli-Palestinian relations with mutual respect is an exciting highlight of their experience in the United States.

13. Richard D. Schwartz, "Arab-Jewish Dialogue in the United States: Toward Track II Tractability," in *Intractable Conflicts and Their Transformation*, eds. Louis Kriesberg, Terrell A. Northrup, and Stuart J. Thorson, (Syracuse, NY: Syracuse University Press, 1989). For a directory of such organizations see: http://www.cehd.umn.edu/ssw/rjp/Arab_Palestinian_Jewish_Project/Directory_Arab_Jewish_Palestinian_Dialogue_Groups.pdf.

14. http://www.adc.org/.

15. Louis Kriesberg, "International Nongovernmental Organizations and Transnational Integration," *International Associations* 24 (11):520–525 (1972); "U.S. and U.S.S.R. Participation in International Non-Governmental Organizations," in *Social Processes in International Relations*, ed. Louis Kriesberg (New York: John Wiley & Sons, 1968); Jackie Smith, Charles Chatfield, and Ron Pagnucco, eds., *Transnational Social Movements and Global Politics: Solidarity Beyond the State* (Syracuse, NY: Syracuse University Press, 1997).

16. C. Wright Mills, *The Power Elite* (New York: Oxford University Press, 1956); Arnold M. Rose, *The Power Structure* (New York: Oxford University Press, 1967).

17. See appendix B in Seymour Melman, *Pentagon Capitalism* (New York: McGraw-Hill, 1970).

18. http://www.military.com/daily-news/2012/08/20/congress-pushes-for-weapons-pentagon-didnt-want.html. Winslow T. Wheeler, *The Wastrels of Defense: How Congress Sabotges U.S. Security* (Annapolis, MD: Naval Institute Press, 2004).

19. Ibid., pp. 66, 71, 85, and 245.

20. Chalmers Johnson, *Blowback: The Costs and Consequences of American Empire* (New York: Henry Holt, 2000), pp. 85–94.

21. Project on Government Oversight was founded in 1981 (see http://www.pogo.org/). Taxpayers for Common Sense was founded in 1995 (see http://www.taxpayer.net/).

22. http://www.pogo.org/about/press-room/releases/2012/ns-wds-20120508-wasteful-defense-spending.html.

23. Robert M. Gates, *Duty: Memoirs of a Secretary at War* (New York: Alfred A. Knopf, 2014).

24. See *Who Pays for Think Tanks* at Fairness & Accuracy in Reporting (http://fair.org/extra-online-articles/who-pays-for-think-tanks/).

25. Edward W. Lollis, *Monumental Beauty: Peace Monuments and Museums around the World* (Knoxville, TN: Peace Partners International, Inc., 2013).

26. Jonah Winter, *Peaceful Heroes* (New York: Arthur A. Levine Books, 2009). Charles De-Benedetti, ed. *Peace Heroes in Twentieth-Century America* (Bloomington, IN: Indiana University Press, 1986). Craig Zelizer and Robert A. Rubinstein, eds., *Peacebuilding: Creating the Structure and Capacity for Peace* (West Hartford, CT: Kumarian, 2009).

27. David Cortright, *Peace: A History of Movements and Ideas* (Cambridge, UK: Cambridge University Press, 2008).

28. Stephen John Stedman, Donald Rothchild and Elizabeth M. Cousens, eds., ed. *Ending Civil Wars: The Implementation of Peace Agreements* (Boulder-London: Lynne Rienner, 2002).

29. Louis Kriesberg, "Peace Movements and Government Peace Efforts," in *Research in Social Movements Conflicts and Change*, ed. Louis Kriesberg, Bronislaw Misztal, and Janusz Mucha

(Greenwich, CT and London: JAI Press, 1988). John Lofland, *Polite Protestors: The American Peace Movement of the 1980s* (Syracuse, NY: Syracuse University Press, 1993).

30. www.peace-action.org/.

31. What we support in www.winwithoutwar.org/; Coalition members include Council for a Livable World, Friends Committee on National Legislation, Peace Action, Physicians for Social Responsibility, and Veterans for Peace.

32. www.unitedforpeace.org/.

33. Murray Polner and Jim O'Grady, *Disarmed and Dangerous: The Radical Life and Times of Daniel and Philip Berrigan, Brothers in Religious Faith and Civil Disobedience* (New York: Basic Books, 1997).

34. The assassination appears to have been committed by a death squad under orders of former Major Roberto D'Aubuisson.

35. Resolution adopted by the UN General Assembly, March 16, 2001, 54/263. Optional protocols to the Convention on the Rights of the Child on the involvement of children in armed conflict and on the sale of children, child prostitution, and child pornography.

36. http://carnegieendowment.org/.

37. In January 2009, *Foreign Policy* magazine ranked WPI as the 16th most influential US think tank out of 1777 in the United States and 5465 worldwide.

38. Barry R. Posen, "Command of the Commons: The Military Foundation of U.S. Hegemony," *International Security*, 28 (1):5–46 (2003).

39. John Mueller, *Overblown: How Politicians and the Terrorism Industry Inflate National Security Threats and Why We Believe Them* (New York: Free Press, 2006); John E. Mueller and Mark G. Stewart., *Terror, Security, and Money: Balancing the Risks, Benefits, and Costs of Homeland Security* (New York: Oxford University Press, 2011).

40. James M. McCormick, "Decision Making in the Foreign Affairs and Foreign Relations Committee," in *Congress Resurgent: Foreign and Defense Policy on Capital Hill*, ed. Randall B. Ripley and James M. Lindsay (Ann Arbor, MI: The University of Michigan Press, 1993).

41. Oral presentation at Syracuse University, November 12, 2013, by Morgan Courtney, on staff of Bureau. See: http://www.state.gov/j/cso/.

42. For example, see Nathan Hodge, *Armed Humanitarians: The Rise of the Nation Builders* (New York, Berlin, London, Sydney: Bloomsbury, 2011), pp. 285–299.

43. Goldstein, Joshua S. 2011. *Winning the War on War: The Decline of Armed Conflict Worldwide*. New York: Penguin. http://www.peacejusticestudies.org/globaldirectory/

44. Bacevich, *Washington Rules: America's Path to Permanent War*.

45. Chalmers Johnson, "737 U.S. Military Bases = Global Empire," *Chalmers Johnson's ZSpace Page* (February 22, 2007). Also see: Chalmers A. Johnson, *The Sorrows of Empire: Militarism, Secrecy, and the End of the Republic* (New York: Metropolitan Books, 2004).

46. Cited on p. 148 in Bacevich, *Washington Rules: America's Path to Permanent War*.

47. Dana Priest, *The Mission: Waging War and Keeping Peace with America's Military*, 1st ed. (New York: W.W. Norton & Co., 2003).

48. http://www.defense.gov/ucc/.

49. Maintaining the huge defense budget is a possible source of several domestic problems. Whether or not it slows economic growth is debatable, and there probably are both negative and positive effects. In the long term, it is likely that there are negative indirect effects when investment spending for education, infrastructure, and other social welfare services are forgone for

high rates of military spending. Uk Heo, "The Relationship Betwen Defense Spending and Economic Growth in the United States," *Political Research Quarterly* 63 (4):760–770 (2010).

50. Robert M. Gates, in *National Defense University* (2008, September 29).

51. Walter Pincus, "Vast Number of Military Bands May Not Be Music to Gates," *Washingtonpost.com* (2010, August 24).

52. Catherine Lutz, ed. *The Bases of Empire: The Global Struggle against U.S. Military Posts* (New York: New York University Press, 2009). www.g2mil.com. G2mil is a collection of articles on military affairs authored by Carlton Meyer,

53. Amnesty International-USA, "U.S. Training of Foreign Police and Soldiers," (http://www.amnestyusa.org/our-work/issues/military-police-and-arms/military-and-police-training: Amnesty International USA, 2013).

54. Randall B. Ripley and James M. Lindsay, "Foreign and Deense Policy in Congress: An Overview and Preview," *Congress Resurgent: Foreign and Defense Policy on Capital Hill*, ed. Randall B. Ripley and James M. Lindsay (Ann Arbor, MI: The University of Michigan Press, 1993), p. 8.

55. James M. Lindsay, *Congress and the Politics of U.S. Foreign Policy* (Baltimore and London: Johns Hopkins University Press, 1994). William G. Howell and Jon C. Pevehouse, *While Dangers Gather: Congressional Checks on Presidential War Powers* (Princeton, NJ: Princeton University Press, 2007).

56. Barbara Sinclair, "Congressional Party Leaders in the Foreign and Defense Policy Arena," in *Congrerss Resurgent: Foreign and Defense Policy on Capital Hill*, ed. Randall B. Ripley and James M. Lindsay (Ann Arbor, MI: The University of Michigan Press, 1993).

57. Lindsay, *Congress and the Politics of U.S. Foreign Policy*, pp. 147–150.

58. Lily J. Goren, *The Politics of Military Base Closings: Not in My District* (New York: Peter Lang, 2003).

59. Wheeler, *The Wastrels of Defense: How Congress Sabotges U.S. Security.*

60. Barbara Hinckley, *Less Than Meets the Eye: Foreign Policy Making and the Myth of the Assertive Congres* (Chicago and London: A Twentieth Century Fund Book. The University of Chicago Press, 1994).

61. Joshua S. Goldstein, *Winning the War on War: The Decline of Armed Conflict Worldwide* (New York: Penguin, 2011), 105–108; Virginia Page Fortna, *Does Peackeeping Work? Shaping Belligerents' Choices after Civil War* (Princeton, NJ: Princeton University Press, 2008). Paul Collier, *Wars, Guns, and Vote: Democracy in Dangerous Places* (New York: Harper, 2009).

62. Some reforms were close to realization during the presidency of George W. Bush, but with John Bolton as the U.S. ambassador to the UN, they failed to occur. James Traub, *The Best Intentions: Kofi Annan and the Un in the Era of American World Power* (New York: Farrar, Straus and Giroux, 2006).

63. United Nations, "The Millenium Development Goals Report 2012," (New York: United Nations, 2012). This should not be confused with the "Millennium Challenge Account," promoted by President George W. Bush. See: Melanie Nakagawa, "The Millennium Challenge Account: A Critical Look at the Newly Focused Development Approach and Its Potential Impact on the U.S. Agency for International Development," *Sustainable Development Law & Policy* 6 (1), Development Goals & Indicators Article 7 (2005).

64. Jeff Faux and Larry Mishel, "Inequality and the Global Economy," in *Global Capitalism*, ed. Will Hutton and Anthony Giddens (New York: The New Press, 2000).

65. "The richest 1% of the world's population (around 60 million) now receive as much income as the poorest 57%, while the income of the richest 25 million Americans is the equivalent of that of almost 2 billion of the world's poorest people. In 1820, Western Europe's per capita income was three times that of Africa's; by the 1990s it was more than 13 times as high." Larry Elliott, "The Lost Decade," *Guardian*, July 9, 2003. http://www.globalpolicy.org/socecon/un/2003/0709lost.htm.

66. Jay Mandle, "Davos and the Real World," *The (Syracuse) Post Standard*, January 27, 2004, p. A-9.

67. B. Welling Hall, "International Law and the Responsibility to Protect," in *The International Studies Encyclopedia*, ed. Robert A. Denemark (Blackwell Reference Online: http://www.isacompendium.com/subscriber/tocnode?id=g9781444336597_chunk_g978144433659711_ss1-32, 2010); Kur Mills and Cian O'Driscoll, "From Humanitarian Intervention to the Responsibility to Protect," Ibid., ed. Robert A. Denemark (Blackwell Reference Online: http://www.isacompendium.com/subscriber/tocnode?id=g9781444336597_chunk_g97814443365978_ss1-28>).

68. International Commission on Interventio and State Soveregnty *The Resonsibility to Protect*, International Development Research Centre (Ottawa, Canada, 2001).

69. Sabine von Schorlemer, "The Responsibility to Protect as an Element of Peace," in *Policy Paper 28* (Bonn: Development and Peace Foundation, 2007). But the value of R2P has also been debated. Gareth Evans, Ramesh Thakur, and Robert A. Pape, "Correspondence: Humanitarian Intervention and the Responsibility to Protect," *International Security* 37 (4):199–214 (2013).

70. http://www.un.org/peacekeeping/operatons/.

71. Goldstein, *Winning the War on War: The Decline of Armed Conflict Worldwide*. pp. 314–316. In a 2007 poll, 72% of Americans supported the idea and only 24% opposed it.

72. Ibid., pp. 118–125.

73. Carolyn M. Stephenson, "NGOs and the Principal Organs of the United Nations," in *The United Nations at the Millennium*, ed. Paul Taylor & A. J. R. Groom (London and New York: Continuum, 2000).

74. Goldstein, *Winning the War on War: The Decline of Armed Conflict Worldwide*; Zelizer and Rubinstein, *Peacebuilding: Creating the Structure and Capacity for Peace*.

Index